W9-ALU-128

Adobe® Photoshop® CS4
The Professional Portfolio

AGAINST THE CLOCK
mastering graphic technology

Managing Editor: Ellenn Behoriam
Cover & Interior Design: Erika Kendra
Copy Editor: Laurel Nelson-Cucchiara
Proofreader: Angelina Kendra

Copyright © 2009 Against The Clock, Inc.
All rights reserved. Printed in the United States of America. This publication is protected by copyright, and permission should be obtained in writing from the publisher prior to any prohibited reproduction, storage in a retrieval system, or transmission in any form or by any means, electronic, mechanical, photocopying, recording, or likewise.

The fonts utilized in these training materials are the property of Against The Clock, Inc., and are supplied to the legitimate buyers of the Against The Clock training materials solely for use with the exercises and projects provided in the body of the materials. They may not be used for any other purpose, and under no circumstances may they be transferred to another individual, nor copied or distributed by any means whatsoever.

A portion of the images supplied in this book are copyright © PhotoDisc, Inc., 201 Fourth Ave., Seattle, WA 98121, or copyright ©PhotoSpin, 4030 Palos Verdes Dr. N., Suite 200, Rollings Hills Estates, CA. These images are the sole property of PhotoDisc or PhotoSpin and are used by Against The Clock with the permission of the owners. They may not be distributed, copied, transferred, or reproduced by any means whatsoever, other than for the completion of the exercises and projects contained in this Against The Clock training material.

Against The Clock and the Against The Clock logo are trademarks of Against The Clock, Inc., registered in the United States and elsewhere. References to and instructional materials provided for any particular application program, operating system, hardware platform, or other commercially available product or products do not represent an endorsement of such product or products by Against The Clock, Inc.

Photoshop, Acrobat, Illustrator, InDesign, PageMaker, Flash, Dreamweaver, Premiere, and PostScript are trademarks of Adobe Systems Incorporated. Macintosh is a trademark of Apple Computer, Inc. QuarkXPress is a registered trademark of Quark, Inc. FrontPage, Publisher, PowerPoint, Word, Excel, Office, Microsoft, MS-DOS, and Windows are either registered trademarks or trademarks of Microsoft Corporation.

Other product and company names mentioned herein may be the trademarks of their respective owners.

10   9   8   7   6   5   4   3   2   978-0-9815216-5-7

mastering graphic technology

4710 28th Street North, Saint Petersburg, FL 33714
800-256-4ATC • www.againsttheclock.com

Adobe® Photoshop® CS4

The Professional Portfolio

AGAINST THE CL CK
mastering graphic technology

Managing Editor: Ellenn Behoriam
Cover & Interior Design: Erika Kendra
Copy Editor: Laurel Nelson-Cucchiara
Proofreader: Angelina Kendra

Copyright © 2009 Against The Clock, Inc.
All rights reserved. Printed in the United States of
America. This publication is protected by copyright,
and permission should be obtained in writing from the
publisher prior to any prohibited reproduction, storage
in a retrieval system, or transmission in any form or by
any means, electronic, mechanical, photocopying,
recording, or likewise.

The fonts utilized in these training materials are the property of Against The Clock, Inc., and are supplied to the
legitimate buyers of the Against The Clock training materials solely for use with the exercises and projects provided
in the body of the materials. They may not be used for any other purpose, and under no circumstances may they be
transferred to another individual, nor copied or distributed by any means whatsoever.

A portion of the images supplied in this book are copyright © PhotoDisc, Inc., 201 Fourth Ave., Seattle, WA 98121,
or copyright ©PhotoSpin, 4030 Palos Verdes Dr. N., Suite 200, Rollings Hills Estates, CA. These images are the sole
property of PhotoDisc or PhotoSpin and are used by Against The Clock with the permission of the owners. They may
not be distributed, copied, transferred, or reproduced by any means whatsoever, other than for the completion of the
exercises and projects contained in this Against The Clock training material.

Against The Clock and the Against The Clock logo are trademarks of Against The Clock, Inc., registered in the
United States and elsewhere. References to and instructional materials provided for any particular application program,
operating system, hardware platform, or other commercially available product or products do not represent
an endorsement of such product or products by Against The Clock, Inc.

Photoshop, Acrobat, Illustrator, InDesign, PageMaker, Flash, Dreamweaver, Premiere, and PostScript are trademarks
of Adobe Systems Incorporated. Macintosh is a trademark of Apple Computer, Inc. QuarkXPress is a registered
trademark of Quark, Inc. FrontPage, Publisher, PowerPoint, Word, Excel, Office, Microsoft, MS-DOS, and Windows
are either registered trademarks or trademarks of Microsoft Corporation.

Other product and company names mentioned herein may be the trademarks of their respective owners.

10   9   8   7   6   5   4   3   2   978-0-9815216-5-7

4710 28th Street North, Saint Petersburg, FL 33714
800-256-4ATC • www.againsttheclock.com

Acknowledgements

ABOUT AGAINST THE CLOCK

Against The Clock has been publishing graphic communications educational materials for more than 17 years, starting out as a Tampa, Florida-based systems integration firm whose primary focus was on skills development in high-volume, demanding commercial environments. Among the company's clients were LL Bean, The New England Journal of Medicine, the Smithsonian, and many others. Over the years, Against The Clock has developed a solid and widely-respected approach to teaching people how to effectively utilize graphics applications while maintaining a disciplined approach to real-world problems.

Against The Clock has been recognized as one of the nation's leaders in courseware development. Having developed the *Against The Clock* and the *Essentials for Design* series with Prentice Hall/Pearson Education, the firm works closely with all major software developers to ensure timely release of educational products aimed at new version releases.

ABOUT THE AUTHORS

Erika Kendra holds a BA in History and a BA in English Literature from the University of Pittsburgh. She began her career in the graphic communications industry as an editor at Graphic Arts Technical Foundation before moving to Los Angeles in 2000. Erika is the author or co-author of more than fifteen books about graphic design software, including QuarkXPress, Adobe Photoshop, Adobe InDesign, and Adobe PageMaker. She has also written several books about graphic design concepts such as color reproduction and preflighting, and dozens of articles for online and print journals in the graphics industry. Working with Against The Clock for more than seven years, Erika was a key partner in developing the new Portfolio Series of software training books.

Gary Poyssick, co-owner of Against The Clock, is a well-known and often controversial speaker, writer, and industry consultant who has been involved in professional graphics and communications for more than twenty years. He wrote the highly popular *Workflow Reengineering* (Adobe Press), *Teams and the Graphic Arts Service Provider* (Prentice Hall), *Creative Techniques: Adobe Illustrator*, and *Creative Techniques: Adobe Photoshop* (Hayden Books), and was the author or co-author of many application-specific training books from Against The Clock.

CONTRIBUTING AUTHORS, ARTISTS, AND EDITORS

A big thank you to the people whose artwork, comments, and expertise contributed to the success of these books:

- **Greg Williams**, Keiser University
- **Don Mangione**, Baker College of Muskegon
- **John R. Craft**, Appalachian State University
- **JoAnn Burkhart**, Dodge City Community College
- **Robin McAllister**, Against The Clock, Inc.
- **Debbie Davidson**, Sweet Dreams Design
- **Dean Bagley**, Against The Clock, Inc.
- **Tim Hubbell**, Tampa, Florida
- **Roger Morrissey**, Lancaster, California

Thanks also to **Laurel Nelson-Cucchiara**, editor, and **Angelina Kendra**, proofreader, for their help in making sure that we all said what we meant to say.

Walk Through

Project Goals

Each project begins with a clear description of the overall concepts that are explained in the project; these goals closely match the different "stages" of the project workflow.

The Project Meeting

Each project includes the client's initial comments, which provide valuable information about the job. The Project Art Director, a vital part of any design workflow, also provides fundamental advice and production requirements.

Project Objectives

Each Project Meeting includes a summary of the specific skills required to complete the project.

Real-World Workflow

Projects are broken into logical lessons or "stages" of the workflow. Brief introductions at the beginning of each stage provide vital foundational material required to complete the task.

Step-By-Step Exercises

Every stage of the workflow is broken into multiple hands-on, step-by-step exercises.

Visual Explanations

Wherever possible, screen shots are annotated so students can quickly identify important information.

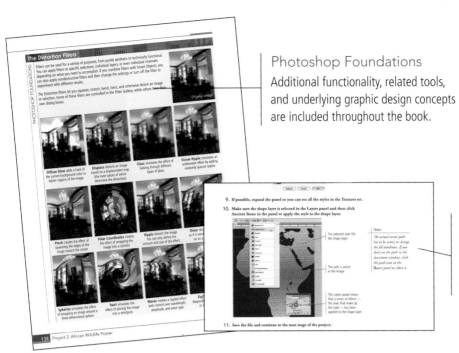

Photoshop Foundations
Additional functionality, related tools, and underlying graphic design concepts are included throughout the book.

Advice and Warnings
Where appropriate, sidebars provide shortcuts, warnings, or tips about the topic at hand.

Project Review
After completing each project, students can complete these fill-in-the-blank and short-answer questions to test their understanding of the concepts in the project.

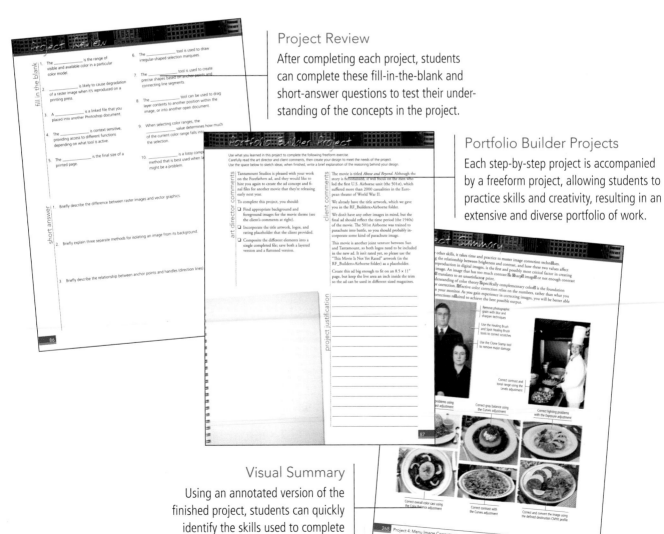

Portfolio Builder Projects
Each step-by-step project is accompanied by a freeform project, allowing students to practice skills and creativity, resulting in an extensive and diverse portfolio of work.

Visual Summary
Using an annotated version of the finished project, students can quickly identify the skills used to complete different aspects of the job.

The *Portfolio Series* is specifically designed to meet the unique needs of graphic arts educators.

The *Portfolio Series* teaches graphic design software tools and techniques entirely within the framework of real-world projects; we introduce and explain skills where they would naturally fall into a real project workflow. For example, rather than offering an entire chapter about printing (which most students find boring), we teach printing where you naturally need to do so — when you complete a print-based project (Project 2).

The project-based approach in the *Portfolio Series* allows you to get in depth with the software beginning in Project 1 — you don't have to read several chapters of introductory material before you can start creating finished artwork.

The project-based approach of the *Portfolio Series* also prevents "topic tedium" — in other words, we don't require you to read pages and pages of information about text (for example); instead, we explain text tools and options as part of a larger project (in this case, as part of a book cover).

Clear, easy-to-read, step-by-step instructions walk you through every phase of each job, from creating a new file to saving the finished piece. Wherever logical, we also offer practical advice and tips about underlying concepts and graphic design practices that will benefit students as they enter the job market.

The projects in this book reflect a range of different types of Photoshop jobs, from creating a magazine ad to correcting menu images to building a Web page. When you finish the eight projects in this book (and the accompanying Portfolio Builder exercises), you will have a substantial body of work that should impress any potential employer.

The eight Photoshop CS4 projects are described briefly here; more detail is provided in the full table of contents (beginning on Page viii).

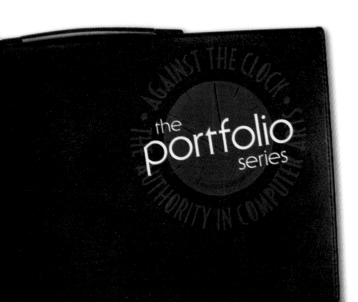

project 1 — Four-Color Movie Ad

- ❏ Setting Up the Workspace
- ❏ Compositing Images and Artwork
- ❏ Creating Silhouettes
- ❏ Managing Multiple Layers
- ❏ Saving Photoshop Files for Print

project 2 — African Wildlife Map

- ❏ Setting Up the Workspace
- ❏ Compositing with Smart Objects
- ❏ Using Filters and Adjustments
- ❏ Creating an Artistic Background
- ❏ Creating Variations

project 3 — Moonscapes Book Cover

- ❏ Setting up the Workspace
- ❏ Working with Text
- ❏ Editing Layers for Visual Impact
- ❏ Outputting Files

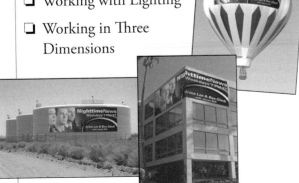

Some experts claim most people use only a small fraction — maybe 10% — of their software's capabilities; this is likely because many people don't know what is available. As you complete the projects in this book, our goal is to familiarize you with the entire tool set so you can be more productive and more marketable in your career as a graphic designer.

It is important to keep in mind that Photoshop is an extremely versatile and powerful application. The sheer volume of available tools, panels, and features can seem intimidating when you first look at the software interface. Most of these tools, however, are fairly simple to use with a bit of background information and a little practice.

Wherever necessary, we explain the underlying concepts and terms that are required for understanding the software. And we're confident that these projects provide the practice you need to be able to create sophisticated artwork by the end of the very first project.

Project 8 PHOTO GALLERY WEB PAGE 447

PREREQUISITES

The entire Portfolio Series is based on the assumption that you have a basic understanding of how to use your computer. You should know how to use your mouse to point and click, as well as how to drag items around the screen. You should be able to resize and arrange windows on your desktop to maximize your available space. You should know how to access drop-down menus, and understand how check boxes and radio buttons work. It also doesn't hurt to have a good understanding of how your operating system organizes files and folders, and how to navigate your way around them. If you're familiar with these fundamental skills, then you know all that's necessary to use the Portfolio Series.

RESOURCE FILES

All of the files that you need to complete the projects in this book are on the provided Resource CD in the **RF_Photoshop** folder. This folder contains nine subfolders, one for each project in the book (including the Interface); you will be directed to the appropriate folder whenever you need to access a specific file. Files required for the related Portfolio Builder exercises are in the **RF_Builders** folder.

The Resource CD also includes a **WIP** folder, which also contains (mostly empty) subfolders for each project in the book. This is where you will save your work as you complete the various projects. In some cases, the location of a file will be extremely important for later steps in a project to work properly; that's why we've provided a specific set of folders with known file names.

Before you begin working on the projects in this book, you should copy the entire WIP folder to your hard drive or some other recordable media such as a flash drive; when we tell you to save a file, you should save it to the appropriate folder on the drive where you put that WIP folder.

ATC FONTS

You must install the ATC fonts from the Resource CD to ensure that your exercises and projects will work as described in the book; these fonts are provided on the Resource CD in the **ATC Fonts** folder. Specific instructions for installing fonts are provided in the documentation that came with your computer. You should replace older (pre-2004) ATC fonts with the ones on your Resource CD.

SYSTEM REQUIREMENTS

As software technology continues to mature, the differences in functionality from one platform to another continue to diminish. The Portfolio Series was designed to work on both Macintosh or Windows computers; where differences exist from one platform to another, we include specific instructions relative to each platform.

One issue that remains different from Macintosh to Windows is the use of different modifier keys (Control, Shift, etc.) to accomplish the same task. When we present key commands, we always follow the same Macintosh/Windows format — Macintosh keys are listed first, then a slash, followed by the Windows key command.

Minimum System Requirements for Adobe Photoshop CS4:

Windows
- 1.8GHz or faster processor
- Microsoft® Windows® XP with Service Pack 2 or Windows Vista® with Service Pack 1
- 512 MB of RAM (1 GB recommended)
- 1 GB of available hard-disk space for installation
- 1,024×768 display with 16-bit video card
- Some GPU-accelerated features require graphics support for Shader Model 3.0 and OpenGL 2.0
- DVD-ROM drive
- QuickTime 7.2 required for multimedia features

Macintosh
- PowerPC® G5 or multicore Intel® processor
- Mac OS X v10.4.11–10.5.4
- 512 MB of RAM (1 GB recommended)
- 2 GB of available hard-disk space for installation
- 1,024×768 display with 16-bit video card
- Some GPU-accelerated features require graphics support for Shader Model 3.0 and OpenGL 2.0
- DVD-ROM drive
- QuickTime 7.2 required for multimedia features

Adobe Photoshop is the industry-standard application for working with pixels — both manipulating existing ones and creating new ones. Mastering the tools and techniques of the application can significantly improve your career potential.

Many Photoshop experts specialize in certain types of work. Photo retouching, artistic painting, image compositing, color correction, and Web site design are only a few subcategories of work you can create with Photoshop. Our goal in this book is to teach you how to use the available tools to create different types of work that you might encounter in your professional career.

Although not intended as a layout design application, you can also use the Photoshop tools to combine type, graphics, and images into a finished design; many people create advertisements, book covers, and other projects entirely in Photoshop. Others argue that Photoshop should never be used for layout design; Adobe InDesign is the preferred page-layout application.

Some projects in this book, such as Projects 4 and 6, focus specifically on image manipulation or creation — which is the true heart of the application. Others, such as Projects 1 and 3, result in finished composite designs. We do not advocate doing *all* or even *most* layout composite work in Photoshop. But because many people use the application to create composite designs, we feel the projects in this book portray a realistic real-world workflow.

As you move forward in your career, it will be your choice to determine which application is appropriate for which task; it is our job to teach you how to use the tools so you can make the best possible decision when that need arises.

The simple exercises in this introduction are designed to let you explore the Photoshop user interface. Whether you are new to the application or upgrading from a previous version, we highly recommend you follow these steps to click around and become familiar with the basic workspace. When you begin Project 1, you will be better prepared to jump right in and start pushing pixels.

Photoshop Menus

PHOTOSHOP FOUNDATIONS

Like most applications, Photoshop has a Menu bar across the top of the workspace; nine menus in Photoshop CS4 or eleven menus in Photoshop CS4 Extended provide access to virtually all of the available options. (Macintosh users have two extra menus. The Apple menu provides access to system-specific commands. The Photoshop menu follows the Macintosh system-standard format for all applications; this menu controls basic application operations such as About, Hide, Preferences, and Quit.) Although you will explore most of the specific menu options as you complete the projects in this book, you should understand what different indicators mean within the application menus.

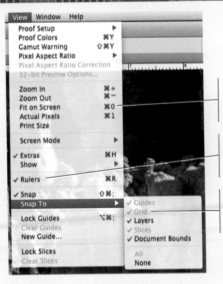

Keyboard shortcuts (if available) are listed on the right side of the menu.

Many menu commands are toggles; the checkmark indicates that an option is visible or toggled on.

If a menu command is grayed out, it is not available for the current selection.

EXPLORE THE PHOTOSHOP INTERFACE

The user interface (UI) is what you see when you launch the Photoshop application. The specific elements you see — including which panels are open and where they appear on the screen — depend on what was done the last time the application was open. The first time you launch Photoshop, you'll see the default workspace settings defined by Adobe. When you relaunch the application after you or another user has quit, the workspace defaults to the last-used settings — including specific open panels and the position of those panels on your screen.

1. **Launch Photoshop.**

2. **Macintosh users: Open the Window menu. If Application Frame is not checked (active), choose that command in the menu.**

Note:

Most screen shots in this book show floating panels so we can focus on the most important issue in a particular image. In our production workflow, however, we make heavy use of docked and iconized panels, and we take full advantage of saved custom workspaces.

The Macintosh Application Frame

PHOTOSHOP FOUNDATIONS

On Windows, each running application is contained within its own frame; all elements of the application — including the Menu bar, panels, tools, and open documents — are contained within the Application frame.

In CS4, Adobe introduced the Application frame concept to Macintosh users as an option for controlling your workspace. When you activate the Application frame, the entire workspace shifts into a self-contained area that can be moved around the screen. All elements of the workspace

(excluding the Menu bar) move when you move the Application frame. The Application frame is active by default, and it can be toggled on or off in the Window menu.

Using the Application frame is purely a matter of personal preference. It can be particularly useful for Windows users who recently made the switch to Macintosh, because the Application frame closely resembles what you are used to seeing on a Windows system. The screen shots throughout this book show the Application frame in use.

When the Application frame is not active, the Application bar appears immediately below the menu bar; in this case, the Application bar can be moved or turned off.

When the Application frame is not active, the desktop is visible behind the workspace elements.

3. Choose Window>Workspace>Essentials.

This step might or might not do anything, depending on what was done in Photoshop before you started this project. If you or someone else changed something and then quit the application, those changes are remembered when Photoshop is relaunched. Because we can't be sure what your default settings show, by completing this step you are resetting the user interface to one of the built-in default workspaces so that your screen shots match ours.

Saved **workspaces** (accessed in the Window>Workspace menu, or in the Workspace switcher on the Application/ Menu bar) provide one-click access to a defined group of tools that might otherwise take ten or more clicks to create each time you need the same toolset.

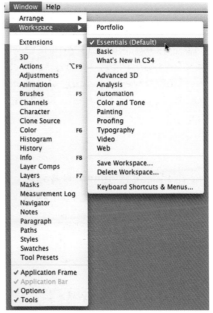

Note:

Options for accessing and managing custom workspaces are available in the Window>Workspace menu, or in the Workspace switcher on the Application/Menu bar.

The Essentials workspace includes the Tools panel on the left of the screen, the Control panel at the top of the screen, and a set of panels attached to the right side of the screen. (The area where the panels are stored is called the **panel dock**.)

On Macintosh systems, the Application bar includes a number of buttons for accessing different view options. On Windows systems, those same options are available on the right side of the Menu bar. We'll come back to these specific options later in this introduction.

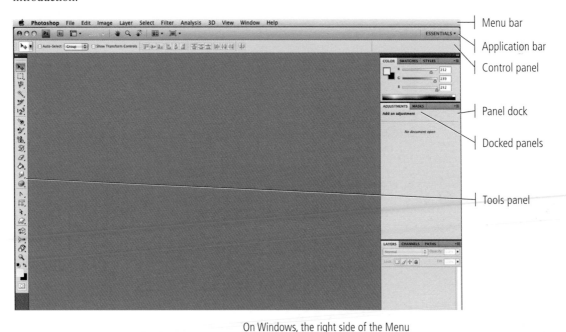

On Windows, the right side of the Menu bar provides access to the same options that are in the Macintosh Application bar.

4. **Click the title bar above the column of docked panels to collapse those panels to icons.**

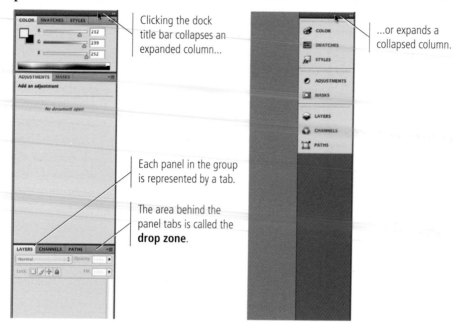

Clicking the dock title bar collapses an expanded column...

...or expands a collapsed column.

Each panel in the group is represented by a tab.

The area behind the panel tabs is called the **drop zone**.

Note:

You can create multiple columns of panels in the dock. Each column, technically considered a separate dock, can be expanded or collapsed independently of other columns.

5. **In the panel dock, click the Styles button.**

Most Photoshop functionality is accessed in one of more than 20 **panels**. Virtually everything you do in Photoshop will require interacting with at least one panel; more often than not you'll use multiple panels to complete any given project.

Note:

*Collapsed panels are referred to as **iconized** or **iconic**.*

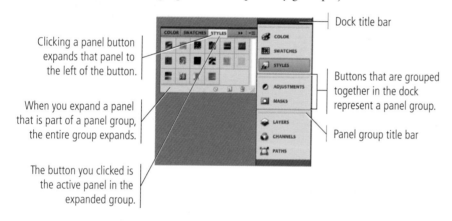

Clicking a panel button expands that panel to the left of the button.

When you expand a panel that is part of a panel group, the entire group expands.

The button you clicked is the active panel in the expanded group.

Dock title bar

Buttons that are grouped together in the dock represent a panel group.

Panel group title bar

6. **Click away from the expanded panel, anywhere in the application workspace.**

By default, expanded panels remain open until you manually close them or expand another panel in the dock.

7. **Control/right-click the title bar above the docked panel icons. Choose Auto-Collapse Iconic Panels in the contextual menu to toggle on that option.**

Control/right-clicking a dock title bar opens the dock contextual menu, where you can change the default panel behavior. If you toggle off the Auto-Collapse Iconic Panels option (which is active by default), a panel will remain open until you intentionally collapse it, or until you open a different panel in the dock.

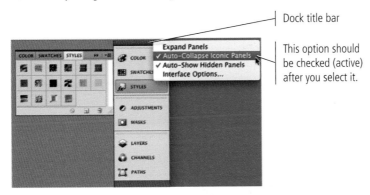

Dock title bar

This option should be checked (active) after you select it.

Note:

If you're using a Macintosh and don't have a mouse with right-click capability, we highly recommend that you purchase one that does. They're inexpensive, can be purchased in most retail stores, and will save you significant amounts of time when accessing contextual options.

8. **In the panel dock, click the Layers button to expand the panel, and then click away from the expanded panel.**

When Auto-Collapse Iconic Panels is toggled on, the expanded panel collapses as soon as you click away from it.

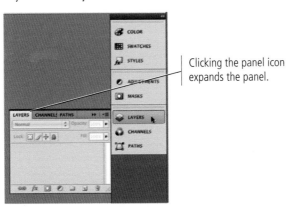

Clicking the panel icon expands the panel.

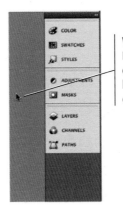

When Auto-Collapse Iconic Panels is active, the expanded panel collapses back to an icon when you click away from the panel.

Note:

The Auto-Collapse Iconic Panels option is also available in the User Interface pane of the Preferences dialog box, which you can open directly from the dock contextual menu.

9. **Click the left edge of the docked panels and drag right.**

When panels are iconized, you can reduce the panel buttons to only the icons. This can be particularly useful once you are more familiar with the application and the icons used to symbolize the different panels.

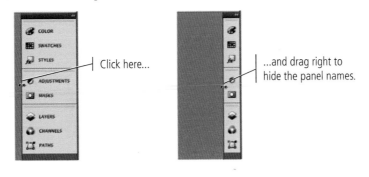

Click here...

...and drag right to hide the panel names.

10. On the left side of the workspace, click the Tools panel title bar.

The Tools panel can't be expanded, but it can be displayed as either one or two columns; clicking the Tools panel title bar toggles between the two modes.

The one- or two-column format is a purely personal choice. The one-column layout takes up less horizontal space on the screen, which can be useful if you have a small monitor. The two-column format fits in a smaller vertical space, which can be especially useful if you have a laptop with a widescreen monitor.

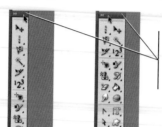

Click the Tools panel title bar to toggle between the one-column and two-column layouts.

Note:

Throughout this book, our screen shots show the Tools panel in the one-column format. Feel free to work with the panel in two columns if you prefer.

11. Continue to the next exercise.

Identifying and Accessing Photoshop Tools

PHOTOSHOP FOUNDATIONS

Photoshop CS4 includes no less than 59 different tools (70 in Photoshop Extended) — a large number that indicates the power of the application. In addition to the basic tool set, the bottom of the Tools panel includes options that control the foreground and background colors, as well as the screen mode you're using. You will learn how to use all of these tools as you complete the projects in this book. For now, you should simply take the opportunity to identify the tools.

Because displaying more than tools individually would be unwieldy at best, the Photoshop Tools panel groups related tools. Any tool with an arrow in the bottom-right corner includes related tools below it. When you click a tool and hold the mouse button (or Control/right-click a tool), the **nested tools** appear in a pop-up menu. When you choose one of the nested tools, that variation becomes the default choice in the Tools panel.

When you hover your mouse over a tool, the pop-up **tool tip** shows the name of the tool, as well as a letter in parentheses. Pressing that letter activates the associated tool. If you don't see tool tips, check the Interface pane of the Preferences dialog box; the Show Tool Tips check box should be active.

This arrow means there are nested tools.

When you hover the mouse cursor over the tool, a tool tip shows the name of the tool.

Click and hold down the mouse button (or Control/ right-click) to show nested tools.

- Move tool
- Rectangular Marquee tool
- Lasso tool
- Quick Selection tool
- Crop tool
- Eyedropper tool
- Spot Healing Brush tool
- Brush tool
- Clone Stamp tool
- History Brush tool
- Eraser tool
- Gradient tool
- Blur tool
- Dodge tool
- Pen tool
- Horizontal Type tool
- Path Selection tool
- Rectangle tool
- 3D Rotate tool
- 3D Orbit tool
- Hand tool
- Zoom tool

Default Foreground and Background colors

Foreground color

- Switch Foreground and Background colors
- Background color
- Edit in Quick Mask mode

Keyboard Shortcuts and Nested Tools

The following chart offers a quick reference of nested tools, as well as the keyboard shortcut for each tool. Not all nested tools can be accessed with a shortcut. In the marquee tools, for example, the shortcut toggles between the rectangular and elliptical variations only.

Also, most nested tools have the same shortcut as the default tool. Photoshop groups related tools into nested sets, so the same shortcut is assigned to the nested variations. By default, you have to press Shift plus the shortcut key to access the nested variations; for example,

press Shift-M to toggle between the Rectangular and Elliptical Marquee tools. You can change this behavior in the General pane of the Preferences dialog box by unchecking the Use Shift Key for Tool Switch option.

Finally, if you press and hold a tool's keyboard shortcut, you can temporarily call the appropriate tool (called **spring-loaded keys**); after releasing the shortcut key, you return to the tool you were using previously. For example, you might use this technique to switch temporarily from the Brush tool to the Eraser tool while painting.

Move tool (V)	Brush tool (B)	Horizontal Type tool (T)
	Pencil tool (B)	*Vertical Type tool (T)*
Rectangular Marquee tool (M)	*Color Replacement tool (B)*	*Horizontal Type Mask tool (T)*
Elliptical Marquee tool (M)		*Vertical Type Mask tool (T)*
Single Row Marquee tool	Clone Stamp tool (S)	
Single Column Marquee tool	*Pattern Stamp tool (S)*	Path Selection tool (A)
		Direct Selection tool (A)
Lasso tool (L)	History Brush tool (Y)	
Polygonal Lasso tool (L)	*Art History Brush tool (Y)*	Rectangle tool (U)
Magnetic Lasso tool (L)		*Rounded Rectangle tool (U)*
	Eraser tool (E)	*Ellipse tool (U)*
Quick Selection tool (W)	*Background Eraser tool (E)*	*Polygon tool (U)*
Magic Wand tool (W)	*Magic Eraser tool (E)*	*Line tool (U)*
		Custom Shape tool (U)
Crop tool (C)	Gradient tool (G)	
Slice tool (C)	*Paint Bucket tool (G)*	3D Rotate tool (K)
Slice Select tool (C)		*3D Roll tool (K)*
	Blur tool	*3D Pan tool (K)*
Eyedropper tool (I)	*Sharpen tool*	*3D Slide tool (K)*
Color Sampler tool (I)	*Smudge tool*	*3D Scale tool (K)*
Ruler tool (I)		
Notes tool (I)	Dodge tool (O)	3D Orbit tool (N)
Count tool (I)	*Burn tool (O)*	*3D Roll View tool (N)*
	Sponge tool (O)	*3D Pan View tool (N)*
Spot Healing Brush tool (J)		*3D Walk View tool (N)*
Healing Brush tool (J)	Pen tool (P)	*3D Zoom View tool (N)*
Patch tool (J)	*Freeform Pen tool (P)*	
Red Eye tool (J)	*Add Anchor Point tool*	Hand tool (H)
	Delete Anchor Point tool	*Rotate View tool (R)*
	Convert Point tool	
		Zoom tool (Z)

EXPLORE THE ARRANGEMENT OF PHOTOSHOP PANELS

As you gain experience and familiarity with Photoshop, you will develop personal artistic and working styles. You will also find that different types of Photoshop jobs often require different but specific sets of tools. Adobe recognizes this wide range of needs and preferences among users; Photoshop includes a number of options for arranging and managing the numerous panels so you can customize and personalize the workspace to suit your specific needs.

We designed the following exercise so you can explore different ways of controlling panels in the Photoshop user interface. Because workspace preferences are largely a matter of personal taste, the projects in this book instruct you regarding which panels to use, but not where to place those elements within the interface.

1. **With Photoshop open, choose Window>Styles.**

   All panels can be toggled on and off using the Window menu.

   - If you choose a panel that is already open but iconized, the panel expands to the left of its icon.

   - If you choose a panel that is already open in an expanded group, that panel comes to the front of the group.

   - If you choose a panel that isn't currently open, it opens in the same position as when it was last closed.

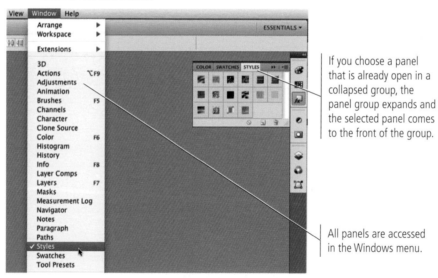

If you choose a panel that is already open in a collapsed group, the panel group expands and the selected panel comes to the front of the group.

All panels are accessed in the Windows menu.

2. **Control/right-click the Styles panel tab and choose Close from the contextual menu.**

   The panel's contextual menu is the only way to close a docked panel. You can also close an entire panel group by choosing Close Tab Group from the contextual menu.

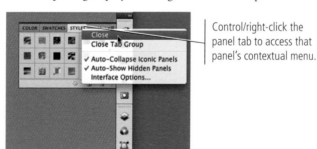

Control/right-click the panel tab to access that panel's contextual menu.

The closed panel is removed from the panel group.

3. Click the drop zone in the remaining panel group (the one with Swatches and Color) and drag away from the dock.

This is the panel group drop zone.

When a group is expanded, click the group's drop zone to move the entire panel group.

When you release the mouse button, the panel group floats freely in the workspace.

Panel group title bar

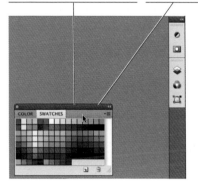

Note:

*Panels and panel groups can be **floated** away from the dock by clicking a panel tab or the panel group's drop zone and dragging away from the dock.*

4. Click the title bar of the panel dock to expand the dock column.

5. Click the title bar of the floating panel group to collapse the group.

Floating panels (and panel groups) can be iconized just like panels in the dock.

Click the title bar at the top of the floating group to collapse or expand it.

Note:

You can independently iconize or expand each floating panel (group) and each column of docked panels.

6. Click the Swatches panel icon (in the floating panel group) and drag the panel into the dock, below the second panel group. Don't release the mouse button.

Individual panels can be dragged to different locations (including into different groups) by dragging the panel's tab. The target location — where the panel will be located when you release the mouse button — is identified by the blue highlight.

The blue highlight shows where the panel will be placed if you release the mouse button.

7. **Drag the Swatches panel onto the drop zone area of the upper panel group in the dock, and then release the mouse button.**

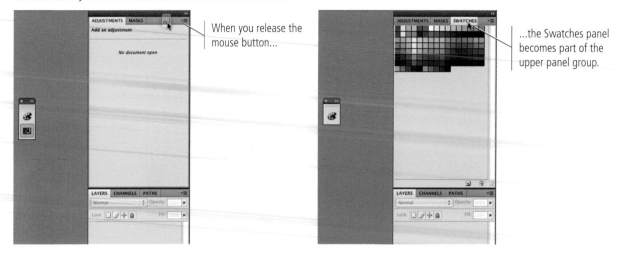

When you release the mouse button...

...the Swatches panel becomes part of the upper panel group.

8. **In the lower docked panel group, click the Layers panel tab and drag left until the blue highlight shows a second column added to the dock.**

As we mentioned previously, you can create multiple columns of panels in the dock. This can be very useful if you need easy access to a large number of panels and you have a monitor with enough available screen space.

This pop-out "drawer" indicates that releasing the mouse button...

...creates a second column in the panel dock.

9. **Click the title bar above the left dock column to collapse that column of panels.**

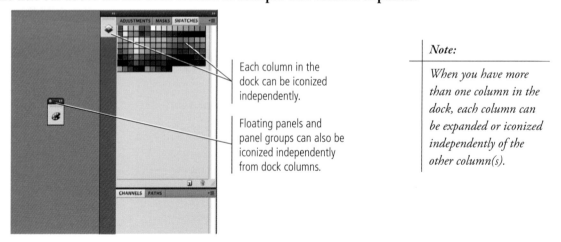

Each column in the dock can be iconized independently.

Floating panels and panel groups can also be iconized independently from dock columns.

Note:

When you have more than one column in the dock, each column can be expanded or iconized independently of the other column(s).

10. **Click the left edge of the right dock column and drag left.**

Dragging the left edge of a dock column changes the width of all panels in that column.

11. **Click the bottom edge of the upper panel group in the right column of the dock and drag up.**

When you drag the bottom edge of a docked group, other panels in the same column expand or contract to fit the available space.

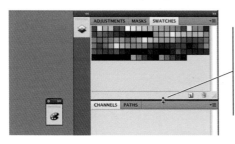

Dragging the bottom edge of a docked panel (group) changes the height of that panel (or group). Other panels in the same column expand or shrink as necessary to fit the column.

12. **Continue to the next exercise.**

CREATE A SAVED WORKSPACE

By now you should understand that you have extensive control over the exact appearance of your Photoshop workspace — what panels are visible, where and how they appear, and even the size of individual panels or panel groups.

Over time you will develop personal preferences — the Colors panel always appears at the top, for example — based on your work habits and project needs. Rather than re-establishing every workspace element each time you return to Photoshop, you can save your custom workspace settings so they can be recalled with a single click.

1. **Click the Workspace switcher in the Application/Menu bar and choose Save Workspace.**

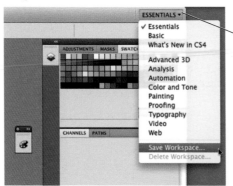

The Workspace switcher shows the name of the last-called workspace.

Note:

The Tools panel can also be floated by clicking its title bar and dragging away from the edge of the screen. To re-dock the floating Tools panel, simply click the title bar and drag back to the left edge of the screen; when the blue line highlights the edge of the workspace, releasing the mouse button puts the Tools panel back into the dock.

Note:

The Delete Workspace option opens a dialog box where you can choose a specific user-defined workspace to delete. You can't delete the default workspaces that come with the application.

2. **In the Save Workspace dialog box, type `Portfolio`. Make sure the Panel Locations option is checked and click OK.**

You didn't define custom keyboard shortcuts or menus, so those two options are not relevant in this exercise.

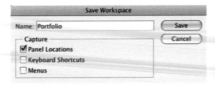

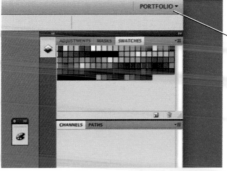

After saving the current workspace, the Workspace switcher shows the name of the newly saved workspace.

3. **Click the Workspace switcher and choose Essentials from the list of available workspaces.**

As we already explained, saved workspaces — whether part of the default set or ones you create — call specific sets of panels in specific locations on your screen. This step restores the default set of panels, iconized without the panel names.

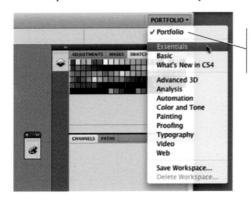

Custom workspaces are listed at the top of the Workspace switcher.

4. **Continue to the next exercise.**

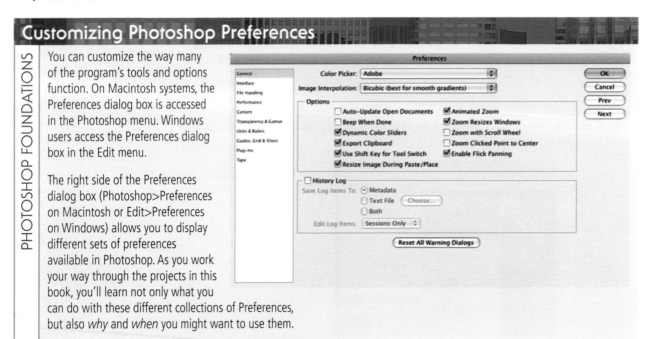

Customizing Photoshop Preferences

PHOTOSHOP FOUNDATIONS

You can customize the way many of the program's tools and options function. On Macintosh systems, the Preferences dialog box is accessed in the Photoshop menu. Windows users access the Preferences dialog box in the Edit menu.

The right side of the Preferences dialog box (Photoshop>Preferences on Macintosh or Edit>Preferences on Windows) allows you to display different sets of preferences available in Photoshop. As you work your way through the projects in this book, you'll learn not only what you can do with these different collections of Preferences, but also *why* and *when* you might want to use them.

EXPLORE THE PHOTOSHOP DOCUMENT VIEWS

There is much more to using Photoshop than arranging the workspace. What you do with those panels — and even which panels you need — depends on the type of work you are doing in a particular file. In this exercise, you open a Photoshop file and explore interface elements that will be important as you begin creating digital artwork.

1. **In Photoshop, choose File>Open.**

2. **Navigate to the RF_Photoshop>Interface folder on your Resource CD and select bryce2.jpg in the list of available files.**

   The Open dialog box is a system-standard navigation dialog. This is one area of significant difference between Macintosh and Windows users.

Note:

Press Command/ Control-O to access the Open dialog box.

PHOTOSHOP FOUNDATIONS

Customizing Keyboard Shortcuts and Menus

Different people use Photoshop for different reasons, sometimes only using a limited set of tools to complete specific projects. Photoshop allows you to define the available menu options and the keyboard shortcuts that are associated with menu commands, panel menus, and tools.

At the bottom of the Edit menu, two options (Keyboard Shortcuts and Menus) open different tabs of the same dialog box. (If you don't see the Keyboard Shortcuts or Menus options in the Edit menu, choose Show all Menu Items to reveal the hidden commands.) Once you've defined custom menus or shortcuts, you can save your choices as a set so you can access the same custom choices again without having to redo the work.

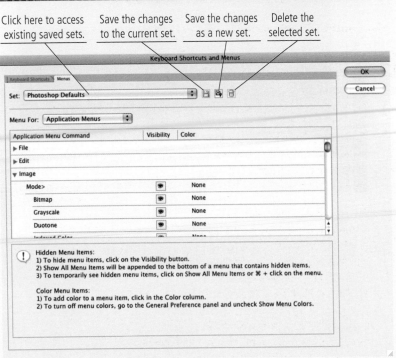

The following labels appear above the dialog box:
- Click here to access existing saved sets.
- Save the changes to the current set.
- Save the changes as a new set.
- Delete the selected set.

3. Press Shift, and then click `bryce3.jpg` in the list of files.

Pressing Shift allows you to select multiple contiguous (consecutive) files in the list.

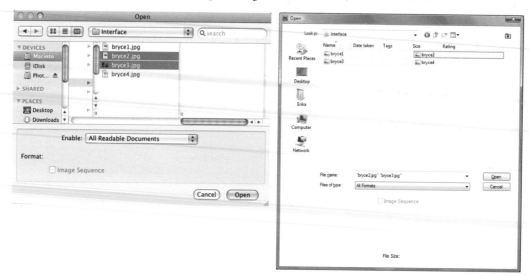

4. Click Open.

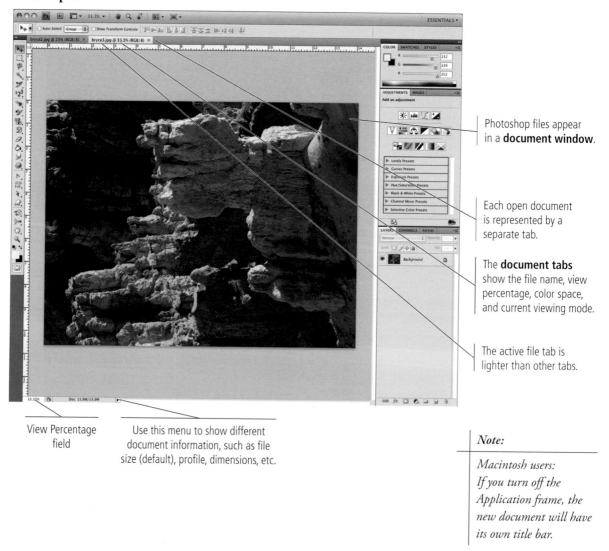

Photoshop files appear in a **document window**.

Each open document is represented by a separate tab.

The **document tabs** show the file name, view percentage, color space, and current viewing mode.

The active file tab is lighter than other tabs.

View Percentage field

Use this menu to show different document information, such as file size (default), profile, dimensions, etc.

Note:

*Macintosh users:
If you turn off the Application frame, the new document will have its own title bar.*

5. **Click the bryce2.jpg tab to make that document active.**

6. **Highlight the current value in the Zoom Level field (in the Application/
Menu bar) and type 40.**

Different people prefer larger or smaller view percentages, depending on a number of factors (eyesight, monitor size, and so on). As you complete the projects in this book, you'll see our screen shots zoom in or out as necessary to show you the most relevant part of a particular file. In most cases we do not tell you what specific view percentage to use for a particular exercise, unless it is specifically required for the work being done.

Note:

You can also type a specific percentage in the View Percentage field in the bottom-left corner of the document window.

Hand tool Zoom tool

Zoom Level field/menu Rotate View tool

View Extras button Arrange Documents button

Launch Bridge button Screen Mode button

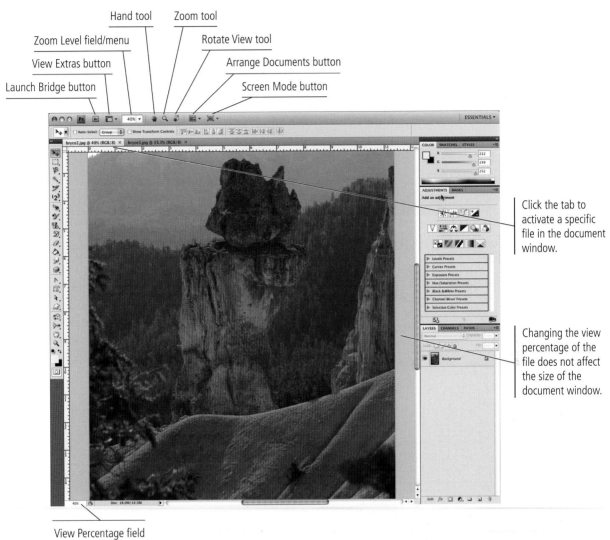

Click the tab to activate a specific file in the document window.

Changing the view percentage of the file does not affect the size of the document window.

View Percentage field

You can zoom a document between approximately 0.098% and 3200%. We say approximately because the actual smallest size is dependent on the original image size; you can zoom out far enough to "show" the image as a single tiny square, whatever that percentage of the image.

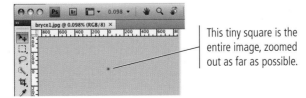

This tiny square is the entire image, zoomed out as far as possible.

7. **Choose View>Fit On Screen.**

These five options affect the view percentage of a file.

The Fit On Screen command automatically calculates view percentage based on the size of the document window.

8. **Click the Zoom tool in the Tools panel, and then review the options in the Control panel.**

Although we will not discuss all 20+ Photoshop panels here, the Control panel deserves mention. This panel appears by default at the top of the workspace below the Menu bar (and the Application bar on Macintosh). It is context sensitive, which means it provides different options depending on which tool is active.

9. **In the Control panel, click the Actual Pixels button.**

This option, the same as the Actual Pixels command in the View menu, changes the image view to 100%.

Note:

The Control panel is also called the Options bar in Photoshop, and is turned on or off by choosing Window>Options. For the sake of consistency, we refer to it as the Control panel throughout this book.

If Resize Windows to Fit is checked, zooming in a floating window affects the size of the actual document window (as much as possible within the available screen space).

If Zoom All Windows is checked, zooming in one window affects the view percentage of all open files.

These four buttons duplicate the same options in the View menu.

The Control panel shows options related to the active tool.

Zoom tool cursor

Zoom tool

10. **Press Option/Alt, and then click anywhere in the document window.**

Clicking with the Zoom tool enlarges the view percentage in specific, predefined percentage steps. Pressing Option/Alt while clicking with the Zoom tool reduces the view percentage in the reverse sequence of the same percentages.

Option/Alt-clicking with the Zoom tool reduces the view percent in the predefined sequence of percentages.

With the Zoom tool active, pressing Option/Alt changes the cursor to the Zoom Out icon.

11. **Click the Hand tool near the bottom of the Tools panel, and then review the options in the Control panel.**

12. **Click in the document window, hold down the mouse button, and drag around.**

The Hand tool is a very easy and convenient option for changing the area of an image that is currently visible in the document window.

Note:

Dragging with the Zoom tool enlarges the selected area to fill the document window.

If Scroll All Windows is checked, dragging in one window affects the visible area of all open files.

These four buttons duplicate the same options in the View menu.

The Control panel shows options related to the active tool.

Hand tool cursor

Hand tool

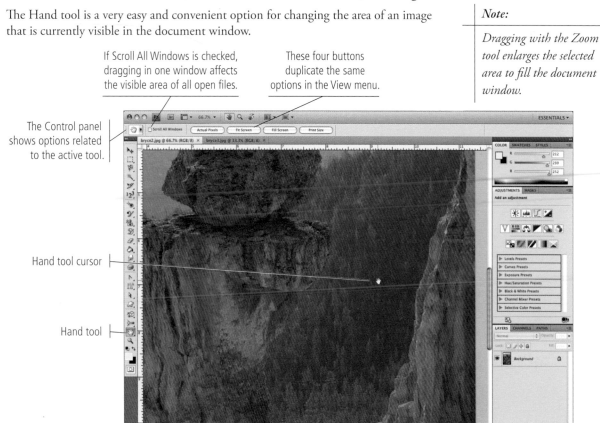

13. **Click the bryce3.jpg tab to make that document active.**

14. **In the Tools panel, Control/right-click the Hand tool and choose the Rotate View tool from the list of nested tools. Click in the document window and drag right to turn the document clockwise.**

The Rotate View tool turns an image without permanently altering the orientation of the file; the actual image data remains unchanged. This tool allows you to more easily work on objects or elements that are not oriented horizontally (for example, working with text that appears on an angle in the final image).

If you are unable to rotate the image view, open the Performance pane of the Preferences dialog box and make sure Enable OpenGL Drawing is checked. You will have to close the file and reopen it after enabling OpenGL Drawing for the change to take effect.

Note:

The Application/Menu bar includes buttons to select the three tools related to the document view (Hand, Zoom, and Rotate View tools).

Note:

OpenGL is a hardware/software combination that makes it possible to work with complex files such as 3D. If this option is not available (grayed out) on your computer, your video card and/or driver does not support OpenGL. You will not be able to rotate the image view.

Type a specific angle in this field to rotate the image view.
Click and drag around this icon to rotate the image view.
Clicking Reset View restores the original image orientation.
If Rotate All Windows is checked, dragging in one window affects the view angle of all open files.

The Control panel shows options related to the active tool.

Rotate View tool cursor

Rotate View tool

The red arrow of the compass indicates the image's original North.

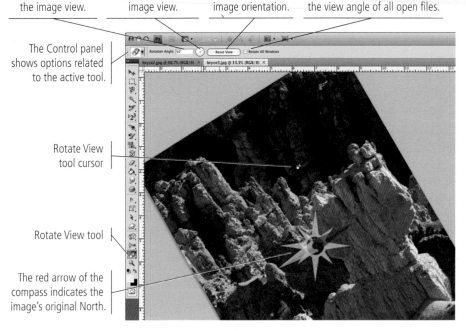

15. **In the Control panel, click the Reset View button.**

As we said, the Rotate View tool is non-destructive. You can easily use the tool's options to define a specific view angle or to restore an image to its original orientation.

Resetting the view restores the image's original orientation.

16. **Continue to the next exercise.**

Most Photoshop projects require some amount of zooming in and out to various view percentages, as well as navigating around the document within its window. As we show you how to complete different stages of the workflow, we usually won't tell you when to change your view percentage because that's largely a matter of personal preference. However, you should understand the different options for navigating around a Photoshop file so you can easily and efficiently get to what you want, when you want to get there.

View Menu

The View menu also provides options for changing the view percentage, including the associated keyboard shortcuts. (The Zoom In and Zoom Out options step through the same predefined view percentages that you see by clicking with the Zoom tool.)

Zoom In	Command/Control-plus (+)
Zoom Out	Command/Control-minus (-)
Fit On Screen	Command/Control-0 (zero)
Actual Pixels (100%)	Command/Control-1

Zoom Tool

You can click with the **Zoom tool** to increase the view percentage in specific, predefined intervals (the same intervals you see in the View Percentage menu in the bottom-left corner of the document window). Pressing Option/Alt with the Zoom tool allows you to zoom out in the same predefined percentages. If you drag a marquee with the Zoom tool, you can zoom into a specific location; the area surrounded by the marquee fills the available space in the document window.

Hand Tool

Whatever your view percentage, you can use the **Hand tool** to drag the file around in the document window. The Hand tool changes only what is visible in the window; it has no effect on the actual pixels in the image.

Mouse Scroll Wheel

If your mouse has a scroll wheel, rolling the scroll wheel up or down moves the image up or down within the document window. If you press Command/Control and scroll the wheel, you can move the image left (scroll up) or right (scroll down) within the document window. You can also press Option/Alt and scroll the wheel up to zoom in or scroll the wheel down to zoom out.

(In the General pane of the Preferences dialog box, the Zoom with Scroll Wheel option is unchecked by default. If you check this option, scrolling up or down with no modifier key zooms in or out and does not move the image within the document window.)

Application/Menu Bar

The Application/Menu bar consolidates many of the view-related tools and options into a single location, which is always visible at the top of the workspace (unless you're on a Macintosh and have turned off the Application frame and Application bar).

Navigator Panel

The **Navigator panel** is another method of adjusting how close your viewpoint is and what part of the page you're currently viewing (if you're zoomed in close enough so you can see only a portion of the page). The Navigator panel shows a thumbnail of the active file; a red rectangle represents exactly how much of the document shows in the document window.

The red rectangle shows the area of the file that is visible in the document window.

Drag the red rectangle to change the visible portion of the file.

Use the slider and field at the bottom of the panel to change the view percentage.

EXPLORE THE ARRANGEMENT OF MULTIPLE DOCUMENTS

You will often need to work with more than one Photoshop file at once. Photoshop CS4 incorporates a number of options for arranging multiple documents. We designed the following simple exercise so you can explore these options.

1. **With `bryce2.jpg` and `bryce3.jpg` open, choose File>Open.**

   The Open dialog box defaults to the last-used location, so you should not have to navigate back to the RF_Photoshop>Interface folder.

2. **Click `bryce1.jpg` in the list to select that file.**

3. **Press Command/Control and click `bryce4.jpg` to add that file to the active selection.**

   Pressing Command/Control allows you to select and open non-contiguous files.

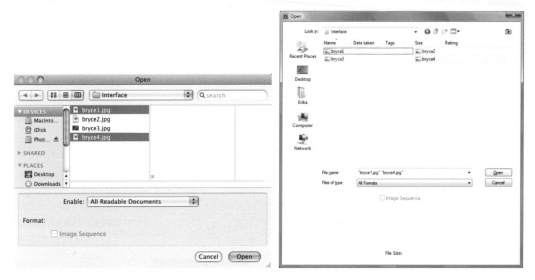

4. **Click Open to open both selected files.**

5. **Click the bryce1.jpg tab at the top of the document window.**

6. **Open the Window menu and choose `bryce2.jpg` at the bottom of the menu.**

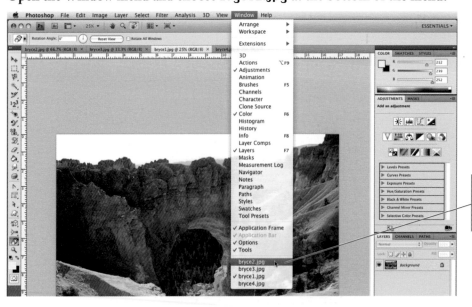

All open files can be activated using the file names at the bottom of the Window menu.

7. **Choose Window>Arrange>Float in Window.**

Floating a document separates the file into its own document window.

The title bar of the separate document window shows the same information that was in the document tab.

8. **In the Application/Menu bar, click the Arrange Documents button to open the panel of defined arrangements.**

9. **Click the 4 Up button in the Arrange Documents panel.**

The defined arrangements provide a number of options for tiling multiple open files within the available workspace. These arrangements manage all open files, including those in floating windows.

Note:

You can separate all open files by choosing Window>Arrange>Float All In Windows.

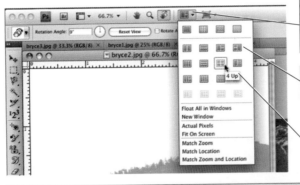

The Arrange Documents panel includes a number of tiling options for arranging multiple open files in the workspace.

The appearance of each icon suggests the result of each option.

Rolling your mouse cursor over an icon shows the arrangement name in a tool tip.

Note:

On Macintosh, the Application bar must be visible to access the Arrange Documents button.

10. Open the Arrange Documents panel again and click the Consolidate All button.

The Consolidate All button (and the Consolidate All to Tabs command in the Window>Arrange menu) restores all floating documents into a single tabbed document window (the same as you see in the default arrangement).

The remaining buttons in the top row separate all open files into separate document windows, and then arrange the different windows as indicated.

The lower options use a specific number of floating documents (2-Up, 3-Up, etc.); if more files are open than an option indicates, the extra files are consolidated as tabs in the first document window.

Note:

When multiple document windows are open, two options in the Window>Arrange menu allow you to cascade or tile the different document windows.

The consolidated document window snaps to fill the available monitor space (within the boundaries of docked panels).

The Consolidate All arrangement restores all open documents into a single document window.

11. In the Application/Menu bar, click the Screen Mode button.

Photoshop has three different **screen modes**, which change the way the document window displays on the screen. The default mode, which you saw when you opened these three files, is called Standard Screen mode.

12. Choose Full Screen Mode with Menu Bar from the Screen Mode menu.

As you saw previously, all open files are listed at the bottom of the Window menu. You can use these menu options to navigate from one file to another. This is particularly useful if you're working in Full Screen Mode with Menu Bar because the document tabs are not visible in this mode.

In Full Screen Mode with Menu Bar, the document window fills the entire workspace.

In Full Screen Mode with Menu Bar, the document tabs are hidden behind the Menu bar.

13. Click the Screen Mode button in the Application/Menu bar and choose Full Screen Mode. Read the resulting warning dialog box, and then click Full Screen.

14. Press the Escape key to return to Normal Screen mode.

Move your mouse cursor to the left edge of the screen to temporarily show the Tools panel.

In Full Screen Mode, the Menu bar, title bar, and all panels are hidden.

Move your mouse cursor to the right edge of the screen to temporarily show docked panels.

15. Click the Close button on the bryce2.jpg tab.

When multiple files are open, clicking the Close button on a document tab closes only that file.

16. Macintosh: Click the Close button in the top-left corner of the Application bar.

Closing the Macintosh Application frame does not quit the application.

On Macintosh, closing the Application frame closes all files open in that frame.

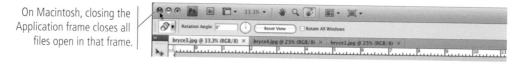

Windows: Click the Close button on each document tab to close the remaining files.

Clicking the Close button on the Windows Menu bar closes all open files *and* quits the application. To close open files *without* quitting, you have to manually close each file.

Click the Close buttons on each document tab to close the open files.

Clicking the Menu bar Close button closes all open files, but also quits the application.

The Undo command (Edit>Undo or Command/Control-Z) only steps back to the last one action you completed; after you use the Undo command, it toggles to Redo. You can also use the Step Backward command (Edit>Step Backward or Command-Option-Z/Control-Alt-Z) to move back in the history one step at a time, or use the History panel (Window>History) to navigate back to earlier stages of your work.

Every action you take is recorded as a state in the History panel. You can click any state to return to that particular point in the document progression. You can also delete specific states or create a new document from a particular state using the buttons at the bottom of the panel.

By default, the History panel stores the last 20 states; older states are automatically deleted. You can change that setting in the Performance pane of the Preferences dialog box. Keep in mind, however, that storing a larger number of states will increase the memory that is required to work with a specific file.

Keep the following in mind when using the History panel:

- The default snapshot shows the image state when it was first opened.

- The oldest state is at the top of the list; the most recent state appears at the bottom.

- The History State slider identifies the active state.

- You can save any particular state as a snapshot to prevent it from being deleted when that state is no longer within the number of states that can be stored.

- The history is only stored as long as the file is open; when you close a file, the history (including snapshots) is not saved.

- When you select a specific state, the states below it are dimmed so you can see which changes will be discarded if you go back to a particular history state.

- Selecting a state and then changing the image eliminates all states that come after it.

- Deleting a state deletes that state and those that came after it. If you choose Allow Non-Linear History in the History Options dialog box (accessed in the History panel options menu), deleting a state deletes only that state.

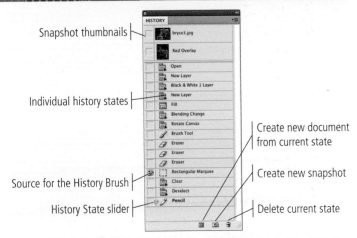

Snapshot thumbnails

Individual history states

Source for the History Brush

History State slider

Create new document from current state

Create new snapshot

Delete current state

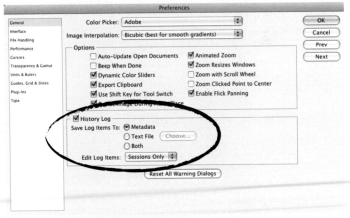

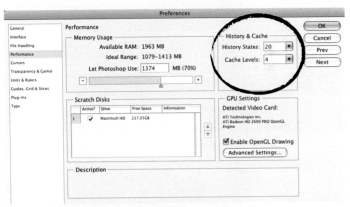

If you need to keep a record of a file's history even after you close the file, you can activate the History Log option in the General pane of the Preferences dialog box. When this option is checked, you can save the history log as metadata, in a text file, or both. You can also determine the level of detail that will be recorded in the history log.

- Sessions Only records each time you launch or quit and each time you open and close individual files.

- Concise adds the text that appears in the History panel to the Sessions information.

- Detailed gives you a complete history of all changes made to files.

Four-Color Movie Ad

Tantamount Studios, one of the largest film production companies in Hollywood, is developing a new movie called "Forefathers." You have been hired to develop advertisements that will be used to announce the movie in several different trade magazines.

This project incorporates the following skills:

❏ Creating a background image that can accommodate multiple trim sizes in a single file

❏ Incorporating vector graphics as rasterized layers and Smart Objects

❏ Compositing multiple photographs and scans, using various techniques to silhouette the focal object in each image

❏ Scaling and aligning different objects in relation to the page and to each other

❏ Managing individual layout elements using layers and layer groups

❏ Working with multi-layer and flattened files

❏ Saving multiple versions of a file to meet different output requirements

Here's a basic synopsis of the movie:

Most American history books teach us that our "forefathers" were esteemed, venerable men who crafted the United States out of lofty and respected ideals. But there's an old saying that history is written by the victors… In other words, who were these men really, and exactly how honorable were they? The movie is about the events during and after the American Revolution — not the war itself, but the personal aspects that drove these individuals to do what they did. It's not a war movie, and it's not a political movie. It's more a study of the human condition… How greed and power can corrupt even the most idealistic of men.

This movie is going to be one of our summer blockbusters, and we're throwing a lot of resources behind it. We'll be putting the same ad in multiple magazines, and they all have slightly different page sizes. We've forwarded the advertising specs for two of them to your art director, since those are the only ones we have right now.

The client loved the initial concept sketch I submitted last week, so we're ready to start building the files. I've had the photographer prepare the images we need, and the client has provided the studio and rating logo files. They also sent me the two magazines' specs:

Magazine 1

– Files should be submitted as native layout files or layered TIFF; CMYK only

– Bleed size: 8.75 × 11.25″

– Trim size: 8.5 × 11″

– Live area: 8 × 10.5″

Magazine 2

– Files should be submitted as native layout files or flattened TIFF; CMYK only

– Bleed size: 8.25 × 10.25″

– Trim size: 8 × 10″

– Live area: 7.5 × 9.5″

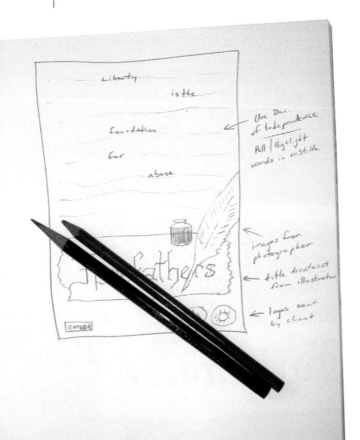

To complete this project, you will:

❏ Create a single file that can contain multiple page sizes

❏ Composite multiple images into a single background file

❏ Incorporate both raster and vector elements into the same design

❏ Use selection techniques to isolate images from their backgrounds

❏ Transform and arrange individual layers to create a cohesive design

❏ Create layer groups and nested groups to easily manage files

❏ Save two different types of TIFF files for different ad requirements

Stage 1 **Setting Up the Workspace**

There are two primary types of artwork: vector graphics and raster images. (Line art, sometimes categorized as a third type of image, is actually a type of raster image.) Photoshop is what some people call a "paint" program — it is primarily used to create and manipulate pixel-based or raster images.

Vector graphics are composed of mathematical descriptions of a series of lines and geometric shapes. These files are commonly created in illustration ("drawing") applications like Adobe Illustrator or in page-layout applications like Adobe InDesign. Vector graphics are **resolution independent**; they can be freely scaled and are automatically output at the resolution of the output device.

Raster images are made up of a grid of individual pixels (rasters or bits) in rows and columns (called a **bitmap**). Raster files are **resolution dependent** — their resolution is determined when you scan, photograph, or create the file.

Why is this information important? The ad you're building in this project will be placed in print magazines, so you have to build the new file with the appropriate settings for commercial printing.

Raster image quality depends directly on the resolution; when you create files in Photoshop, you need to understand the resolution requirements from the very beginning of the process:

- **Pixels per inch (ppi)** is the number of pixels in one horizontal or vertical inch of a digital raster file.

- **Lines per inch (lpi)** is the number of halftone dots produced in a horizontal or vertical linear inch by a high-resolution imagesetter in order to simulate the appearance of continuous-tone color.

- **Dots per inch (dpi)** or **spots per inch (spi)** is the number of dots produced by an output device in a single line of output. Dots per inch is sometimes used interchangeably with pixels per inch.

When reproducing a photograph on a printing press, the image must be converted into a set of different-size dots that fool the eye into believing it sees continuous tones. The result of this conversion process is a halftone image; the dots used to simulate continuous tone are called **halftone dots**. Light tones in a photograph are represented as small halftone dots; dark tones become large halftone dots. Prior to image-editing software, photos were converted to halftones with a large graphic-arts camera and screens. The picture was photographed through the screen to create halftone dots. Different screens produced different numbers of dots in an inch, hence the term "dots per inch."

Understanding Line Art

PHOTOSHOP FOUNDATIONS

Line art is a raster image made up entirely of 100% solid areas. The pixels in a line-art image have only two options: they can be all black or all white. Examples of line art are UPC bar codes or pen drawings.

The rule for line-art reproduction is to scan the image at the same resolution as the output device. Think about it like this: a 600 dpi (dots per inch) printer can create a maximum of 600 × 600 (360,000) dots in one square inch. With line art we want to give the printer the most information available, which in this case would be 600 pixels per inch. If the art is created and printed at only 300 ppi, then the printer would have to skip to every other possible space to put a dot. The result is known as "stair-stepping" or "bitmapping."

Most laser printers today image at 600 to 1200 dpi, but film on an imagesetter is typically produced at a much higher resolution, possibly 2400 dpi or more. Fortunately, the human eye is not sensitive enough to discern bitmapping beyond 1200 dpi, so you can be fairly safe capturing line art at 1200 ppi.

A bitmap or line-art image has only two colors — black and white.

Screen Ruling

The screens used with old graphic-arts cameras had a finite number of available dots in a horizontal or vertical inch. That number was the **screen ruling**, or lines per inch of the halftone. A screen ruling of 133 lpi means that in a square inch there are 133 × 133 (17,689) possible locations for a halftone dot. If the screen ruling is decreased, there are fewer total halftone dots, producing a grainier image; if the screen ruling is increased, there are more halftone dots, producing a clearer image.

Line screen is a finite number based on a combination of the intended output device and paper. You can't randomly select a line screen. Ask your printer what line screen will be used before you begin creating your images. If you can't find out ahead of time, or you're unsure, follow these general guidelines:

- Newspaper or newsprint: 85–100 lpi

- Magazine or general commercial printing: 133–150 lpi

- Premium-quality-paper jobs (such as art books or annual reports): 150–175 lpi; some specialty jobs might use 200 lpi or more

Image Resolution

When a printer creates halftone dots, it calculates the average value of a group of pixels and generates a spot of appropriate size. An image's resolution controls the quantity of pixel data the printer can read. Regardless of their source — camera, scanner, or files you create in Photoshop — images need to have sufficient resolution for the output device to generate enough halftone dots to create the appearance of continuous tone.

Ideally, the printer has four pixels for each halftone dot created. The relationship between pixels and halftone dots defines the rule of resolution for all raster-based images — the resolution of an image should be two times the screen ruling (lpi) that will be used for printing.

All of this can be confusing. If you're preparing a document to be printed commercially, remember this general rule: Most raster images (except line art) should have about twice the pixel resolution as the line screen that will be output.

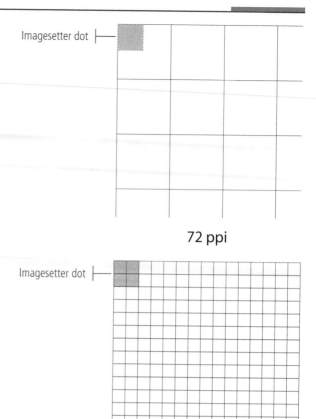

72 ppi

300 ppi

Each white square symbolizes a pixel in a digital image. The gray area shows the pixel information used to generate a halftone dot or spot. If an image only has 72 pixels per inch, the output device has to generate four halftone dots per pixel, resulting in poor printed quality.

The same raster image is reproduced here at 300 ppi (left) and 72 ppi (right). Notice the obvious degradation in quality when the resolution is set to 72 ppi.

CREATE THE NEW FILE

1. **On your desktop, copy the Liberty Ad folder from the WIP folder on your Resource CD to the WIP folder where you're saving your work.**

   Save all files for this project in your WIP>Liberty Ad folder.

2. **In Photoshop, choose File>New.**

   If Clipboard is showing in the Preset menu, the new file settings will match the current contents of the system clipboard (whatever you last copied in any application).

   You can create new files based on a number of included presets, including standard paper sizes (U.S. Paper, International Paper, and Photo) and standard sizes for different devices (Web, Mobile & Devices, and Film & Video).

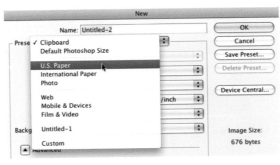

Note:

The New File dialog box defaults to the Clipboard preset (if you have anything copied) or to the last-used settings.

   If you choose one of these presets, the Size menu shows secondary options for the selected preset (such as Letter, Legal, or Tabloid for U.S. Paper). Choosing any of these presets automatically changes the values in the other fields of the dialog box.

Note:

Choosing U.S. Paper in the Preset menu automatically converts the Width and Height measurement units to inches. Choosing International in the Preset menu changes the default measurement units to millimeters.

3. **Highlight the Name field and type Movie Ad.**

   When you save the file, the file name defaults to the name you define when you create the file (in this case, "Movie Ad"). The name you assign here also appears in the Window menu and on the document tab at the top of the document window.

4. **Press Tab to highlight the next field (Width) of the dialog box.**

   Similar to most applications, you can press Tab to move through the fields of a dialog box. Pressing Shift-Tab moves to the previous field in the dialog box.

Note:

You can change the default unit of measurement in the Preferences>Units & Rulers dialog box.

5. **Click the menu to the right of the Width field and choose inches.**

   When you change one unit of measurement (width), the other (height) changes too.

Don't worry about the default values. You're going to define exactly what you need in the following steps.

The Image Size area shows the base file size of the file you're defining. This number changes dynamically whenever you change an option in this dialog box.

6. **With the Width field highlighted, type 8.75 in the field and press Tab.**

   As soon as you change any field, the Preset menu switches to "Custom" — you are defining a "custom" file size.

7. **Change the highlighted Height field to 11.25 and press Tab.**

8. **Change the Resolution field to 300; make sure the menu shows pixels/inch.**

   Pixels/cm is primarily used in countries that use the metric system of measurement (just about anywhere other than the U.S.). But if you inadvertently set the field to 300 pixels/cm, you'll create a file that is 762 pixels/inch — far more than you need for most applications.

9. **Click the Color Mode menu and choose CMYK.**

10. **Choose White in the Background Contents menu.**

    You can set the default background of any new file to White, the current Background Color, or Transparent. You can change this setting at any time after the file has been created.

Note:

Although designers trained in traditional (non-digital) methods are sometimes comfortable talking about picas or ciceros, most people use inches as the standard unit of measurement in the U.S.

Note:

Although many magazines are printed at 133 lpi, some are printed at 150 lpi. By setting the resolution to 300, your file will work for any magazine that prints at 133 or 150 lpi.

Use this menu to determine the default background color of the file (if any).

When you changed color modes, the Image Size changed to reflect the impact on the file's size.

11. **If the Advanced options are collapsed (the arrow button is pointing down), click the arrow button to show the Advanced options.**

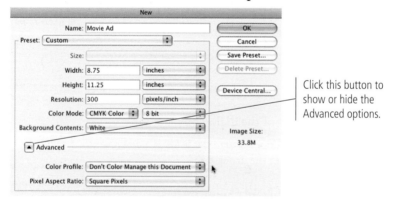

Click this button to show or hide the Advanced options.

12. **Click the Color Profile menu and choose Don't Color Manage this Document from the top of the menu.**

    Color management is basically a process for controlling color shift from one color space to another. You'll learn about color management in Project 3; for now, we're going to (mostly) ignore it.

13. **Leave the Pixel Aspect Ratio menu set to Square Pixels.**

    The options in this menu are primarily used for editing video. Since this is a print project, you don't want to alter the pixel ratio.

14. Click OK to create the new file.

15. If you don't see rulers on the top and left edges, choose View>Rulers to toggle rulers on.

As we explained in the Interface chapter, the panels you see depend on what was done the last time you (or someone else) used the Photoshop application. Because workspace arrangement is such a personal preference, we tell you what panels you need to use but we don't tell you where to put them.

In our screen shots we typically float panels over the relevant area of the document; this allows us to focus on the most important part of the file at any time. As you complete the projects in this book, feel free to dock the panels, grouped or ungrouped, iconized or expanded, however you prefer.

Note:

Remember: Panels can always be accessed in the Window menu.

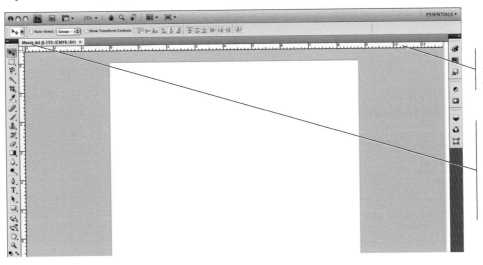

Rulers display the selected unit values.

As we mentioned earlier, the document tab shows the file name you already defined. This makes it much easier to work with multiple files, rather than a long list of Untitled1, Untitled2, etc.

16. Choose File>Save As.

Understanding Color Modes

PHOTOSHOP FOUNDATIONS

The **color mode** (or color space) defines the structure of the colors in your file.

Bitmap color reproduces all pixels in the image as either black or white; there are no shades of gray.

Grayscale color reproduces all tones in the file as shades of gray. This type of image has only one channel (you learn about color channels later in this book).

RGB creates color by combining different intensities of red, green, and blue light (collectively referred to as the "additive primaries"). Computer monitors and television sets display color in RGB, which has a **gamut** or range of more than 16.7 million different colors. An RGB file has three color channels, one for each of the additive primaries.

CMYK ("process") color is based on the absorption and reflection of light. Four process inks — cyan, magenta, yellow, and black (collectively referred to as the "subtractive primaries") — are used in varying combinations and percentages to produce the range of printable colors in most commercial printing. A CMYK file has four color channels, one for each of the four subtractive primaries.

Theoretically, a mixture of equal parts of cyan, magenta, and yellow would produce black. Pigments, however, are not pure, so the result of mixing these colors is a muddy brown (called **hue error**). To obtain vibrant colors (and so elements such as type can be printed cleanly), black ink is added to the three primaries. Black is represented by the letter "K" for "key color."

LAB color is device independent; the colors it describes don't depend upon the characteristics of a particular printer, monitor, or scanner. In theory, LAB bridges the gap between the various color models and devices; it is used as the background when converting images from one color space to another.

The problem with using RGB for print jobs is that the RGB colors eventually need to be converted to CMYK separations for a commercial printing press. Photoshop includes sophisticated tools that allow you to control this conversion, which you'll learn about in Project 5. Since you're creating this file for print, it's a better idea to create it in the color mode that will ultimately be used — CMYK — so you won't have to convert and correct colors later.

17. **Navigate to your WIP>Liberty Ad folder as the location for saving this file.**

    Because you named the file when you created it (in the New dialog box), the Save As field is automatically set to the file name you already assigned. The extension is automatically added on both Macintosh and Windows computers.

18. **Choose Photoshop in the Format menu.**

    You can save a Photoshop file in a number of different formats, all of which have specific capabilities, limitations, and purposes. While you are still working on a file, it's best to keep it as a native Photoshop (PSD) file. You'll use some of the other available formats as you complete the projects in this book.

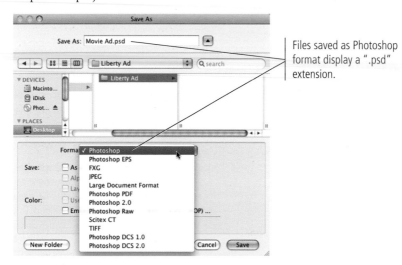

Files saved as Photoshop format display a ".psd" extension.

Note:

Also called "native", the PSD format is the most flexible format to use while building files in Photoshop.

19. **Leave any remaining options unchecked and click Save.**

    Since this is a very basic file with only a white background, most of these options are not available.

20. **Continue to the next exercise.**

    Since this is the first time you're seeing this series of dialog boxes (New and Save As), we explained a fairly large number of options. In the following projects, the basic file set-up instructions will be considerably shorter. Whenever you create a new file, refer to this section if you need help.

 ## DEFINE THE BACKGROUND

Now that the file has been created, the next step is to add a custom background color. When you defined the file, you had three options — transparent, white, or background color. You could have defined the background color before opening the New dialog box, but it is more common to create the file first, and then set the background.

1. **With Movie Ad.psd open, choose View>Fit On Screen.**

2. **Click the Default Foreground and Background Colors button near the bottom of the Tools panel.**

    By clicking this button, you can always return to the basic black/white options.

Note:

The foreground and background color swatches default to the last-used values.

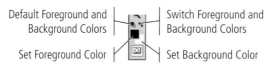

Default Foreground and Background Colors | Switch Foreground and Background Colors

Set Foreground Color | Set Background Color

3. **Click the Set Background Color button to open the Color Picker.**

You can use the same process to define the foreground color, except you click the foreground swatch in the Tools panel instead of the background swatch.

4. **In the lower-right corner of the dialog box, change the C (Cyan) field to 0, the M (Magenta) field to 35, the Y (Yellow) field to 0, and the K (Black) field to 100, and then click OK.**

Since you're working on a file in CMYK mode, you should define colors as percentages of CMYK.

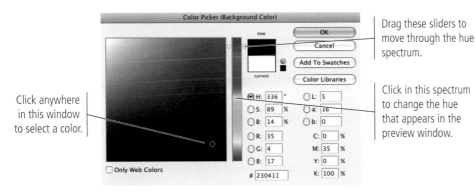

Drag these sliders to move through the hue spectrum.

Click in this spectrum to change the hue that appears in the preview window.

Click anywhere in this window to select a color.

Note:

*This type of color — 100% black and some percent of another color — is called **rich black** or **superblack**. It might seem like 100% black is black, but when the inks are printed, adding another ink to solid black enhances the richness of the solid black. Adding magenta typically creates a warmer black, while adding cyan typically creates a cooler black.*

5. **Look at the Layers panel.**

Every file you create has at least one layer. If you use the Transparent option in the New dialog box, the default layer is called "Layer 1". If you define the file with a white or other color background, the default layer is named "Background".

This Background layer cannot be moved, as indicated by the Lock icon. It can, however, be painted.

Note:

When the default layer is "Layer 1" instead of "Background," it is unlocked; you can move it within the image window or within the Layers panel.

6. **With nothing selected in the file, choose Edit>Fill.**

7. **Choose Background Color in the Use menu and click OK.**

The file has only one layer, so that layer is selected by default. Because no area of the file is currently selected, the Fill process fills the entire selected layer. (Depending on the accuracy of your monitor, you'll see the "rich" magenta color underneath the black — hence the name "rich black").

8. **Save the file and continue to the next exercise.**

PLACE PAGE GUIDES

The final step in preparing the workspace is defining the live area of the page. If you were creating an ad for a single magazine, this task would be relatively simple. Since the file you're building needs to fit several page sizes, you have to complete a few additional steps.

According to your client, the larger magazine trim size is 8.5 × 11 and the smaller magazine size is 8 × 10. (**Trim size** is the actual size of a page once it has been cut out of the press sheet.)

The outside dimensions of your file need to be big enough to fill the larger size. You might have noticed that you created the file 0.25″ larger than the larger file size. That's because the file has to incorporate **bleeds** that will print right up to the edge of the paper; to create this effect, you have to extend the page elements and background beyond the page trim size (called **bleed allowance**). Most applications require at least 1/8″ bleed allowance on any bleed edge.

All of the important elements of the design need to fit inside the smaller page size, so you need to mark those edges as well.

Note:

You should familiarize yourself with the most common fraction-to-decimal equivalents:

1/8 = 0.125

1/4 = 0.25

3/8 = 0.375

1/2 = 0.5

5/8 = 0.625

3/4 = 0.75

7/8 = 0.875

1. **With Movie Ad.psd open, click the horizontal page ruler and drag a guide to the 1/8″ (0.125″) mark.**

   Because the file has a very dark background, it's difficult to see the guide you're dragging. If you watch the vertical ruler, you can see a marker indicating the position of the cursor. When you see it at the 1/8″ mark, release the mouse button.

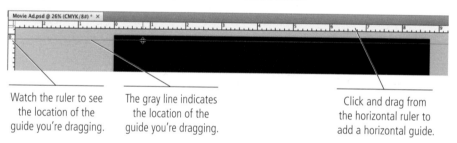

Watch the ruler to see the location of the guide you're dragging.

The gray line indicates the location of the guide you're dragging.

Click and drag from the horizontal ruler to add a horizontal guide.

2. **Drag another horizontal guide to the 11.125″ mark.**

3. **Click the vertical ruler and drag a guide to the 0.125″ mark.**

   Watch the marker on the horizontal ruler to judge the guide's position.

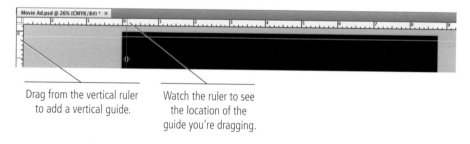

Drag from the vertical ruler to add a vertical guide.

Watch the ruler to see the location of the guide you're dragging.

Note:

It might be helpful to look at the Info panel while you drag guides to specific locations.

4. **Drag a second vertical guide to the 8.625″ mark.**

   At this point you should have four guides – two vertical and two horizontal, each 1/8″ from the file edges.

5. **Drag vertical guides 0.375″ from the left and right edges.**

Note:

When you drag guides onto the page, zooming in can help you place guides at precise measurements.

6. Drag horizontal guides 0.625″ from the top and bottom edges.

These guides mark the trim area of the smaller magazine size (8 × 10″). The smaller magazine needs to be exactly centered inside the larger magazine area. This is how we determined where to put these guides:

11.25 − 10 = 1.25 / 2 = 0.625, so each horizontal guide is 0.625″ from the edge

8.75 − 8 = 0.75 / 2 = 0.375, so each vertical guide is 0.375″ from the edge.

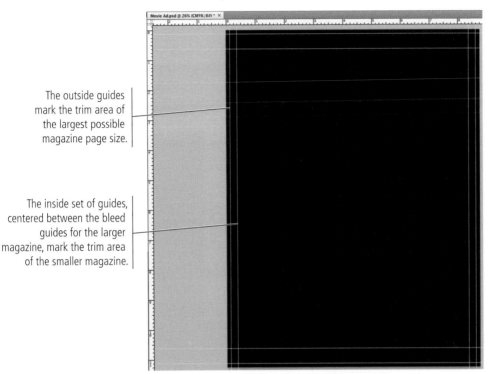

The outside guides mark the trim area of the largest possible magazine page size.

The inside set of guides, centered between the bleed guides for the larger magazine, mark the trim area of the smaller magazine.

The final step is to mark the live area of the smaller page size, or the area where important pieces should fit. Because there is inherent variation in the mechanical printing and trimming process, most magazines define a live area. All important design elements (especially text) should stay within this live area.

7. In the top-left corner of the document window, click the zero-point crosshair and drag to the top-left corner of the smaller page size.

You can reposition the zero point to the top-left corner by double-clicking the zero-point crosshairs.

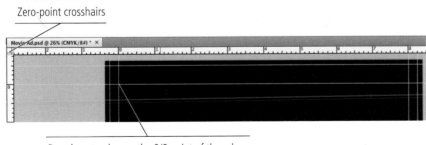

Zero-point crosshairs

Drag here to change the 0/0 point of the rulers. This new zero point is the reference point for any measurements you make in this file.

Note:

Use the Move tool to reposition placed guides. Remove individual guides by dragging them back onto the ruler.

If you try to reposition a guide and can't, choose View>Lock Guides. If this option is checked, guides are locked; you can't move them until you toggle this option off.

8. **Drag guides 0.25″ inside each trim guide for the smaller page size.**

These guides mark the live area of the smaller magazine. All important elements of the ad design must fit inside this space.

9. **Click the View menu and make sure a checkmark appears to the left of Lock Guides. If no checkmark is there, choose Lock Guides to toggle on that option.**

After you carefully position specific guides, it's a good idea to lock them so you don't accidentally move or delete them later. If you need to move a guide at any point, simply choose View>Lock Guides to toggle off the option.

Note:

Press Option/Alt and click a guide to change it from vertical to horizontal (or vice versa). The guide rotates around the point where you click, which can be useful if you need to find a corner based on the position of an existing guide.

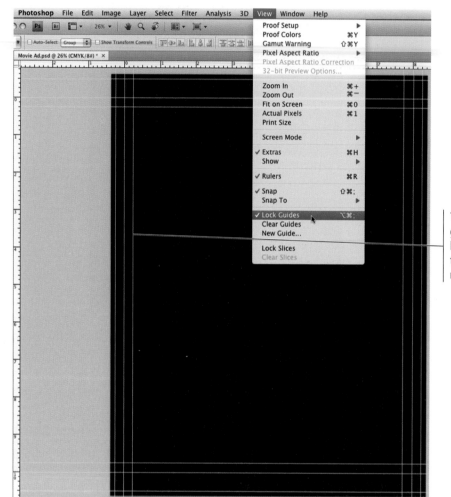

The inside guides mark the live area within the smaller magazine size.

Note:

If you choose View>New Guide, you can place a new guide in a specific position (horizontally or vertically) using a simple dialog box.

10. **Save the file and continue to the next stage of the project.**

Stage 2 Compositing Images and Artwork

Many of the projects you complete in Photoshop — including this one — involve compositing two or more images into the same file. Technically speaking, **compositing** is the process of combining any two or more objects (images, text, illustrations, etc.) into an overall design. When we talk about compositing in Photoshop, we're typically referring to the process of combining multiple images into a single cohesive image. Image compositing might be as simple as placing two images into different areas of a background file, and then adding blurred edges; or it could be as complex as placing a person into a group photo, carefully clipping out the individual's background, and adjusting the shadows to match the lighting in the group.

The movie ad you're building in this project requires compositing three individual images — one that has been scanned and two digital photographs. You'll also incorporate title treatment and logo files that were created in Adobe Illustrator by other members of your creative team. The various elements that make up the ad are fairly representative of the type of work you can (and probably will) create in Photoshop as your career progresses.

NAVIGATE FILES WITH ADOBE BRIDGE

When you created the background file for this project, you created a raster image that contains pixels (Photoshop files are almost always pixel-based). Digital photographs and scans are also pixel-based, which is why you use Photoshop to edit and manipulate those types of files.

Compositing multiple images in Photoshop is a fairly simple process — or at least, it starts out that way. But there are a number of technical and aesthetic issues you must resolve whenever you combine multiple images into a single design.

Note:

Adobe Bridge is a complete stand-alone application. However, this is a book about Photoshop, not Bridge. We're simply introducing you to the Bridge interface and showing you how to use Bridge to navigate and access files. We encourage you to read the Bridge documentation (accessed in the Help menu when you are in the Bridge application).

1. **In Photoshop, make sure Movie Ad.psd is open.**

2. **Click the Launch Bridge button in the Application/Menu bar.**

Launch Bridge button

3. **If you don't see a navigation window in Bridge, choose File>New Window.**

   Adobe Bridge is a stand-alone application that ships and installs along with Photoshop. This asset-management tool enables you to navigate, browse, manage, and access files anywhere on your system. If you have the entire Adobe Creative Suite, Bridge can also help streamline the workflow as you flip from one application to another to complete a project.

4. **In Bridge, navigate to the RF_Photoshop>Liberty Ad folder on your Resource CD.**

   Bridge is primarily a file manager, so you can think of it as a media browser. If some panels aren't visible, you can access them in the Bridge Window menu.

   The following image shows all the available Bridge panels. If one isn't showing in your application, you can open it in the Bridge Window menu.

   - The Folders panel on the left is used to navigate anywhere on your hard drive or networked devices (if you're connected to a network).

   - The Favorites panel provides quick access to saved "Favorite" folders. A number of these folders are defined by the Bridge Preferences (accessed in the Bridge menu on Macintosh or the Edit menu on Windows). You can also drag any folder into the Favorites panel to add it to the list.

- The Filter panel finds and sorts files based on specific, user-defined criteria.
- The Collections panel accesses specific, user-defined groups of files. Collections can be created based on virtually any criteria.
- The Content panel shows thumbnails of images in the selected folder. You can use the slider at the bottom to change the thumbnail size.
- The Preview panel shows a larger thumbnail of the selected file. You can click the preview image to view a specific area of the image at 100% magnification.
- The Metadata and Keywords panels allow you to add or review existing file information. Metadata and keywords are two of the most important aspects of true file management, allowing more logical and intuitive searches and easier tracking, to name only a few benefits.

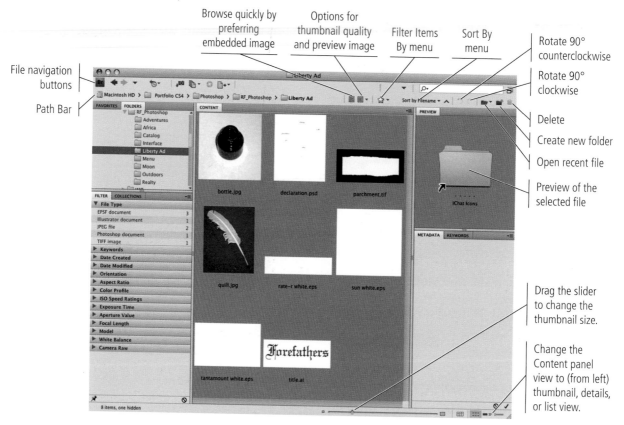

5. **Click the parchment.tif thumbnail in the Content panel.**

6. **In the Metadata panel, use the arrow buttons to collapse all but the File Properties.**

Depending on the size of your monitor, you might need to drag the bar separating the Preview and Metadata panels to show both panels at once.

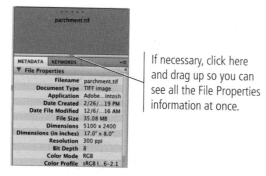

If necessary, click here and drag up so you can see all the File Properties information at once.

7. Review the file information.

The most important information in File Properties is the resolution and color mode. This image is a scan of an actual piece of torn parchment; it was scanned at 300 dpi (appropriate for print) in RGB color mode (most scans are RGB).

8. Double-click the parchment.tif thumbnail to open that file in Photoshop.

In this case, Bridge is an alternative to the File>Open method for opening files in Photoshop. The Bridge method can be useful because it provides more information than Photoshop's Open dialog box.

9. Navigate back to Bridge.

If you can't see the Bridge window behind Photoshop, use the Dock (Macintosh) or the Task bar (Windows) to re-activate the Bridge application.

10. Click the bottle.jpg thumbnail to select it.

11. Press Command/Control and click the quill.jpg thumbnail to select it, too.

You can open multiple images by simply selecting what you want and double-clicking. If you press Shift, you select multiple contiguous (adjacent) files. Pressing Command/Control allows you to select multiple non-contiguous files.

Note:

When the parchment image opens in Photoshop, the Bridge application remains open in the background.

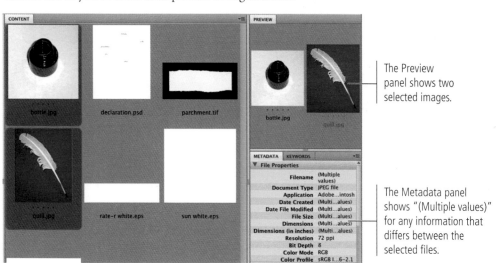

The Preview panel shows two selected images.

The Metadata panel shows "(Multiple values)" for any information that differs between the selected files.

12. Double-click either of the selected files to open both in Photoshop.

You should now have four images open in Photoshop — the background file you created earlier, the parchment scan, and the bottle and quill photographs.

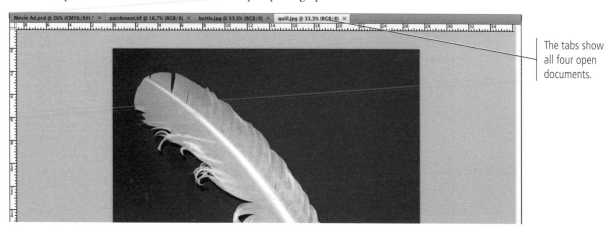

The tabs show all four open documents.

13. **In the Application/Menu bar, open the Arrange Documents panel and choose the 4 Up document arrangement.**

As you saw in the Interface chapter, these options are useful for arranging and viewing multiple open files within your workspace.

14. **Continue to the next exercise.**

 ## COMPOSITE MULTIPLE IMAGES

Now that the four files are open, you have to get the images into your background file. This is a fairly simple process of selecting what you want to import, and then copying it into the background.

1. **With all four images (the Movie Ad file you created and the three supplied photos) open and tiled in Photoshop, click the parchment window to activate that file.**

Like the file you created, this file has only one layer — Background. Every scan and digital photograph has this characteristic.

2. **With nothing selected, choose the Move tool at the top of the Tools panel.**

Adobe Bridge: Four Useful Tools for Graphics Professionals

Capturing Images from a Camera

The Get Photos from Camera button in Bridge (📷) opens the Photo Downloader dialog box, where you can pull images from your digital camera, name them logically (according to your instructions), and store them somewhere on your hard drive or network.

Batch Renaming

If you choose Tools>Batch Rename in Bridge, you can change the names of multiple files in a single action. For example, we frequently use this command to add the appropriate codes to screen captures ("_PSCS4_06" for images in Project 6 of our Photoshop CS4 book). Rather than manually type this into every file name, we use the Batch Rename function to add the information for us. You have full control over what's used for the new file names, including dates, locations, custom text, and more.

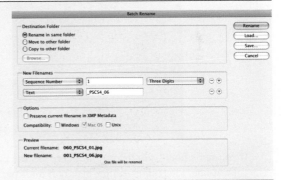

Accessing the Metadata Placard

Bridge's **Metadata Placard** shows technical photographic data, including virtual film speed, shutter settings, and a host of other information relative to images brought in from higher-end digital cameras. You can toggle it on or off in the Metadata panel Options menu.

Managing Camera RAW-Formatted Files

Most professional photographers rely on cameras that are a combination of digital and traditional SLR (single-lens reflex) technology. The file format of these high-end cameras contains far more data than Photoshop was originally designed to handle. To resolve this problem, manufacturers developed the RAW format, which stores more data — particularly in color ranges, hue, lighting, density, and other specifications.

Both Bridge and Photoshop CS4 include the necessary tools to open and work with RAW images, making fine and detailed adjustments without losing any of the extra information stored in the RAW format. Click the Open in Camera Raw button in Bridge (⚙) to access these options.

3. Click in the parchment file window and drag to the Movie Ad.psd file window.

Since you didn't select anything specific in the parchment file, you can drag the entire image layer into another file.

Move tool

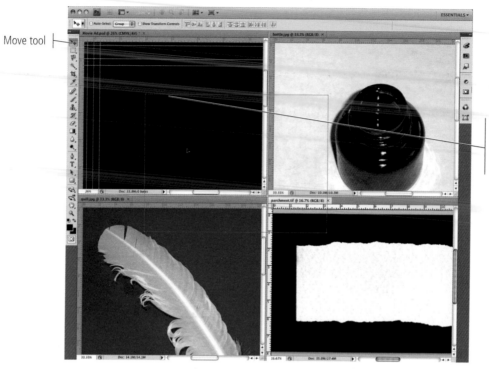

This outline shows the shape of the layer you're dragging from one document to another.

If you remember from the previous exercise, the parchment image was 300 dpi in RGB color mode. Photoshop cannot maintain multiple color modes in a single file. The RGB parchment image is automatically converted to the CMYK color mode you're using in the background file. (If you were using color management, you would see a warning about this conversion. Later in this book, you will learn how to control the process; for now, you should just know that the conversion occurred.)

The Movie Ad.psd file now has two layers: Background (the one you created) and Layer 1 (the parchment image you just copied). When you copy or drag a layer from one file into another, it is automatically placed on a new layer with the default name "Layer *n*", where "n" is a sequential number.

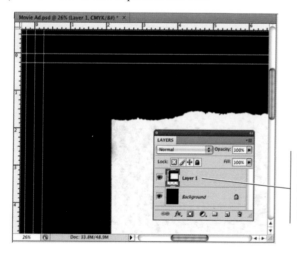

Dragging the Parchment file onto the Movie Ad automatically generates a new layer (Layer 1) for the dragged image.

Note:

You might notice that the parchment image doesn't fit into the background. You'll fix this problem later.

4. **Click the bottle.jpg window to activate that file. If you can't see the entire bottle, zoom out until you can.**

5. **Choose the Rectangular Marquee tool in the Tools panel.**

   In addition to dragging entire files into other files, you can also composite specific areas of a file using one of the selection tools.

   Note:

   Use the marquee tools to create simple-shape selections such as rectangular, elliptical, single row of pixels, or a single column of pixels.

6. **Using the Rectangular Marquee tool, click in the bottle.jpg window and drag around the entire shape of the bottle.**

   By default, dragging with the selection tool creates a new selection. You can use the buttons on the left end of the Control panel to add to the current selection, subtract from the current selection, or intersect with the current selection.

Rectangular Marquee tool

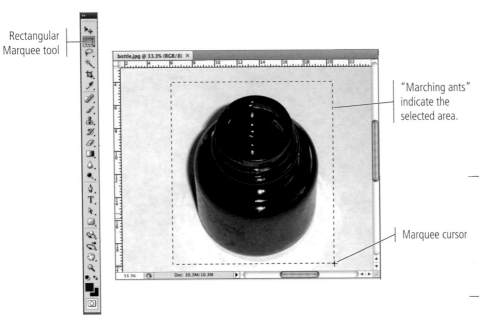

"Marching ants" indicate the selected area.

Marquee cursor

Note:

***Marching ants** is an industry term for the animated edge of an active selection marquee.*

Note:

Press Shift while dragging a new marquee to constrain the selection to a square (using the Rectangular Marquee tool) or circle (using the Elliptical Marquee tool).

7. **Click the Subtract From Selection button on the Control panel.**

   When one of the marquee tools is selected, the Control panel gives you better control over what you are selecting.

New Selection   Add to Selection   Subtract from Selection   Intersect Selections

Access saved presets for the selected tool

Feather (soften) the edges of a selection by a specified number of pixels

Choose a normal selection, a fixed-ratio selection, or a fixed-size selection

Control precise attributes of the selection preview

Note:

Press Option/Alt while using a selection tool to subtract from the current selection.

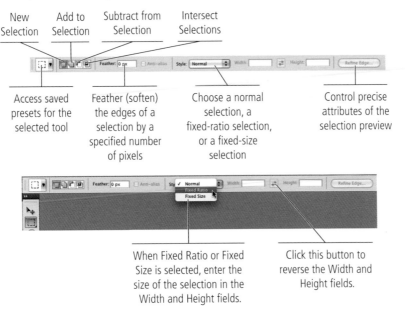

When Fixed Ratio or Fixed Size is selected, enter the size of the selection in the Width and Height fields.

Click this button to reverse the Width and Height fields.

8. **Drag a new marquee that overlaps the upper corner of the first selection, but doesn't include any part of the bottle.**

   When you release the mouse button, the selection is the area of the first marquee, minus the area of the second marquee. (This isn't particularly necessary in this case, but you should know how to add to and subtract from selections.)

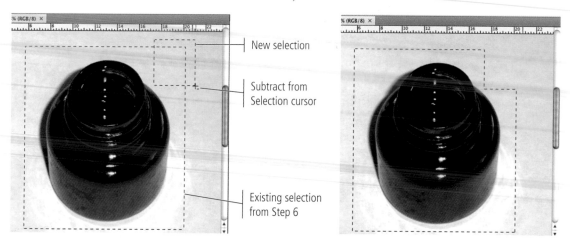

New selection

Subtract from Selection cursor

Existing selection from Step 6

9. **Choose Edit>Copy.**

10. **Click the Movie Ad.psd file window to activate that file and choose Edit>Paste.**

   The standard Cut and Paste options are available in Photoshop, just as they are in most applications. Whatever you have selected will be copied to the Clipboard, and whatever is in the Clipboard will be pasted.

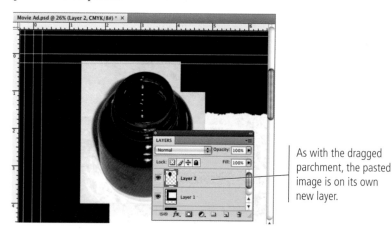

As with the dragged parchment, the pasted image is on its own new layer.

Note:

You can also press Shift to add to the current selection or press Option/Alt to subtract from the current selection.

11. **Click the quill.jpg window to activate that file, and zoom out so you can see the entire image.**

12. **Select the Lasso tool in the Tools panel.**

   The lasso tools allow you to make irregular selections — in other words, selections that aren't just rectangular or elliptical.

13. Drag a shape around the entire quill.

When you release the mouse button, the end point automatically connects to the beginning point of the selection.

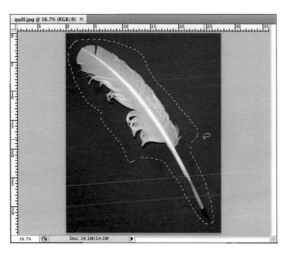

The Lasso Tools

The basic **Lasso tool** works like a pencil, following the path where you drag the mouse.

The **Polygonal Lasso tool** creates selections with straight lines, anchoring a line each time you click the mouse. To close a selection area, you must click the first point in the selection.

The **Magnetic Lasso tool** snaps to edges of high contrast in the image.

With the Magnetic Lasso tool, you can use the Control panel (Window>Options) to control the way Photoshop detects the edges of an image. **Width** is the distance away from the edge the cursor can be and still detect the edge; if you set this value higher, you can move the cursor farther from the edge (such as 20 pixels away). **Contrast** is how different the foreground can be from the background and still be detected; if there is a very sharp distinction between the foreground and background (as in the case of the white quill against the blue background, you can set this value higher). **Frequency** is the number of points that will be created to make the selection; setting this number higher creates finer selections, while setting it lower creates smoother edges.

It isn't uncommon for a mouse to unexpectedly jump when you don't want it to — which can be particularly troublesome if you're drawing a selection with the Polygonal or Magnetic Lasso tools. If you aren't happy with your Polygonal or Magnetic Lasso selection, press Esc to clear the selection and then try again.

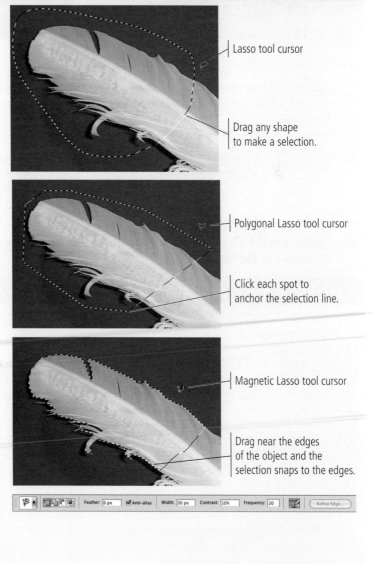

Lasso tool cursor

Drag any shape to make a selection.

Polygonal Lasso tool cursor

Click each spot to anchor the selection line.

Magnetic Lasso tool cursor

Drag near the edges of the object and the selection snaps to the edges.

14. **Copy the selection and paste it into the Movie Ad.psd file window, just as you did for the bottle selection.**

15. **Close the parchment, bottle, and quill files.**

16. **Choose View>Fit On Screen to fit the image into the document window.**

    You now have a file with four layers, but the composited images are simply stacked one on top of another. You'll fix this problem as you complete the rest of the project.

Note:

After closing the other open files, notice that the Movie Ad document window expands to fill the available space.

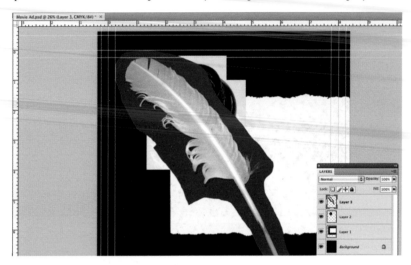

17. **Choose File>Save.**

    Because this is the first time you've saved the file after adding new layers, you should see the Photoshop Format Options dialog box, with the Maximize Compatibility check box already activated. It's a good idea to leave this check box selected so your files will be compatible with other CS4 applications and other versions of Photoshop.

Note:

If you don't see this dialog box, check the File Handling pane of the Preferences dialog box. You can set the Maximize PSD and PSB File Compatibility menu to Always, Never, or Ask.

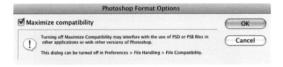

18. **Make sure the Maximize Capability check box is selected and click OK. Continue to the next exercise.**

Resizing Raster and Vector Images (Effective Resolution)

PHOTOSHOP FOUNDATIONS

You might have noticed (either in Bridge or from the rulers) that the bottle and quill images were physically very large — both over 26 inches wide — but they are only 72 dpi. When you copied these images into the Movie Ad file, however, they were nowhere near 26 inches wide. This is because, like color mode, copied images adopt the resolution of the file you paste them into. On the surface this seems simple; but you should understand what is actually happening behind the scenes so you don't accidentally lose image quality.

In the file's metadata, you can see that the file dimensions of bottle.jpg are 1887 × 1917 at 72 dpi. The dimensions shown here are measured in pixels; in other words, the bottle image has 1887 pixels in a horizontal row. If you divide 1887 pixels by 72 pixels/inch, you end up with the size in inches: the image is approximately 26.21 inches wide.

When the image is copied into a 300 dpi file, the bottle has the same 1887 pixels across. But when those 1887 pixels are divided by 300 dpi, the pasted image is about 6.3 inches wide. This is why the bottle you pasted into the Movie Ad file was so much smaller than it appeared in its own file window — the same number of pixels takes up a much smaller space when more pixels fit into an inch.

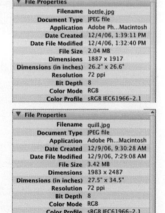

RASTERIZE A VECTOR FILE

As you already know, vector graphics are based on a series of mathematical descriptions that tell the computer processor where to draw lines. Logos and title treatments — such as the ones you use in this project — are commonly created as vector graphics. Although Photoshop is typically a "paint" (pixel-based) application, you can also open and work with vector graphics created in illustration programs like Adobe Illustrator.

1. **With Movie Ad.psd open, choose File>Open and navigate to the RF_Photoshop>Liberty Ad folder.**

2. **Select title.ai in the list of files.**

   This is an Adobe Illustrator file of the movie title text treatment. The Format menu defaults to Photoshop PDF because Illustrator uses PDF as its underlying file structure.

3. **Click Open.**

   When you open a vector file (Illustrator, EPS, or PDF) in Photoshop, it is rasterized (converted to a raster graphic). The Import PDF dialog box allows you to determine exactly what and how to rasterize the file. The default values in this box are defined by the contents of the file you're opening.

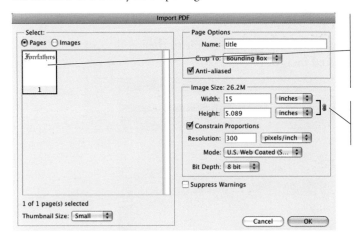

If you're opening a multi-page PDF or an Illustrator file with more than one Artboard, this window shows thumbnail previews of each "page" in the file.

When this chain icon appears, the width and height are constrained.

The Crop To options determine the size of the file you import. Depending on the type of file you're importing and how it was created, some of these values might be the same as others:

- **Bounding Box** is the outermost edges of the artwork in the file.
- **Media Box** is the size of the paper as defined in the file.
- **Crop Box** is the size of the page including printer's marks.
- **Bleed Box** is the trim size plus any defined bleed allowance.
- **Trim Box** is the trim size as defined in the file.
- **Art Box** is the area of the page as defined in the file.

The Image Size fields default to the settings of the bounding box you select. You can change the size, resolution, color mode, and bit depth by entering new values.

Note:

If you double-clicked this file in Adobe Bridge, it would default to open in Adobe Illustrator — its native application, or the application in which it was created. You could, however, Control/right-click the thumbnail in Bridge and choose Open With>Adobe Photoshop CS4 from the contextual menu.

4. **Highlight the Width field and type 8.**

   You know the page size of the smaller ad you're building is 8″ wide, so you can import this file at a size small enough to fit into that space.

   Because the Constrain Proportions option is checked by default, the height changes proportionally to match the new width.

5. **Make sure the Resolution field is set to 300 pixels/inch, and then choose CMYK Color from the Mode menu.**

6. **Click OK.**

   The title treatment file opens in Photoshop. The checked area behind the text indicates that the background is transparent. If you look at the Layers panel, you'll see that Layer 1 isn't locked; because it's transparent, it is not considered a background layer.

7. **Using the Arrange Documents panel in the Application/Menu bar, display the open documents using the 2 Up (side-by-side) arrangement.**

8. **Using the Move tool, click in the title window and drag the layer into the main file (the one with the other composited images).**

9. **Close title.ai without saving.**

   Because the title text file has a transparent background, the other layers are visible behind the text in the background file.

10. **Save Movie Ad.psd and continue to the next exercise.**

PLACE VECTOR GRAPHICS

Vector graphics offer several advantages over raster images, including sharper edges and free scaling without deteriorating image quality. To take advantage of these benefits, you might want to maintain vector files as vector objects instead of rasterizing them. Photoshop CS4 gives you the option to do exactly that — maintaining vector information and raster information in the same file.

1. **With Movie Ad.psd open, choose File>Place.**

   The Place dialog box is virtually the same as the Open dialog box. You can use this function any time you want to place one entire file directly into another without dragging or copying and pasting (as you did in the previous exercises).

2. **Navigate to and select rate-r white.eps and click Place.**

   In the background file, the placed file appears with bounding box handles and crossed diagonal lines. The placement isn't final until you press Return/Enter; if you press the Escape key, the file will not be placed.

3. **Press Return/Enter to commit (finalize) the placement.**

   After you finalize the placement, the bounding box handles and crossed diagonal lines disappear. In the Layers panel, the placed file has its own layer (just as the copied layers do). This layer, however, is automatically named, based on the name of the placed file.

   The layer's thumbnail indicates that this layer is a **Smart Object** — it is linked to the file that you placed. Because you are essentially placing a link to the vector file, it isn't rasterized into the Photoshop file; the vector information is maintained.

Note:

You can place either raster or vector files as Smart Objects. If you place a raster file as a Smart Object, double-clicking the thumbnail opens the placed raster file in another Photoshop window.

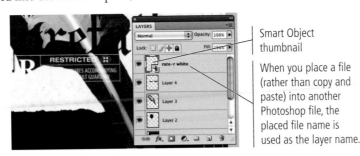

Smart Object thumbnail

When you place a file (rather than copy and paste) into another Photoshop file, the placed file name is used as the layer name.

Double-clicking the thumbnail would open the placed file in its native application — in this case, it would open the EPS file in Adobe Illustrator. If you edit the native file and save your changes (with the same file name in the same location), those changes would automatically update and reflect in the Photoshop file.

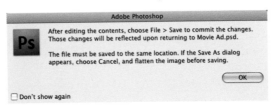

4. **Repeat Steps 2–3 to place the two remaining logo files (sun white.eps and tantamount white.eps) as Smart Objects into the movie ad.**

When you place Smart Objects, they are automatically placed into the center of the file. So right now, you have a fairly incomprehensible mess of four raster images and three vector objects all piled on top of one another. You'll start to make sense of these files in the next stage.

Note:

If you have the entire Adobe Creative Suite, Smart Objects provide extremely tight integration between Adobe Photoshop and Adobe Illustrator. You can take advantage of the sophisticated vector-editing features in Adobe Illustrator, and then place those files into Photoshop without losing the ability to edit the vector information.

5. **Save the file and continue to the next stage of the project.**

Stage 3 Creating Silhouettes

At this stage of the project, you have a single file that contains all of the necessary graphic elements, but you still have a few issues to resolve: the images are stacked on top of one another, some images don't fit into the page area, and some images have border edges that don't fit into the overall design (the blue background around the quill, for example). In this stage, you start fixing these problems.

Virtually any Photoshop project involves making some kind of selection. Making selections is so important, in fact, that there are no fewer than nine tools dedicated specifically to making selections, as well as a whole Select menu and a few other options for making and refining selections.

In an earlier lesson you learned how to use the marquee and lasso tools to draw selections. In the next series of exercises, you use several other selection methods to isolate the graphics from their backgrounds (called **silhouetting**).

 TRANSFORM A LAYER

Before you start silhouetting the different elements of the ad, it's a good idea to make them fit into the page area. Photoshop makes scaling, rotating, and other transformations fairly easy to implement.

1. **With Movie Ad.psd open, look at the Layers panel.**

2. **Click the eye icons to hide all but Layer 1.**

Toggling layer visibility is an easy way to see only what you want to see at any given stage in a project.

Note:

To show or hide a series of contiguous layers, click the visibility icon (or empty space) for the first layer you want to affect, hold down the mouse button, and drag down to the last layer you want to show or hide.

3. Double-click the Layer 1 layer name and type `parchment`.

You can rename any layer by simply double-clicking the name and typing. It's always a good idea to name your layers because it makes managing the file much easier — especially when you work with files that include dozens of layers. Even with only four unnamed layers in this file, it would be tedious to have to toggle each layer on to find the one you want.

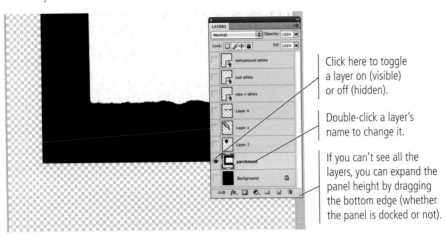

Click here to toggle a layer on (visible) or off (hidden).

Double-click a layer's name to change it.

If you can't see all the layers, you can expand the panel height by dragging the bottom edge (whether the panel is docked or not).

4. Choose Edit>Transform>Scale.

You can use this menu to apply any specific transformation to a layer or selection.

When you use the transform options, bounding box handles surround the selection; although the parchment doesn't fit inside the area of your file, you can still see the edges outside the page area. Since the parchment file is so much wider than the background file you created, some of the handles might not be visible.

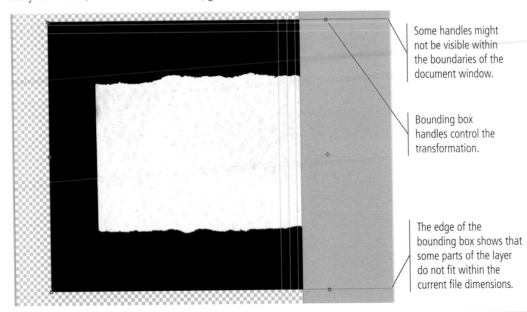

Some handles might not be visible within the boundaries of the document window.

Bounding box handles control the transformation.

The edge of the bounding box shows that some parts of the layer do not fit within the current file dimensions.

5. **Choose View>Zoom Out until you can see all eight bounding box handles.**

6. **Place the cursor within the bounding box. Drag until the left edge of the bounding box snaps to the left edge of the image.**

7. **Press Shift, click the bottom-right bounding box handle, and then drag up and left until the right edge of the bounding box is just past the right edge of the file.**

   The image dynamically changes as you scale the layer. Pressing Shift while you drag a handle constrains the image proportions as you resize it. When you release the mouse button, the handles remain in place until you finalize ("commit") the transformation.

8. **Look at the Control panel.**

   While you're manually transforming a layer or selection, the Control panel shows the specifics. You can also type into these fields to apply specific numeric transformations.

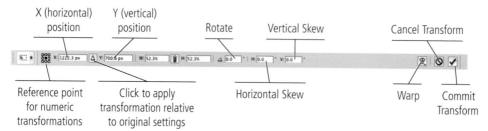

9. **Type 51 in the Control panel Width field, and then click the Constrain button.**

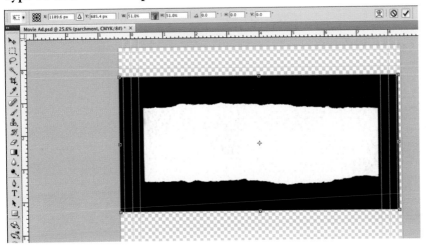

10. **Click the Commit Transform button on the Control panel or press Return/ Enter to apply the transformation.**

11. **Choose the Move tool and drag the selected layer until it's approximately centered in the file area.**

    While the Move tool is active, pressing the Arrow keys nudges the selected layer by a few pixels at a time. This method is useful for slight movements.

12. **Choose Edit>Transform>Scale again and look at the Control panel.**

    Once you commit the transformation, it is final. Looking at the Control panel now, you can see that it shows the layer at 100% instead of the 51% from Step 9.

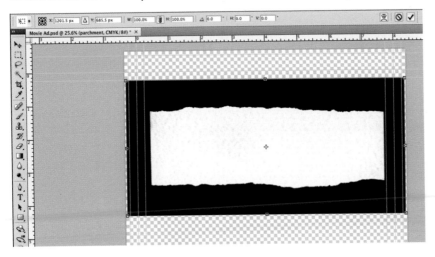

13. **Click the Cancel button in the Control panel or press the Escape key.**

14. **Save the file and continue to the next exercise.**

Note:

*The Control panel includes a "hidden" feature called the **scrubby slider**. If you place your cursor over a field name, it turns into a pointing hand with left- and right-facing arrows. While you see this cursor, you can drag across the Control panel to increase (drag right) or decrease (drag left) the value in the selected field.*

MAKE AND REFINE A QUICK SELECTION

Rather than drawing a selection area, you can make selections based on the color in an image. This technique is especially useful when you want to select large areas of solid color, or in photos with significant contrast between the foreground and background.

1. **With Movie Ad.psd open, choose the Quick Selection tool (nested with the Magic Wand tool) in the Tools panel.**

   As with the other selection tools, the Quick Selection tool can create a new selection, add to the existing selection, or subtract from the existing selection (using the three buttons on the left side of the Control panel).

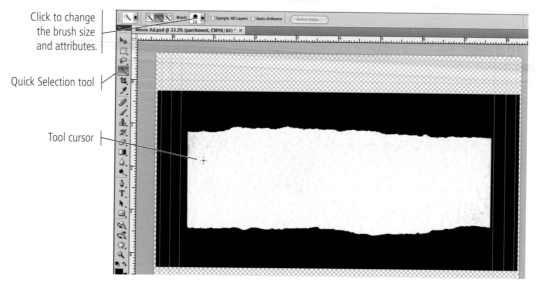

Click to change the brush size and attributes.

Quick Selection tool

Tool cursor

2. **Click at the left edge of the parchment and drag to the right.**

   The Quick Selection tool essentially allows you to "paint" a selection. As you drag, the selection expands and automatically finds the edges in the image. Because the varying shades in the parchment aren't significantly different, the resulting selection should closely — but not exactly — match the parchment edges.

Note:

If you stop dragging and then click in a nearby area, the selection grows to include the new area.

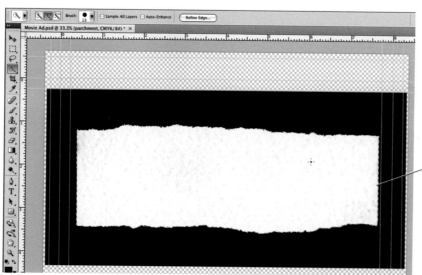

Marching ants surround the piece of parchment.

3. **Click the Refine Edge button on the Control panel.**

4. **If it is not already selected, click the On White preview button.**

   The five preview options allow you to change the way your image appears in the document window while you refine the edges within the dialog box.

   - **Standard** shows the basic selection (including the marching ants).
   - **Quick Mask** shows the selection using the current Quick Mask settings.
   - **On Black** shows the selection in color against a black background.
   - **On White** shows the selection in color against a white background.
   - **Mask** shows the selection in white and the unselected areas in black.

Note:

In a dialog box such as Refine Edge, pressing Option/Alt changes the Cancel button to Reset. If you press Option/Alt and click Reset, you restore the default values in the dialog box without closing the dialog box.

The On White preview shows the selected area (the parchment).

The remaining black edges are easily visible using the On White preview.

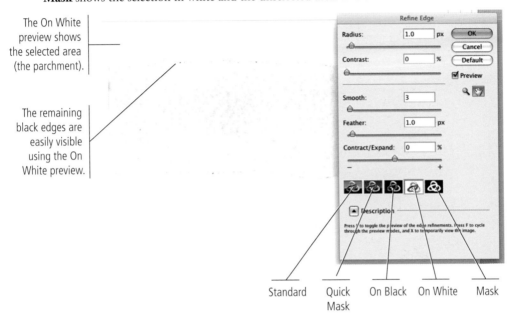

Standard   Quick Mask   On Black   On White   Mask

5. **Click the Zoom tool in the Refine Edge dialog box, and then click in the image window (where the parchment is located).**

   It might help to work with a closer view while you refine edges. We're working at 100% magnification in these screen shots.

At 100%, you can see how much of the black edge remains.

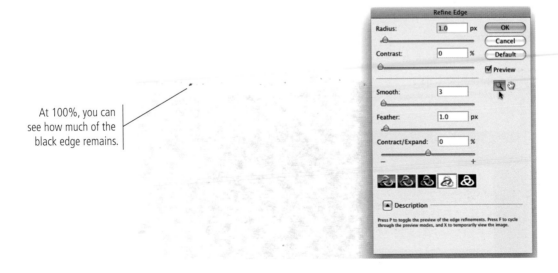

6. **Experiment with the five adjustment sliders until you're satisfied with the selection edge.**

- **Radius** is the number of pixels around the edge that are affected. Higher radius values (up to 250 pixels) improve the edge in areas of fine detail.

- **Contrast** is the degree of variation allowed in the selection edge. Higher Contrast values (up to 100%) mean sharper selection edges.

- **Smooth** reduces the number of points that make up your selection and, as the name suggests, makes a smoother edge. You can set smoothness from 0 (very detailed selection) to 100 (very smooth selection).

- **Feather** softens the selection edge, resulting in a transition that does not have a hard edge (in other words, blends into the background). You can feather the selection up to 250 pixels.

- **Contract/Expand** shrinks or grows the selection edge by the defined percentage (from –100% to 100%).

Note:

If you increase the Contract/Expand value high enough, you essentially increase the contrast of the edge and create a fairly hard, "refined" edge on the image.

Your numbers don't have to exactly match what we show here, but your finished layer should be close to ours.

7. **Click OK to accept your refined selection.**

8. **Fit the view back in the window (View>Fit on Screen).**

The black border is still there; don't be fooled by the On White preview you saw in the Refine Edge dialog box. Now you have to remove that black edge.

9. **Choose Select>Inverse.**

This command reverses the selection, so now everything except the parchment is selected.

Note:

We adjusted the Refine Edge sliders and arrived at these numbers visually. You'll often be in the same situation – performing actions partially by eye and partially "by the numbers."

10. **Press Delete/Backspace to remove anything within the current selection (the area other than the parchment).**

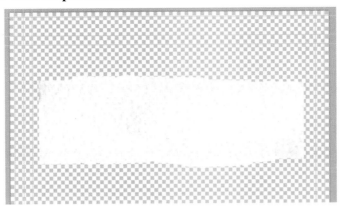

11. **Choose Select>Deselect to turn off the active selection.**

12. **Save the file and continue to the next exercise.**

 DRAW A VECTOR PATH

In some cases, the image content makes it difficult (or at least tedious) to select by color. The bottle image in this ad, for example, has only black colors — the bottle is black, the shadow is a medium black, and the background is a mottled light gray. Selecting by color range will almost certainly result in some of the selection intruding into the bottle shape, and some of the background/shadow area being omitted from the selection. The good news is that Photoshop has other ways for making selections, including several that are specifically designed for selecting areas with hard edges — such as this bottle.

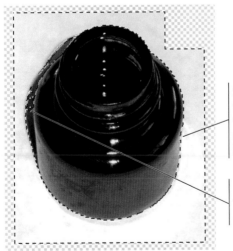

Slight variation between the background color and the bottle glass lets the selection intrude into the bottle shape.

Mottled background meeting the shadow area makes it difficult to select by color.

Note:

Photoshop clipping paths can be used to make selections in Photoshop; but if you save an image with a clipping path, the path can also be accessed in layout applications like Adobe InDesign.

Understanding Anchor Points and Handles

An **anchor point** marks the end of a line **segment**, and the point **handles** determine the shape of that segment. That's the basic definition of a vector, but there is a bit more to it than that. (The Photoshop Help files refer to handles as direction lines, and distinguishes different types of points with different names. Our aim here is to explain the overall concept of vector paths, so we use the generic industry-standard terms. For more information on Adobe's terminology, refer to the Photoshop CS4 Help files.)

Each segment has two anchor points and two associated handles. We first clicked to create Point A and dragged (without releasing the mouse button) to create Handle A1. We then clicked and dragged to create Point B and Handle B1; Handle B2 is automatically created as a reflection of B1 (Point B is a **symmetrical point**).

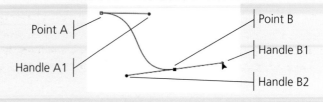

This image shows the result of dragging Handle B1 to the left instead of to the right. Notice the difference in the curve here, as compared to the curve above. By dragging the handle, the segment arcs away from the direction of the handle.

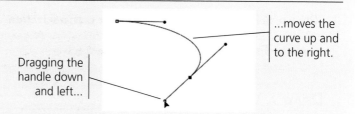

It's important to understand that a segment is connected to two handles. In this example, Handle A1 and Handle A2 determine the shape of Segment A. Dragging either handle to the right pulls out the arc of the connected segment.

Clicking and dragging a point creates a symmetrical point; both handles start out at equal length, directly opposite one another. Dragging one handle of a symmetrical point also changes the opposing handle of that point. (In the example here, dragging Handle B also moves Handle A, which affects the shape of Segment A.)

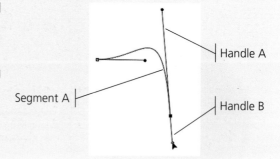

You can create corner points by simply clicking with the Pen tool instead of clicking and dragging. Corner points do not have their own handles; the connected segments are controlled by the handles of the other associated points.

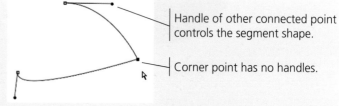

Handle of other connected point controls the segment shape.

Corner point has no handles.

You can convert a symmetrical point into a corner point by clicking the point with the Convert Point tool [↖] (nested under the Pen tool). You can also add a handle to only one side of an anchor point by Option/Alt-clicking a point with the Convert Point tool and dragging.

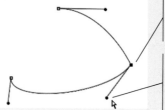

Option/Alt-click this point with the Convert Point tool and drag to create only one handle.

This handle controls the connected segment; the handle is not reflected on the other side of the point.

1. **With Movie Ad.psd open, hide the Parchment layer and show Layer 2.**

2. **Choose Select>Deselect to make sure any selection marquees from previous exercises are turned off.**

3. **Double-click the Layer 2 name and rename it bottle.**

4. **Zoom in so you can more clearly see the bottle edges.**

   When drawing paths, it helps to work with high view percentages so you can see the edges more clearly. We're using 66.7% in our screen shots; you should use whatever works best for you. It isn't necessary to keep the entire image in the project window if you're more comfortable working at higher percentages; you can scroll around the project window while you create paths.

5. **Choose the Pen tool in the Tools panel.**

   The Pen tool can be used to create shape layers or paths. Shape layers are vector-based, which means they have mathematically defined edges and can be filled with colors or pixel-based images. Paths are also vector-based, but they do not create their own layers and cannot be directly filled; instead, paths (or clipping paths, to use their full name) are most commonly used to isolate certain portions of an image.

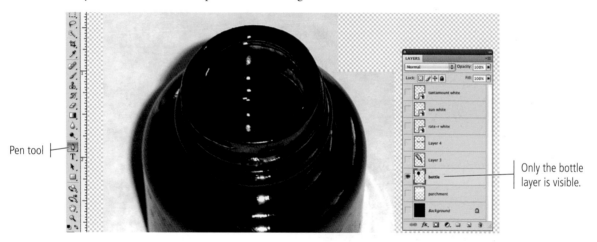

Pen tool

Only the bottle layer is visible.

You can use the Control panel to determine what type of path you want to create. The Pen tool defaults to create a shape layer. Regardless of which option is selected, you can select any of the vector drawing tools from the group of eight buttons; you see the same buttons when you choose one of the Pen or Shape tools directly from the Tools panel.

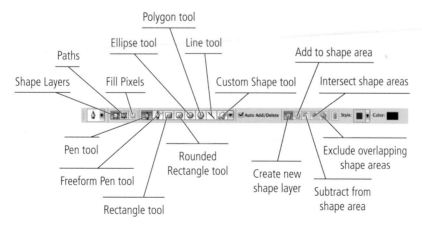

The Auto Add/Delete option, active by default, allows you to add or remove points on an active path without manually switching to the Add Anchor Point or Delete Anchor Point tool (nested under the Pen tool).

Note:

Pressing Command/ Control-D deselects selections more quickly and easily than choosing Select>Deselect from the Menu bar.

You should learn – and use – keyboard shortcuts wherever you can. They result in measurable time savings.

Note:

The options for shape layers and paths are virtually the same. One exception, however, is the Create New Shape Layer button, which is not available if you are creating a path; new paths are created using the Paths panel.

The final options for the Pen tool, which are only available when you create shape layers, are explained in Project 2.

6. **On the Control panel, click the Paths button to draw a path instead of a shape layer.**

7. **Click in the image where the bottle opening meets the side of the bottle.**

Click here with the Pen tool to add a single anchor point.

8. **Move your cursor down and to the right along the curved edge of the bottle. Click to add an anchor point and drag down and to the right before releasing the mouse button.**

When you click and drag with the Pen tool, you are defining the handles for the anchor point. Without getting too heavily into detailed explanations of geometry, you should simply understand that the anchor points determine the ends of line segments, and the handles determine the curve shape of the segments that are connected to that point.

Click here and hold down the mouse button …

… then drag down and to the right; the curve takes shape as you drag.

9. **Move the cursor down and to the right, then click and drag down to create another anchor point and handles.**

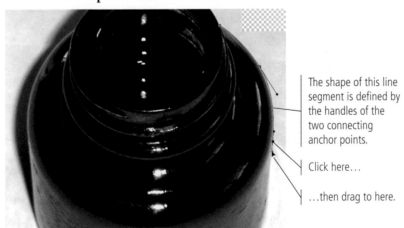

The shape of this line segment is defined by the handles of the two connecting anchor points.

Click here…

…then drag to here.

Note:

As you work more with paths, anchor points, and handles, you'll become more comfortable with how changing a handle affects the associated line segments. In this case, the best teacher is practice.

10. **Move the cursor down and click to add another anchor point. For this point, don't drag a handle.**

When you click without dragging, no handles are created for that point. This creates a corner point.

Click here without dragging. The result is a corner point.

11. **Move down and to the left, and then click and drag to the left to create another smooth anchor point.**

12. **Continue clicking and dragging points until you have outlined the entire bottle. Use a corner point where the left side of the bottle opening meets the left side of the bottle.**

13. **When you reach the first point you created, place your cursor over the point and click to close the path.**

This small hollow circle in the cursor icon indicates that clicking will close the path.

Note:

A smooth point allows the path to flow continuously from one segment to another. A corner point creates a sharp angle, allowing you to change directions of the path.

Click a smooth point to change it to a corner point. Click and drag a corner point with the Convert Point tool to change a corner point to a smooth point.

Don't worry if your path isn't perfect. You can edit a path at any point, which you will do next.

Some parts of the path aren't as smooth as they should be.

Some portions of the image are not within the path.

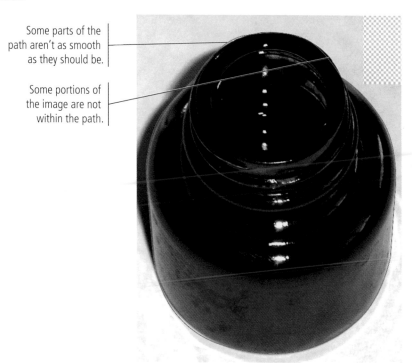

14. **Save the file and continue to the next exercise.**

EDIT A VECTOR PATH

In most cases, the first path you draw won't be perfect; you'll probably need to edit at least one or two points or segments, move existing points, or even add or delete points before your path exactly matches the shape you're outlining. As you complete this exercise, we show you how to correct the path in our screen shots. You should follow the general directions to correct the path that you drew in the previous exercise.

1. **With Movie Ad.psd open, open the Paths panel.**

   When you use the Pen tool to draw a path, it automatically appears in the Paths panel as the Work Path (in italics).

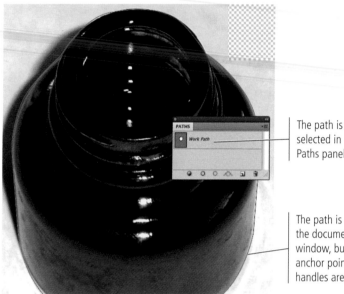

The path is selected in the Paths panel.

The path is visible in the document window, but the anchor points and handles are not.

2. **Click the empty area in the Paths panel (below the work path).**

   This effectively "turns off" the path; it is still in the Paths panel, but the points and handles are no longer visible in the file window.

Note:

Once you close a path, you can click in other places to create a different (nonconnected) piece of the same path; the Add to Path option is selected by default. If you want to create an entirely new path, you have to click in the Panel area below the work path to deselect it, and then draw the new path.

Note:

If you deselect the work path and then draw a new path, your first work path will be lost. You have to manually save the work path if you want to access it again later.

3. **Click Work Path in the Paths panel to show the current work path in the document window.**

4. **Choose the Path Selection tool in the Tools panel and click the path in the document window.**

   The Path Selection tool selects the entire path.

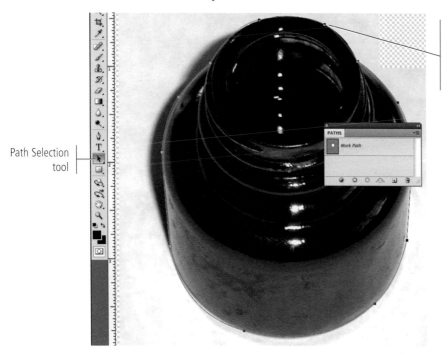

Path Selection tool

When the path is selected with the Path Selection tool, the anchor points are visible.

5. **Choose the Direct Selection tool (nested under the Path Selection tool).**

   The Direct Selection tool selects individual points and segments of a path.

6. **Zoom in if necessary, and then click one of the segments of your path that needs to be edited.**

   When you select a segment with the Direct Selection tool, you can see the handles that are associated with that segment.

Note:

If you click a point with the Direct Selection tool, the point appears solid. Unselected points appear hollow.

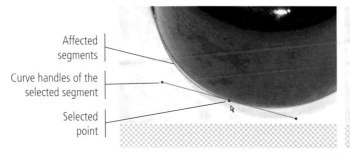

Affected segments

Curve handles of the selected segment

Selected point

7. **Drag the handle and/or point to correct the bad segment.**

8. **Continue editing the path until you are satisfied with the result. If you need to add or remove points from the path, use the related tools nested under the Pen tool.**

9. **When you're satisfied with your path, open the Paths panel Options menu and choose Save Path.**

Click here to open the Paths panel Options menu.

10. **In the Save Path dialog box, name the path bottle outline and click OK.**

   Trust us — when you get into very complicated files with multiple paths, you'll thank yourself for using names that indicate the purpose of a layer, path, or other element.

   After you save a path, it stays in the Paths panel; if you draw a new path now, you create a new work path.

11. **Save the file and continue to the next exercise.**

 ## CREATE A LAYER MASK

You now have a path that outlines the bottle shape, but the bottle background is still in the image. Since you've already selected the shape (with the path), you can remove the background.

One option for completing this task is to make a selection based on the path (choose Make Selection in the Paths panel Options menu) and simply delete the pixels outside the selection. This is a pixel-based option, even though the path is a vector. When you make the selection, it will be a rendered version of the original vector path.

The second option for isolating an object with a path is to create a layer mask. This option maintains the vector data as the outside edge of the image; areas of the image outside the vector path are hidden but not deleted, so you can later edit the path to change whatever part of the image is visible.

1. **With Movie Ad.psd open, make sure the bottle outline path is selected in the Paths panel.**

2. **Display the Layers panel and make sure the bottle layer is selected.**

3. **Choose Layer>Vector Mask>Current Path.**

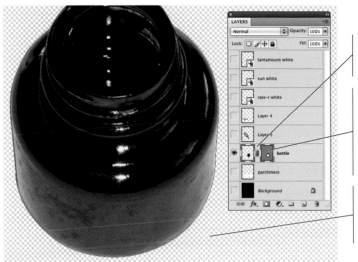

The new linked icon indicates that the layer has a vector mask applied.

As long as the vector mask is linked to the layer, the mask will move along with the layer. You can click this icon to unlink the layer from its mask.

When the vector mask is applied, any pixels on that layer that are outside the mask disappear.

4. **Control/right-click the Vector Mask icon and choose Disable Vector Mask from the contextual menu.**

When you disable the vector mask, the background pixels are again visible. This is one of the advantages of using masks — the background pixels are not permanently removed, they are simply hidden. You can safely edit the vector mask just as you edit any vector path; moving the vector mask path changes what is visible in the layer.

Note:

Creating selections, reversing them, and then deleting the pixels surrounding an object is a common method for creating silhouettes — but not necessarily the best method. Masks protect the original pixels while providing exactly the same result.

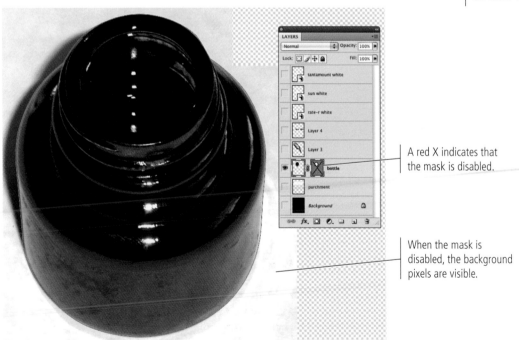

A red X indicates that the mask is disabled.

When the mask is disabled, the background pixels are visible.

5. **Control/right-click the Vector Mask icon and choose Enable Vector Mask from the contextual menu.**

6. **Save the file and continue to the next exercise.**

SELECT A COLOR RANGE

As we said earlier, there is a host of selection options in Photoshop CS4, each with its own advantages and disadvantages. You've already used the marquee tools and lasso tools to select general areas of images; you've used the Quick Selection tool to easily select an entire background, and then refined the edges of that selection; and you've used the Pen tool to select an object with a well-defined edge.

Some images aren't quite as clear-cut as the ones you've silhouetted so far. In fact, many images have both hard and soft edges, and/or very fine detail that needs to be isolated from its background (think of a model's blowing hair overlapping the title on the cover of a magazine). In this type of image, other tools can be used to create a very detailed selection based on the color in the image.

1. **With Movie Ad.psd open, hide the bottle layer and show Layer 3.**

2. **Rename Layer 3 as quill and zoom out so you can see the entire feather.**

3. **Choose the Magic Wand tool (under the Quick Selection tool). In the Control panel, make sure the New Selection button is active and set the Tolerance field to 32.**

   The Magic Wand tool is an easy way to select large areas of solid color.

   The first four options in the Control panel are the same as those for the Marquee tools (New Selection, Add to Selection, Subtract from Selection, and Intersect with Selection).

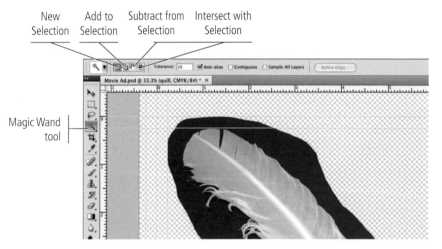

Tolerance is the degree of variation between the color you click and the colors Photoshop will select; higher tolerance values select a larger range based on the color you click. If you're trying to select a very mottled background (for example), you should increase the tolerance; be careful, however, because increasing the tolerance might select too large a range of colors if the parts of the foreground object falls within the tolerance range.

The **Anti-alias** check box, selected by default, allows edges to blend more smoothly into the background, preventing a jagged, stair-stepped appearance.

When **Contiguous** is selected, the Magic Wand tool only selects adjacent areas of the color; unchecking this option allows you to select all pixels within the color tolerance, even if some pixels are non-contiguous (for example, inside the shape of the letter Q).

By default, selections relate to the active layer only. You can check Sample All Layers to make a selection of all layers in the file.

The **Refine Edge** button opens the same dialog box you used when you isolated the parchment image with the Quick Selection tool.

Note:

The 'W' key automatically picks and toggles between the Magic Wand and the Quick Selection tools (both in the same place on the Tools panel).

Note:

Using any of the selection tools, press Shift and select again to add to the current selection. Press Option/Alt and select again to subtract from the current selection. If you use these modifier keys, you'll see a plus sign (Add To) or minus sign (Subtract From) in the tool cursor.

Note:

Anti-aliasing is the process of blending shades of pixels to create the illusion of sharp lines in a raster image.

4. Click anywhere in the blue area of the image.

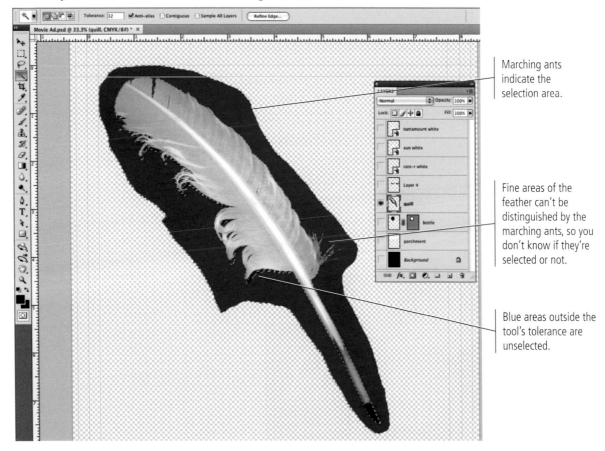

Marching ants indicate the selection area.

Fine areas of the feather can't be distinguished by the marching ants, so you don't know if they're selected or not.

Blue areas outside the tool's tolerance are unselected.

PHOTOSHOP FOUNDATIONS

Selecting Localized Color Clusters

The Localized Color Clusters option can be used to select specific areas of a selected color. When this option is checked, the Range slider defines how far away (in physical distance) a color from the point you click can be located and still be included in the selection.

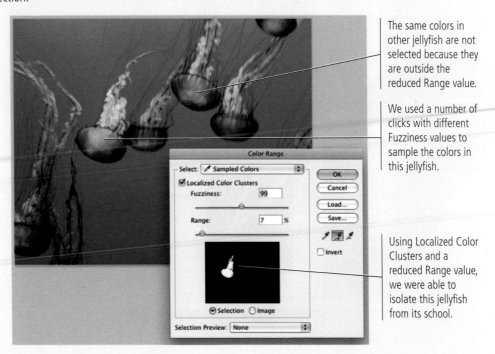

The same colors in other jellyfish are not selected because they are outside the reduced Range value.

We used a number of clicks with different Fuzziness values to sample the colors in this jellyfish.

Using Localized Color Clusters and a reduced Range value, we were able to isolate this jellyfish from its school.

5. **Choose Select>Deselect to turn off the current selection.**

   Although you could keep adding to the selection with the Magic Wand tool, the marching ants can't really show the fine detail, and they don't show shades of gray. There's a better way to isolate the feather from its blue background.

6. **Choose Select>Color Range.**

7. **Make sure the Localized Color Clusters option is unchecked.**

8. **Set the Fuzziness value to 24 and click anywhere in the blue area around the feather image (in the document window).**

   Fuzziness is similar to the Tolerance setting for the Magic Wand tool. Higher Fuzziness values allow you to select more variation from the color you click.

Note:

Press Command/ Control-D to turn off the current selection.

The low Fuzziness value doesn't select a large enough range of blues.

9. **Change the Fuzziness value to 60 and watch the effect on the dialog box preview.**

   Changing the Fuzziness value expands (higher numbers) or contracts (lower numbers) your selection. Be careful, however, since higher fuzziness values also eliminate very fine lines and details.

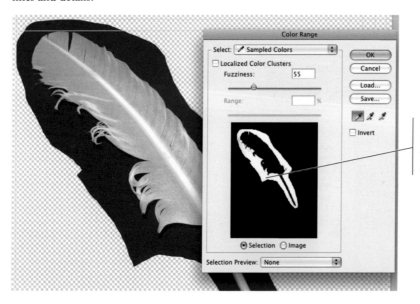

Increasing the Fuzziness value allows you to select areas of greater color variation.

10. Choose White Matte in the Selection Preview menu.

By changing the Selection Preview mode, you can more easily determine exactly what is selected. Using the White Matte preview, anything visible is selected.

You can preview color range selections in the image window as grayscale (areas outside the selection are shown in shades of gray), against a black matte (unselected areas are shown in black), against a white matte (unselected areas are shown in white), or using the default Quick Mask settings. If you choose None in the Selection Preview menu, the document window displays the normal image.

Note:

Because the dialog box preview is so small, we prefer to rely on the preview in the document window, which is controlled in the Selection Preview menu at the bottom of the dialog box.

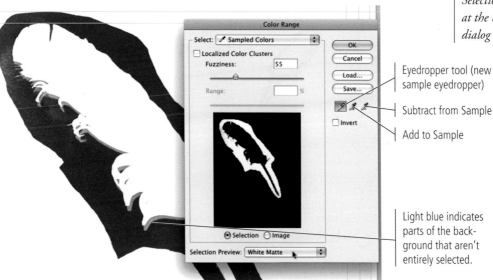

Eyedropper tool (new sample eyedropper)

Subtract from Sample

Add to Sample

Light blue indicates parts of the background that aren't entirely selected.

Depending on where you clicked, your selection might not exactly match what you see in our screen shot. For now, the important point is to know that the visible areas indicate the current selection.

11. Click the Add to Sample eyedropper and click in the image where parts of the blue background are not shown in full strength (light blue).

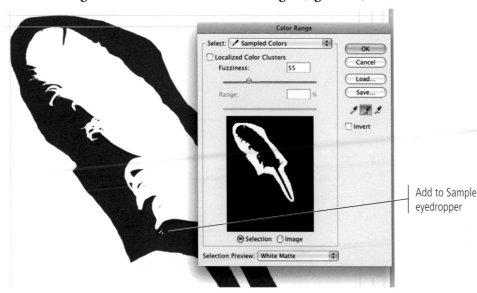

Add to Sample eyedropper

12. **Check the Invert box in the Color Range dialog box.**

Because your goal is to isolate the feather and not the background, it helps to look at what you want to keep instead of what you want to remove.

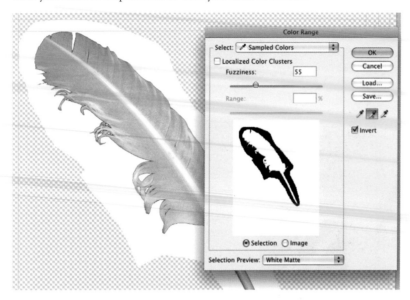

13. **Continue adding to (or subtracting from, if necessary) your selection until you are satisfied that all the blue background is gone.**

14. **Click OK when you're satisfied with your selection.**

When you return to the image window, the marching ants indicate the current selection. In the Color Range dialog box, you selected the blue and inverted the selection — in other words, your selection is everything that isn't blue.

If you zoom out to see the entire file, you'll see the marching ants surround the file as well as the blue background. Since the transparent area is not blue, it is included in the selection.

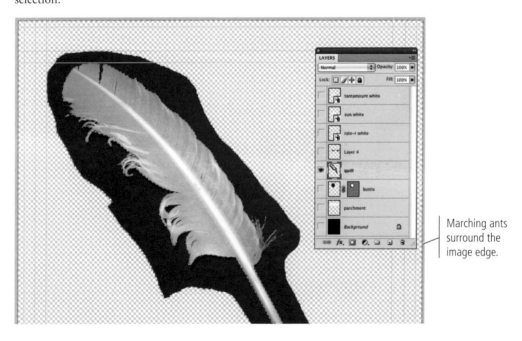

Marching ants surround the image edge.

15. **Choose the Magic Wand tool in the Tools panel and choose the Subtract from Selection option on the Control panel.**

16. **Click anywhere in the transparent area (the gray-and-white checkerboard) to remove that area from the selection.**

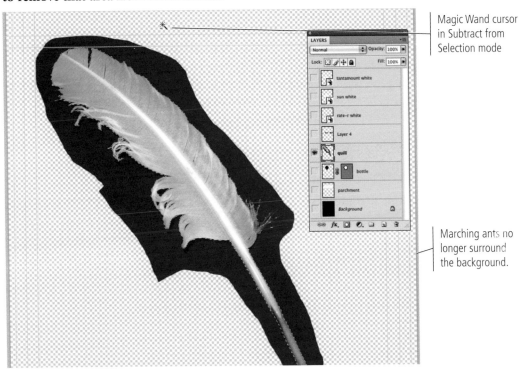

Magic Wand cursor in Subtract from Selection mode

Marching ants no longer surround the background.

17. **In the Layers panel, click the Add Layer Mask button.**

Similar to the vector mask you created in the previous exercise, this layer mask shows a new icon linked to the layer icon. A layer mask works on the same principle as the vector mask, except that the layer mask is raster-based instead of vector-based. You can disable the layer mask in the same way you disabled the vector mask in the previous exercise.

Layer Mask thumbnail

Add Layer Mask button

18. **Save the file and continue to the next stage of the project.**

Stage 4 **Managing Multiple Layers**

Your ad file has most of the necessary pieces. If you show all of the layers, however, you'll still see a bunch of stacked images. It's not yet an actual design, just a pile of images. When you composite images into a cohesive design, you almost certainly need to manipulate and transform some of the layers to make all the pieces work together.

Photoshop includes a number of tools for managing layers, from resizing the layer (as you did for the parchment) to rotating and flipping layers, to aligning different layers to each other, to grouping individual layers so you can work on multiple images at once.

 ## MANIPULATE AND ARRANGE LAYERS

1. **With Movie Ad.psd open, hide the quill layer and show the Background, parchment, and Layer 4 layers.**

2. **Rename Layer 4 as title.**

   Right now the title is too large to fit into the parchment layer, so you need to resize it.

3. **Using the Move tool, drag the title layer to be approximately centered over the parchment image.**

Note:

Press Command/ Control-T to display the transform handles.

4. **With the title layer selected in the Layers panel, choose Edit>Transform>Scale.**

5. **Click one of the corner handles, press Shift, and drag until the Control panel shows the layer at approximately 85%. Press Return/Enter to commit (finalize) the rescaling.**

   Because you pressed Shift, the layer automatically rescales proportionally.

Keep an eye on the Control panel as you transform (scale) the layer.

Once you've resized the title to fit into the parchment, you need to reposition the title in the center of the parchment. You could do this manually, but Photoshop includes tools that make this task much easier.

6. **In the Layers panel, press Command/Control and click the parchment layer name.**

   Since the title layer was already selected, the parchment layer should now be a second selected (highlighted) layer.

Note:

Command/Control-clicking a layer thumbnail results in a selection around the contents of that layer.

Note:

You can select noncontiguous layers by pressing Command/Control. You can select contiguous layers by pressing Shift while you click.

7. **On the Control panel, click the Align Vertical Centers button.**

   When more than one layer is selected, the align buttons become available. This method is far more precise than simply dragging by eye, and far easier than manually calculating positions by the numbers.

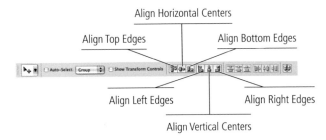

8. **Click the Align Horizontal Centers button while the two layers are selected.**

   The title and parchment should now be evenly positioned horizontally and vertically in relation to one another.

   Since these two layers function as a single element in the overall design, it's a good idea to combine them so they can function as one unit. You could merge the two layers, but that would require flattening the pixels in the two layers into a single layer. Once flattened, you would no longer be able to edit the individual layers.

Note:

Deselect all layers by clicking in the empty area at the bottom of the Layers panel.

9. **In the Layers panel, click the title layer and drag down. When a heavy black bar appears between the bottle and parchment layers, release the mouse button.**

You can move a layer to any position in the **stacking order** (the top-to-bottom position of a layer) by simply dragging it to a new position in the Layers panel.

Note:

Step 9 isn't particularly necessary; you can group selected layers even if they aren't contiguous. We simply want to make sure you know how to reposition layers in a file.

10. **With the title layer selected, press Shift and click the parchment layer to select it as well.**

11. **Click the button in the top-right corner of the panel to open the Layers panel Options menu. Choose New Group from Layers.**

This option creates a group that automatically contains the selected layers. You can also create an empty group by choosing New Group (this option is available even when no layer is selected) or by clicking the New Group button at the bottom of the panel.

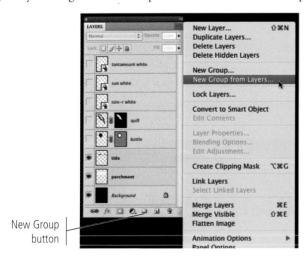

New Group button

Note:

You can create a group from selected layers by dragging the selected layers onto the New Group button at the bottom of the panel. In this case, the new group is automatically named "Group N" (N is a placeholder for a sequential number); of course, you can rename a layer group just as easily as you can rename a layer.

12. **In the New Group from Layers dialog box, type** Parchment Title **in the Name field and click OK.**

As with any other layer, you should name groups based on what they contain so you can easily identify them later.

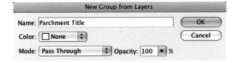

13. Click the arrow left of the Parchment Title group name to expand the layer group.

The two selected layers are now part of the group.

14. Collapse the group by clicking the arrow left of the group name.

15. With the Parchment Title group selected in the Layers panel, use the Move tool to position the Parchment Title group in the bottom third of the document window.

Because the current selection is the layer group, both layers contained within that group are moved in the document window.

16. Save the file and continue to the next exercise.

CREATE A NESTED GROUP

1. With **Movie Ad.psd** open, show and select the bottle layer.

2. Scale the bottle layer to 40% (proportionally).

3. Using the Move tool, drag the bottle until it is directly above the "he" in the title.

4. Show and select the quill layer, and then resize it to 65% proportionally.

5. With the quill layer still selected, choose Edit>Transform>Flip Horizontal.

6. Using the Move tool, drag the selected layer so the quill image overlaps the "er" in the title, and the tip is just within the edges of the parchment. (Use the following image as a placement guide.)

Note:

When the Move tool is active, you can move the selected object or layer 1 pixel by pressing the Arrow keys. Pressing Shift with any of the Arrow keys moves the selected object/layer by 10 pixels.

7. In the Layers panel, select the bottle and quill layers and group them together in a group named **Bottle and Quill**.

8. **Click the new layer group and drag down. When a black border appears around the Parchment Title group, release the mouse button.**

   This places the Bottle and Quill group inside the Parchment Title group (called nesting).

9. **Expand the Parchment Title layer group.**

   The nested group is automatically placed at the bottom of the group's stacking order, so the bottle and quill are behind the parchment.

10. **Click the Bottle and Quill layer group and drag it up above the parchment and title layers within the group.**

11. **Collapse the Parchment Title layer group, save the file, and then continue to the next exercise.**

1. With **Movie Ad.psd** open, show the three remaining layers (the logo Smart Objects).

2. Resize the Sun logo to 13% and drag it to the bottom-right corner (inside the live area guides of the smaller ad).

3. Resize the Tantamount logo to 20% and drag it to the bottom live area guide, about 1/4″ to the left of the Sun logo.

4. Resize the rating logo to 45%. Drag it to the bottom-left corner of the live area.

5. Select all three logo layers and align their vertical centers.

6. Combine the three logo layers in a layer group named **Logos**.

7. Drag the Parchment Title layer group directly above the logos, centered horizontally on the page.

8. Choose File>Place to place the file **declaration.psd** (from the **RF_Photoshop>Liberty Ad** folder) as a Smart Object.

9. Make sure the placed file is scaled at 100% and reaches all edges of the image.

    Placed files are sometimes automatically scaled below 100% when you place them. To check, choose Edit>Transform>Scale and look at the W or H field in the Control panel.

10. In the Layers panel, drag the declaration layer below the Parchment Title layer group.

    Be careful that you don't drop the declaration layer onto the Parchment Title group folder, which would place it inside that group instead of behind it.

Note:

If you use the Control panel to resize a Smart Object, the scale percentage is maintained even after you finalize the change (unlike scaling a regular layer, where the layer reverts to 100% once you finalize the scaling).

11. Save the file and continue to the final stage of the project.

Stage 5 Saving Photoshop Files for Print

At the beginning of the project, you saved this file in Photoshop's native format (PSD). However, many Photoshop projects require saving the completed file in at least one other format. Many artists prefer to leave all files in the PSD format since there is only one file to track. Others prefer to send only flattened TIFF files of their artwork because the individual elements can't be changed. Ultimately, the format (or formats, if the file is being used in multiple places) you use will depend on where and how the file is being placed.

As a general rule, many Photoshop projects are pieces of a larger composition; the overall project defines the format you need to use when you save a complete project. The ad you've created, for example, will be placed in magazine layouts, which will be built in a page-layout application like Adobe InDesign or QuarkXPress.

Although the current versions of both industry-standard page-layout applications can support native layered PSD files, older versions can't import those native files. If a magazine is being designed in QuarkXPress 4, for example (and many still are), you can't place a layered PSD file into the QuarkXPress 4 layout. As the Photoshop artist, you would have to save your work in a format that is compatible with the magazine layout.

As you know, the ad you created will be placed in multiple magazines, and different publishers have provided different file requirements. You need to save two different versions of the ad to meet those requirements.

SAVE A LAYERED TIFF FILE

The magazine with the 8.5 × 11″ trim size suggests that ads created in Photoshop be submitted as layered TIFF files. Since you designed the ad to incorporate bleeds for pages up to 8.5 × 11″, all you have to do for this version is save the file in the appropriate format.

1. **With Movie Ad.psd open, choose File>Save As.**

2. **Navigate to your WIP>Liberty Ad folder as the target location for saving the final files.**

   The Save As dialog box defaults to the last-used location. If you continued the entire way through this project without stopping, you won't have to navigate.

3. **Click the Format menu and choose TIFF.**

4. Make sure the Layers check box is selected in the lower half of the dialog box.

Because this file contains layers, this option is probably checked by default. If your file contained alpha channels, annotations, or spot colors, those check boxes would also be available. The As a Copy check box can be used if you want to save multiple versions of the same file with different options (which you'll do in the next exercise).

Choosing a different format automatically changes the file's extension.

5. Click Save.

Most file formats include additional options, which you should understand before you simply click OK.

6. In the TIFF Options dialog box, make sure the None radio button is selected.

TIFF files can be compressed (made smaller) using one of three schemes:

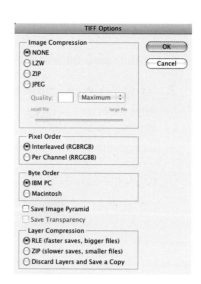

- **None** (as the name implies) applies no compression to the file. This option is safe if file size is not an issue, but digital file transmission often requires files to be smaller than a full-page, multi-layered Photoshop file.

- **LZW** (Lempel-Ziv-Welch) compression is lossless, which means all file data is maintained in the compressed file.

- **ZIP** compression is also lossless, but is not supported by all desktop publishing software (especially older versions).

- **JPEG** is a **lossy** compression scheme, which means some data will be thrown away to reduce the file size. If you choose JPEG compression, the Quality options determine how much data can be discarded. Maximum quality means less data is thrown out and the file is larger. Minimum quality discards the most data and results in the smaller file size.

7. Leave the Pixel Order radio button at the default value, and choose the IBM PC byte order.

Pixel Order determines how channel data is encoded. The Interleaved (RGBRGB) option is the default; Per Channel (RRGGBB) is called "planar" order.

Byte Order determines which platform can use the file, although this is somewhat deceptive. Even in older versions of most desktop publishing software, Macintosh systems can read the PC byte order but Windows couldn't read the Macintosh byte order. If you don't know which platform will ultimately be used, choose IBM PC.

Save Image Pyramid creates a tiered file with multiple resolution versions; this isn't widely used or supported by other applications, so you can typically leave it unchecked.

If your file contains transparency, the Save Transparency check box will be available. If you don't choose this option, transparent areas will be white in the saved file.

Note:

Older desktop publishing software doesn't always support compressed TIFF files. When saving for those workflows, you might have to save the file without compression, regardless of the resulting file size.

8. **In the Layer Compression area, make sure the RLE option is selected.**

   These three options explain — right in the dialog box — what they do.

9. **Click OK to save the file.**

   Photoshop warns you that including layers will increase the file size.

10. **Click OK to dismiss the warning and save the file.**

11. **Continue to the next exercise.**

Note:

If you don't see the warning, it's possible that someone checked the Don't Show Again check box. If you want to make sure that you see all warnings and messages, click Reset All Warning Dialogs in the General Preferences.

Save a Flattened TIFF File

The smaller of the magazines (the 8 × 10 version) is still using an older page-layout application that doesn't support layered TIFF or PSD files. This company requires ads to be submitted as either native page-layout format or flattened TIFF files. To meet these requirements, you have to flatten the Photoshop file, and then save it in a different TIFF format. One extra step — cropping it to the appropriate bleed size — will prevent the ad from being placed incorrectly in the magazine layout.

1. **With Movie Ad.tif open in Photoshop, choose the Crop tool in the Tools panel.**

   If you continued directly from the previous exercise, this is the version you just saved. If you quit before you began this exercise, make sure you open the TIF version and not the PSD version from your WIP>Liberty Ad folder.

2. **Click in the image window and drag a marquee with the Crop tool.**

   The crop marquee has eight handles, which you can drag to change the size of the cropped area.

   When you draw a marquee with the Crop tool, the area outside the marquee is masked by a darkened overlay so that you can get an idea of what will remain after you finalize the crop. You can turn off this preview by unchecking the Shield box on the Control panel; you can also change the color and opacity of the shield.

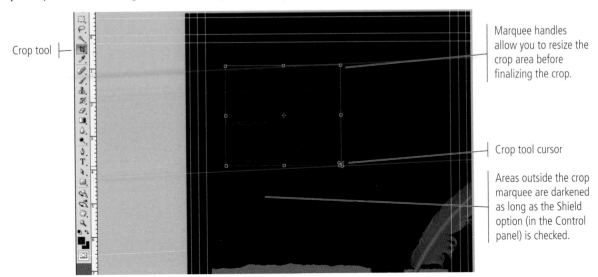

Crop tool

Marquee handles allow you to resize the crop area before finalizing the crop.

Crop tool cursor

Areas outside the crop marquee are darkened as long as the Shield option (in the Control panel) is checked.

3. **Drag the crop marquee handles to the smaller page trim guides (8 × 10).**

Remember: anything that runs to the page edge has to incorporate a bleed allowance.

4. **Extend the crop marquee 1/8″ outside each trim guide.**

Use the rulers to include the 1/8″ bleed allowance within the crop marquee.

Remember, you moved the zero point to the smaller magazine trim. You can use the marks on the rulers to easily find 1/8 inch outside this trim edge.

Note:

You can rotate a crop marquee by placing the cursor slightly away from a corner handle.

Note:

You can press the Escape key to cancel the crop marquee and return to the uncropped image.

5. **Press Return/Enter to finalize the crop.**

6. **Choose File>Save As.**

Since you started this exercise with the TIFF file from the previous exercise, the format and file name extension already reflect the TIFF options.

7. **Uncheck the Layers check box.**

The As a Copy box is now selected by default. A warning shows that the file must be saved as a copy when the Layers option is unchecked. This is basically a failsafe built into Photoshop that prevents you from overwriting your layered file with a flattened version.

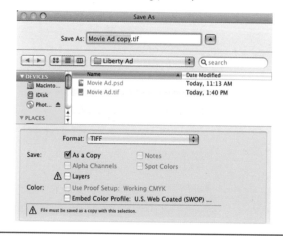

Note:

You can manually flatten a file by choosing Layer>Flatten Image.

8. **In the Save As field, replace the word "copy" with 8x10 to distinguish it from the larger version.**

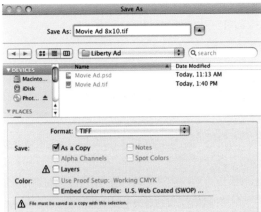

9. **Click Save. In the resulting TIFF Options dialog box, make sure the None compression option is selected and the Byte Order is set to IBM PC.**

10. **Click OK to save the second version of the file.**

11. **When the save is complete, choose File>Close. Click Don't Save when asked.**

   When you finished the previous exercise, you saved the ad as an 8.5 × 11″ layered TIFF; that TIFF file remained open at the end of the exercise (not the original PSD file). In this exercise, you used the options in the Save As dialog box to save another copy of the TIFF file, this one with layers flattened and a small file size.

   The open file is still the original Movie Ad.tif file, which you saved for the 8.5 × 11″ trim requirement. You've made changes, though (you cropped the image), so Photoshop asks if you want to save your changes before closing. If you click Save, you will overwrite the 8.5 × 11″ version with the cropped version.

Common File Formats

PHOTOSHOP FOUNDATIONS

Photoshop, with the extension PSD, is the native format.

Photoshop EPS can maintain vector and raster information in the same file, and can maintain spot color channels.

JPEG is a lossy compressed file format that does not support transparency.

Large Document Format, using the extension PSB, is used for images larger than 2 GB (the limit for PSD files); this format supports all Photoshop features including transparency and layers.

Photoshop PDF can contain all required font and image information in a single file, which can be compressed to reduce file size.

Photoshop 2.0 saves a flattened file that can be opened in Photoshop 2.0; all layer information is discarded.

Photoshop Raw supports CMYK, RGB, and grayscale images with alpha channels, and multichannel and LAB images without alpha channels; this format does not support layers.

Scitex CT is used for high-end image processing on proprietary Scitex computers. (Although rarely used today, this format is still used occasionally, so we include it here.)

TIFF is a raster-based image format that supports layers, alpha channels, and file compression.

Photoshop DCS 1.0 creates a separate file for each color channel in a CMYK image, plus a fifth composite file that can be used for placement.

Photoshop DCS 2.0 is a later variation of DCS 1.0; version 2 supports spot color channels, and can be saved as multiple files (one for each channel) or as a single file.

1. The _____ is the range of visible and available color in a particular color model.

2. _____ is likely to cause degradation of a raster image when it's reproduced on a printing press.

3. A _____ is a linked file that you placed into another Photoshop document.

4. The _____ is context sensitive, providing access to different functions depending on what tool is active.

5. The _____ is the final size of a printed page.

6. The _____ tool is used to draw irregular-shaped selection marquees.

7. The _____ tool is used to create precise shapes based on anchor points and connecting line segments.

8. The _____ tool can be used to drag layer contents to another position within the image, or into another open document.

9. When selecting color ranges, the _____ value determines how much of the current color range falls into the selection.

10. _____ is a lossy compression method that is best used when large file size might be a problem.

1. Briefly describe the difference between raster images and vector graphics.

2. Briefly explain three separate methods for isolating an image from its background.

3. Briefly describe the relationship between anchor points and handles (direction lines) on a vector path.

Portfolio Builder Project

Use what you learned in this project to complete the following freeform exercise.
Carefully read the art director and client comments, then create your design to meet the needs of the project.
Use the space below to sketch ideas; when finished, write a brief explanation of the reasoning behind your design.

art director comments

Tantamount Studios is pleased with your work on the Forefathers ad, and they would like to hire you again to create the ad concept and final files for another movie that they're releasing early next year.

To complete this project, you should:

❏ Find appropriate background and foreground images for the movie theme (see the client's comments at right).

❏ Incorporate the title artwork, logos, and rating placeholder that the client provided.

❏ Composite the different elements into a single completed file; save both a layered version and a flattened version.

client comments

The movie is titled *Above and Beyond*. Although the story is fictionalized, it will focus on the men who led the first U.S. Airborne unit (the 501st), which suffered more than 2000 casualities in the European theater of World War II.

We already have the title artwork, which we gave you in the RF_Builders>Airborne folder.

We don't have any other images in mind, but the final ad should reflect the time period (the 1940s) of the movie. The 501st Airborne was trained to parachute into battle, so you should probably incorporate some kind of parachute image.

This movie is another joint venture between Sun and Tantamount, so both logos need to be included in the new ad. It isn't rated yet, so please use the "This Movie Is Not Yet Rated" artwork (in the RF_Builders>Airborne folder) as a placeholder.

Create this ad big enough to fit on an 8.5 × 11″ page, but keep the live area an inch inside the trim so the ad can be used in different sized magazines.

project justification

_____
_____
_____
_____
_____
_____
_____
_____
_____
_____
_____
_____
_____
_____
_____

Making selections is arguably the most important skill you will learn to do in Photoshop. Selections are so important that Photoshop dedicates an entire menu to the process.

As you created the four-color magazine ad in this project, you used a number of skills and techniques that you will apply in many (if not all) projects you build in Photoshop. You learned a number of ways to make both simple and complex selections — and you'll learn additional methods in later projects. You also learned that after you make a selection, you can create composite images, move pixels to silhouette an object against its background, and much more.

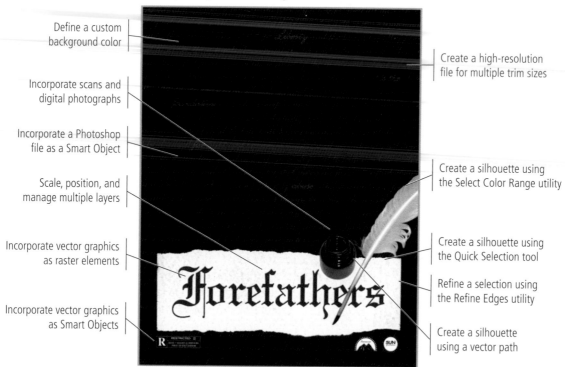

Define a custom background color

Incorporate scans and digital photographs

Incorporate a Photoshop file as a Smart Object

Scale, position, and manage multiple layers

Incorporate vector graphics as raster elements

Incorporate vector graphics as Smart Objects

Create a high-resolution file for multiple trim sizes

Create a silhouette using the Select Color Range utility

Create a silhouette using the Quick Selection tool

Refine a selection using the Refine Edges utility

Create a silhouette using a vector path

African Wildlife Map

Your client, the Global Wildlife Fund (GWF), is a not-for-profit organization dedicated to preserving wildlife resources around the world. Every year GWF does a direct-mail fundraising drive, offering premiums for certain levels of membership donations. This year they want to offer a series of limited-edition art prints. Anyone who donates at least $100 will be allowed to pick one of the prints; people who donate over $1000 will receive the entire set of six prints. Your job is to create the first piece in the series as a sample.

This project incorporates the following skills:

❑ Using a small, low-resolution image as a drawing template

❑ Navigating back in time using the History panel and snapshots

❑ Creating complex, scalable vector shape layers

❑ Compositing images as Smart Objects

❑ Creating and modifying selections and layer masks

❑ Applying filters and adjustments to create artistic effects

❑ Developing custom artistic backgrounds

❑ Presenting multiple layout variations using layer comps

client comments

This is our 25th anniversary, and we want our fundraising drive to set records. In the past, we've sent out address labels, note pads, and even beanie animals as incentives for donating. This year we want to commission a series of paintings that we could reproduce as limited-edition prints for people who contribute a certain amount of money.

We're a not-for-profit organization, and we try to keep most of our finances dedicated to conservation activities. A colleague suggested that we might be able to find someone who can do what we want with Photoshop, and probably do it much faster and for far less money than a traditional artist.

Here's what we want: We thought each piece in the series could be the shape of a different continent with various indigenous animals inside each continent. We're going to skip Antarctica because there isn't much wildlife there. We have a lot of animal photos from our travels over the years, and you can use anything we have access to. We'd rather not have to pay for stock images when we already have so many of our own images in-house.

art director comments

I downloaded a comp image with a map of Africa that we can use to get the shape right, and then incorporate their photos into the map outline. I think the ideal size for the final piece is 10 × 12 inches, since that's a standard size for framing.

Photoshop is ideal for this type of job; there are dozens of filters for making photographs look like artwork. You're going to have to be creative with the background; Africa is surrounded by water, and we don't want to give them a plain, flat blue background.

Since we're creating this artwork digitally, we have options that traditional painters don't have. I want you to use different filters and options to try a couple of variations, so the client can choose which one they prefer.

project objectives

To complete this project, you will:

❏ Resize a raster graphic to change resolution

❏ Create a compound shape layer using variations of the Pen tool

❏ Composite and work with multiple images as Smart Objects

❏ Create a clipping mask from a vector shape layer

❏ Modify selections to create soft-edged layer masks

❏ Use the brush tools to refine a layer mask

❏ Apply artistic filters using the Filter Gallery

❏ Use patterns, blending modes, and filters to create a custom background

❏ Use layer comps to present multiple options to your client

Stage 1 Setting Up the Workspace

Any project you build in Photoshop — especially an oversize project like this map — requires some amount of zooming in and out to various view percentages, as well as navigating around the document within its window. As we show you how to complete different stages of the workflow, we usually won't tell you when to change your view percentage because that's largely a matter of personal preference. But you should understand the different options for navigating around a Photoshop file so you can easily and efficiently get to what you want, when you want to get there.

To review information from the Interface chapter, keep in mind that you have a number of options for navigating around a document:

- Click with the Hand tool to drag the image around in the document window.

- Click with the Zoom tool to zoom in; Option/Alt-click to zoom out.

- Use the Zoom Level field/menu on the Application/Menu bar.

- Use the options in the View menu (or the corresponding keyboard shortcuts).

- Use the Navigator panel.

Note:

As you complete the exercises in this project, use any of these methods to zoom in or out on different areas of the file.

REVIEW AND RESAMPLE THE EXISTING SOURCE IMAGE

As we stated in Project 1, the best way to start any new project is to set up an efficient workspace. This project — like many others you'll build throughout your career — starts with an existing image, which you'll open and use as the basis for the rest of the project. Whenever you start with an existing file, it's best to evaluate what you already have before you make any changes.

1. **On your desktop, copy the Africa folder from the WIP folder on your Resource CD to the WIP folder where you are saving your work.**

   You will save all files for this project in your WIP>Africa folder.

2. **In Photoshop, open africa.jpg from the RF_Photoshop>Africa folder.**

3. **Make sure your image displays at 100% and the rulers are visible, and then choose Image>Image Size.**

   The Image Size dialog box shows the number of pixels in the image, as well as the image dimensions and current resolution. You can change any value in this dialog box, but you should understand what those changes mean before you do so.

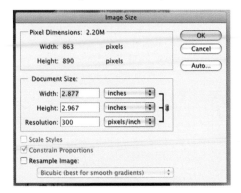

The africa.jpg file is slightly less than 3″ wide by 3″ high, with a resolution of 300 dpi. In Project 1, you learned that commercial printing typically requires 300 dpi, so this image would be considered "print quality." However, you need to build the final artwork at 10 × 12″ — nearly 4 times the current size.

4. **At the bottom of the dialog box, make sure the Resample option is unchecked.**

Resampling means maintaining the existing resolution for the new dimensions. When the Resample option is checked, Photoshop adds pixels if you enlarge the image or throws away pixels if you reduce the image.

5. **Highlight the Height field and type 12.**

Resizing without resampling basically means dividing the same number of pixels over a different area. When you resize an image without resampling, you do not change the number of pixels in the image.

You can see how changing one of the linked fields (Height) directly affects the other linked fields (Width and Resolution). By resizing the image to be 12″ high, you would have only 74.167 dpi — which is not enough to be considered "print quality."

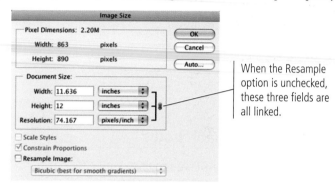

When the Resample option is unchecked, these three fields are all linked.

6. **Press Option/Alt and click the Reset button to restore the original image dimensions.**

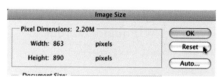

Note:

Pressing Option/Alt changes the Cancel button to a Reset button, which can be very useful for canceling your choices without closing the dialog box. (This is true in many of the Photoshop dialog boxes.)

7. **Check the Resample option at the bottom of the dialog box.**

Resampling an image effectively means adding or deleting pixels. When this option is turned on, you can change the dimensions of an image without affecting the resolution, or you can change the resolution of an image (useful for removing excess resolution or **downsampling**) without affecting the image size.

8. **Highlight the Height field and type 12.**

When you change the height with resampling turned on, you do not change the resolution. To maintain 300-dpi resolution at the new size, Photoshop needs to literally add pixels to the image. You can see at the top of the dialog box that this setting will change the total number of pixels from 863 × 890 to 3491 × 3600 — a huge number of pixels to generate.

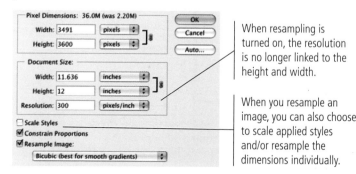

When resampling is turned on, the resolution is no longer linked to the height and width.

When you resample an image, you can also choose to scale applied styles and/or resample the dimensions individually.

Note:

You can also see the effect of more pixels on file size — more pixels at larger sizes means much higher (potentially huge) file sizes.

9. **Click OK to return to the document window.**

The map image, which was originally crisp and clear, is now blurry and pixelated. You no longer have clean lines to use as the basis for the map outline.

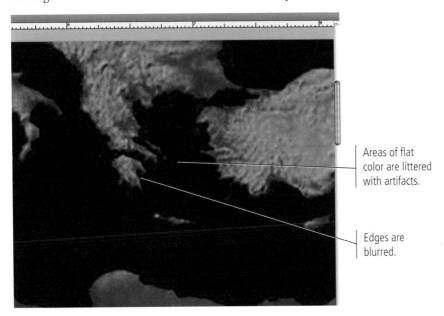

Areas of flat color are littered with artifacts.

Edges are blurred.

10. **Choose Edit>Undo Image Size to return the file to its original size.**

The Photoshop Undo command is a single-action toggle; after you use the command, it becomes Redo for the same action. To move back through more than one action, you must use the Step Backward command or the History panel.

11. **Save the file as a Photoshop file named africa_working.psd in your WIP>Africa folder, and then continue to the next exercise.**

Note:

Press Command/Control-Z to undo the previous action.

Press Command-Option-Z/Control-Alt-Z to step backward one action at a time through the file history.

 ## CREATE A VECTOR SHAPE LAYER

As you learned in the previous exercise, one of the disadvantages of raster images is that they are what they are — meaning the size you start with is (more or less) the size you have to work with. Photoshop is very powerful, but it simply can't create enough pixels at good enough quality to generate a 14″ image from a 4″ image.

Vector graphics, on the other hand, are based on mathematically defined lines and points instead of pixels. When you output a vector file, the output device calculates the position of those lines and points as necessary to create the final version at whatever size you need. Because of this, vectors can be resized as large as you need without losing a single pixel of quality.

To work around the problem of your original map image, you're going to create a vector shape layer using the original map as a guide.

1. **With africa_working.psd open, choose the Pen tool in the Tools panel.**

In Project 1, you used the Pen tool to create a precise outline of an ink bottle. You're going to use the same principle to create the outline of the African continent.

The shape of Africa is far more complex and detailed than the clean edges of an ink bottle. For this project, your ultimate goal is an artistic rendering — which means you don't have to precisely match the individual points and curves of the continental shape.

Rather than creating every anchor point and precisely pulling every curve, you can use the Freeform Pen tool to draw as you would with a pencil.

Every raster image has a defined, specific resolution that is established when the image is created. If you scan an image to be 3″ high by 5″ wide at 150 ppi, that image has 450 pixels in each vertical column and 750 pixels in each horizontal row. Simply resizing the image stretches or compresses those pixels into a different physical space, but does not add or remove pixel information. If you resize the 3 × 5″ image to 6 × 10″ (200% of the original), the 450 pixels in each column are forced to extend across 6″ instead of 3, causing a marked loss of quality.

The **effective resolution** of an image is the resolution calculated after any scaling is taken into account. This number is equally — and sometimes more — important than the original image resolution. The effective resolution can be calculated with a fairly simple equation:

> Original resolution / (% magnification / 100) =
> Effective resolution

If a 300-ppi image is magnified 150%, the effective resolution is:

> 300 ppi / 1.5 = 200 ppi

In other words, the more you enlarge a raster image, the lower its effective resolution becomes. In general, you can make an image 10% or 15% larger without significant adverse effects; the more you enlarge an image, however, the worse the results. Even Photoshop, which offers very sophisticated formulas (called "algorithms") for sizing images, cannot guarantee perfect results.

Downsizing

You can take advantage of effective resolution if you want to print a low-resolution image that is a large enough physical size. Consumer-level digital cameras work on this principle.

The camera captures all images at a set resolution (usually 72 ppi). The different quality settings (high, medium, and low, or some similar variations) do not change the capturing resolution. Instead, they affect the physical size of the resulting image; "high" quality settings produce very large pictures, while "low" settings produce small pictures.

When you first open a "high" quality picture in Photoshop, you might have a picture that is 28″ wide at 72 ppi. If you resize the image to 25%, or 7″ wide, you will increase the effective resolution to 288 ppi — enough for most printing applications.

Resampling

In general, you should always scan your images to the size you will use in your final job. If you absolutely must resize a digital image, you can use resampling to achieve better results than simply changing the image size. Photoshop CS4 offers five types of resampling algorithms to generate extra pixel data (when increasing the image size) or to determine which pixels to discard (when reducing the image size).

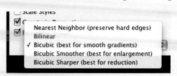

- **Nearest Neighbor** is a low-quality but quick resampling method. Nearest neighbor interpolates new pixel information based on only one of the squares in the grid, usually resulting in an image with a blocky appearance.

- **Bilinear** is a medium-quality resampling method. Bilinear resampling averages adjacent pixels to create new information.

- **Bicubic** creates the most accurate pixel information for continuous-tone images; it also takes the longest to process and produces a softer image. To understand how this option works, think of a square bisected both horizontally and vertically — bicubic resampling averages the value of all four of those squares (pixels) to interpolate the new information.

- **Bicubic Smoother** is useful for enlarging images with smoother results than basic bicubic resampling.

- **Bicubic Sharper** is useful for reducing the size of an image and maintaining sharp detail.

Discarding Pixels

Higher resolution means larger file sizes, which translates to longer processing time for printing or longer download time over the Internet. When you scale an image to a smaller size, simply resizing can produce files with far greater effective resolution than you need. Resampling allows you to reduce the physical size of an image without increasing the resolution, resulting in a smaller file size.

The caveat here is that once you discard (delete) pixels, they are gone. If you later try to re-enlarge the smaller image, you will not achieve the same quality as the original (before it was reduced). You should always save reduced images as copies instead of overwriting the original.

2. **In the Control panel, click the Freeform Pen tool icon and make sure the Shape Layers option is selected.**

3. **In the Control panel, click the arrow button to the right of the tool variations to access the options for the Freeform Pen tool.**

The Curve Fit field determines how close the resulting curve will match the path you drag with the tool. Lower values (minimum 0.5 pixels) result in more anchor points and curves that more closely match the path you draw; higher values (up to 10 pixels) create fewer anchor points and smoother curves with greater variation from the path you draw.

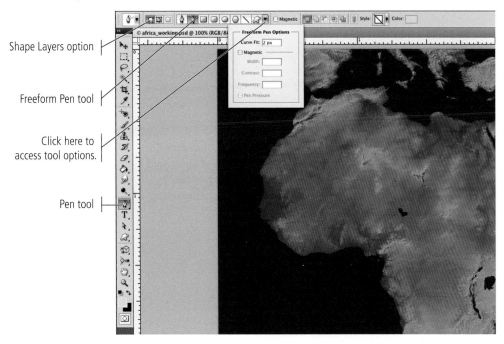

Shape Layers option

Freeform Pen tool

Click here to access tool options.

Pen tool

4. **Set the Curve Fit field to 2 px and press Return/Enter to close the options dialog box.**

This field remembers the last-used value; 2 px is the application default value, but this setting might have been changed by another user.

5. **In the Control panel, click the Style button and choose the No Style option.**

The Style and Color options maintain the last-used settings. You're simply making sure no style is automatically applied to the new shape. We'll return to the idea of styles later in this project.

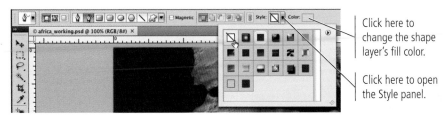

Click here to change the shape layer's fill color.

Click here to open the Style panel.

6. **Click the Color swatch to open the Color Picker. In the resulting Color Picker dialog box, select a color that will be visible against the background map image, and then click OK.**

This step determines the color that will fill the shape you are about to create. We used a light blue, which will stand out well against the background image.

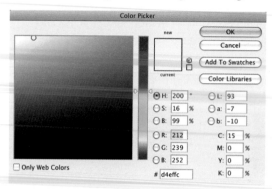

7. **Zoom in to Madagascar (the island east of the main African continent).**

8. **With the Freeform Pen tool active, click near the top of Madagascar to establish the starting point, hold down the mouse button, and then drag to trace the outside edge of the island.**

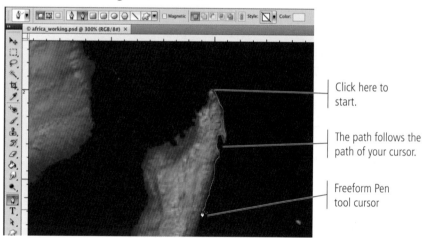

Click here to start.

The path follows the path of your cursor.

Freeform Pen tool cursor

9. **Release the mouse button about half-way down the east side of the island.**

When you release the mouse button, the shape you drew fills with whatever color shows in the Color swatch on the Control panel. This happens even when you draw a shape that isn't a closed path.

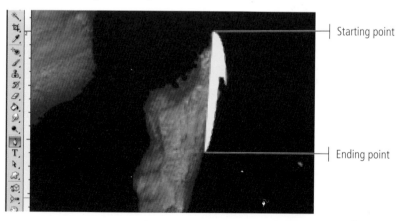

Starting point

Ending point

Note:

When you draw by holding down a button (mouse button or the button on a graphics tablet/pen) it is not uncommon for the line to "jump" where you don't want it to jump. If this happens, press Esc to remove your selection or path and start drawing again.

10. Place the mouse cursor over the point where you stopped dragging.

When the Pen tool cursor is over the end of an open path, the small slash in the icon indicates that you can click to continue drawing the same path.

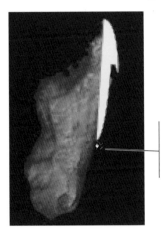

The slash in the tool cursor indicates that clicking will continue the existing path.

Note:

Even if the cursor is not directly over the open endpoint, you can double-click with the Freeform Pen tool in magnetic mode to close the shape.

11. Click over the open end point and continue tracing the outline of the island.

When you return to the original starting point, a small circle in the tool cursor indicates that you are closing the shape. If you release the mouse button when you see the circle, the entire island shape will fill with the shape color.

Tool cursor shows that releasing the mouse button here will close the shape.

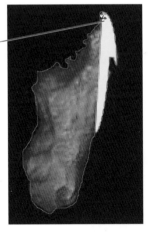

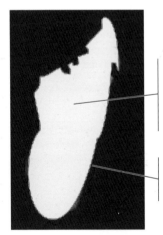

Releasing the mouse button fills the entire shape with the color you selected in the Color Picker.

The resulting path can be edited with the Direct Selection tool.

12. Look at the Layers panel.

When you draw with a Pen tool in Shape Layer mode, the resulting vector shape exists on its own layer.

This is the layer fill color. This color is visible within the area of the vector mask.

This is the vector mask, which you drew with the Freeform Pen tool.

13. Save the file and continue to the next exercise. If you get a warning about maximizing capability, click OK.

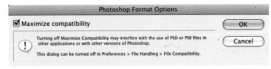

ADD TO AN EXISTING SHAPE LAYER

The Freeform Pen tool is very useful for drawing custom vector shapes, whether you're tracing a map or drawing original freeform art. When using this tool, however, you must hold down the mouse button the entire time you draw (unless you have a graphics tablet).

In this case, however, you have a better option because you don't need to precisely match the shape of the continent. The Freeform Pen tool has a Magnetic mode that snaps to edges of high contrast in the image. Using this method will make it far easier to complete the outline you need.

1. **With africa_working.psd open, zoom out to see the entire image.**

2. **With the Freeform Pen tool active, check the Magnetic option in the Control panel.**

3. **Click the button to the right of the tool variations to access the tool options.**

   You can still define the Curve Fit option when drawing in Magnetic mode. You also have three new options:

   - **Width** determines how far from an edge you have to drag (1–256 pixels) for Photoshop to still find the edge.

   - **Contrast** determines how much variation (1–100%) must exist between pixels for Photoshop to define an edge.

   - **Frequency** determines the rate at which Photoshop places anchor points. Higher values (up to 100) create anchor points faster than lower values (down to 0).

4. **Set the Width to 40, the Contrast to 20%, and the Frequency to 25.**

   This image has very high contrast between the land and the water, so you can use a lower contrast value and still find the edges.

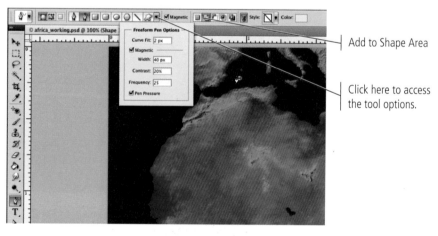

Add to Shape Area

Click here to access the tool options.

Note:

The Pen Pressure option only applies if you have a pressure-sensitive graphics tablet. When this option is turned on, higher pressure decreases the Width tolerance.

5. **In the Control panel to the right of the Magnetic check box, choose the Add to Shape Area option.**

   You want to create a single shape layer with all the land masses, so you must make sure each new disconnected shape is added to the previous shapes.

6. **Click at the northeast point of Somalia to place the first anchor point, release the mouse button, and then drag around the shape of the African continent.**

You don't have to hold down the mouse button when you draw with the Freeform Pen tool in Magnetic mode. In fact, you can click specific points while you draw to manually place anchor points along the way. Otherwise, Photoshop automatically draws the path and points as necessary to create the shape.

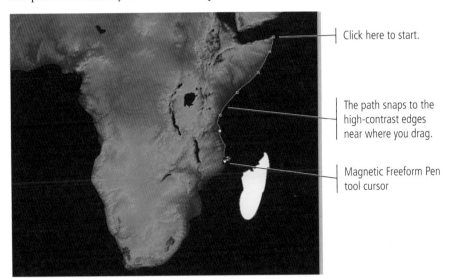

Click here to start.

The path snaps to the high-contrast edges near where you drag.

Magnetic Freeform Pen tool cursor

Note:

Manually clicking while using the Magnetic Freeform Pen tool option is a good way to make sharp turns along thin areas, which you'll see shortly.

7. **When you get to the point where Africa meets the Arabian Peninsula, drag across the Suez Canal. Photoshop will find and recognize the edge where Africa meets the Red Sea.**

8. **Drag around to the original starting point and click to close the shape.**

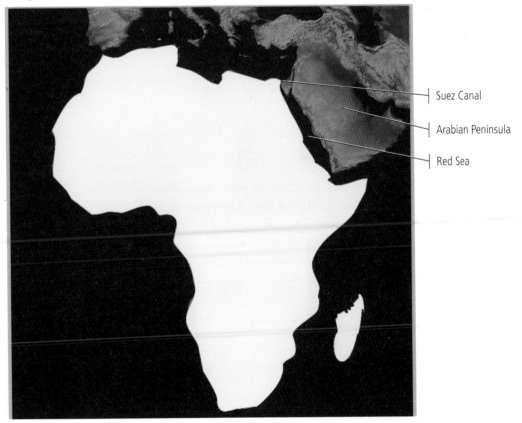

Suez Canal

Arabian Peninsula

Red Sea

9. **Look at the Layers panel.**

The mask thumbnail shows both shapes because you used the Add to Shape Area option to create a single shape of multiple closed paths (called a compound path).

10. **Save the file and continue to the next exercise.**

 ## CONTROL AND EDIT A SHAPE LAYER

When you outlined the shape of Africa, the Magnetic Freeform Pen tool made the work much easier than manually tracing the shape — but the path is not perfectly matched to the original. In this case, the result is acceptable because you don't need precision to achieve your ultimate goal. In many other cases, however, the path you first draw will be a good starting point, but will need some (if not significant) refinement before you can call it complete.

1. **In the open africa_working.psd file, zoom in to the southern part of Europe at the top of the image.**

2. **Using the Freeform Pen tool in Magnetic mode and adding to the existing shape layer, click to anchor the path where Italy meets the top edge of the image.**

3. **Drag around Italy to create the path.**

When you drag around the tip of the "boot," the area is too narrow for Photoshop to accurately create the outline.

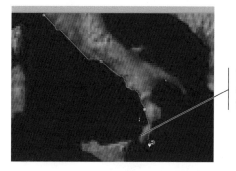

The path can't accurately snap to the tip of the boot.

4. **Drag back to the tip of the boot and click to manually place an anchor point, and then continue dragging around the outline. Anywhere the path doesn't accurately snap to the edge, click to manually create a point.**

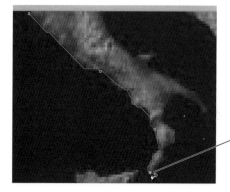

Click to manually anchor a point while drawing with the Freeform Pen tool in Magnetic mode.

5. **Click over the original starting point to close the shape.**

When you close the shape, the shape probably needs some help. For example, it's nearly impossible to draw a straight line using only the Magnetic Freeform Pen tool.

6. **Use the information you learned about the Pen tool in Project 1 to fine-tune your outline of Italy.**

This is one place where we can't give you specific instructions because everyone's path will be a bit different. Keep the following points in mind as you refine your shape.

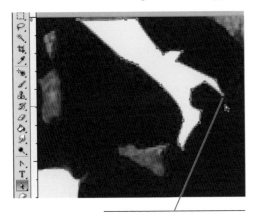

Click to manually anchor a point while drawing with the Freeform Pen tool in Magnetic mode.

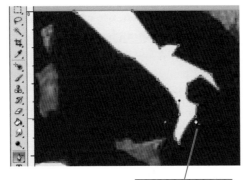

Use the Delete Anchor Point tool to delete a point from the path.

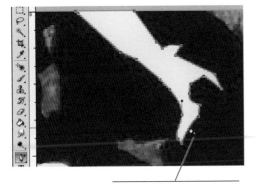

Use the Add Anchor Point tool to add a point to a path.

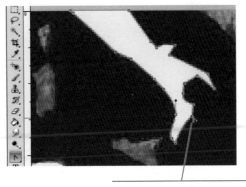

Use the Convert Anchor Point tool to change a smooth point to a corner point (and vice versa).

This is our final result.

7. **Save the file and continue to the next exercise.**

 ## SUBTRACT FROM A SHAPE LAYER

You now have a single shape layer made up of three different shapes. This type of object — when more than one closed path comprises a single shape — is called a **compound path**. Compound paths can also be used to remove inner areas from a shape, such as the interior of the letter A or the number 9.

1. **With africa_working.psd open, use what you have learned about drawing shape layers to add the remaining land areas to the existing shape layer. Use the following guidelines as you create the shapes:**

   - Make sure all the points that touch the image edges are corner points, with no extraneous points on the segments that touch the image edge.

   - Include the larger islands in the Mediterranean Sea (Sicily, Corsica, Sardinia, Crete, and Cyprus).

   - For now, don't worry about tracing the Black and Caspian Seas above the Arabian Peninsula. You'll remove those in the next few steps.

   When you've finished drawing the outlines, you're almost done — except that you covered two large seas and at least five major lakes within the African continent. You'll fix that problem next.

Note:

We used the Freeform Pen tool without the Magnetic option because we prefer the control of the line exactly following the mouse cursor. This decision is entirely up to you, especially since the shape you're drawing doesn't have to be perfect.

2. **In the Layers panel, change the Shape Layer opacity to 50%.**

   You can change the opacity of any layer, including a shape layer. By reducing the layer opacity, you can see the underlying layers enough to trace the seas and lakes.

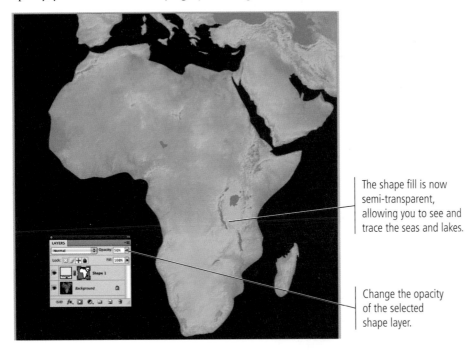

The shape fill is now semi-transparent, allowing you to see and trace the seas and lakes.

Change the opacity of the selected shape layer.

3. **With the Freeform Pen tool active (with or without Magnetic mode), click the Subtract from Shape Area option in the Control panel.**

4. **Using the same techniques you used to create the existing shape layer, trace the outline of the Caspian Sea.**

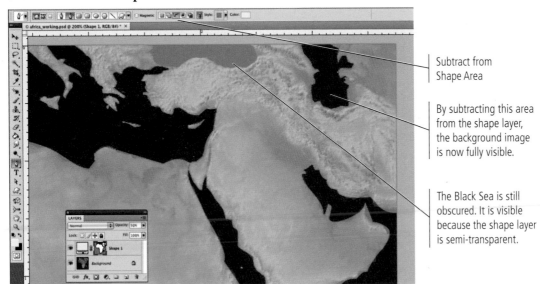

Subtract from Shape Area

By subtracting this area from the shape layer, the background image is now fully visible.

The Black Sea is still obscured. It is visible because the shape layer is semi-transparent.

5. **Continue removing the areas of any large bodies of water from the shape layer. Make sure you exclude the larger African lakes identified in the following image.**

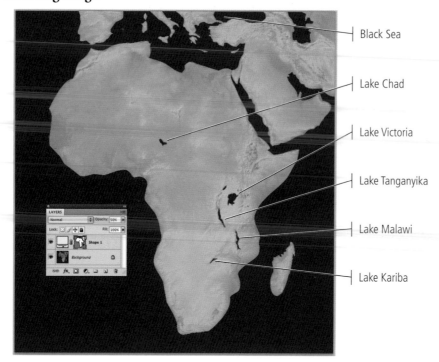

Black Sea
Lake Chad
Lake Victoria
Lake Tanganyika
Lake Malawi
Lake Kariba

6. **Save the file and continue to the next exercise.**

RESAMPLE THE SHAPE LAYER AND CHANGE THE CANVAS SIZE

You now have a complete compound shape layer that outlines all the land areas in the original image. The file, however, is still only about 4″ wide. Before you add the animal images, you need to convert the file to the appropriate size so the placed animal pictures are not resampled when you enlarge the image.

1. **With `africa_working.psd` open, choose Image>Image Size.**

2. **In the Image Size dialog box, make sure the Resample check box is active.**

3. **Change the Height field to 12 [inches] and click OK.**

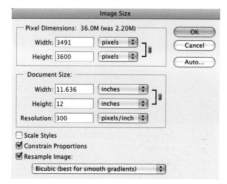

You're adding a sizeable amount of information to this file, so the resampling process might take a few minutes. Depending on the power and speed of your computer, you might see a progress bar as the image size is remapped.

4. **When the Progress bar disappears, change the view percentage to 100%.**

5. **In the Layers panel, return the shape layer to 100% opacity. Click away from the shape layer to turn off the vector path in the document window.**

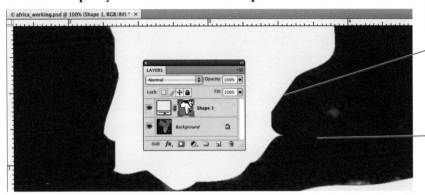

The vector edge of the shape layer is still just as sharp as it was when you created it at the original size.

The background image is still badly pixelated, just as it was when you resized it earlier.

6. **Change your view to fit the entire image in the document window.**

7. **Choose Image>Canvas Size.**

When you resampled the image to 12″ high, you might have noticed that the width was proportionally changed to 11.636″. That's slightly larger than the 10″ you want, so you need to crop the image to the correct dimensions.

In Project 1, you used the Crop tool to crop a file to a specific size. If you know the exact size you need, you can change the size of the canvas to change the size of an image.

The Anchor area shows the reference point around which the canvas will be enlarged or cropped. If the center point is selected, for example, reducing the width by 1″ would remove 0.5″ from the left and right edges of the image.

8. **Change the Width field to 10 [inches] and click OK.**

Note:

If you are enlarging the canvas, you can define the color that will be used in the new area outside the existing image size. Your choices are Foreground, Background, Black, White, Gray, or a custom color.

Note:

If you activate the Relative check box, you can define how much you want to add or subtract instead of defining a specific height and width. For example, you can reduce the height by 1″ by typing −1 in the height field.

The inward-pointing arrows show that space will be removed from the top and bottom of the image.

When you reduce a canvas size, you're warned that elements outside the new dimensions will be clipped (removed).

9. **Click Proceed to crop the canvas to 10″ wide.**

10. **Save the file and continue to the next exercise.**

 ADD COLOR AND TEXTURE TO THE SHAPE LAYER

Aside from their usefulness as scalable vector paths, shape layers can be filled with solid color (which yours is now), with styles or patterns (which you will add in this exercise), or even with other images (which you will do later).

Most of the shape layer in this file is going to be filled with pictures of animals, but some areas will visible. Adding a texture to the whole shape layer will create an effective background in areas where the animal pictures don't cover the shape layer.

1. **With africa_working.psd open, click the Eye icon of the shape layer to hide that layer.**

   You're going to pull a color from the placed image to use as the layer's fill color. To do that, you must be able to see the underlying layer.

2. **In the Layers panel, double-click the Color icon to the left of the (hidden) shape layer.**

   In the Color Picker dialog box, you can numerically define a color in any of the available color modes; you can click in the Color Picker window; or you can use the Eyedropper tool to click in the image window and "pick up" a color from the image.

3. **Click the eyedropper cursor in one of the gold areas of the image.**

   We used the one on the left edge of the Arabian Peninsula.

Note:

You can change the fill of a shape layer by double-clicking the Color icon in the Layers panel, or by clicking the Color swatch in the Control panel. These methods work even when the layer is not visible.

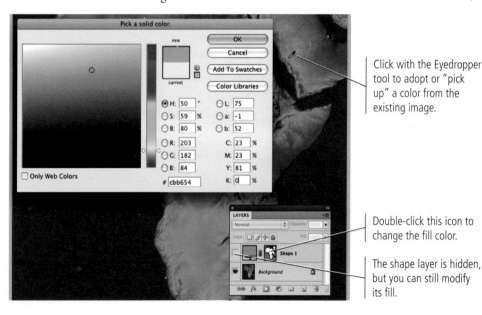

Click with the Eyedropper tool to adopt or "pick up" a color from the existing image.

Double-click this icon to change the fill color.

The shape layer is hidden, but you can still modify its fill.

4. Click OK to close the Color Picker, then make the shape layer visible again.

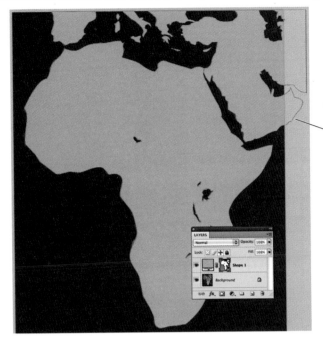

Cropping an image (as you did in the previous exercise) does not cut the vector shape layer.

Note:

The shape layer fill changes as soon as you choose a color in the Color Picker dialog box; you can't see this effect because the layer is currently hidden.

5. Make sure the Pen tool is selected. In the Control panel, click the arrow to the right of the Style button.

This panel shows the predefined styles that can be applied to a shape layer. The icons give you an idea of what the styles do, but these small squares can be cryptic.

6. Click the arrow in the top-right corner of the Control panel and choose Large List from the Options menu.

We prefer the list view because the style names provide a better idea of what the styles do. The Large List option displays a bigger style thumbnail than the Small List view.

Note:

*A Photoshop **style** is simply a saved group of effects that can be applied with a single click. You can create your own styles using the Layer Effects dialog box (which you will do in Project 3).*

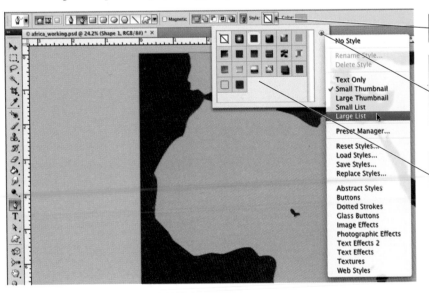

Click here to open the Style panel.

Click here to open the Style panel Options menu and access built-in libraries of styles.

By default, panels appear in Small Thumbnail view.

7. **Open the Style panel Options menu again and choose Textures near the bottom of the list.**

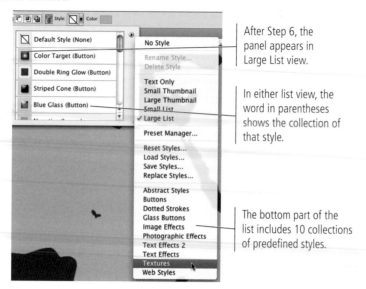

After Step 6, the panel appears in Large List view.

In either list view, the word in parentheses shows the collection of that style.

The bottom part of the list includes 10 collections of predefined styles.

Note:

The same style options can also be accessed and applied in the Styles panel (Window>Styles).

8. **Click OK to replace the current set with the Textures set.**

When you call a new set of styles, Photoshop asks if you want to replace the current set or append the new set to the existing set(s).

9. **If possible, expand the panel so you can see all the styles in the Textures set.**

10. **Make sure the shape layer is selected in the Layers panel and then click Ancient Stone in the panel to apply the style to the shape layer.**

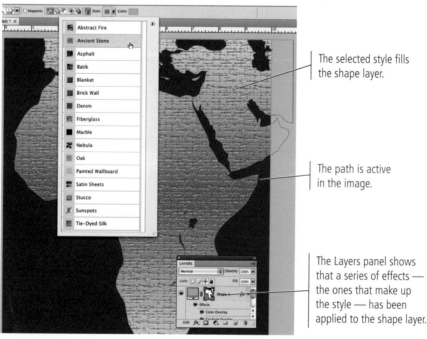

The selected style fills the shape layer.

The path is active in the image.

The Layers panel shows that a series of effects — the ones that make up the style — has been applied to the shape layer.

Note:

The actual vector path has to be active to change the fill attributes. If you don't see the path in the document window, click the path icon in the Layers panel to select it.

11. **Save the file and continue to the next stage of the project.**

Stage 2 **Compositing with Smart Objects**

Your client provided a number of animal pictures that you can use in the finished artwork. In Project 1, you learned the two basic methods for compositing files into another file — copy and paste (or drag) and placing a file as a Smart Object. Your ultimate goal determines which of these methods is most appropriate for a specific job.

Smart Objects are layers that preserve source content, which means you can apply non-destructive transformations to the layer. (**Non-destructive** means you do not alter the actual image data; you can restore the original image content, or make changes to the transformations that you apply, without negatively affecting the image quality.)

Smart Objects also allow you to apply non-destructive image filters. When you apply a Photoshop filter to a regular layer, the pixels on the layer are permanently affected (unless you undo the filter or step back through the History panel). Using Smart Objects means you can apply non-destructive filters to a layer since you aren't affecting the actual file data.

Note:

In addition to placing files as Smart Objects, you can also open a file as a Smart Object in the File menu.

COMPARE SMART OBJECT LAYERS TO NORMAL LAYERS

In this exercise, you apply layer masks and filters to the client's animal pictures. However, you don't want to modify the actual photo files, and you want to be able to change the filter settings if the client doesn't like the initial results. To accomplish both of these objectives, you will place the animal images as Smart Objects.

1. With `africa_working.psd` open, choose File>Place.

2. Navigate to `addax.tif` in the `RF_Photoshop`>`Africa` folder, click Place, and then press Return/Enter to finalize the placement in the document window.

3. Repeat Step 2 to place `lion.tif` into your working file.

4. Choose File>Open. Select `giraffe.jpg` and `gorilla.tif` and click Open.

5. Use the Arrange Documents panel in the Applications/Menu bar to show all three documents at once within the workspace.

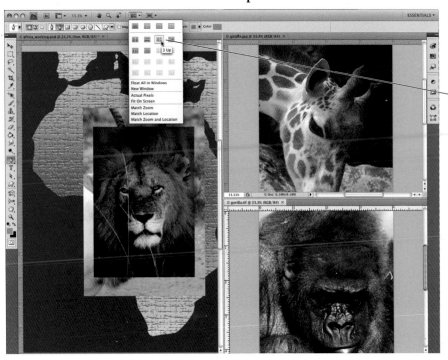

We used the 3 Up arrangement in the Arrange Documents panel.

6. **Choose the Move tool in the Tools panel.**

7. **Click the Giraffe window to activate that file, and then drag the giraffe image into your working map file. Close the giraffe file.**

8. **Repeat Step 7 for the gorilla file.**

9. **Fit the entire working file into the document window, and then review the Layers panel.**

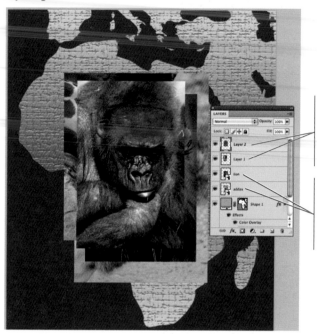

The giraffe layer (Layer 1) and gorilla layer (Layer 2) are regular Photoshop layers. They are not linked to external files.

The lion and addax layers are Smart Object layers; the layer names are defined by the names of the files you placed.

Note:

In a later exercise, you will explore the different way that Photoshop manages masks for regular layers compared to Smart Layers.

10. **Rename the two regular layers to reflect which animals reside on those layers.**

Remember: To rename a layer, simply double-click the layer name in the Layers panel and then type the new name.

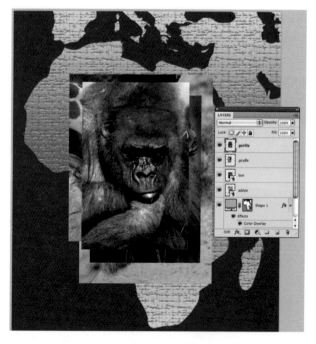

11. **Save the file and continue to the next exercise.**

PHOTOSHOP FOUNDATIONS

You need a bit of background about channels to understand what's happening in the Quick Mask you're using. (You'll use channels extensively in later projects.)

Every image has one channel for each component color. An RGB image has three channels: Red, Green, and Blue; a CMYK image has four channels: Cyan, Magenta, Yellow, and Black. Each channel contains the information for the amount of that component color in any given pixel.

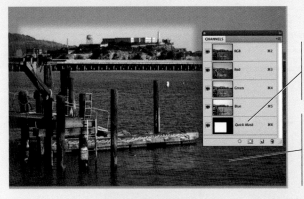

An RGB image has three channels, one for each additive primary.

A CMYK image has four channels, one for each subtractive primary plus one for black.

In RGB images, the three additive primaries can have a value of 0 (none of that color) to 255 (full intensity of that color). Combining a value of 255 for each primary results in white; a value of 0 for each primary results in black.

In CMYK images, the three subtractive primaries plus black are combined in percentages from 0 (none of that color) to 100 (full intensity of that color) to create the range of printable colors. Channels in a CMYK image represent the printing plates or separations required to output the job.

When you work in Quick Mask mode, an extra Alpha channel is created to temporarily store the selection area. An Alpha channel functions similar to a regular channel, in that it has the same range of possible values as a regular color channel (0–255 in an RGB image, 0–100 in a CMYK image). However, the Alpha value determines the degree of transparency in a color. In other words, a 50% value in the Alpha channel means that area of the image will be 50% transparent (semi-opaque).

Alpha channels allow you to design with degrees of transparency. You can blend one image into another, blend one layer into another, or blend an entire image into a background in a page-layout application (both Adobe InDesign and QuarkXPress support embedded Alpha channels).

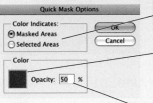

The Quick Mask channel stores the degree of transparency based on the current selection.

The semi-transparent red overlay shows areas being masked (i.e., the areas outside the current selection).

You can change the appearance of masks by double-clicking the Quick Mask button in the Tools panel, or double-clicking the Quick Mask thumbnail in the Channels panel.

Change the mask to overlay the masked area instead of the selected area.

Click here to change the color of the mask in the image window.

Use this option to make the mask more or less transparent. This setting only affects the appearance of the mask in Photoshop; it doesn't change the transparency values in the actual Alpha channel.

Quick Masks are useful when you need to work with a temporary selection or if you are still defining the exact selection area. As long as you stay in Quick Mask mode, the temporary Alpha channel remains in the Channels panel (listed in italics as "Quick Mask"). If you return to Standard mode, the Quick Mask disappears from the window and the panel.

Once you've created a complex selection, you can save it as a permanent Alpha channel by dragging the Quick Mask channel onto the New Channel button at the bottom of the Channels panel. Doing so adds a channel named "Quick Mask copy" (not in italics), which will be a permanent part of the file even if you exit Quick Mask mode.

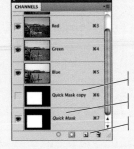

Permanent Alpha channel

Temporary Quick Mask channel

New Channel button

WORK WITH FEATHERED SELECTIONS IN QUICK MASK MODE

In the Interface chapter, we said that making selections is so important that Photoshop has an entire menu dedicated to that task. In Project 1, you learned several methods for creating selections. To complete the map in this project, you'll expand on the skills you learned in Project 1 to create soft-edged layer masks that blend the edges of the animal pictures into the background.

1. With **africa_working.psd** open, hide all the layers except the background and the lion.

2. Click the lion layer in the Layers panel to select that layer.

3. Drag with the Elliptical Marquee tool to create a selection around the lion's face.

4. Choose Select>Modify>Feather.

Feathering means to soften the edge of a selection so the image blends into the background instead of showing a sharp line around the edge. The Smooth, Expand, and Contract options are rather self-explanatory. The **Border** option creates a specific number of pixels around the active selection (think of the stroke/border around a shape in an illustration program).

Note:

Press Option/Alt to draw a selection marquee from the center out.

5. In the Feather Selection dialog box, type 25 in the Feather Radius field.

The Feather Radius defines the distance from solid to transparent.

Note:

If you choose Transform Selection in the Select menu, the selection marquee shows bounding box handles, which you can use to transform the marquee just as you would transform a layer.

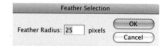

6. Click OK to return to the image window.

There's no apparent difference in the selection because the marching ants can't show shades of a selection. The selection is feathered, but you can't see it yet.

7. **Click the Quick Mask button at the bottom of the Tools panel to toggle into Quick Mask mode.**

   This mode creates a temporary Alpha channel that shows the graded selection.

The mask edge shows the feathered part of the selection.

Click this button to toggle between Quick Mask mode and Standard mode.

8. **Click the Quick Mask button at the bottom of the Tools panel to toggle off the Quick Mask.**

9. **In the Layers panel, click the Add Layer Mask button.**

   A layer mask is basically an Alpha channel connected to a specific layer.

The feathered-selection-turned-layer-mask allows the lion image to blend into the background instead of ending abruptly.

The layer mask is linked to the selected layer.

Add Layer Mask button

Note:

If you don't turn off the Quick Mask mode, Step 9 will create an empty layer mask.

Alternatively, you could Command/Control-click the Quick Mask in the Channels panel to show the marching ants, and then click the Add Layer Mask button in the Layers panel.

10. **Hide the lion layer and show the gorilla layer. Click the gorilla layer in the Layers panel to make that the active layer.**

11. **Use the same basic technique from Steps 3–9 to create a feathered mask around the gorilla's face.**

    Even though one of these layers is a Smart Object and one is a regular layer, the technique and the result are basically the same. Both layers show the appropriate layer mask in the Layers panel.

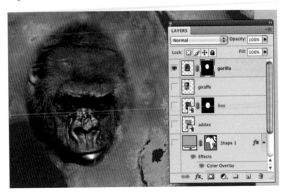

Note:

When a masked layer is selected in the Layers panel, the layer mask appears in the Channels panel as a temporary Alpha channel.

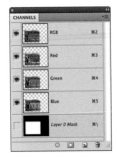

12. **Hide the gorilla layer, save the file, and continue to the next exercise.**

APPLY A LAYER MASK TO A SMART OBJECT LAYER

It's important to understand that when you place an image file as a Smart Object, the placed Smart Object is not linked to the original file you placed. If you're familiar with page-layout software such as InDesign or QuarkXPress, this is the opposite of what you expect when you "place" an image file in those programs.

An image Smart Object in Photoshop is actually linked to an internal copy of the original file. Editing the original file has no effect on the placed Smart Object layer, and editing the Smart Object has no effect on the original file. This workflow protects your original images, while still allowing you to make destructive and non-destructive changes to the Smart Object.

In the previous exercise, you created a feathered layer mask for a Smart Object layer; you added the layer mask within the main africa_working Layers panel, so the layer mask did not affect the original file. Depending on the project you're building, you might want to create a layer mask once and have it affect all instances of that Smart Object. In this case, you should edit the actual Smart Object instead of affecting the placed instance.

1. **In africa_working.psd, show the addax layer.**

   Remember, you placed this image as a Smart Object.

2. **Double-click the layer thumbnail to open the Smart Object file in its own window. If you see a warning message, click OK.**

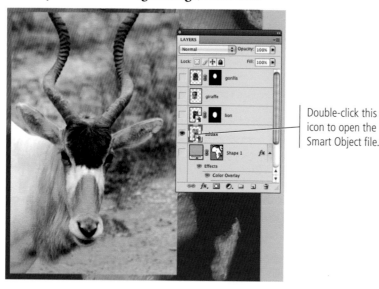

Double-click this icon to open the Smart Object file.

Note:

If you don't see this message, you can open the Photoshop General Preferences dialog box and click the Reset All Warning Dialogs button.

This message tells you that you must save the Smart Object with the same name for the changes to reflect in the africa_working file. You can't use the Save As function to save the file with a different name or in a different location.

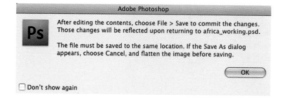

The addax file opens separately, appearing by default as a separate tab at the top of the document window.

3. **Using the Rectangular Marquee tool, drag a selection around the addax's head, and then feather the selection by 25 pixels.**

    In the Layers panel, the Add Layer Mask option is not available because the file has only one layer — Background. You can't apply a layer mask to the Background layer of a file.

4. **In the Layers panel, double-click the Background layer to see your options.**

    The addax image is a flat image, which means it has only a Background layer that is locked. You can't apply a layer mask to the locked Background layer, so you have to first convert the Background layer to a regular layer.

5. **In the New Layer dialog box, leave the options at their default values and click OK.**

    The former Background layer is now a regular unlocked layer named Layer 0. You could have renamed it, but that is unnecessary for this exercise because you will eventually delete this layer.

6. **With the feathered selection still active, click the Add Layer Mask button at the bottom of the Layers panel.**

Click here to create the layer mask.

7. **Choose File>Save (or press Command/Control-S).**

   The TIFF Options dialog box appears because your file now has new layer information. Even though the file has only one layer, that layer is partially transparent.

   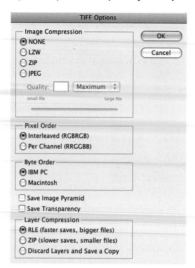

Note:

This technique wouldn't work if you placed a JPEG file as a Smart Object. To save a JPEG file with layer information, you must save the file as a copy — and you would see a related warning if you tried to do so. Saving as a copy means saving the file under a different file name, which would defeat the purpose and function of Smart Objects.

8. **Leave the TIFF options at their default values and click OK. If you see a warning about including layers, click OK again.**

9. **Close the addax.tif file.**

   When you look at the africa_working file, you can see that the layer mask has been applied to the addax image, but the Layers panel doesn't show the layer mask thumbnail. That's because the mask is applied in the Smart Object, not in the main file.

   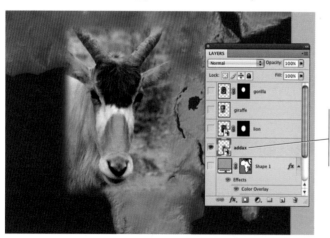

   The addax layer has no applied layer mask; the mask exists only in the Smart Object file.

10. **Save the file, clicking OK to the warning about maximizing layer compatibility. Continue to the next exercise.**

EDIT A LAYER MASK

Creating a layer mask from a selection is easy enough, and it's sometimes sufficient for a particular job (as was the case for the lion). But in other cases, you may want to create a mask that is beyond what you can easily accomplish with the basic selection tools. If necessary, you can paint directly on a layer mask to achieve virtually any effect — such as a mask that better outlines the addax in the map you're building.

1. **With `africa_working.psd` open, double-click the addax layer thumbnail to open the Smart Object file.**

2. **In the Layers panel, click the layer mask thumbnail to select it.**

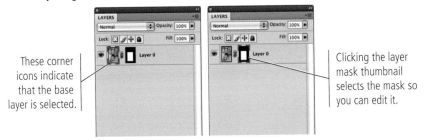

These corner icons indicate that the base layer is selected.

Clicking the layer mask thumbnail selects the mask so you can edit it.

3. **In the Channels panel, make sure the Layer 0 Mask channel is visible.**

   Layer masks are not visible by default; you have to turn them on in the Channels panel to see them. This isn't necessary, since you can paint a mask without seeing it. By painting on a layer mask, you're not really "painting" anything; instead, you're actually "painting" the visibility of the associated layer. We find it easier (at least when you're first learning) to be able to see what you're painting.

Making the mask channel visible allows you to see the red overlay in the image window.

4. **Double-click the Layer 0 Mask channel thumbnail, and then change the Opacity value to 100% in the Layer Mask Display Options dialog box.**

5. **Click OK to return to the image window.**

   Remember, this change only affects the transparency of the mask, not the degree of transparency applied to the layer. By setting the mask opacity to 100%, you know that anything solid red will be hidden and anything with no red will be visible.

6. **Choose the Brush tool in the Tools panel, and then click the Default Foreground and Background Colors button at the bottom of the Tools panel.**

If you look at the layer mask thumbnail for the layer, you can see it's just a black-and-white shape. White areas of the thumbnail show which parts of the layer are visible in the main document; the black parts of the mask hide the associated areas of the layer. This is an important distinction: painting with black on a layer mask hides those areas; painting with white on a layer mask reveals those areas.

Brush tool

Click here to return the foreground to black and the background to white.

7. **In the Control panel, click the Brush button to access the tool options.**

This panel shows the different brushes included with Photoshop. The default brush set includes a number of specific-diameter hard- and soft-edge brushes, as well as some artistic options farther down the panel. The number below each brush icon shows the size of the brush. If you click a specific brush in the panel, the same number displays in the Master Diameter field.

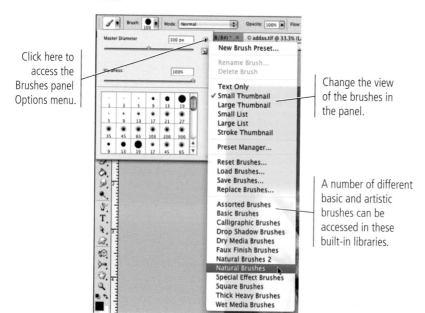

Click here to access the Brushes panel Options menu.

Change the view of the brushes in the panel.

A number of different basic and artistic brushes can be accessed in these built-in libraries.

Note:

You'll use brushes extensively in Project 7; for now, you only need to know how to select a brush and how to paint with it.

8. **Click the 200-pixel soft-edge brush in the panel to select it.**

9. **Click once between the addax's horns.**

   The Brush tool paints with whatever is defined as the foreground color, which is black in this case. Because you're using a soft-edge brush, the place where you click blends from solid black to nothing — resulting in a soft edge to the brush stroke (or dot in this case).

Even though you're painting with black, the stroke appears as red because that's the defined mask color.

The Brush tool cursor reflects the size of the brush you're using.

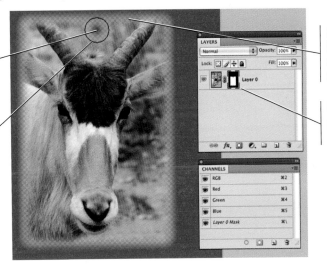

Using a soft-edge brush adds a feathered edge to what you paint in the mask.

Remember, you're painting on the layer mask.

10. **Using the brush, drag to paint the entire area between the horns and to the right of the animal's head.**

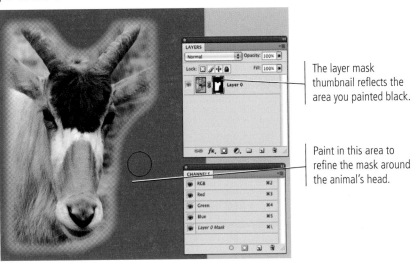

The layer mask thumbnail reflects the area you painted black.

Paint in this area to refine the mask around the animal's head.

11. **Click the Switch Foreground and Background Colors button near the bottom of the Tools panel.**

Note:

You can change the Brush tool cursor in the Cursors pane of the Preferences dialog box. Standard shows only the tool icon; Precise shows a crosshair icon; Normal shows the solid-area brush size; Fill Size expands the normal brush to include the feathered area. You can also choose to show a crosshair icon in the center of the brush area.

12. Paint over the area where the tip of the left ear should be.

Because you're painting with white, you're basically removing area from the mask. You can also use the Eraser tool on a mask. Be careful, though, because erasing an area of the mask when the foreground color is white has the same effect as painting with black — "erasing" on the mask actually adds to the mask.

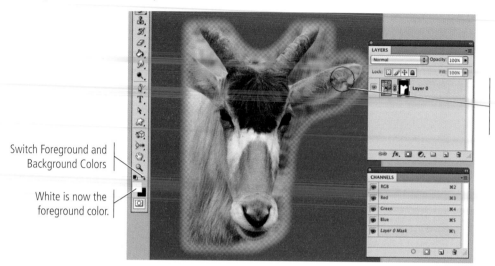

Switch Foreground and Background Colors

White is now the foreground color.

Paint on the mask with white to reveal the addax's ear.

13. Continue refining the mask until you're satisfied with the result. You should have no hard edges around the outside of the image.

14. Save the addax file and close it.

Remember, you're working in a Smart Object file, so don't choose Save As or save the file with a different name. Once the process has updated, you see the refined layer mask in the africa_working file.

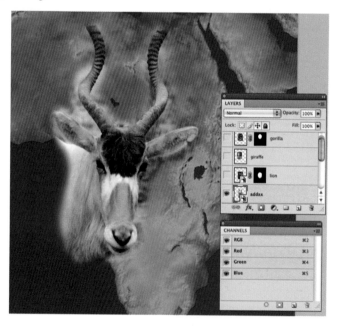

Note:

You can create a layer mask from scratch by adding the mask with nothing selected, and then painting and erasing as necessary to mask the areas you want to hide. You can even use a black-to-white gradient on a layer mask to create unique effects in a non-specific shape.

15. Save the map file and continue to the next exercise.

PHOTOSHOP FOUNDATIONS

In the first part of this project, you learned how to access additional sets of built-in styles. You can use the same basic technique to access any of the twelve built-in brush libraries from the Brushes panel Options menu. If you call a brush library from the menu, you have the choice of appending the brushes to the current set or replacing the current set with the new library (just as you do with built-in style libraries).

Click here to access the Brushes panel Options menu.

Change the view of the brushes in the panel.

A number of different basic and artistic brushes can be accessed in these built-in libraries.

New Brush Preset...

Rename Brush...
Delete Brush

Text Only
✓ Small Thumbnail
Large Thumbnail
Small List
Large List
Stroke Thumbnail

Preset Manager...

Reset Brushes...
Load Brushes...
Save Brushes...
Replace Brushes...

Assorted Brushes
Basic Brushes
Calligraphic Brushes
Drop Shadow Brushes
Dry Media Brushes
Faux Finish Brushes
Natural Brushes 2
Natural Brushes
Special Effect Brushes
Square Brushes
Thick Heavy Brushes
Wet Media Brushes

USE THE MASKS PANEL

In the previous exercises, you learned how to create a feathered selection and a layer mask based on that selection. You also learned how to use black and white to paint directly on a layer mask. These same techniques work for both normal layers and Smart Object layers. The Masks panel provides another option for creating and managing layer masks. This panel consolidates mask-related options from multiple locations in a single, convenient interface.

1. **With africa_working.psd open, hide the addax layer and show the giraffe layer. Click the giraffe layer to select it.**

2. **Choose the Lasso tool in the Tools panel. Drag to create a selection roughly matching the shape of the giraffe's head.**

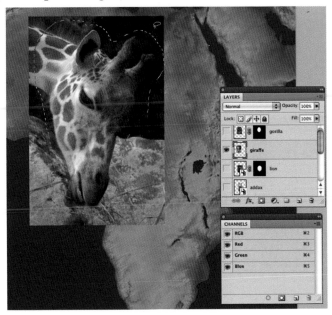

3. Open the Masks panel, and then click the Add a Pixel Mask button.

Clicking this button in the Masks panel is basically the same as clicking the Add Layer Mask button in the Layers panel. The active selection automatically becomes a mask for the selected layer. In this case, the selection has a hard edge because you didn't feather the selection.

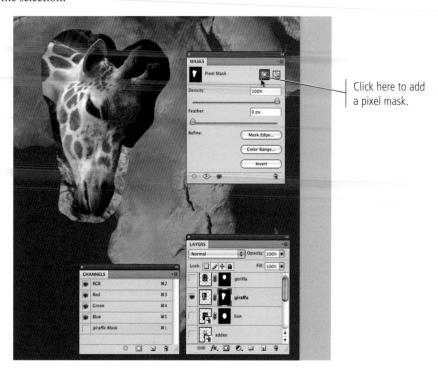

Click here to add a pixel mask.

4. In the Masks panel, drag the Feather slider until the field shows 25 px.

When you feather a selection and then make a layer mask from that selection, the feathering becomes a permanent part of the mask (unless you manually paint the mask to remove the feathering).

The Masks panel allows you to adjust the feathering of a hard-edged mask, and then later change or even remove the feathering if necessary, without manually painting on the layer mask.

5. Choose the Brush tool from the Tools panel.

6. In the Control panel, click the Brush button and choose one of the hard-edge brushes. At the top of the panel, use the slider to change the Master Diameter to 100 px.

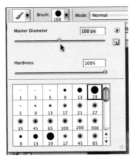

7. In the Layers panel, click the giraffe layer mask thumbnail to select the layer mask instead of the actual layer.

8. Make sure white is the foreground color and paint around the edges of the giraffe's horns.

The mask should closely follow the shape of the horns. If you paint over part of a horn (or anything else you want to keep, simply change the foreground color to black and paint that area back onto the mask.

Although you are painting with a hard-edged brush, the result is a soft edge because the mask is feathered in the Masks panel.

9. In the Masks panel, change the Feather value to 0 px.

Remember, you were painting with a hard-edge brush, so the edges where you painted have a hard edge. Because the Masks panel allows you to change the Feather value, you can easily turn feathering on or off to monitor your progress.

10. Change the Feather value to 25 px.

11. Save the file and continue to the next exercise.

CONVERT LAYERS TO SMART OBJECTS

Your file currently has two layers that you simply copied into the map file. You need to change these layers to Smart Objects before you apply filters. You can convert a regular layer to a Smart Object layer (or vice versa) rather easily. It is important, however, to know what to expect before you start converting in either direction.

1. **With africa_working.psd open, Control/right-click the giraffe layer name in the Layers panel.**

   When you Control/right-click a layer name, you see a contextual menu of options that are specific to the selected layer. Different options are available when you Control/right-click the layer thumbnail icons.

2. **Choose Convert to Smart Object in the menu.**

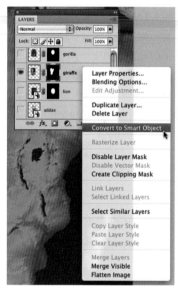

   Remember, you copied the giraffe image into the map file, so it was not originally placed as a Smart Object.

   Depending on the size of the file and the speed of your computer, this conversion might take a while; a Progress bar might show the Merging Layers message.

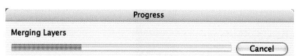

   When the process is complete, the Layers panel shows that the giraffe layer is now a Smart Object.

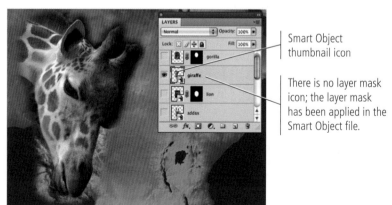

Smart Object thumbnail icon

There is no layer mask icon; the layer mask has been applied in the Smart Object file.

3. **Double-click the giraffe Smart Object thumbnail to open the file, and then review the Layers panel.**

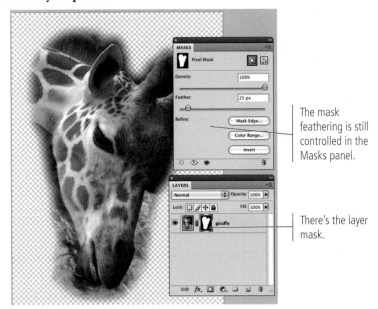

The mask feathering is still controlled in the Masks panel.

There's the layer mask.

4. **Close the giraffe file.**

5. **In your map file, repeat this process to convert the gorilla layer to a Smart Object.**

   You now have four Smart Objects, each with a layer mask. However, one of the layer masks (for the lion) is applied within the map file instead of within the Smart Object file. For the sake of uniformity (and to show you how to do it), you're going to move that layer mask into the Smart Object layer in the map file.

6. **Look closely at the thumbnail of the gorilla layer.**

   You might notice that nothing is visible in the thumbnail. That's because the layer was hidden when you converted it to a Smart Object.

7. **Double-click the gorilla layer thumbnail to open that file.**

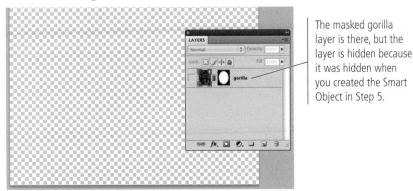

The masked gorilla layer is there, but the layer is hidden because it was hidden when you created the Smart Object in Step 5.

8. **Show the gorilla layer, save the gorilla file, and then close it.**

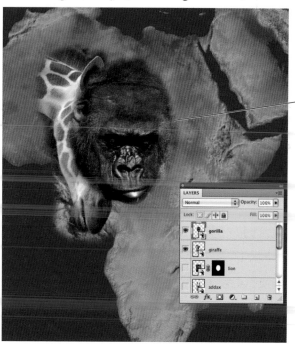

In the main file, the gorilla is now visible because that Smart Object layer is visible and the appropriate layer is now visible within the Smart Object file.

9. **Show the lion layer. Control/right-click the lion layer and choose Convert to Smart Object from the contextual menu.**

Although the layer is already a Smart Object, you must complete this step to move the existing layer mask from the map file into the Smart Object.

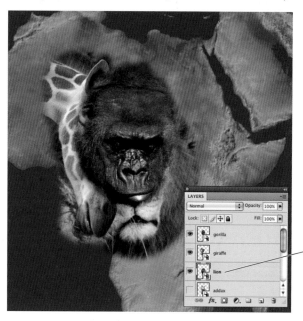

By converting the layer to a Smart Object, the layer mask is removed from the map file layer and placed inside the Smart Object file.

10. **Double-click the lion Smart Object thumbnail to open that file.**

The file contains the original Smart Object, as well as the layer mask you created. The more Smart Objects you have (including nested ones), the larger your file size. To avoid unnecessary bloating, you can eliminate the nested Smart Object.

11. Control/right-click the lion layer in the Layers panel and choose Rasterize Layer from the contextual menu.

To access the contextual menu for a specific layer, you have to Control/right-click in the area to the right of the layer name.

The Smart Object file has a nested Smart Object.

The layer mask from the map file has been moved to this Smart Object file.

Rasterizing the Smart Object basically removes the link to any external file, making the Smart Object a part of the file in which it has been placed.

The former nested Smart Object is now a regular layer.

12. Save the lion file and close it.

Other than the missing layer mask thumbnail, there is no apparent change in the map. By completing the last few steps, you reduced the complexity of the file you're building — a good thing since you're going to add more layers later.

13. Save the map file and continue to the next exercise.

Rasterizing Smart Objects with Masks

PHOTOSHOP FOUNDATIONS

If a Smart Object file has a layer mask, and you rasterize that Smart Object, the layer mask in the Smart Object will be applied before the file becomes a part of the master file.

In the following image, the gorilla Smart Object had a layer mask in the placed file before the Smart Object was rasterized. Rasterizing the gorilla layer converts the Smart Object layer to a regular layer, but the layer mask from the placed file is no longer available or editable.

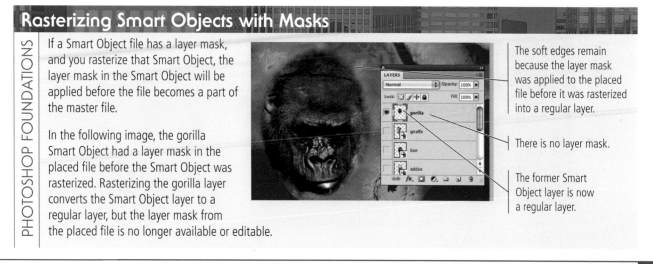

The soft edges remain because the layer mask was applied to the placed file before it was rasterized into a regular layer.

There is no layer mask.

The former Smart Object layer is now a regular layer.

CREATE A CLIPPING MASK

You now have four masked animals and the shape of the map. But your client wants the animal pictures to appear *inside* the map shape. You can accomplish this task by using the map shape as a clipping mask. It's relatively easy to create a clipping mask from any layer. As with Smart Objects, however, you should know what to expect when you create a clipping mask. Specifically, you should understand how the different layers will behave and interact with one another.

1. **With africa_working.psd open, make all layers visible.**

2. **Using the Move tool, drag the giraffe to fill the bottom portion of the African continent. Move the lion layer into the top-left area, move the addax so its ear fills the right area of the continent, and move the gorilla into the space between the lion and the addax.**

3. **Control/right-click the gorilla layer and choose Create Clipping Mask from the contextual menu.**

   A clipping mask is another way to show only certain areas of a layer; in this case, using the shape of one layer (giraffe) to hide parts of the layer above it (gorilla). Because no part of the gorilla layer is inside the area of the giraffe layer, the gorilla is now hidden.

Note:

To access the contextual menu for a specific layer, you have to Control/ right-click in the area to the right of the layer name.

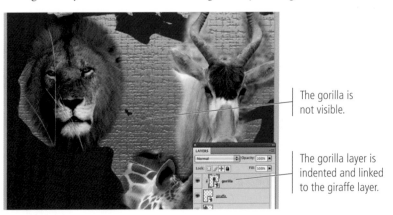

The gorilla is not visible.

The gorilla layer is indented and linked to the giraffe layer.

Since you want to put the animals inside the map shape and not in the shape of the other animals, this isn't what you want.

4. **Control/right-click the gorilla layer and choose Release Clipping Mask from the contextual menu.**

As with layer masks, clipping masks do not permanently modify the pixels in the layer, so you can always hide or remove clipping masks without damaging the masked image.

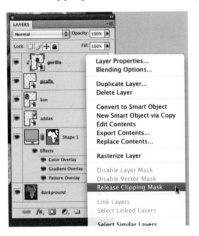

5. **Shift-click to select all four animal layers. Control/right-click any of the selected layers and choose Create Clipping Mask from the contextual menu.**

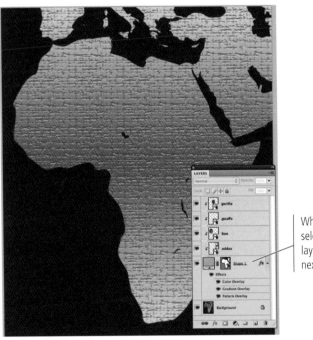

When multiple layers are selected, all the selected layers are clipped by the next-lowest layer.

This highlights a problem that occurs when working with a shape layer filled with a pattern (this shape layer is filled with the Ancient Stone pattern/style). This style includes overlays, which are technically overlaying the animal layers you placed inside the clipping mask. In other words, the pattern overlay completely obscures the animal layers.

If you don't need or want to maintain the layer style, you can simply clear the layer style using the layer's contextual menu. Because you want to keep the style but prevent it from overlaying the clipped animal images, you need to use a different technique.

6. **Click the Shape layer in the Layers panel to select it, and then choose Layer>Layer Style>Create Layers.**

   This command converts each applied effect to a separate layer, which are placed into the shape layer's clipping path to contain the new layers within the shape.

7. **When you see a warning that some effects cannot be reproduced with layers, click OK.**

   Nine times out of ten, you'll see this warning. However, we prefer to let the conversion happen and review the results before we make a final design decision. If you're not satisfied with the result, you can always undo the conversion and try again.

8. **Review the image and the Layers panel.**

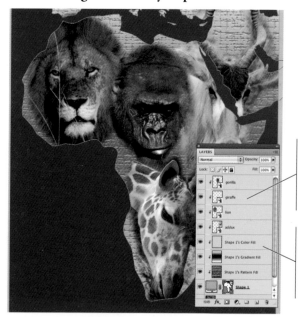

The animals are still clipped by the shape layer, and they are higher than the fill layers created from the effects.

The effects layers are now individual layers, which are placed into the shape layer as a clipping mask.

Note:

Now that you can see how the animals appear within the continent shape, it's easier to see where changes might be necessary.

9. Use the Move tool to reposition the animal layers as necessary to fill the continent. (Our solution is shown in the following image).

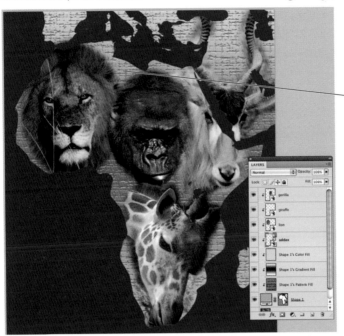

It's okay if some areas aren't filled; that's why you applied the pattern style to the shape layer — to add texture in areas that aren't covered by animal images.

Note:

The client supplied a large number of animal photos (in the RF_Photoshop>Africa folder). Feel free to add more animals to your artwork if you want to experiment further with masking techniques.

10. Save the file and continue to the next stage of the project.

Stage 3 Using Filters and Adjustments

Your client originally wanted a traditional painter to create this job, but decided instead on a digital version to save time and money. The advantage of using Photoshop is that you can easily create an art-like version of existing files using the built-in filters. You can make images look like pencil sketches, paintings, or any of dozens of other options. You can even compound multiple filters to create unique effects that would require extreme skill in traditional art techniques such as oil painting.

 ## APPLY NON-DESTRUCTIVE FILTERS TO SMART OBJECTS

Because the animals are placed into the map file as Smart Objects, the filters you apply do not affect the placed file data. In other words, they are non-destructive. This means you can later change the filter settings, add additional filters, or even delete a filter effect without damaging the placed file.

Note:

Filters apply to the selected layer, not to the entire file.

1. **With africa_working.psd open, click the giraffe layer in the Layers panel to select it.**

2. **Choose Filter>Artistic and review the options.**

   Photoshop ships with more than 100 filters divided into 13 categories; some of these are functional while others are purely decorative. You'll use some of the art filters in this project and experiment with some of the functional filters in later projects to accomplish specific goals.

Note:

You can choose Filter> Filter Gallery to open the Filter Gallery showing the last-used settings.

3. Choose Dry Brush in the Artistic menu.

The "Art" filters are controlled in a separate dialog box called the Filter Gallery. This gallery opens when you choose one of the Artistic, Brush Strokes, Dissolve, Sketch, Stylize, or Texture filters in the menu.

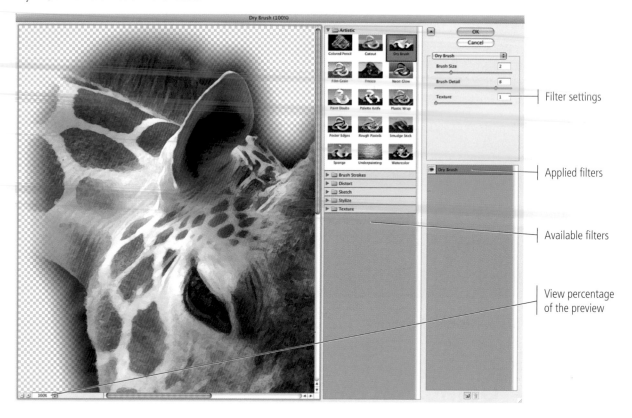

Filter settings

Applied filters

Available filters

View percentage of the preview

4. In the filter settings area, drag the Brush Size slider to 3.

When you change the filter settings, the preview window dynamically changes to show the new options. You can reduce the preview viewing percentage, but it's a good idea to look at your changes at 100% to get a good idea of what you're applying.

5. Change the Brush Detail slider to 6, and set the Texture slider to 1. Click OK to close the Filter Gallery and apply your choices.

The filter might not be obvious in the image window, especially if you're viewing the file at a low view percentage (we're using 33% in these screen shots). That's why we recommend previewing at 100% in the Filter Gallery.

In the Layers panel, a new icon appears in the giraffe layer, and a Smart Filters layer appears indented below it.

Click this button to collapse (hide) the Smart Filters options in the panel.

Double-click this icon to change the filter's blending options.

Double-click the filter name to re-open the Filter Gallery and make changes.

Click any of these eye icons to temporarily turn off the filter.

Note:

You can choose any of the available filters from the menu above the filter settings.

Note:

We thought about providing a long list of the different filters and what they do, but the best way to learn the available options is to simply open a file and start clicking. The preview shows you the different effects, and the individual filters have indicative thumbnails to show what they will produce.

6. **Double-click the Dry Brush item in the Layers panel to reopen the Filter Gallery.**

7. **In the bottom-right corner of the Filter Gallery, click the New Effect Layer button.**

    As we mentioned earlier, you can apply multiple filters to a single layer to create unique effects. When you add a new filter layer, it defaults to the same settings as the previous filter (in this case, Dry Brush). The preview shows the effect of compounding the Dry Brush filter two times.

8. **With the bottom Dry Brush layer selected, click the arrow to the left of the Brush Strokes filter set to expand the folder.**

9. **In the Brush Strokes set, click Dark Strokes to apply that filter.**

10. **In the filter settings area, adjust the settings until you are satisfied with the result.**

Note:

You might want to zoom in to get a better idea of the filter gallery results.

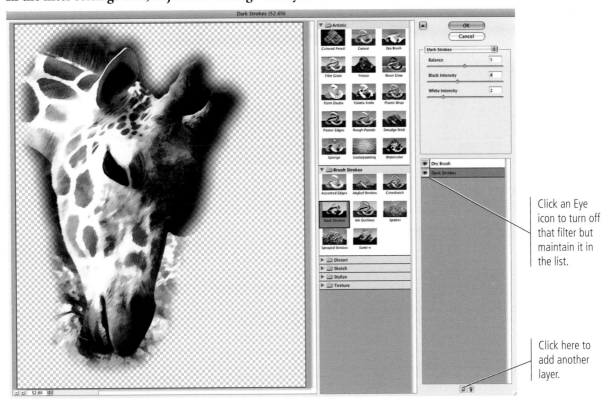

Click an Eye icon to turn off that filter but maintain it in the list.

Click here to add another layer.

11. **Click OK to close the Filter Gallery and apply your changes.**

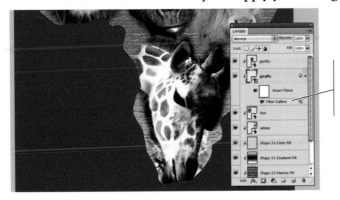

Since multiple filters are applied, this item now says Filter Gallery instead of Dry Brush.

Note:

You can reorder filter layers in the Layers panel just as you can reorder regular layers. Filters are applied from the bottom up; when you want to create a unique effect, experiment with multiple filters, as well as the order in which they are applied.

12. **Apply the Dry Brush and Dark Strokes filters to the remaining animal layers.**

You can simplify this process by Option/Alt-dragging the Filter Gallery listing in the Layers panel to the layers where you want to apply the same settings.

13. **In the Layers panel, click the buttons to collapse the Smart Filter information for each animal layer.**

Click these buttons to hide or show the Smart Filter information.

14. **Save the file and continue.**

 APPLY DESTRUCTIVE FILTERS TO REGULAR LAYERS

The previous exercise highlighted the Filter Gallery, and the benefits of applying non-destructive filters to Smart Objects. If you're working with regular layers, however, filters are destructive; they can't be edited or removed (although they can be undone).

1. **With africa_working.psd open, select the Shape 1 Pattern Fill layer.**

2. **Choose Filter>Distort>Glass. Adjust the filter options until you are satisfied with the result.**

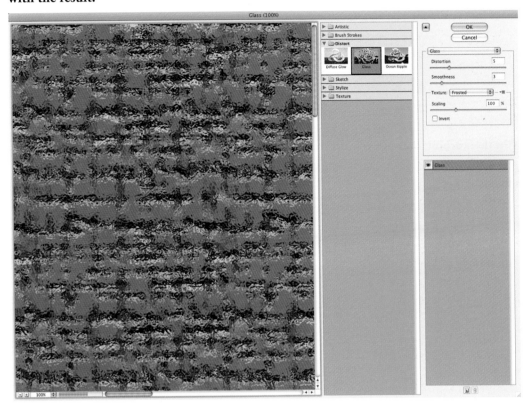

3. **Click OK to apply the filter.**

In the image, the pattern behind the animals is now much softer and less defined. Filtering the pattern layer helps you achieve the goal of a "painting" effect.

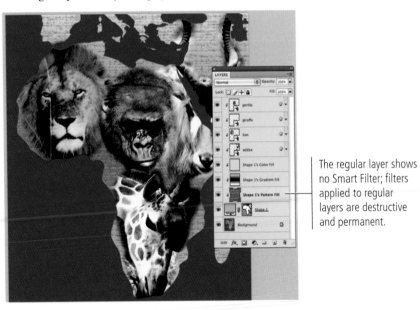

The regular layer shows no Smart Filter; filters applied to regular layers are destructive and permanent.

The only remaining problem is the sharp edges of the vector shape layer — a "real" painting would not have these sharp edges.

4. Select the Shape 1 layer and choose Filter>Stylize>Diffuse.

Functional filters such as Diffuse are not applied in the Filter Gallery; instead, each filter has its own dialog box. However, before you can access the Diffuse dialog box, you have to rasterize the shape layer.

Note:

Webster's dictionary defines diffuse as "to pour, spread out, or disperse in every direction; spread or scatter wildly." The Photoshop Diffuse filter reflects the second half of that definition: scattering the pixels in the selected layer.

5. Click OK in the warning message to rasterize the shape layer.

The Diffuse dialog box shows a preview of the layer. In this case, you're editing a large area of flat color, so there appears to be no effect.

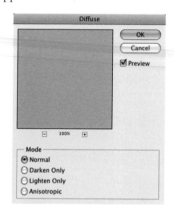

Note:

You can't apply filters to vector shape layers.

6. While the Diffuse dialog box is open, use the keyboard shortcuts to zoom the image to 100% in the document window.

You can change the view percentage of a file even when a dialog box is open. You can also scroll a document if you have scroll-wheel capabilities on your mouse.

Note:

You can also drag within the preview area of the dialog box. Simply click in the preview and drag to change the area that appears.

Fading Effects

PHOTOSHOP FOUNDATIONS

The Fade option (Edit>Fade) changes the opacity and blending mode of the last-used filter, painting tool, or color adjustment; you can also fade the effects of using the Extract filter, Liquify filter, and Brush Strokes filters. The Fade blending modes are the same as those available for layers. (The Behind and Clear modes are reserved for only the painting tools.) The following example shows the result of fading the Emboss filter that was applied in the left image.

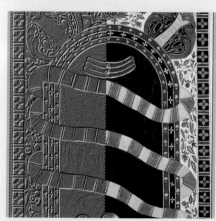

The Stylize Filters

In addition to the options in the Filter Gallery, other artistic filters can also be found in the various Filter submenus. The Stylize filters (Filter>Stylize) generate artistic effects, typically referred to as *painted* or *impressionist*.

Keep the following points in mind when you use filters:

- Filters can be applied to the entire selected layer or to an active selection.
- Some filters work only on RGB images; if you are in a different color mode, some or all filter options — including the Filter Gallery — will be unavailable.
- All filters can be applied to 8-bit images; available filter options are limited for 16-bit and 32-bit images.
- If you don't have enough available RAM to process a filter effect, you might get an error message.

Original Image

Diffuse shuffles pixels to soften focus.

Emboss makes an image look like it was pushed out from (embossed) or into (debossed) the surface.

Extrude creates a 3D texture of raised blocks or pyramids, using a defined or random depth for the resulting grid.

Find Edges identifies areas with significant transitions and emphasizes the edges with dark lines.

Glowing Edges identifies color edges and adds a neon-like glow.

Solarize blends a negative and a positive image version of the image.

Tiles splits an image into a grid, and then offsets the resulting tiles with your choice of "grout" or gap fill.

Trace Contour finds the transitions of major brightness areas and thinly outlines them for each color channel.

Wind adds tiny horizontal lines in the image to create a windblown effect.

The Distortion Filters

Filters can be used for a variety of purposes, from purely aesthetic to technically functional. You can apply filters to specific selections, individual layers, or even individual channels depending on what you need to accomplish. If you combine filters with Smart Objects, you can also apply nondestructive filters and then change the settings or turn off the filter to experiment with different results.

The Distortion filters let you squeeze, stretch, bend, twist, and otherwise distort an image or selection. Some of these filters are controlled in the Filter Gallery, while others have their own dialog boxes.

Original Image

Diffuse Glow adds a haze of the current background color to lighter regions of the image.

Displace distorts an image based on a displacement map (the tone values of which determine the distortion).

Glass simulates the effect of looking through different types of glass.

Ocean Ripple simulates an underwater effect by adding randomly spaced ripples.

Pinch creates the effect of squeezing the edges of the image toward the center.

Polar Coordinates creates the effect of wrapping the image into a cylinder.

Ripple distorts the image. You can only define the amount and size of the effect.

Shear distorts the image as if it were being reflected on an angled mirror.

Spherize simulates the effect of wrapping an image around a three-dimensional sphere.

Twirl simulates the effect of placing the image into a whirlpool.

Waves creates a rippled effect with control over wavelength, amplitude, and wave type.

ZigZag distorts pixels diagonally, out from the center, or around the center.

7. **Move the mouse cursor over an edge in the document window. Click to change the preview area of the dialog box.**

When you see the edges, you can see the effect of the diffusion. (If the layer had more than just flat color, you'd see the effect right away.) The diffused pixels allow the shape edges to blend into the background instead of ending at an abrupt, sharp edge.

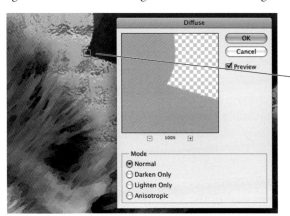

When the Diffuse dialog box is open, clicking in the image changes the visible area in preview window.

Note:

Normal *diffusion scatters pixels randomly.*

Darken Only *replaces light pixels with dark ones.*

Lighten Only *replaces dark pixels with light ones.*

Anisotropic *scatters pixels where there is the least difference in color.*

8. **Leave the mode set to Normal and click OK.**

9. **Save the file and continue to the next stage of the project.**

Lens Correction

The **Lens Correction** filter (Filter>Distort>Lens Correction) is designed to remove inherent distortion from an image. You can also rotate an image or fix perspective problems caused by a tilted camera.

Remove Distortion corrects lens barrel or pincushion distortion. The slider straightens horizontal and vertical lines that bend either away from or toward the center of the image. (You can also use the Remove Distortion tool to make this type of correction.)

The **Chromatic Aberration** options clean up flaws such as color fringes or streaks around edges, as well as light-related problems caused by the lighting of the lens.

The **Vignettes** options correct dark edges caused by lens faults or shading when the photograph was taken.

The **Transform** options correct out-of-perspective images caused by camera tilt. The Vertical slider controls vertical lines and the Horizontal slider controls horizontal lines. The Angle option rotates the image to a specific degree.

The **Edge** options determine what will fill the empty areas that result when you remove distortion.

Remove Distortion tool
Straighten tool
Move Grid tool

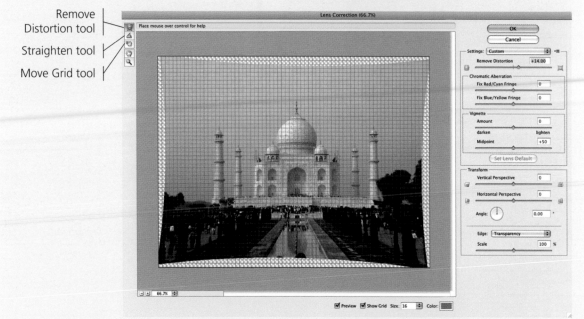

Stage 4 Creating an Artistic Background

Since the background image (the original map) is badly deteriorated from resampling, you're going to use several built-in Photoshop tools to create a custom artistic background. Doing so gives you an advantage: you can create any effect you want instead of using the flat blue color in the existing background image. In this series of exercises, you combine Photoshop's filters with a custom gradient and a pattern fill, and then liquify the background to create a watery effect, reminiscent of Monet.

CREATE A CUSTOM GRADIENT

A **gradient** (sometimes called a blend) is a fill that creates a smooth transition from one color to another or across a range of multiple colors. Photoshop can create several different kinds of gradients (linear, radial, etc.) from one color to another, and you can access a number of built-in gradients. You can also create your own custom gradients, which you will do in this exercise.

1. **With africa_working.psd open, chose the Gradient tool in the Tools panel.**

2. **In the Control panel, click the arrow to the right of the gradient sample bar to show the Gradient Editor.**

   Similar to the Styles and Brushes panels, the Gradient Editor shows a set of predefined gradients, including black-to-white, foreground-to-transparent, foreground-to-background, and several other common options. You can also access additional sets of gradient libraries in the Gradient panel Options menu.

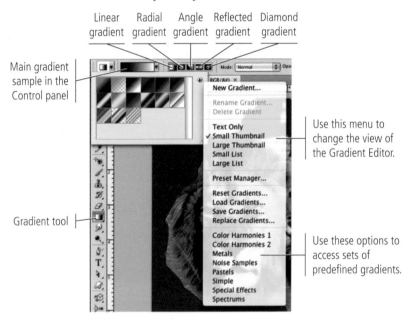

3. **Click the gradient sample in the Control panel to open the Gradient Editor dialog box.**

   You can use this dialog box to edit existing gradients or create new ones.

Note:

At this point it doesn't matter which gradient is selected because you are going to define a custom gradient.

4. **Click the color stop at the left end of the gradient ramp.**

As soon as you click the color stop, the name changes to Custom because you're defining a custom gradient.

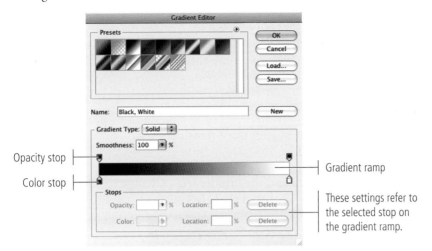

Opacity stop

Color stop

Gradient ramp

These settings refer to the selected stop on the gradient ramp.

5. **Click the Color swatch at the bottom of the dialog box.**

6. **When the Select Stop Color dialog box appears, move the cursor over the water area in the image window and click with the Eyedropper tool.**

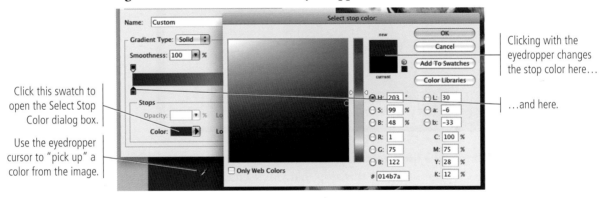

Click this swatch to open the Select Stop Color dialog box.

Use the eyedropper cursor to "pick up" a color from the image.

Clicking with the eyedropper changes the stop color here…

…and here.

7. **Click OK to close the Color Picker.**

8. **Select the right color stop on the ramp and apply the same color you applied to the first stop.**

Note:

The Eyedropper tool works the same way; it is used to change the Foreground or Background swatch to a color that you pick up from an image on your monitor.

9. **Click below the gradient ramp to add a stop, and then drag the new stop until the Location field displays 50%.**

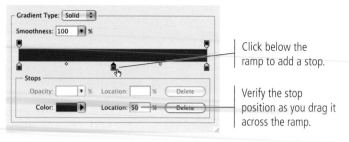

Click below the ramp to add a stop.

Verify the stop position as you drag it across the ramp.

Note:

Drag a stop off the gradient ramp to remove it from the gradient.

When you add a stop along the ramp, it adopts a color as necessary, based on the existing gradient.

10. **Add a new stop halfway between the left stop and the middle stop. Change the color of this new stop to a teal color (we used R=0 G=120 B=110).**

11. **Repeat Step 10 to add a fifth stop, halfway between the center stop and the right stop. Use the same color for this stop that you used in Step 10.**

12. **Type Ocean Blues in the Name field and click the New button.**

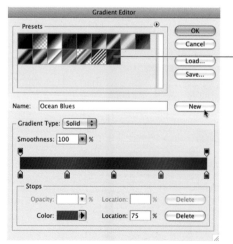

Clicking the New button adds the new swatch to the list of gradient options.

Note:

Press Option/Alt-Shift-drag a stop on the gradient to copy it to another location on the gradient.

13. **Click OK to close the dialog box.**

14. **Save the file and continue to the next exercise.**

CREATE A GRADIENT FILL LAYER

Once you have the gradient you want, applying it is fairly easy: add a layer (if necessary), select the type of gradient you want to create, and then click and drag.

1. **With africa_working.psd open, click the Background layer to select it.**

2. **Click the New Layer button at the bottom of the Layers panel. Name the new layer Ocean.**

   When you add a new layer, it is automatically added directly above the selected layer.

Note:

If you added a new layer between any of the layers in the Shape Layer clipping mask set, the new layer would become the basis of the clipping path for any layers above it.

3. **Make sure the Gradient tool is selected and the Ocean Blues gradient swatch is selected in the Gradient panel.**

4. **Choose the Linear gradient option in the Control panel.**

5. **Click in the top-left side of the image and drag to the bottom-right side.**

   Use the following image as a guide. You can drag anywhere you want, but this is our solution.

Ocean Blues gradient is selected.

Linear Gradient option is selected.

Gradient tool is selected.

Click here…

…and drag to here.

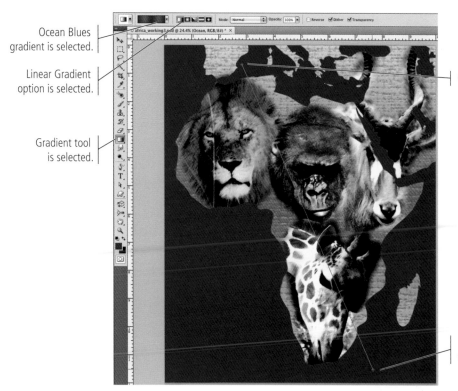

When you release the mouse button, the layer fills with the gradient. Areas before and after the line you draw with the Gradient tool fill with the start and stop colors of the gradient (in this case, they're both the dark blue color).

6. **Save the file and continue to the next exercise.**

 ## CREATE A PATTERN FILL LAYER

The gradient layer is a good start for your art background, but it needs some texture to look more like a painting. A pattern fill will create the texture you need.

1. **With africa_working.psd open, create a new layer named Waves above the Ocean layer.**

2. **Choose the Paint Bucket tool (nested under the Gradient tool) and review the Control panel.**

   When you click with the Paint Bucket tool, it fills areas of similar color (similar to the Magic Wand tool you used in Project 1). You can define the Paint Bucket tool tolerance in the Control panel, just as you did for the Magic Wand tool.

Fill with a color or pattern.

Click this button to open the Pattern panel.

Paint Bucket tool

3. **Choose Pattern in the left menu of the Control panel, and then open the Pattern panel.**

4. **In the Pattern panel Options menu, choose Small List to see the names of the various patterns.**

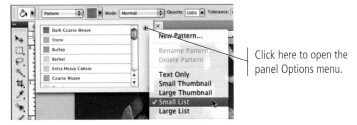

Click here to open the panel Options menu.

5. **Choose Artist Surfaces in the Options menu to show that set of pre-defined patterns.**

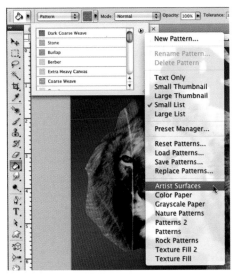

6. **When you see a warning that the patterns will replace the current set, click OK.**

   By now, this interface sequence should look familiar. You've seen the same thing in the Styles, Brushes, and Gradient panels.

7. **Scroll through the list and click Oil Pastel on Canvas.**

8. **Place the cursor anywhere in the image window and click.**

Because there is nothing on the currently selected layer, every pixel in the layer is within the tool's tolerance — the entire layer fills with the pattern.

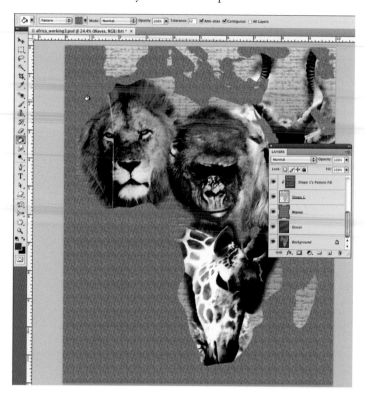

9. **Save the file and continue.**

 ## ADJUST LAYER ORDER AND BLENDING MODE

The pattern fill layer is currently on top of the gradient layer. You need to reverse that order, and then blend the two layers together to create the textured, colored ocean background.

1. **With africa_working.psd open, drag the Waves layer below the Ocean layer in the Layers panel.**

Now the gradient obscures the pattern, which isn't right either. To blend the two layers together, you have to change the top layer's blending mode.

2. **With the Ocean layer selected, click the Blending Mode menu at the top of the Layers panel.**

Photoshop provides access to 25 different layer blending modes (the default is Normal, or no blending applied).

3. Choose Overlay in the Blending Mode menu.

The texture of the pattern is now visible behind the gradient. The pattern is very obvious, however, which doesn't lend well to the "painting" effect you're trying to create.

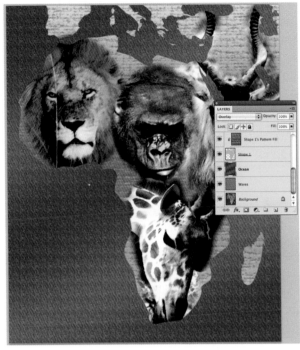

4. Select the Waves layer and open the Filter Gallery.

5. In the Filter Gallery window, apply two filters in the following order:

Top filter: Smudge Stick (Artistic)
                 Settings: Stroke Length = 2, Highlight Area = 7, Intensity = 10

Bottom filter: Ocean Ripple (Distort)
                 Settings: Ripple Size = 3, Ripple Magnitude = 9

Distinguishing Photoshop Blending Modes

When working with blending modes, think of the top layer as the "blend" layer and the next lowest layer as the "base".

- **Normal** is the default mode (no blending applied).

- **Dissolve** results in a random scattering of pixels of both the blend and base colors.

- **Darken** returns the darker of the blend or base color. Base pixels that are lighter than the blend color are replaced; base pixels that are darker than the blend color remain unchanged.

- **Multiply** multiplies (hence the name) the base color by the blend color, resulting in a darker color. Multiplying any color with black produces black; multiplying any color with white leaves the color unchanged (think of math — any number times 0 equals 0).

- **Color Burn** darkens the base color by increasing the contrast. Blend colors darker than 50% significantly darken the base color by increasing saturation and reducing brightness; blending with white has no effect.

- **Linear Burn** darkens the base color similar to Color Burn; using Linear Burn, the brightness is reduced about twice as much for blend colors in the mid-tone range.

- **Darker Color** compares the channel values of the blend and base colors, resulting in the lower value.

- **Lighten** returns whichever is the lighter color (base or blend). Base pixels that are darker than the blend color are replaced; base pixels that are lighter than the blend color remain unchanged.

- **Screen** is basically the inverse of Multiply, always returning a lighter color. Screening with black has no effect; screening with white produces white.

- **Color Dodge** brightens the base color. Blend colors lighter than 50% significantly increase brightness; blending with black has no effect.

- **Linear Dodge (Add)** is similar to Color Dodge, but creates smoother transitions from areas of high brightness to areas of low brightness.

- **Lighter Color** compares channel values of the blend and base colors, resulting in the higher value.

- **Overlay** multiplies or screens the blend color to preserve the original lightness or darkness of the base.

- **Soft Light** darkens or lightens base colors depending on the blend color. Blend colors lighter than 50% lighten the base color (as if dodged); blend colors darker than 50% darken the base color (as if burned).

- **Hard Light** combines the Multiply and Screen modes. Blend colors darker than 50% are multiplied, and blend colors lighter than 50% are screened.

- **Vivid Light** combines the Color Dodge and Color Burn modes. Blend colors lighter than 50% lighten the base by decreasing contrast; blend colors darker than 50% darken the base by increasing contrast.

- **Linear Light** combines the Linear Dodge and Linear Burn modes. If the blend color is lighter than 50%, the result is lightened by increasing the base brightness. If the blend color is darker than 50%, the result is darkened by decreasing the base brightness.

- **Pin Light** preserves the brightest and darkest areas of the blend color; blend colors in the mid-tone range have little (if any) effect.

- **Hard Mix** pushes all pixels in the resulting blend to either all or nothing. The base and blend values of each pixel in each channel are added together (e.g., R 45 [blend] + R 230 [base] = R 275). Pixels with totals over 255 are shown at 255; pixels with a total lower than 255 are dropped to 0.

- **Difference** inverts base color values according to the brightness value in the blend layer. Lower brightness values in the blend layer have less of an effect on the result; blending with black has no effect.

- **Exclusion** is very similar to Difference, except that mid-tone values in the base color are completely desaturated.

- **Hue** results in a color with the luminance and saturation of the base color and the hue of the blend color.

- **Saturation** results in a color with the luminance and hue of the base color and the saturation of the blend color.

- **Color** results in a color with the luminance of the base color and the hue and saturation of the blend color.

- **Luminosity** results in a color with the hue and saturation of the base color and the luminance of the blend color (basically the opposite of the Color mode).

When using a painting tool (Brush, Paint Bucket, Pencil, etc.), you have two additional blending mode options:

- **Behind** paints only on the transparent part of a layer.
- **Clear** paints each pixel and makes it transparent.

6. **Click OK to close the Filter Gallery.**

   The pattern is now less obvious, and the filters have added (and more random) texture.

7. **With the Waves layer selected, choose Filter>Blur>Blur.**

   This filter does not have a dialog box interface; it simply blurs the pixels in the selected layer. If you want more control over the blur, you must use one of the more sophisticated blur filters (which you will do in a later project).

Note:

The result of the Blur filter might not be apparent unless you're viewing the image at 100% magnification.

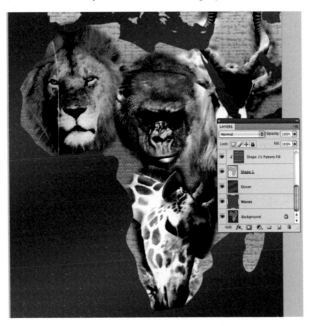

8. **Save the file and continue to the next exercise.**

 LIQUIFY A LAYER

You're nearly done, but the background layers still have a strong patterned feel — which makes sense, since you created them with a pattern fill. In this exercise, you use the Liquify filter to push around the background layer pixels in a freeform style to create a unique, non-patterned background.

1. **With africa_working.psd open, Shift-click the Ocean and Waves layers to select both.**

2. **Choose Merge Layers from the Layers panel Options menu.**

3. **With the resulting Ocean layer still selected, choose Filter>Liquify.**

   The Liquify filter has its own interface and tools. Depending on which tool you select, different options become available in the right side of the dialog box.

4. **In the Liquify filter dialog box, use the View Percentage menu to fit the layer in the view.**

5. **Click the Turbulence tool in the top-left corner and review your options in the top-right corner.**

   For any of the distortion tools, you have to define a brush size, density (feathering around the edges), and pressure (how fast distortions are made).

   Some tools also allow you to define the brush rate (how fast distortions are made when you click without dragging). If you use the Turbulence tool, you can set the Turbulent Jitter (how tightly pixels are scrambled by the effect).

Note:

If necessary, you can press Command/Control-Z to undo your last brush stroke in the Liquify dialog box.

6. **Using the Turbulence tool, select a large brush size, medium density, high pressure, and mid-to-high jitter.**

   Our settings are shown in the screen shot after Step 7.

7. **Drag in the preview where the green blends into the blue, starting at the left side and dragging to the right.**

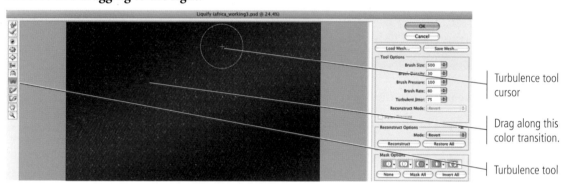

Turbulence tool cursor

Drag along this color transition.

Turbulence tool

8. **Continue adding turbulence to the blend lines, and then experiment with some of the other tools. Our solution, shown here, made heavy use of the Forward Warp tool to push the pixels around.**

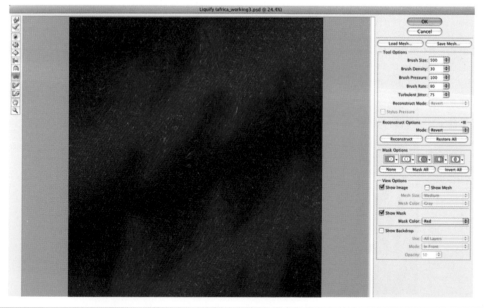

PHOTOSHOP FOUNDATIONS

Several tools in the Liquify dialog box distort the brush area when you drag. The distortion is concentrated at the center of the brush area, and the effect intensifies as you hold down the mouse button or repeatedly drag over an area. Some of the tools (Twirl, Pucker, Bloat, and Turbulence) have airbrush-like effects, applying more distortion when you hold down the mouse button for a longer period of time.

Use the following as a guide when you want to create unique effects with the Liquify filter:

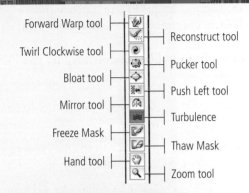

- The **Forward Warp tool** pushes pixels in the direction you drag.
- The **Reconstruct tool** restores distorted pixels to their original state.
- The **Twirl Clockwise tool** rotates pixels clockwise as you hold down the mouse button or drag. Press Option/Alt to twirl pixels counterclockwise when you hold down the mouse button or drag.
- The **Pucker tool** moves pixels toward the center of the brush, creating a zoomed-out effect if you simply hold down the mouse button without dragging.
- The **Bloat tool** moves pixels away from the center of the brush, creating a zoomed-in effect if you simply hold down the mouse button without dragging.

- The **Push Left tool** moves pixels left when you drag up, and moves pixels right when you drag down. You can also drag clockwise around an object to increase its size, or drag counterclockwise to decrease its size. Press Option/Alt to reverse the direction of the distortion.
- The **Mirror tool** copies pixels to the brush area. Drag to mirror the area perpendicular to the direction of the stroke. Press Option/Alt to mirror the area in the direction opposite to that of the stroke.
- The **Turbulence tool** scrambles pixels.
- The **Freeze Mask tool** protects areas where you paint from being liquified.
- The **Thaw Mask tool** removes the protection created by the Freeze Mask tool.
- The **Hand** and **Zoom tools** have the same function here as in the main Photoshop interface.

Using Masks

By freezing areas of the Liquify Filter preview, you protect those areas from distortion with a mask that looks and behaves like Quick Mask mode in the main Photoshop interface. You can use the Mask options to freeze areas based on existing selections, transparent areas, or layer masks in the original image. Each button has a pop-up menu, where you can choose one of those options (if they are available):

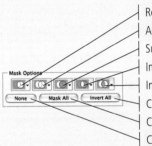

- **Replace Selection** creates a new mask from the selection, transparency, or mask.
- **Add to Selection** adds the selection, transparency, or mask to the currently thawed area.
- **Subtract from Selection** adds the selection, transparency, or mask to the currently frozen area.

- **Intersect with Selection** creates a mask with any areas that are frozen in the preview and in the selection, transparency, or mask from the original image.
- **Invert Selection** inverts the mask in the preview image within the boundaries of the selection, transparency, or mask from the original image.

9. **Click OK to return to the image.**

10. **Save the file and continue to the next stage of the project.**

Stage 5   Creating Variations

The map image is now virtually done, but the colors in the animal layers seem a bit harsh in some areas. In this exercise, you use a color adjustment layer to reduce that harshness, and then give your client two PDF files showing the different options from which he can choose.

 ## UNIFY EFFECTS WITH A SOLID COLOR OVERLAY

Each animal image has a unique color range, which doesn't create the feeling of a "whole composition." You can unify the disparate elements in the clipping mask by blending a single color fill into all of the animal images.

Note:

Hiding the clipping mask layer (the Shape 1 layer) hides all layers clipped by that layer.

1. **With africa_working.psd open, hide all the layers except the Background layer.**

2. **Click the Foreground swatch in the Tools panel to open the Color Picker.**

3. Click with the eyedropper in a gold area of the original map image to pick up that color as the new foreground color, and then click OK.

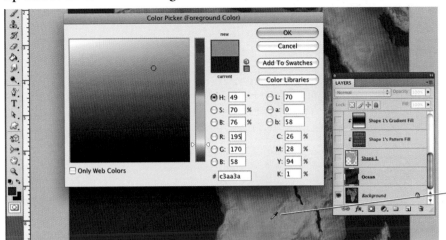

Click one of the gold areas to change the foreground color.

4. Show all the layers, and then click the highest layer in the Layers panel stack to select it.

5. Create a new layer at the top of the stack named **Gold Tone**.

6. With the new layer selected, choose Edit>Fill.

7. In the Use menu, choose Foreground Color.

8. Click OK to fill the selected layer with the solid color.

9. In the Layers panel, make sure the Gold Tone layer is selected, and then change the blending mode to Soft Light.

Note:

You could accomplish the same thing using fill adjustment layers, which you'll do in Project 5.

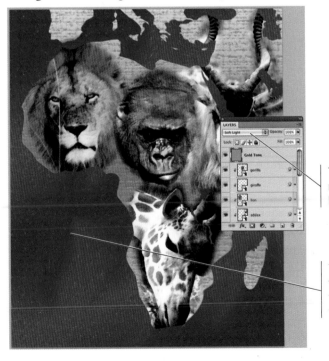

The Soft Light blending mode is applied to the layer you just filled.

The fill blends into the water background too, which isn't what you want.

10. **Control/right-click the Gold Tone layer and choose Create Clipping Mask.**

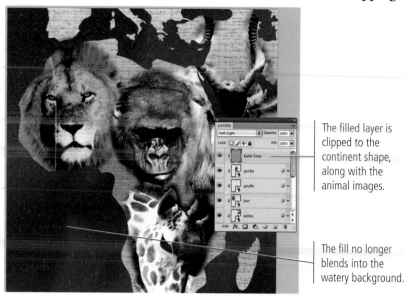

The filled layer is clipped to the continent shape, along with the animal images.

The fill no longer blends into the watery background.

11. **Delete the background layer from the file.**

12. **Save the file and continue to the next exercise.**

 ## CREATE LAYER COMPS

The Layer Comps feature allows you to save multiple iterations of a file at one time. A layer comp can store the position and visibility of individual layers, as well as any effects applied. This feature is useful when you want to experiment with the position of specific layers, but you want to keep a record of earlier positions of the layers — or, as in this case, when you want to present two versions of a file: one version with a layer visible, and one version with a layer hidden.

It's important to know that layer comps do not store pixel information. Modifying the actual pixel data on a layer will not be undone by reverting to an earlier layer comp. To undo that kind of change, you must use the History panel and snapshots, assuming you haven't closed the file since you created the snapshots.

1. **With africa_working.psd open, display the Layer Comps panel.**

2. **Without changing anything in the file (the Gold Tone layer should be visible), click the New Layer Comp button.**

3. **In the New Layer Comp dialog box, name the comp Final Golden. Make sure the Visibility option is checked, and then click OK.**

Note:

Smart Filter settings are not stored in a layer comp.

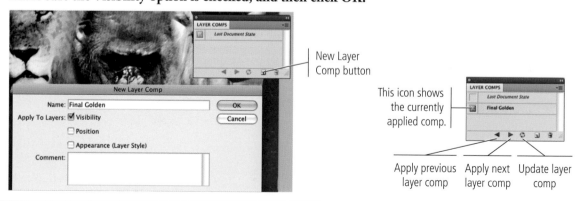

New Layer Comp button

This icon shows the currently applied comp.

Apply previous layer comp — Apply next layer comp — Update layer comp

4. In the Layers panel, hide the Gold Tone layer.

5. Create a second layer comp named **Final Plain**, again including only the layer visibility attributes in the comp.

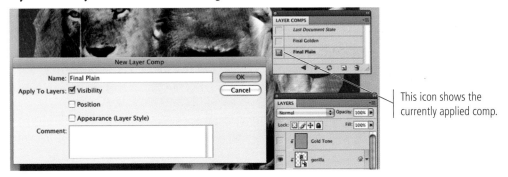

This icon shows the currently applied comp.

6. **Choose File>Scripts>Layer Comps to Files.**

This is a common workflow step, which is why Adobe provides a predefined script to make it easy to create each version of the file as a PDF in one pass.

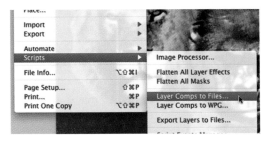

7. **In the Layer Comps to Files dialog box, choose PDF in the File Type menu, and leave the lower options at their default values.**

8. **Type africa in the File Name Prefix field.**

This script creates separate files for each layer comp. The target location defaults to the same location as the working file, and the file name defaults to the current file name. The new file names begin with what you define in the File Name Prefix field.

9. **Click Run.**

The process could take a while to complete, since you are exporting two versions of a very large file. Don't panic and don't get impatient. When the file is done, you'll see the message shown to the right.

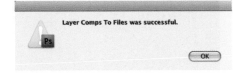

10. **Click OK to close the message, and then close the Photoshop file.**

1. You can toggle on _____ to see the feathered areas of a soft-edged mask.

2. When resizing an image, unchecking the _____ option redistributes the same number of existing pixels into the new physical dimensions.

3. The _____ dialog box is used to enlarge or reduce the document's physical size; the image resolution is not affected by this change.

4. In RGB mode, a _____ value of each color channel results in black.

5. The _____ tool can be used to fill areas with solid colors or patterns.

6. A _____ is a smooth transition from one color to another.

7. A _____ is a resolution-independent, vector-based layer that can be filled with a solid color or pattern.

8. The _____ command is used to show only areas of one layer that fall within the area of the underlying layer.

9. Pressing the _____ key in most Photoshop dialog boxes changes the Cancel button to Reset.

10. The _____ allows you to experiment with different filters and filter settings, and compound multiple filters to create unique artistic effects.

1. Briefly describe the concept of resampling, and how it relates to effective resolution.

2. Briefly describe the advantages and disadvantages of placing files as Smart Objects.

3. Briefly explain the concept of alpha channels.

Use what you learned in this project to complete the following freeform exercise.
Carefully read the art director and client comments, then create your design to meet the needs of the project.
Use the space below to sketch ideas; when finished, write a brief explanation of the reasoning behind your design.

art director comments

The Global Wildlife Fund is very happy with your work on the Africa poster. They chose the original version without the color overlay. They would like you to create at least two more of the pieces in the series. If you only have time for two, use North America and Asia.

To complete this project, you should:

❏ Search the Internet for maps you can use as templates to create the continent shapes.

❏ Save the animal images in the TIFF format if you want to place them as Smart Objects.

❏ Create each piece with styles similar to the ones you used in the Africa map.

❏ Create each poster at 10 × 12″ for the final size.

client comments

Remember, this is a series of pieces that make up an entire collection, so each piece should be similar. We really like the style you created in the first version, and we want the other pieces to have a similar feel. Use the same style as the Africa artwork (without the overlay) for each of the other pieces.

One thing we do want is a similar-but-different background for each piece. Of course they're all water, but the water isn't exactly the same around the entire globe. Make sure there's some variation from one background to the next — maybe a slightly different color or a different pattern.

We have some images you can use; we sent them to you in the RF_Builders>Maps folder. We know there aren't enough for most of the continents, so please find other images as necessary to fill out each continent. Just make sure the animals you put into each continent actually live in those areas. Keep in mind, we'd like to avoid a huge stock-image bill.

Our campaign kicks off in a little less than two months; can you complete the work in two weeks?

project justification

_____

_____

_____

_____

_____

_____

_____

_____

_____

_____

_____

_____

_____

Project Summary

This project extended many of the concepts you learned in Project 1, adding new options for compositing multiple images into a single cohesive piece of artwork. Smart Objects, which played a major role in this project, are one of the most significant advances in image compositing technology. They allow you to apply effects and filters without affecting or damaging the original image data. You also learned how to create and edit soft-edge layer masks to smooth the transitions between layer edges, and you learned how to manage those layer masks in regular layers and Smart Objects.

This project also introduced some of the creative tools that can turn photos and flat colors into painting-like artwork. You learned to use the Filter Gallery — with its many options, custom gradients, gradient and pattern fill layers, and blending modes — and the Liquify filter. You will use these options many times in your career as you complete different types of projects in Photoshop.

Create a compound vector shape layer using a low-resolution image as a template

Add a pattern and fill color to the vector shape layer

Composite multiple images using Smart Objects

Create a clipping mask to place images into the vector shape layer

Use soft-edged layer masks to blend one image into another

Apply filters to images to create a "painting" effect

Use gradients and patterns to create a custom background

Liquify pixels to create unique effects

Change blending modes to merge one layer into another

Moonscapes Book Cover

Your client publishes high-end "coffee-table" books on a variety of pop culture subjects. The company is planning a special edition of a book called *Moonscapes*, which will be published on July 20, 2009, to celebrate the 40th anniversary of the Apollo 11 lunar landing. The book includes a collection of images taken from various space missions over the last 40 years, some of which have never been published before.

This project incorporates the following skills:

❏ Working with color-managed files

❏ Defining working color spaces

❏ Building an accurate page grid

❏ Creating and formatting type layers

❏ Managing point and area type

❏ Converting type to a shape

❏ Working with layer styles and opacity

client comments

This book is going to be quite a production, since one of our board members is a retired astronaut — he suggested the title, and it's his "pet project."

We've provided three images that we think would be good for the cover; you can use any or all of them, however you prefer. We sent two text files that you can use, too. One is simply a list of lunar geographic features that most people are familiar with. The other is a poem by William Wordsworth that's in the public domain; we thought it might be nice to use the poem somewhere, if you can figure out a good way to do it.

The complete title of the book is *Moonscapes: Images of Exploration, Discovery, & Imagination.* The title needs to be on the front cover and the spine; the subtitle needs to be at least on the front cover.

This is going to be a case-bound (hard-back) book that will be 8 × 8″ when assembled. The cover you're designing will be glued to hard boards, and then wrapped around and attached to the printed book block.

art director comments

There are some special considerations in this type of layout. First, you need to add an extra 5/8″ on all four sides of the job for the part that will be folded onto the inside of the boards. The board is 1/8″ thick, which leaves 1/2″ that is glued on the inside of the boards.

Second, you need to remember that case-bound books have hinged covers. If you look at a hard-back book, you can see the hinge about 1/4″ from the spine, where the spine side of the board ends. Make sure you keep any important elements of the design out of the hinge area.

Third, you have to build the spine width into the layout. According to the printer, the spine for this book needs to be 7/8″ wide.

Finally, remember that you're designing for commercial printing, which means high-resolution files. Since you're using Photoshop to compose the entire layout, you should work in CMYK color mode for the base file. I've looked at the images the client sent; one is RGB, but two are already CMYK, so you'll have to manage the color conversions when you incorporate the images into the cover.

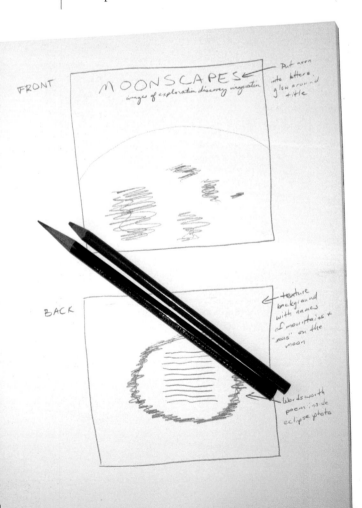

project objectives

To complete this project, you will:

❏ Create a color-managed file with a specific embedded profile

❏ Manage file conversion from one color mode to another

❏ Create and format area and point type

❏ Convert type to a shape that can contain other objects

❏ Silhouette objects using the Extract filter

❏ Create visual effects with layer styles and opacity

❏ Print a composite proof

Stage 1 Setting up the Workspace

The book cover you create in this project will be printed, which means the file ultimately has to be in the CMYK color mode. However, there are two schools of thought about which color mode to use when building files in Photoshop. Some people argue that all Photoshop files should be created in RGB; others vary between CMYK and RGB, depending on the type of job.

In this project, you use Photoshop to compose an entire print layout. Much of this work could be (and is, in many cases) created in a page-layout application such as Adobe InDesign. When you work in InDesign, you typically build print files in CMYK; so if you're using Photoshop for the same function (i.e., page layout), why would you start in RGB? For this type of work, we argue that it's easier to start in CMYK, instead of building a file in RGB, and then converting colors later.

When you become more familiar and comfortable working in CMYK, you'll be able to predict the ink percentages you need to reproduce a specific color. In fact, there are swatch books of various CMYK ink combinations that you can use to find a specific color. For example, you're going to define a super-black background color for this book cover with the values C=35 K=100, which prints as a cool black with a cyan tint. And if you know the ink percentages you want, there is really no reason to create the colors in RGB and then later convert them to CMYK. Doing so would introduce an extra, unnecessary step that might result in the wrong output color if you don't manage the conversion correctly.

Of course, many images you open or place into Photoshop exist in RGB. Almost all scanners and digital cameras capture color in RGB; most stock photo libraries maintain files in the RGB color space; and many digital artists create their original images in RGB. In this project, one of the client's images is in the RGB color space, and two are already converted to CMYK. You need to understand how to manage the conversion for these images into the color space you will use for your background file.

You can't accurately reproduce color without a basic understanding of color theory, so we present a very basic introduction to color theory in the following pages. We highly recommend you read this information. Be aware that there are entire, weighty books written about color science; we're providing the condensed version of what you absolutely must know to work effectively with files in any color mode.

Some might argue that the beginning of Project 3 is too early to discuss something as complex as color management. While it's true that color management science can be extremely complex and beyond the needs of most graphic designers, applying color management in Photoshop is more intimidating than difficult. We believe the following foundational information on color management will make you a more effective and practically grounded designer.

Additive vs. Subtractive Color Models

The most important thing to remember about color theory is that color is light, and light is color. You can easily prove this by walking through your house at midnight; you will notice that what little you can see appears as dark shadows. Without light, you can't see — and without light, there is no color.

The **additive color** model (RGB) is based on the idea that all colors can be reproduced by combining pure red, green, and blue light in varying intensities. These three colors are considered the **additive primaries**. Combining any two additive primaries at full strength produces one of the **additive secondaries** — red and blue light combine to produce magenta, red and green combine to produce yellow, and blue and green combine to produce cyan. Although usually considered a "color," black is the absence of light (and, therefore, of color). White is the sum of all colors, produced when all three additive primaries are combined at full strength.

Note:

Although composing a book cover is a more common project in Adobe InDesign, the workflow in this project is not an unrealistic example. Many people use Photoshop to compose entire layouts, including book covers like this one and the ad you built in Project 1.

Note:

Unfortunately, too many people use color management features without understanding what happens when they click a certain option. This can be as bad — if not worse — than not managing the conversion at all.

Note:

Additive color theory is practically applied when a reproduction method uses light to reproduce color. A television screen or computer monitor is black when turned off. When the power is turned on, light in the monitor illuminates at different intensities to create the range of colors you see.

Printing pigmented inks on a substrate is a very different method of reproducing color. Reproducing color on paper requires **subtractive color theory**, which is essentially the inverse of additive color theory. Instead of adding red, green, and blue light to create the range of colors, subtractive color begins with a white surface that reflects red, green, and blue light at equal and full strength. To reflect (reproduce) a specific color, you add pigments that subtract or absorb only certain wavelengths from the white light. To reflect only red, for example, the surface must subtract (or absorb) the green and blue light.

Remember that the additive primary colors (red, green, and blue) combine to create the additive secondaries (cyan, magenta, and yellow). Those additive secondaries are also called the **subtractive primaries**, because each subtracts one-third of the light spectrum and reflects the other two-thirds:

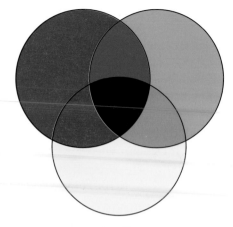

Subtractive color model

- Cyan absorbs red light, reflecting only blue and green light.

- Magenta absorbs green light, reflecting only red and blue light.

- Yellow absorbs blue light, reflecting only red and green light.

A combination of two subtractive primaries, then, absorbs two-thirds of the light spectrum and reflects only one-third. As an example, a combination of yellow and magenta absorbs both blue and green light, reflecting only red.

Color printing is a practical application of subtractive color theory. The pigments in the cyan, magenta, yellow, and black inks are combined to absorb different wavelengths of light. To create the appearance of red, the green and blue light must be subtracted or absorbed, thus reflecting only red. Magenta absorbs green light, and yellow absorbs blue light; combining magenta and yellow inks on white paper reflects only the red light. By combining different amounts of the subtractive primaries, it's possible to produce a large range (or gamut) of colors.

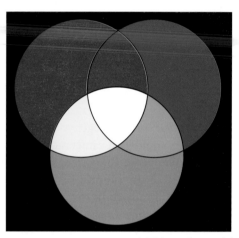

Additive color model

Because white is a combination of all colors, white paper should theoretically reflect equal percentages of all light wavelengths. However, different papers absorb or reflect varying percentages of some wavelengths, thus defining the paper's apparent color. The paper's color affects the appearance of inks printed on that paper.

Understanding Gamut

Different color models have different ranges or **gamuts** of possible colors. A normal human visual system is capable of distinguishing approximately 16.7 million different colors. Color reproduction systems, however, are far more limited. The RGB model has the largest gamut of the output models. The CMYK gamut is far more limited; many of the brightest and most saturated colors that can be reproduced using light cannot be reproduced using pigmented inks.

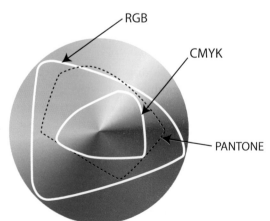

This difference in gamut is one of the biggest problems graphic designers face when working with color images. Digital image-capture devices (including scanners and digital cameras) work in the RGB space, which, with its larger gamut, can more closely mirror the range of colors in the original scene. Printing, however, requires images to first be converted or **separated** into the CMYK color space.

The usual goal in color reproduction is to achieve a color appearance equivalent to the original. Depending on the image, at least some colors in the RGB color model likely cannot be reproduced in the more limited gamut of the CMYK color model. These **out-of-gamut** colors pose a challenge to faithfully reproducing the original image. If the conversion from RGB to CMYK is not carefully controlled, **color shift** can result in drastic differences between the original and printed images.

Color Management in Brief

Color management is intended to preserve color predictability and consistency as a file is moved from one color mode to another throughout the reproduction process. Color management can also eliminate ambiguity when a color is only specified by some numbers. For example, you might create a royal purple in the Photoshop Color Picker; but without color management, that same set of RGB numbers might look more lilac (or even gray) when converted to CMYK for printing. A well-tuned color-management system can translate the numbers that define a color in one space to numbers that can better represent that same color in another space.

It's important to have realistic expectations for color management, and to realize that color management isn't a replacement for a thorough knowledge of the color-reproduction process. Even at its best, color management can't fix bad scans or bad photos — all it can do is introduce consistency and predictability to a process that otherwise rarely has either.

Color management relies on **color profiles**, which are simply data sets that define the reproduction characteristics of a specific device. A profile is essentially a recipe that contains the ingredients for reproducing a specific color in a given color space. The color recipes in profiles are known as **look-up tables** (LUTs), which are essentially cross-reference systems for finding matching color values in different color spaces.

Source profiles are the profiles of the device (scanner, digital camera, or monitor in the case of original digital artwork) used to capture the image. **Destination profiles** are the profiles of output devices used in the process. Most professional-level devices come with profiles you can install when you install the hardware; a number of generic and industry-specific destination profiles are also built into Photoshop.

LAB (or L*a*b*, or CIELAB) is a theoretical color space that represents the visible spectrum. This device-independent color space can represent any possible color. By moving device-dependent RGB and CMYK colors into LAB as an intermediary space, you can convert color from any one space to any other space, eliminating the need for specific LUTs for every possible combination of spaces, models, and devices.

The **Color Management Module** (CMM) is the engine that drives color conversions via the LUT numbers. The engine doesn't do much other than look up numbers and cross-reference them to another set of numbers.

The mechanics of color-managed conversions are quite simple. Regardless of the specific input and output spaces in question, the same basic process is followed for every pixel in the image:

1. The CMM looks up the color values of a pixel in the input-space profile to find a matching set of LAB values.

2. The CMM looks up the LAB values in the output-space profile to find the matching set of color values that will display the color of that pixel accurately in the output space.

Note:

Color shift can also result when converting from one type of CMYK to another, or (though less likely) from one version of RGB to another. Whatever models are being used, color management gives you better control over the conversion process.

Note:

Color profiles are sometimes also called "ICC profiles," named after the International Color Consortium (ICC), which developed the standard for creating color profiles.

Note:

If you convert an image's color space using the Image>Mode menu, Photoshop converts the image to the default working space for the mode you choose.

DEFINE COLOR SETTINGS

To ensure that you can control color shift in the client's supplied images, you're going to build this project in a color-managed environment. Photoshop's color management system allows you to set up a fully managed color workflow — from input device through output device. You can use Adobe's predefined color settings or create custom settings that pertain to the equipment you use.

1. **In Photoshop, choose Edit>Color Settings.**

   The Color Settings dialog box defines default working spaces for RGB, CMYK, gray, and spot colors, as well as general color management policies.

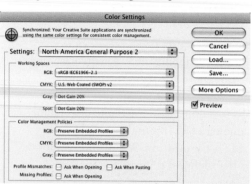

Note:

Your default options might be different than what you see here, depending on what previous users have defined.

Color Management in Theory and Practice

PHOTOSHOP FOUNDATIONS

RGB and CMYK are very different entities. The two color models have distinct capabilities, advantages, and limitations. There is no way to exactly reproduce RGB color using the CMYK gamut because many of the colors in the RGB gamut are simply too bright or too saturated. Rather than claiming to produce an exact (impossible) match from your monitor to a printed page, the true goal of color management is to produce the best possible representation of the color using the gamut of the chosen output device.

A theoretically ideal color-managed workflow resembles the following:

- Image-capture devices (scanners and digital cameras) are profiled to create a look-up table that defines the device's color-capturing characteristics.

- Images are acquired using a profiled device. The profile of the capturing device is tagged to every image captured.

- The image is opened in Photoshop and viewed on a calibrated monitor. The monitor's profile is defined in Photoshop as your working space.

- Photoshop translates the image profile to your working space profile.

- You define a destination (CMYK) profile for the calibrated output device that will be used for your final job.

- The image is converted from RGB to CMYK, based on the defined working space and destination profiles.

Notice that two of the "ideal workflow" steps mention a form of the word "calibrate." To **calibrate** something means to check and correct a device's characteristics. Calibration is an essential element in a color-managed workflow; it is fundamentally important to achieving consistent and predictable output.

You cannot check or correct the color characteristics of a device without having something to compare the device against. To calibrate a device, a known target — usually a sequence of distinct and varying color patches — is reproduced using the device. The color values of the reproduction are measured and compared to the values of the known target. Precise calibration requires adjusting the device until the reproduction matches the original.

As long as your devices are accurately calibrated to the same target values, the color acquired by your RGB scanner will exactly match the colors displayed on your RGB monitor and the colors printed by your RGB desktop printer. Of course, most devices (especially consumer-level desktop devices that are gaining a larger market share in the commercial graphics world) are not accurately calibrated, and very few are calibrated to the same set of known target values.

Keeping in mind these ideals and realities, the true goals of color management are to:

- Compensate for variations in the different devices
- Accurately translate one color space to another
- Compensate for limitations in the output process
- Better predict the final outcome when an image is reproduced

2. Choose North America Prepress 2 in the Settings menu.

Photoshop includes four saved groups of options that are common in North America, which can be accessed in the Settings menu. You can also make your own choices and save those settings as a new preset by clicking Save, or you can import settings files created by another user by clicking Load.

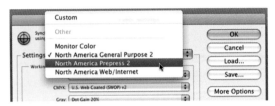

3. In the Working Spaces area, choose the RGB profile for your monitor. If your specific monitor isn't available, choose Adobe RGB (1998).

If you use a color-managed workflow, each color mode must be defined as a particular type of color space. As there are different types of monitors, there are different types of RGB color spaces; the same is true of the other color spaces. The Working Space menus define exactly which version of each space is used to define color within that space.

For color management to work properly, you must have accurate, device-specific profiles for every device in the workflow. However, you can use generic settings such as Adobe RGB (1998) in a "better-than-nothing" color environment — which is almost a direct contradiction to the concept of color management. We're showing you how to use the tools in Photoshop, but it's up to you to implement true color management by profiling your devices and using those profiles for specific jobs.

Note:

*In Photoshop, a **working space** is the default profile used for each of the different color modes.*

Note:

When you choose a profile that isn't part of the saved settings, the Settings menu automatically changes to "Custom."

4. In the CMYK menu, choose U.S. Sheetfed Coated v2.

There are many CMYK profiles — each different printer and press has a gamut unique to that individual device.

This is a United States industry-standard profile for a common type of printing (sheetfed printing on coated paper). In a truly color-managed workflow, you would actually use a profile for the specific printing press/paper combination being used for the job. Again, we're using the default profiles to show you how the process works.

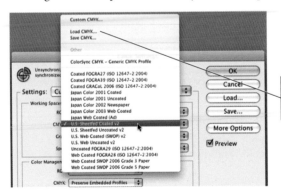

Use the Load CMYK option to access profiles supplied by your output provider.

5. **Leave the Gray and Spot working space menus at their default settings.**

The Gray working space defines how grayscale images will translate when the images are printed. Gray working space options include:

- **ColorSync Gray** (Macintosh only). This is the profile designated as the ColorSync standard for converting monitor space to print.

- **Dot Gain** (of varying percentages). These options compensate for the spread of a halftone dot in a grayscale image.

- **Gray Gamma.** This option allows you to set the monitor's gamma to compensate for differences between the monitor's presentation of an image and the actual grayscale image on press.

The Spot working space is similar to the Gray working space, but you can only specify dot gain percentages (not gamma).

6. **In the Color Management Policies area, make sure Preserve Embedded Profiles is selected for CMYK and Gray, RGB is turned off, and all three check boxes are selected.**

These options tell Photoshop what to do when you open an existing image. When an option here is turned off, color is not managed for that mode. If you choose Preserve Embedded Profiles, images that have a profile retain the embedded profile; images with no profile use the current working space. If you choose Convert to Working Space, images with an embedded profile are converted to the current working profile; images with no profile are assigned the current working profile.

For profile mismatches, you can display a warning when opening or pasting an image with an embedded profile that does not match the working profile. When an image doesn't have an embedded profile, you can display a warning by checking the Missing Profiles Ask When Opening option.

Note:

The check boxes allow you to control Photoshop's behavior when the application encounters a profile mismatch or an image that does not have an embedded profile.

7. **Click the More Options button and review your options.**

The **Engine** option determines the system and color-matching method used to convert between color spaces:

- **Adobe (ACE)** stands for Adobe Color Engine; this is the default, and Adobe recommends it for most users.

- **Apple CMM** (Macintosh only) uses the Apple ColorSync engine.

- **Microsoft ICM** (Windows only) uses the Microsoft ICM engine.

The **Intent** menu defines how the engine translates source colors outside the gamut of the destination profile.

When the **Use Black Point Compensation** option is selected, the full range of the source space is mapped into the full-color range of the destination space. This method can result in blocked or grayed-out shadows, but it is most useful when the black point of the source is darker than that of the destination.

When the **Use Dither** option is selected, colors in the destination space are mixed to simulate missing colors from the source space. Using this option can result in larger file sizes for Web images.

The **Desaturate Monitor Colors** option is useful for visualizing the full range of color, including colors outside the monitor's range. When the option is deselected, however, colors that were previously distinct may appear as a single color, and they may print as a single color, as well.

The **Blend RGB Colors Using Gamma** option inputs a gamma curve to avoid artifacts. A gamma of 1.00 is considered "colorimetrically correct." If this option is deselected, RGB colors are blended using only the document's color space.

Note:

*The **Compensate for Scene-Referred Profiles** option relates to the increasingly popular use of Photoshop to perform color correction — and color profile matching — for video scene enhancement.*

8. **Click Save in the Color Settings dialog box. In the resulting navigation dialog box, change the Save As field to Moonscapes and click Save.**

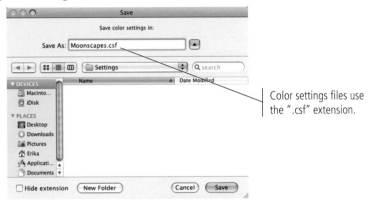

Color settings files use the ".csf" extension.

Note:

Getting ready for this project requires you to change a few of the default color settings. By saving these changes as a CSF file, you can easily restore the same settings later if someone else changes the computer's settings while you're in the middle of this project.

By default, custom color settings are saved in a Settings folder in a specific location where your system stores user preferences for different applications. Settings files saved in the application's default location are available in the Settings menu of the Color Settings dialog box.

If you are working on a shared computer or a network where you can't save to the system files, you might want to save the custom Color Settings file in your WIP folder. In this case, you'd have to click the Load button to locate the CSF file.

9. **In the Color Settings Comment dialog box, type Use this for PS CS4 Project 3.**

Understanding Rendering Intents

PHOTOSHOP FOUNDATIONS

LAB color has the largest gamut, RGB the next largest, and CMYK the smallest. If you need to convert an image from an RGB space to a more limited CMYK space, you need to tell the CMS how to handle any colors that exist outside the CMYK space. You can do this by specifying the **rendering intent** that will be used when you convert colors.

- **Perceptual** presents a visually pleasing representation of the image, preserving visual relationships between colors. All colors in the image — including those available in the destination gamut — are shifted to maintain the proportional relationship within the image.

- **Relative Colorimetric** maintains any colors in both the source and destination profiles. Any source colors outside the destination gamut are shifted to fit into the destination gamut. The Relative Colorimetric method is a good choice, especially when most source colors are in-gamut. This method adjusts for the whiteness of the background media.

- **Absolute Colorimetric** maintains colors in both the source and destination profiles. Any colors outside the destination gamut are shifted to a color within the destination gamut, based on the color's appearance on white paper.

- **Saturation** compares the saturation of colors in the source profile and shifts them to the nearest possible saturated color in the destination profile. Saturation is a good method for images with high levels of saturation, such as pie charts and graphs. The focus is on saturation instead of actual color value, which means this method can produce drastic color shift.

Defining Custom CMYK Spaces

You can define a custom CMYK working space to match the output characteristics of a specific device by choosing Custom CMYK from the CMYK Working Space menu of the Color Settings dialog box. (This process should typically be left to people with a thorough understanding of color science and reproduction. We're explaining it here to give you an idea of what happens behind the scenes when you apply a working space.) The Custom CMYK dialog box allows you to define the variables used to print a job. The Ink Colors menu lists the ink sets typically used in commercial printing.

Understanding Dot Gain

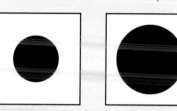

Dot gain (also called **tone value increase**) is the degree to which a physical dot of ink enlarges when it comes in contact with paper. All paper is, to some degree, naturally absorbent; when wet ink hits the paper, it is absorbed and spreads (think of a drop of coffee hitting the morning newspaper; the same principle applies to dot gain). For example, when a 50% ink dot is laid onto paper, it might spread to present the visual appearance of a 70% dot. If you don't compensate for dot gain before images are printed, images appear very dark and quality is compromised.

Dot gain varies depending on the ink/paper/press combination used to print a job. The predefined CMYK profiles use percentages defined for "standard" conditions on a specific type of press. If you need to define specific dot gain characteristics for a CMYK profile, you can do so by choosing Curves from the Dot Gain menu in the Custom CMYK dialog box.

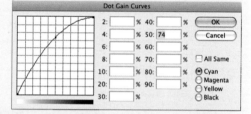

The Dot Gain Curves dialog box presents a curve that you can adjust by clicking on the line or entering dot gain values in the percentage fields. The horizontal axis of the curve is the input value, and the vertical axis is the output value. You can adjust the dot gain curve for each ink using the radio buttons, or you can select the All Same check box.

Understanding Separation Options

There is a limit to the amount of ink that can be applied on the same spot of paper without compromising quality. The ink/paper/press combination defines the **maximum ink coverage**, although 280–300% is considered a safe range for most applications (except newsprint, which generally requires no more than 240% total ink coverage). The two Separation Type options in the Custom CMYK dialog box — GCR (Gray Component Replacement) and UCR (Undercolor Removal) — are methods for maintaining acceptable maximum ink coverage, while still achieving quality color.

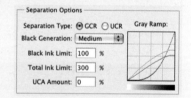

Gray Component Replacement. The three primary ink colors combine to create shades of gray. Black ink also creates shades of gray. To keep maximum ink coverage within the allowed range, gray component replacement removes neutral CMY components and replaces them with gray.

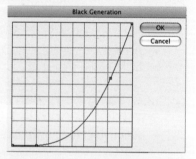

- The **Black Generation** menu defines how much black is used when RGB colors are translated to CMYK. You can choose from None (no black plate is generated), Light, Medium (the default), Heavy, and Maximum. You can also choose Custom to define the curve of black generation. The curve to the right shows that no black will be replaced for colors below 20%; at 20%, the curve gets steeper, which means CMY neutrals greater than 20% are affected.

- The **Black Ink Limit** field defines the maximum dot of black ink that can be used in the separation.

- The **Total Ink Limit** field defines the total ink coverage as defined by your service provider.

- The **UCA Amount** field determines how much Undercolor Addition (UCA) to incorporate. When you replace the CMY component with K, you can lose density in those areas of the image. To compensate for this loss of density, you can specify a UCA amount to return some of the CMY component that was originally removed.

Undercolor Removal. Undercolor Removal affects only the neutral areas of an image, or those areas where the cyan, magenta, and yellow ink percentages are equal. The equal CMY percentages are replaced with a corresponding percentage of black ink. When the UCR radio button is selected, you can only define the Black Ink Limit and Total Ink Limit values; the Black Generation and UCA Amount options are not available.

10. **Click OK to return to the Color Settings dialog box.**

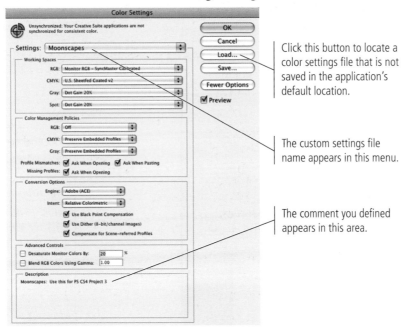

Click this button to locate a color settings file that is not saved in the application's default location.

The custom settings file name appears in this menu.

The comment you defined appears in this area.

11. **Click OK to close the Color Settings dialog box and apply your settings, and then continue to the next exercise.**

BUILD A COLOR-MANAGED FILE

The Color Settings dialog box defines the default working spaces for RGB, CMYK, Gray, and Spot Color spaces. Once you've made your choices in the Color Settings dialog box, those working spaces are automatically applied when you create a new file.

1. **On your desktop, copy the Moon folder from the WIP folder on your Resource CD to the WIP folder where you're saving your work.**

   Save all files for this project in your WIP>Moon folder.

2. **Choose File>New and type moonscapes in the Name field.**

3. **Change the page size to 18.125″ wide by 9.25″ high.**

   Remember, the final book is 8 × 8″. You also need to add 5/8″ to each side, and 7/8″ to the width for the spine.

4. **Make sure the resolution is set to 300 dpi, set the color mode to 8-bit CMYK, and define White as the default background color.**

Note:

We created a custom workspace named Moonscape for this project, including the Info, Layers, Channels, Character, and Paragraph panels. As with the projects you already completed, you should place panels and workspace elements wherever you feel most comfortable.

5. **In the Advanced area, click the Color Profile menu and review the options.**

The Color Profile menu defaults to the working space for the selected color mode; in this case, it automatically shows Working CMYK: U.S. Sheetfed Coated v2.

You can also choose a different profile in the menu if you occasionally need to work in a space other than the default working space for a specific color mode.

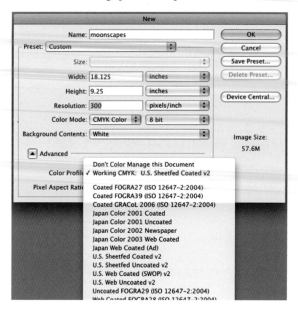

Note:

Web printing is done on larger presses and fed from huge rolls of paper, with the actual pages being cut off the roll only after the ink has been laid down. Although web presses are typically cheaper to operate for long print runs, they generally do not produce the same quality of color as their sheetfed counterparts.

Sheetfed presses place ink on sheets of paper that have already been cut to press-sheet size from a large roll of paper. Sheetfed presses are typically considered higher quality, with appropriately higher costs associated with the job.

6. **Click OK to create the new file.**

7. **Drag ruler guides to mark the 5/8″ (0.625″) area around the page, which is required for the foldovers.**

8. **Move the zero point to the intersection of the top and left guides, and then drag vertical guides to mark the spine area (8″ from the left, and then 7/8″ from that guide).**

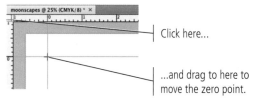

Click here...

...and drag to here to move the zero point.

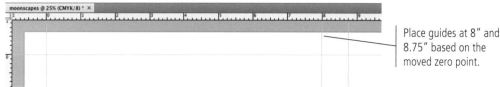

Place guides at 8″ and 8.75″ based on the moved zero point.

9. **Add two more vertical guides 1/2″ from each side of the spine to mark the hinge area.**

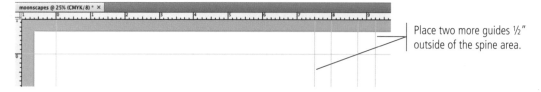

Place two more guides ½″ outside of the spine area.

10. Double-click the intersection of the rulers to reset the original zero point to the top-left corner of the image.

11. Click the Background Color swatch in the Tools panel and define the background color as C=30 M=0 Y=0 K=100.

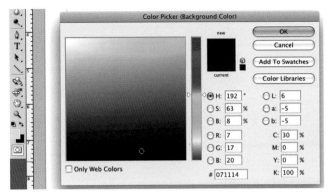

Note:

If you create a file using a profile other than the default working profile for that space, the document tab (or title bar, if you're not using the Macintosh Application frame) shows an asterisk next to the color space information.

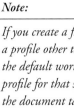

12. Choose Edit>Fill and fill the layer with the background color.

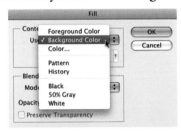

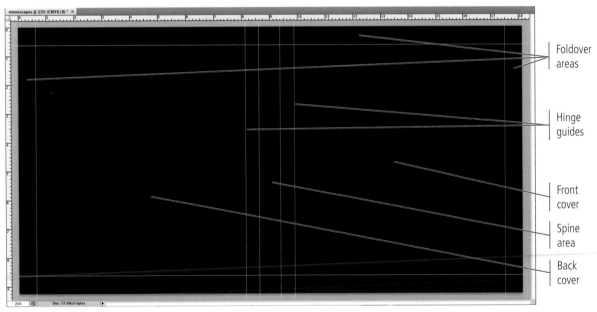

Foldover areas

Hinge guides

Front cover

Spine area

Back cover

13. Save the file in the PSD format in your WIP>Moon folder (using the default name moonscapes.psd) and continue to the next exercise.

In the Color Settings dialog box, you told Photoshop how to handle images with profiles that don't match your working profiles, as well as images that don't have embedded profiles. These issues become important any time you work with files from more than a single source — and especially with client-supplied images, which often come from a wide variety of sources.

1. **With moonscapes.psd open, open the file moon1.jpg from the RF_Photoshop>Moon folder.**

   This is an RGB image, which you can see in the title bar. But as you know, the RGB gamut is much larger than the CMYK gamut, so you should check what will happen when you paste this image into your background file. Fortunately, Photoshop makes this process very easy.

2. **Choose View>Gamut Warning and carefully examine the image.**

   This shows a gray overlay of any pixels that are outside the working CMYK space.

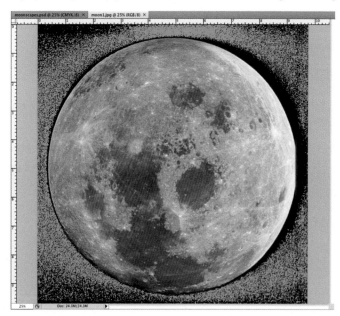

   In this case, there is significant coverage in the black area around the moon; but since the moon has so much gray to begin with, it's hard to tell if anything inside the moon will be affected when you convert the colors.

3. **Open the Transparency & Gamut pane of the Preferences dialog box.**

Note:

On Macintosh, Preferences are accessed in the Photoshop menu. On Windows, Preferences are accessed in the Edit menu.

4. **Click the Gamut Warning Color swatch, and then choose a bright red color in the Color Picker.**

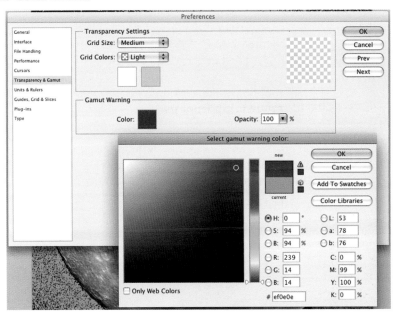

5. **Click OK, and then click OK again to return to the image window.**

6. **Choose View>Gamut Warning, and then immediately choose View>Gamut Warning again to toggle the option off and then back on.**

Using a red overlay instead of gray, you can better see areas outside the working CMYK gamut. The bad news is that there's a significant area outside the CMYK working space. The good news is that you're going to silhouette the moon out of its background. In this case, you don't need to make any color corrections because the area you will ultimately use (the moon) appears to be entirely within the working CMYK gamut.

Note:

For some reason, you have to toggle the Gamut Warning off and then on again to reflect the new warning color.

7. **Use the Document Arrangement menu to show both open files in the document window. Drag the moon1.jpg file from its image window into the moonscapes.psd file.**

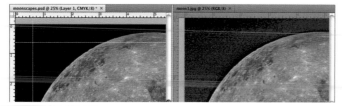

8. **Close moon1.jpg.**

9. **Open the file moon2.jpg from the RF_Photoshop>Moon folder.**

   This image does not have an embedded profile, and (as you specified in the Color Settings dialog box) Photoshop asks how you want to handle the file.

   It's quite common to find images that don't have embedded color profiles, especially when you work with older (legacy) files. In this case, color management will be imperfect at best since you don't know how the image was captured.

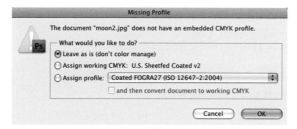

10. **Choose Leave As Is and click OK. Arrange the two open files so you can see both images in the document window.**

11. **Drag the moon2.jpg file into the moonscapes.psd file.**

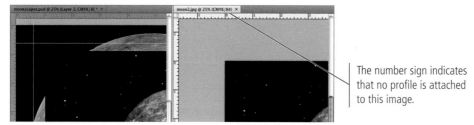

The number sign indicates that no profile is attached to this image.

12. **Close moon2.jpg, and then open eclipse.jpg from the RF_Photoshop>Moon folder.**

   This image is already in CMYK mode, but it has a different profile than your defined CMYK working space. Similar to the image with no profile, you can determine how you want to manage this mismatch.

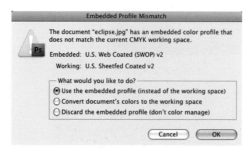

13. **Select the Use the Embedded Profile option and click OK. Arrange the two open files so you can see both images in the document window.**

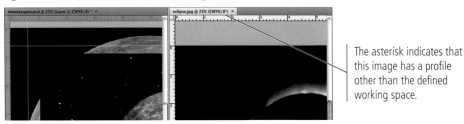

The asterisk indicates that this image has a profile other than the defined working space.

14. **Choose View>Proof Colors.**

This option allows you to preview the image in the defined working space without permanently converting the image data. In this case, you don't see a significant difference; in other images (especially RGB images with vibrant blues or greens) you will see a significant color shift in areas outside the CMYK gamut.

15. **Drag this image into the moonscapes.psd file.**

You see another warning about the profile mismatch, which you asked for in the Color Settings dialog box (dragging is essentially the same as pasting).

16. **Click the Convert radio button, and then click OK.**

Because you activated the Ask When Pasting option in the Profile Mismatches section of the Color Settings dialog box, you see a dialog box that allows you to override the policy settings. (In this project, you chose Preserve Embedded Profiles for CMYK images.)

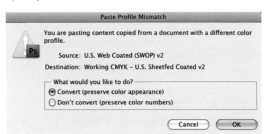

The Convert option converts the pasted image colors to the color profile of the file where you're pasting, preserving the color appearance. The Don't Convert option preserves the color data in the pasted information.

17. **Close eclipse.jpg, save moonscapes.psd, and continue to the next stage of the project.**

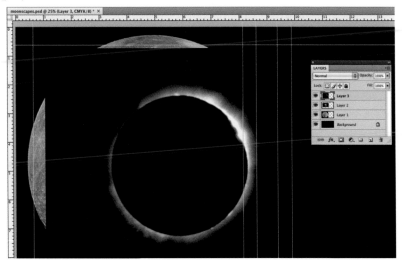

Note:

Using the Move tool to drag one image onto another is the same as copying a selection from one file and pasting it into another; in both cases the process is considered "pasting content".

Stage 2 Working with Text

Type is naturally a vector-based element. As long as you maintain type as vectors, the letter shapes can be resized and transformed without losing quality. And as you know, Photoshop can combine raster and vector objects into a single composition.

Many Photoshop jobs require some kind of text. Although Photoshop is not a typesetting tool by definition, its type capabilities are robust enough for creating and manipulating type in a variety of ways. To complete this book cover, you are going to create and format several text elements.

The Anatomy of Type

Before we jump into the exercises in this section, you should understand the terms that you'll often hear when people talk about type. Keep the following terms in mind as you work through the following exercises.

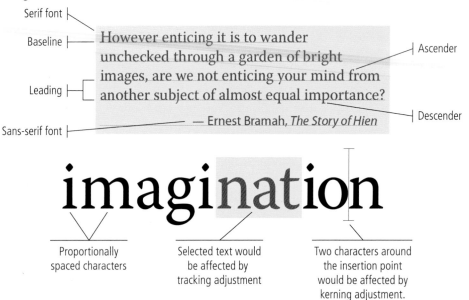

Type is typically divided into two basic categories: serif and sans serif. **Serif type** has small flourishes on the ends of the letterforms; **sans-serif** has no such decorations (*sans* is French for "without"). The actual shape of letters is determined by the specific **font** you use; each character in a font is referred to as a **character** or **glyph**.

Fonts can be monospaced or proportionally spaced. In a monospace font, each character takes up the same amount of space on a line; in other words, a lower-case "i" and "w" will occupy the same horizontal space. In a proportionally spaced font, different characters occupy different amounts of horizontal space as necessary.

When you set type in a digital application, the letters rest on a non-printing line called the **baseline**. If a type element has more than one line in a single paragraph, the distance from one baseline to the next is called **leading** (pronounced "ledding"). Most applications set the default leading as 120% of the type size, but you can change the leading to any value you prefer.

The **x-height** of type is the height of the lower-case letter "x." Elements that extend below the baseline are called **descenders** (as in "g," "j," and "p"); elements that extend above the x-height are called **ascenders** (as in "b," "d," and "k").

The size of type is usually measured in **points** (there are approximately 72 points in an inch). When you define a specific type size, you determine the distance from the bottom of the descenders to the top of the ascenders (plus a small extra space above the ascenders called the **body clearance**).

Note:

There are other types of special fonts, including script, symbol, dingbat, decorative, and image fonts. These don't fit easily into the serif/sans-serif distinction.

PLACE AND FORMAT POINT TEXT

You can create two basic kinds of type in Photoshop: point type and area type. **Point type** is created by simply clicking in the image window with the Type tool. A point type element can exist on one line or multiple lines. However, point type can continue into apparent infinity without starting a new line; if you want to start a new line, you have to manually tell Photoshop where to create the break.

1. **With moonscapes.psd (from your WIP>Moon folder) open, hide all layers except the Background layer.**

   When you're hiding or showing more than one layer at a time, hold down the mouse button and drag over the visibility icon of the layers you want to affect; they'll all turn on or off as you drag the cursor. You can even drag away from the panel to skip specific layers, and then drag back to the panel to affect non-contiguous layers.

   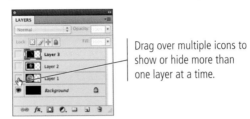

   Drag over multiple icons to show or hide more than one layer at a time.

2. **Choose the Type tool in the Tools panel and review the options in the Control panel.**

   You can access the basic type options in the Control panel. Additional options are available in the Character and Paragraph panels.

   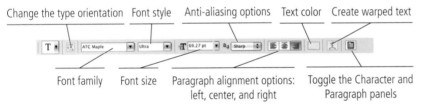

   Change the type orientation · Font style · Anti-aliasing options · Text color · Create warped text

   Font family · Font size · Paragraph alignment options: left, center, and right · Toggle the Character and Paragraph panels

PHOTOSHOP FOUNDATIONS

Anti-Alias Options for Type

Although type is vector-based, it will eventually be rendered (rasterized) at some point — even if that doesn't happen until the final output. Anti-aliasing produces smooth-edge type by partially filling the edge pixels, which allows the edges of the type to better blend into the background when the type is rendered. (Be aware that anti-aliasing small type might distort the letter shapes.)

Photoshop supports five options for anti-aliasing type. The effects of each method are best viewed at higher zoom percentages.

- None applies no anti-aliasing.
- Sharp creates the sharpest type.
- Crisp makes type appear slightly sharp.
- Strong makes type appear heavier.
- Smooth makes type edges appear very smooth.

None

Sharp

Crisp

Strong

Smooth

3. **Macintosh users: Choose ATC Oak in the Font Family menu, and choose Bold in the Font Style menu.**

   Windows users: Choose ATC Oak Bold in the Font Family menu.

4. **Change the font size to 48 pt and make sure the left paragraph alignment option is selected.**

5. **Click the Text Color swatch to open the Color Picker.**

6. **Change the text color to C=5 M=3 Y=0 K=0 and click OK.**

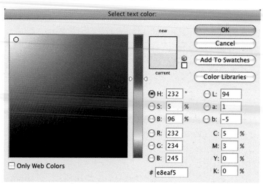

Note:

The text color defaults to the current foreground color.

7. **Click once anywhere in the image window and type Moonscapes.**

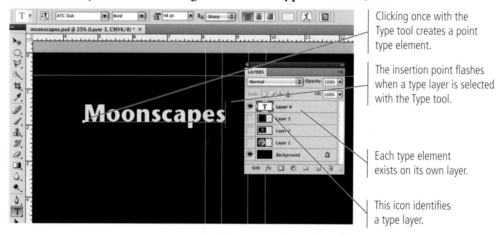

Clicking once with the Type tool creates a point type element.

The insertion point flashes when a type layer is selected with the Type tool.

Each type element exists on its own layer.

This icon identifies a type layer.

The Character Panel in Depth

PHOTOSHOP FOUNDATIONS

The changes you make in the Character panel affect selected characters only. If you make changes before typing, the changes apply to all characters you type from the same insertion point.

The Type Style buttons are (from left): Faux Bold, Faux Italic, All Caps, Small Caps, Superscript, Subscript, Underline, and Strikethrough. Whenever possible, you should use actual font variants instead of applying these artificial type styles — such as ATC Oak Bold instead of ATC Oak Normal with faux bold applied.

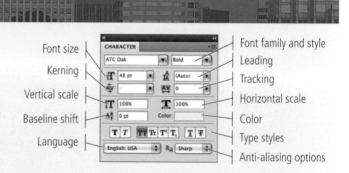

Font size

Kerning

Vertical scale

Baseline shift

Language

Font family and style

Leading

Tracking

Horizontal scale

Color

Type styles

Anti-aliasing options

8. **Choose the Move tool from the Tools panel.**

   Using the Move tool, you can move and manipulate type layers like any other layer, but you can't edit the actual text. As soon as you select a different tool (other than the Type tool), the type layer adopts its new name based on the text you typed on the layer. Your type layer is now named Moonscapes.

   Note:

   You can click the Commit button in the Control panel to finalize the type, but it isn't necessary. Choosing the Move tool accomplishes the same thing.

9. **In the Layers panel, drag the Moonscapes layer to the top of the layer stack if necessary.**

10. **Drag the type layer in the document window until the M snaps to the top and left guides of the front cover area.**

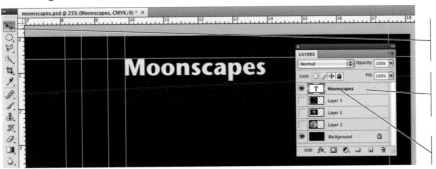

When the layer is selected with the Move tool, the insertion point is not visible.

The Moonscapes layer should be on top of the layer stack.

The layer name is adopted from the text on the layer.

11. **Change to the Type tool and single-click between the "s" and the "c" in the word Moonscapes.**

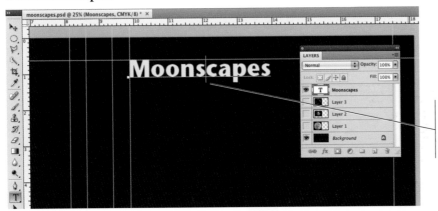

You have to use the Type tool to place the insertion point or select type in an existing type layer.

12. **Double-click the word "Moonscapes" to select all the characters, and then display the Character panel.**

13. **Click the All Caps style button.**

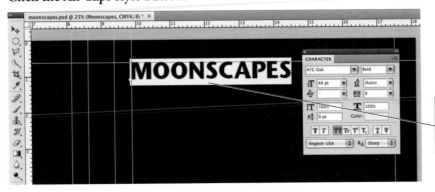

You have to first select the specific text that you want to format using the Character panel.

14. **Save the file and continue to the next exercise.**

TRANSFORM A TYPE LAYER

Type layers in Photoshop are similar to most other layers. You can drag and transform type layers using most of the same tools you use to transform other kinds of layers. You can scale or skew type layers; change their opacity, fill, and blending mode; apply layer styles; and even add warp effects — while still maintaining the type as editable text. The only options you can't apply to live text are the Distort and Perspective transformations, custom warps, and filters. (To use these features, you must first rasterize the type layer.)

1. **In the open moonscapes.psd file, make sure the Moonscapes type layer is selected and the Move tool is active.**

2. **Choose Edit>Free Transform.**

When you transform a type layer with point type, the bounding box automatically adopts the smallest necessary size to fit the text on the layer.

The Transform cursor assumes different shapes, depending on where it's positioned.

3. **Shift-click the bottom-right bounding box handle and drag until the right side of the text meets the right margin guide.**

Shift-dragging the corner handle allows you to resize the object proportionally.

4. **Click the bottom-center bounding box handle and drag down until the text is about 1″ high.**

5. **Press Return/Enter to commit the change.**

This action distorts the text, making it higher than it is wide. However, the distorted text remains an editable type layer.

Dragging the bottom-center handle allows you to make the object higher without making it wider.

6. **Using the Type tool, place the insertion point anywhere in the word "Moonscapes" and review the Character panel.**

   Even though you resized the type layer (proportionally and disproportionally), it is still live text — you can still place the insertion point and edit as necessary.

The Type Size field shows the result of resizing the type layer.

7. **Place the insertion point between the "M" and the "O", and then change the Kerning field to –25.**

Note:

Press Option/Alt-Left Arrow key to apply -20 kerning units or Option/Alt-Right Arrow key to apply +20 kerning units at the current insertion point.

   Kerning and tracking control the spacing between individual characters. **Kerning** adjusts the spacing between two specific characters (called a **kerning pair**). **Tracking** (also called range kerning) is applied over a range of selected text.

   Professional-quality fonts include predefined kerning and tracking tables in the font data; however, you should still check the letter spacing when you set headline type, use All Caps or Small Caps type styles, or apply any other artificial manipulation such as the stretching you applied in Steps 3 and 4.

Kerning and tracking are largely a matter of personal taste. In this project, you want the letters to be very tightly spaced, but not touching.

8. **Continue adjusting the kerning between the letters in the title until you are satisfied with the results.**

9. **Choose Edit>Free Transform again, and Shift-drag the bottom-right handle of the bounding box back to the right margin guide.**

Note:

Kerning values are based by default on the type metrics (the values stored in the font data). The Optical option in the Kerning menu is useful for fonts that don't have built-in kerning values; Photoshop applies optical kerning based on how it perceives the letter shapes.

   The guides on a book cover layout like this one can be a bit deceptive, even when you create the guides yourself.

Note:

While the Text cursor is inside a line of text, holding the Command/Control key displays the bounding box for the type layer.

   The left guide (where the "M" starts) marks the front cover hinge. The right guide (where the "S" ends) and the top guide are actually edges of the front cover. The area above and right of those guides is the part that folds over to the inside of the cover boards.

   If you leave the title as it is now, the title would print all the way to the top and right edges of the book — which would be a mistake.

10. Using the Control panel, scale the type layer to 95% proportionally.

11. Place the title text so it meets the hinge guide in the front cover area. The tops of the letters should be 3/8″ from the top edge guide.

Hinge guide

Cover top edge

Cover left edge

Cover right edge

12. Press Return/Enter to finalize the transformation.

13. Save the file and continue to the next exercise.

 CREATE AN ADDITIONAL TYPE LAYER

You can have as many type layers as you need in a Photoshop file. Each new type element is created on its own type layer.

1. In the open **moonscapes.psd** file, select the Type tool and click once in the empty area below the existing title.

Clicking places the insertion point in a new point type element, creating a new type layer.

2. Type **Images of Exploration, Discovery, & Imagination**

By default, the Type tool remembers the last settings you manually applied (it doesn't remember the scaling applied in Free Transform mode).

If someone changed the type settings since you completed the previous exercise, your type layer might look different than ours. That's okay, because you're going to change all the settings in the next few steps.

Point type exists entirely on a single line unless you manually insert a line break. Using the current type settings, the entire sentence doesn't fit in the space allowed.

3. **With the insertion point anywhere in the new type layer, choose Select>All.**

   When the insertion point is flashing, this command highlights (selects) all the text in the active type layer.

4. **In the Character or Control panel, change the font to ATC Laurel Black Italic and then type 16 in the Size field. Turn off the All Caps type style option.**

   Because 16 pt. isn't one of the built-in sizes, you have to manually type 16 in the Size field.

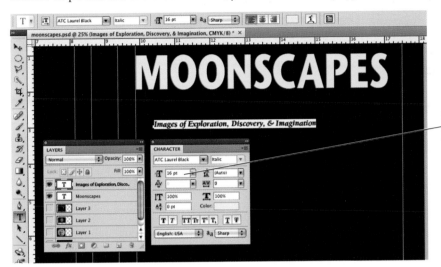

Highlight this field and type "16" to change the type size.

5. **With the subtitle text still selected, show the Paragraph panel.**

   When you work with point type, paragraph attributes apply to all text on a single line. If you have more than one line, you can apply different paragraph format options to each line in the element.

6. **Change the active type element to right paragraph alignment.**

   When you change the alignment of point type, the text moves around the origin point of the element.

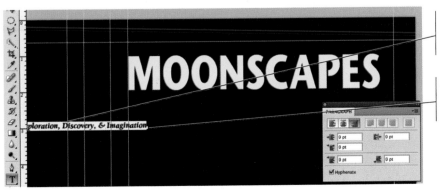

The text is now right aligned, based on the position of the type origin point.

The point doesn't move when you change the paragraph alignment.

7. **Using the Move tool, drag the type layer so the text appears approximately 1/4″ below the book title.**

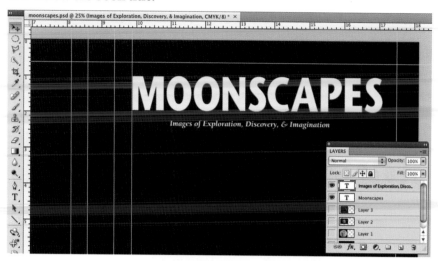

8. **Select both type layers in the Layers panel.**

9. **In the Control panel, click the Align Right Edges button.**

As we said earlier, you can control type layers in the same way you control other layers. The Align buttons are useful for precisely aligning multiple layers relative to each other.

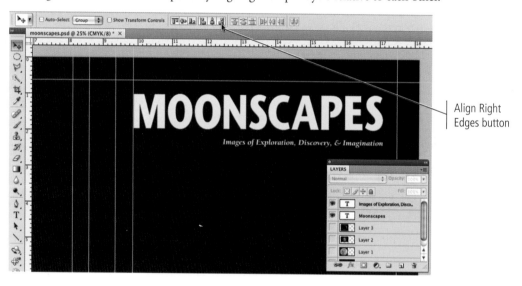

Align Right Edges button

10. **Save the file and continue to the next exercise.**

You can change a number of paragraph attributes, including alignment and justification, indents, and space above and below paragraphs. The Justification options are only available when you work with area type (which you'll do shortly), and some options are not relevant for point type that only occupies a single line.

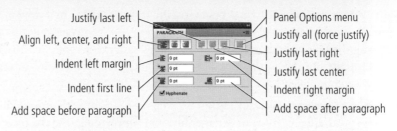

Justify last left
Align left, center, and right
Indent left margin
Indent first line
Add space before paragraph

Panel Options menu
Justify all (force justify)
Justify last right
Justify last center
Indent right margin
Add space after paragraph

Hyphenation Options

When the Hyphenate option is selected, text in area type hyphenates automatically, based on the Hyphenation options in the Paragraph panel Options menu. You can control the minimum length of a word before it can be hyphenated, as well as the minimum number of characters that must appear before or after a hyphen. Formal rules of typography typically suggest that only words longer than six characters should be hyphenated, and at least three characters should exist before or after a hyphen.

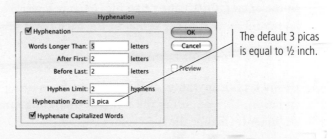

The default 3 picas is equal to ½ inch.

The **Hyphen Limit** field defines how many hyphens can appear at the ends of consecutive lines; formal rules of typography recommend limiting consecutive hyphens to three, and preferably no more than two.

The **Hyphenation Zone** determines the distance from the right edge of a type area where automatic hyphens can exist. If this field is set to 1/2", for example, the automatic hyphen would have to fall within a half inch of the type area edge for a word to be automatically hyphenated.

The final option, **Hyphenate Capitalized Words**, can be used to prevent automatic hyphenation in proper names such as corporate or product names (many companies seriously frown on their trademarks being split across lines).

Justification Options

When you work with area type, you can justify paragraphs inside the type area. Justified type stretches horizontally to fill the width of the area. The last line of the paragraph can be aligned left, centered, or right, or it can be stretched based on your choice in the Paragraph panel. When text is justified, it's stretched based on the defined Justification options, which can be changed by choosing Justification in the Paragraph panel Options menu.

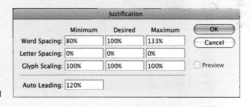

The Minimum and Maximum values define the acceptable spacing for justified paragraphs. The Desired value defines the *preferred* spacing for paragraphs:

- The Word Spacing fields control the space between words (anywhere you press the space bar). A 100% value means the word spacing remains the same when you justify a paragraph.

- The Letter Spacing fields control the space between letters, including kerning and tracking values. A 0% value means the letter spacing remains the same when you justify a paragraph.

- The Glyph Scaling fields control the width of individual characters. A 100% value means they are not stretched.

The Auto Leading field applies to both area type and point type that occupies more than one line. By default, automatic leading is set to 120% of the type size. You can change this automatic value, but it is usually better to change the leading for individual type instances instead of changing the default automatic value.

CREATE AND CONTROL A MULTI-LINE POINT TYPE LAYER

In many cases your clients will provide specific text to include in a design, whether that text comes in an email message or it's saved in a word-processing file. If the client-supplied text is only a couple of words, it's easier to retype the text into your Photoshop file. But when the supplied text is longer, there's no point in making extra work by retyping what has already been typed.

You can't however, place or import external text files directly into a Photoshop file. If you want to use text from an external file, you simply open the file in a text editor, copy it, and paste it into a Photoshop type layer.

1. **In the open moonscapes.psd file, rename Layer 3 as Eclipse, show that layer, and move it to the center of the back cover area.**

2. **Select the Type tool.**

3. **Before typing anything, change the type formatting to ATC Laurel, Black variation, 10.5 pt., using the Sharp anti-aliasing option and left paragraph alignment. Change the type color to white.**

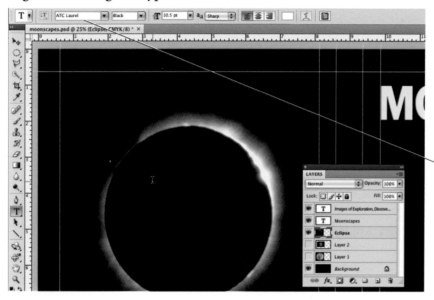

Change these settings before clicking to define the formatting for the new type layer.

4. **Double-click the file ode.txt in the RF_Photoshop>Moon folder (on your desktop) to open it in a word-processing application.**

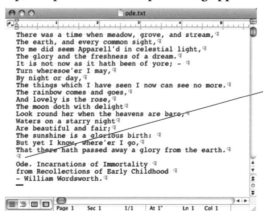

Note the extra paragraph return that separates the poem from the citation.

Note:

We used Microsoft Word as our word processor. This image shows "non-printing" elements — paragraph returns, spaces, tabs, and other items that affect text but don't show on printed output.

5. **Select all the text in the file and copy it, then close the text file and return to Photoshop.**

6. **In Photoshop, click once with the Type tool on top of the Eclipse image to create a new type layer with a point type element.**

7. **Choose Edit>Paste.**

8. **Using the Move tool, drag the new type layer until the first line of the poem fits directly inside the outline of the eclipse (use the following image as a guide).**

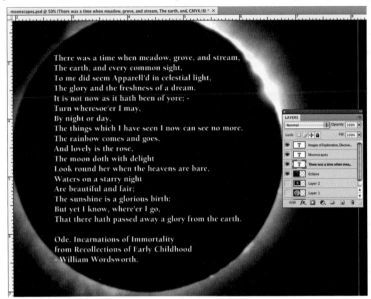

9. **Using the Type tool, place the insertion point before the word "Apparell'd" in the third line and press Return/Enter.**

   Many things can happen when text is saved in a text-only file, including loss of certain formatting attributes. When you import text in this manner, you should check it carefully.

   In addition to the missing paragraph break, the text-only file also stripped out the indents that should be applied to certain lines in the poem. You're going to use the paragraph formatting options to fix this problem.

10. **Place the insertion point in the second line of the poem. In the Paragraph panel, change the Indent Left Margin field to 15 pt.**

The insertion point is in this line.

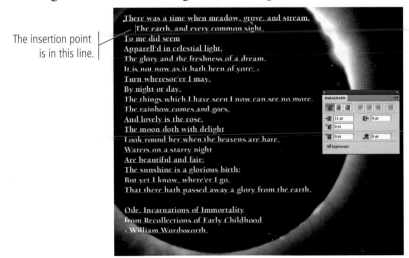

11. **Apply the same indent to lines 4, 7, 13, 16, and 17.**

12. **Apply a 30-pt. left indent to lines 3, 8, 10, 11, 12, 14, and 15.**

When you apply the same paragraph formatting to consecutive lines, you can select all the consecutive lines and change them all at once. You need to select only a part of any paragraph you want to affect.

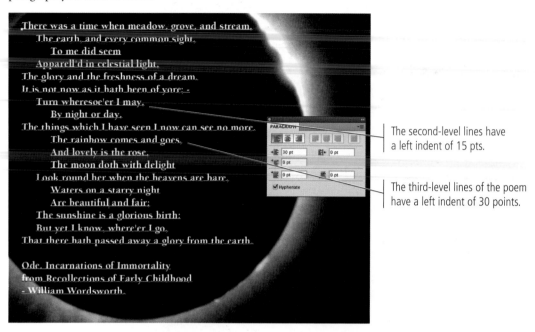

The second-level lines have a left indent of 15 pts.

The third-level lines of the poem have a left indent of 30 points.

13. **Delete the extra paragraph return between the poem and the citation.**

14. **Place the insertion point in the first line of the citation and change the Space Before field to 6 pt.**

In most cases, a full paragraph return adds too much space between lines. Rather than use extra paragraph return characters (which you can't actually see in Photoshop), you have better control over line spacing using the Space Before and Space After options.

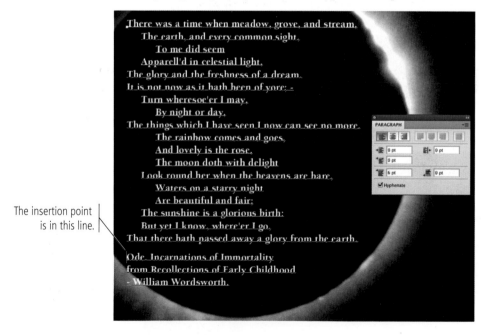

The insertion point is in this line.

15. **Select all the text in the three lines of the citation and change it to 10-pt. ATC Laurel Bold Italic. Change the left indent of the three lines to 50 pt.**

   You can apply different character attributes to different text on the same type layer. But remember: to change the character formatting, every character you want to change must be selected.

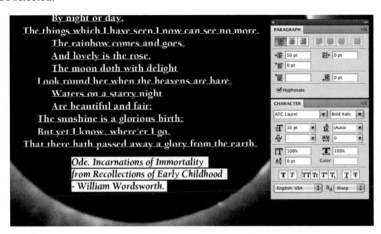

16. **Save the file and continue to the next exercise.**

PLACE AND FORMAT AREA TYPE

The final type element you need to create for this project is a long list of lunar geographic features. This layer needs to fill a specific space — the entire image area. The best way to accomplish this task is to create a type area that you can manipulate to the specific size you need.

1. **In the open `moonscapes.psd` file, hide all layers except the Background layer. Select the Background layer to make it active.**

2. **Choose the Type tool. Change the formatting to 18-pt. ATC Laurel Black Italic, and set the Left Indent and Space Before values back to 0.**

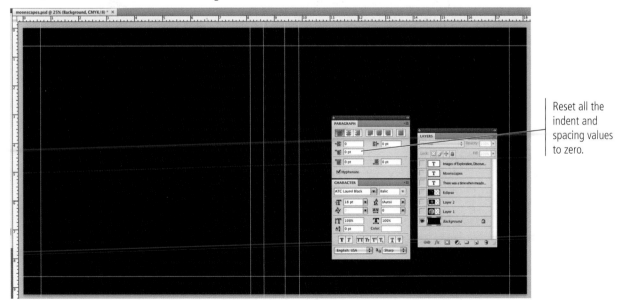

Reset all the indent and spacing values to zero.

3. **On your desktop, open the file `geography.txt` in a text editor and copy all the text. Close the text file and return to Photoshop.**

4. **In Photoshop, click with the Type tool and drag to create a type area on the back cover area.**

   When you release the mouse button, you have a type area with bounding box handles that you can drag to change the area's shape.

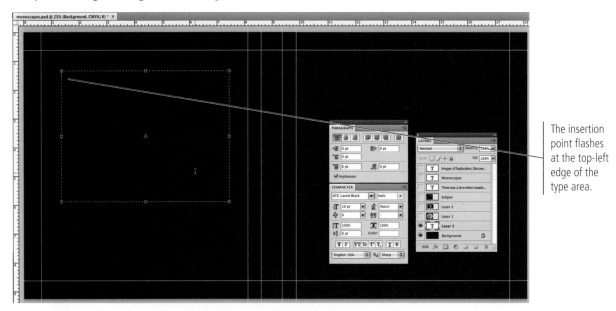

The insertion point flashes at the top-left edge of the type area.

5. **Paste the copied text into the type area.**

   The pasted text automatically adopts the formatting you defined in Step 2. Of course, the entire body of text doesn't fit in the small area we drew.

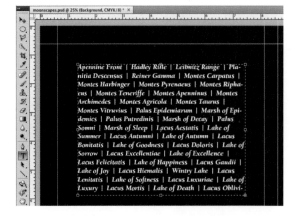

6. **Zoom out until you can see the entire image.**

7. **Drag the top-left bounding box handle to the top-left corner of the image.**

   When you resize the type area by dragging the bounding box handles, you do not affect the type; you change the type *container*, which allows more (or less, depending on how you drag) of the text to show.

   Type also wraps within the type area. You don't have to manually define where new lines begin; simply press Return/Enter to start a new formal paragraph.

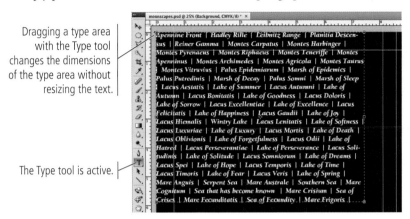

Dragging a type area with the Type tool changes the dimensions of the type area without resizing the text.

The Type tool is active.

8. **Drag the bottom-right handle to the bottom-right corner of the image.**

   You should be able to see how changing the type area affects the wrap of the text within the area. Now you don't have enough text to fill the area, which doesn't work well for a background.

   Make sure to use the Type tool when you want to change the dimensions of a type area. If you press Command/Control-T or choose Edit>Free Transform, stretching or otherwise resizing the type area bounding box resizes the type it contains. You used this technique to create the Moonscapes title for the book cover title.

9. **Select all of the text in the area and copy it.**

10. **Place the insertion point at the end of the existing text, and paste the copied text to fill the type area.**

11. **Click the Type tool anywhere in the visible text to place the insertion point, and then click the Justify All button in the Paragraph panel.**

   Because all of this text is technically one paragraph, you don't have to select all the text to apply the justified paragraph alignment; simply place the insertion point somewhere within the paragraph.

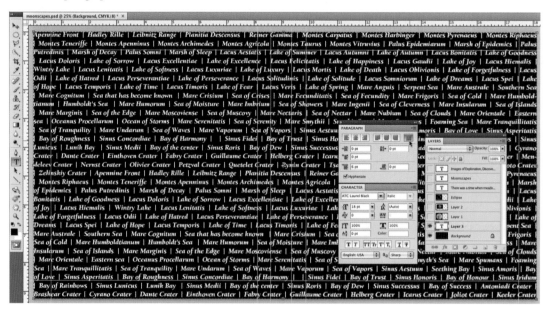

12. **Save the file and continue to the next stage of the project.**

Stage 3 Editing Layers for Visual Impact

At this point, your project contains numerous disparate elements; but if you show all the layers, you see that the project is quite a mess. Creating a single, unified composition requires a little bit of organization, some functional adjustments, and a touch of artistic creativity. Photoshop includes all the tools you need to accomplish this goal.

CREATE EFFECTS WITH LAYER OPACITY

The type area you created in the previous exercise is supposed to add a subtle texture to the black background. Right now, the text is pure white, which is in stark contrast to the background — hardly subtle by any estimation.

To create the desired effect, you can choose from several techniques:

- Experiment with the type color until you find one you like

- Manually calculate a specific percentage of the background color and apply that color to the text

- Change the type color and adjust the blending mode of the type layer

- Make the type layer semi-transparent so that the white text blends into the background color

Note:

We prefer the fourth option since it's basically a one-click change.

1. **In the open moonscapes.psd file, make sure all layers except the layer with the area type and the Background layer are hidden.**

   Because these two layers will combine to make a single element of the design, you should move the layers in the panel so they are directly on top of one another. You can't move the Background layer, so you have to move the type layer.

2. **With the Apennine Front type layer selected, click the Lock Position button at the top of the Layers panel.**

   Locking the layer position prevents you from accidentally moving it as you experiment with different design options.

   You can lock three different layer attributes individually, or you can lock the entire layer at once. (The first two options are not available for type layers.)

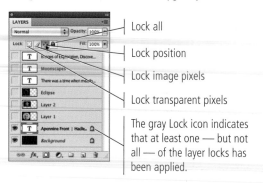

Lock all

Lock position

Lock image pixels

Lock transparent pixels

The gray Lock icon indicates that at least one — but not all — of the layer locks has been applied.

Note:

If the Opacity field is unavailable, check the Lock options. When you use the Lock Position option, you can still affect the opacity of the layer. When you use the Lock All option, however, you can't change the layer opacity.

3. **With the layer still selected, click the Opacity menu and drag the slider to about 20%.**

   The Opacity percentage option changes the opacity of the entire layer, including applied styles and effects. The Fill percentage option changes the opacity of the actual layer pixels, but none of the applied effects or styles. In this case, the layer doesn't yet have any applied styles or effects, so both controls would have the same effect.

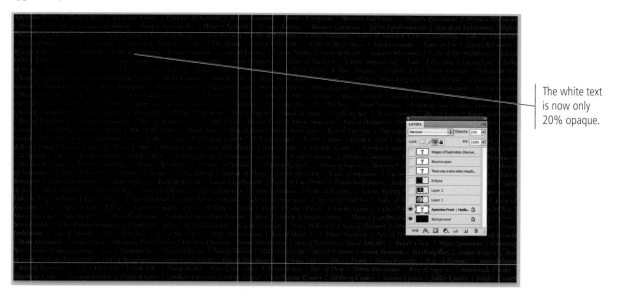

The white text is now only 20% opaque.

4. **Click the Lock All button at the top of the Layers panel.**

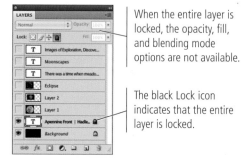

When the entire layer is locked, the opacity, fill, and blending mode options are not available.

The black Lock icon indicates that the entire layer is locked.

5. **Save the file and continue to the next exercise.**

REMOVE THE MOONS FROM THEIR BACKGROUNDS

Reducing the area type opacity is a good start, and you can begin to see the background effect that will be created when the file is printed. But if you show the two images for the front and back cover areas, you see that the black backgrounds in those images hide the text-texture background you just created. To fix this problem, you need to remove the image backgrounds so the images function as part of the entire composition.

1. **In the open moonscapes.psd file, show the Eclipse layer and the type layer with the poem for the back cover. Select the Eclipse layer in the Layers panel to make it active.**

2. **Using any method you learned in Project 1 or 2, create a feathered layer mask to remove the black background, leaving only the eclipse and the purple glow.**

   We used the Magic Wand tool to select the black area outside of the eclipse, then inverted the selection, feathered the selection (Select>Modify>Feather), and created a layer mask. We then used a large soft-edged brush to paint the edges of the mask where necessary.

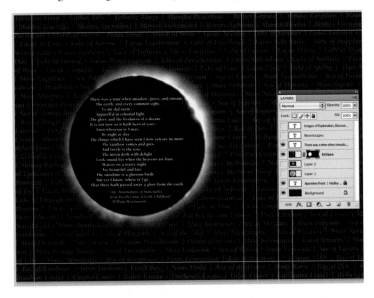

3. **In the Layers panel, select both the Eclipse layer and the type layer with the poem.**

4. **In the Layers panel Options menu, choose New Group from Layers.**

   This option allows you to create a group from the selected layers, which is a good way to manage layers when you know exactly where to place your design elements.

5. Name the new group Back Cover Elements, and then drag the group immediately above the Apennine Front type layer.

Layer groups can have their own blending modes; the default mode is Pass Through, which means no specific blending mode has been applied to the group itself.

6. Show Layer 1, and rename it Cover Moon. Using the Move tool, drag the Cover Moon layer image to the front cover area.

7. Choose Edit>Free Transform. Using the Control panel, resize the cover moon to 95% proportionally.

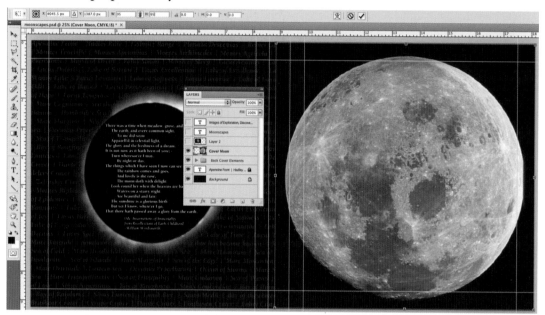

8. Choose the Magnetic Lasso tool.

This tool is particularly useful for selecting an area with high-contrast edges. In most parts of this image, the edge of the moon is considerably different than the black background, so the Magnetic Lasso is a good option for separating the foreground moon from the background color.

9. In the Control panel, set the Width to 20 px, set the Contrast to 10%, and set the Frequency to 20.

The Width value determines how far away from an edge the cursor can be for the line to still snap to the edge. The Contrast value establishes how different the foreground can be from the background and still be detected as an edge. Frequency determines how often points are added along the line.

Note:

If you're working with the insertion point flashing in a type layer, (or you have a dialog box open with the cursor in a field), you can't use the keyboard shortcuts to access different tools.

10. **Place the Magnetic Lasso tool cursor near the top edge of the moon. Click to establish the selection origin, and then drag around the shape of the moon, staying as close as possible to the edge.**

The Magnetic Lasso tool works just like the Freeform Pen tool in Magnetic mode, which you used in Project 2. The only difference is the result: The Pen tool can create a shape layer or path, while the Magnetic Lasso tool only creates selections.

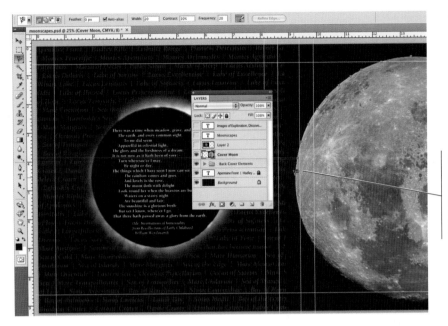

Stay close to the edge as you drag; the contrast setting (especially for this image) will result in a fairly tight selection.

11. **When you get back to your original starting point, release the mouse button.**

You don't need to be exact, but try to stay as close as possible to the edge. Near the bottom of the moon, the Magnetic Lasso tool will have problems because there is little contrast between the background color and the shadowed areas of the moon surface. If some areas are included or are not in the selection, you can fine-tune your selection later as necessary.

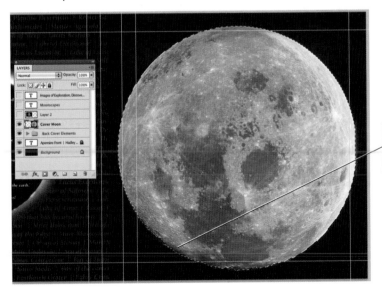

The lower left of the selection may be a bit jagged and imperfect.

Note:

Don't be afraid to mix selection methods — even ones as different as a Magnetic Lasso tool and the Magic Wand tool — to achieve a specific result.

12. **Open the Masks panel. With the selection from Step 11 still active, click the Add a Pixel Mask button.**

    As you saw in Project 2, the Masks panel makes it very easy to change the overall and edge density of any layer mask, at any time in the design process, and as many times as necessary.

Note:

Pixel mask *is simply another term for a raster-based layer mask.*

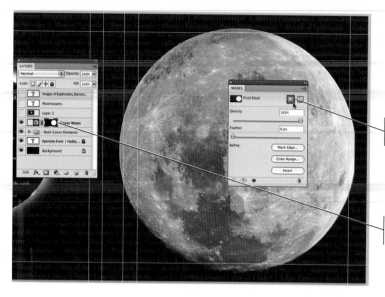

Click here to add a pixel mask.

The layer mask is selected in the Layers panel.

13. **Drag the Feather slider to 2 px.**

    Feathering slightly softens the edges of the mask, which can help to prevent visible imperfections that might result from the imprecise selection method of the Magnetic Lasso tool.

Note:

You might want to zoom in close to see the effect of the feather.

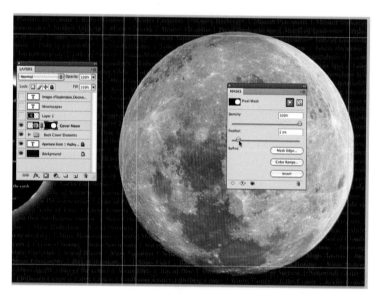

14. **Choose the Brush tool in the Tools panel. In the Control panel, choose a hard-edge round brush from the Brushes panel.**

15. **Click the Default Foreground and Background Colors button near the bottom of the Tools panel.**

16. **With the layer mask selected in the Layers panel, paint over areas of the moon that were excluded by the Magnetic Lasso tool.**

Remember from Project 2: White areas of the mask indicate visible image areas. By painting on the mask with white, you reveal more areas of the image.

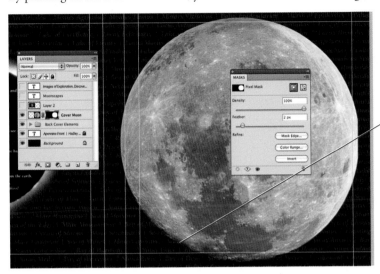

Use what you've already learned about masks to clean up the edges and expose portions of the moon that were hidden by the original mask.

17. **Save the file and continue to the next exercise.**

PLACING IMAGES INTO TYPE

At this point, you have four type layers — three are point type and one is area type. Two of the type layers have multiple lines of text, and two have a single line of text. One type layer has been stretched and resized using the Free Transform option, and one has been made semi-transparent to become a subtle part of the background. One fact that is consistent across all four layers is that the text is "live" — meaning the words and characters can be selected and edited with the Type tool.

In some cases, maintaining a type layer with live text is either unnecessary (e.g., you know the book title isn't going to change) or it prevents you from applying certain changes (e.g., you can't apply filters to a type layer). When you find an effect or change that won't work with live text, you must convert the type layer in one way or another.

You can simply rasterize a type layer by choosing Layer>Rasterize>Type, which converts the editable, vector-based type to a regular pixel-based layer. Once rasterized, you can't edit the text, but you can apply filters and use the layer as a clipping mask.

As we stated earlier, type is fundamentally based on vectors. Rather than simply rasterizing type, you can convert a type layer to a vector-based shape layer by choosing Layer>Type>Convert to Shape. Converting a type layer to a shape means the type is no longer editable, but you can still manipulate the letterforms as you would any other vector shape layer. By converting type to a shape layer, you can use the Distort or Perspective transformation to create custom warps for the layer. You still can't apply filters, however, since filters work on rasterized layers only. (If you try to apply a filter to a shape layer, you will see a message asking if you want to rasterize the shape layer.)

Note:

Each of these type options is useful in different situations, depending on what you need to accomplish.

When you convert a type layer to a shape layer, the shape layer adopts the original text color as the fill color.

If you need to apply filters, custom warps, or transformations to type, but you want to maintain the type layer as live (editable) text, you can convert the type layer to a Smart Object in the layer's contextual menu (Layer>Smart Objects>Convert to Smart Object). You can apply the transformations or filters in the main document, but still edit the text in the Smart Object file.

In the master file you can transform and filter the text as a Smart Object.

The Smart Object file maintains the live text.

Finally, you can use the vector information of type to create a work path (Layer>Type>Create Work Path), which you can then save as a regular path in the Paths panel. In this case, the type layer is maintained as an editable type layer, but you can use the path for any purpose you choose.

When you create a work path from a type layer, you can edit the path using the Path Selection tool.

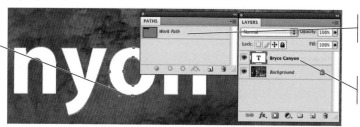

The work path appears in the Paths panel.

The original type layer is maintained.

PHOTOSHOP FOUNDATIONS

Creating Type Selections

The final option for artistically manipulating type actually starts before you create the type layer. You can use one of the Type Mask tools (horizontal or vertical) to create a selection in the shape of letters. When you click with one of the Type Mask tools, you automatically enter a kind of Quick Mask mode; the letters you type are removed from the mask to show what will be selected. (If you press Command/Control while the red mask is visible, you can drag the type selection around in the image window.)

When you've finished typing, switching to the Move tool shows the marching ants that make up the type-shaped selection. This type of selection is similar to any other selection you can make — it just happens to be in the shape of letters. You can manipulate it, create a layer mask with it, save it as an Alpha channel, and so on.

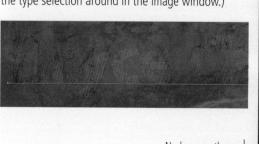

No layer, path, or channel is created when you use one of the Type Mask tools.

1. In the open **moonscapes.psd** file, hide the Cover Moon layer. Show Layer 2 the Moonscapes type layer.

2. Rename Layer 2 as **Title Moon**, and select it as the active layer.

   Your goal is to place the Title Moon layer inside the shapes of the letters in the title.

3. In the Layers panel, drag the Title Moon layer above the Moonscapes layer.

4. Control/right-click the Title Moon layer name and choose Create Clipping Mask from the contextual menu.

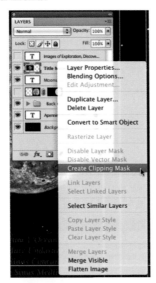

   Once you've created the clipping mask, the Title Moon layer might or might not be visible in the image window, depending on the layer's position. In our file, the Title Moon layer does not overlap the area of the Moonscapes title text, so you can only see the fill of the shape layer.

The Title Moon layer is only visible where the two layers overlap.

5. Using the Move tool, drag the Title Moon layer image until the image on the layer fills the shape of the letters (none of the type fill color should be visible).

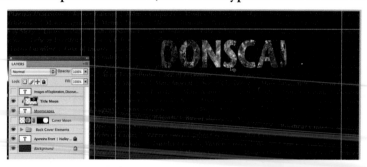

6. In the Layers panel, select the Moonscapes and Title Moon layers, and then choose New Group from Layers in the panel Options menu. Name the new group Main Title.

These two layers function as a single design element, so it makes sense to group them.

7. Show the subtitle type layer (Images of …), and then select that layer and the Main Title layer group.

8. Using the panel Options menu, create another new group named Title All from the selected layer and layer group.

9. Show the Cover Moon layer and select it as the active layer.

10. Use the Move tool to position the Cover Moon layer image so the top edge of the moon is about 1/2″ below the subtitle, and the sides of the moon extend into the spine area on the left and on the foldover area on the right.

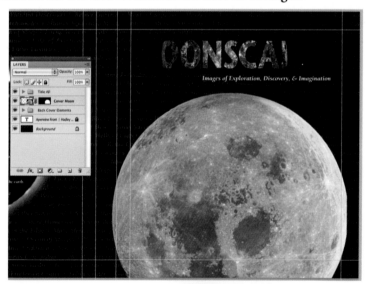

11. Save the file and continue to the next exercise.

CREATE EFFECTS WITH LAYER STYLES

All the design elements are starting to work together now, and your book cover is almost complete. If you look at the title, however, the black in the clipped image gets lost in the black background. Plus, the title and subtitle are rather stark, and they seem to float on the cover instead of functioning as an integrated part of the design. You're going to use layer styles to solve those problems.

You worked with layer styles in Project 2, even if you didn't realize it. In that project, you applied predefined styles and textures to the map shape layer using the Photoshop Style libraries. Those styles are simply saved groups of layer style settings that you can apply with a single click. In this project, you're going to learn how to apply and control the individual components that make up those predefined styles.

1. **In the open `moonscapes.psd` file, expand the Title All and nested Main Title folders in the Layers panel.**

2. **Select the Moonscapes type layer and choose Layer>Layer Style>Outer Glow.**

When you open the Layer Style dialog box, the preview option is automatically checked. You can see the effects of your selections in the image behind the dialog box.

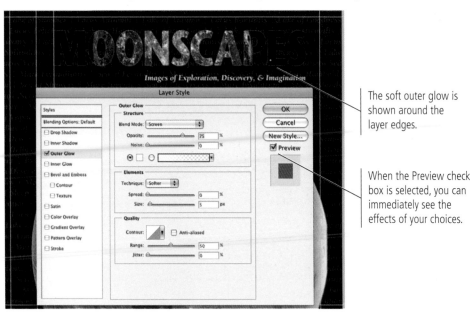

The soft outer glow is shown around the layer edges.

When the Preview check box is selected, you can immediately see the effects of your choices.

3. **Click the color swatch below the Noise slider.**

4. **When the Color Picker appears, click the eyedropper cursor on a light gray-purple color in the Cover Moon.**

   The default outer glow color is yellow, but there is no yellow anywhere else in this composition. Using a color from the existing image makes more sense and will help unify the title with the rest of the cover elements.

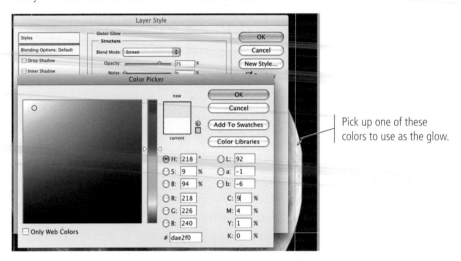

Pick up one of these colors to use as the glow.

5. **Increase the size of the glow to 25 pixels and click OK.**

Layer styles appear in the Layers panel as Effects. You can show or hide these individually or (if more than one is applied) all at once.

6. **Click the arrow to the right of the *fx* icon in the Moonscapes layer to collapse the Effects listing.**

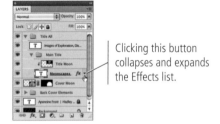

Clicking this button collapses and expands the Effects list.

7. **Duplicate the Main Title layer group and change the name of the duplicate to** Title Spine. **Drag the duplicate group to the top of the Layers panel (out of the Title All layer group).**

   You need to put the title on both the spine and front cover. Since the main title is done, you can simply copy the layer group and put it in place for the spine. At least, it's almost that simple.

8. **With the Title Spine group selected, choose Edit>Transform>Rotate 90° CW (clockwise), and then move the Title Spine group to the spine area (you don't have to be precise yet).**

   This transformation follows centuries of design convention for book titles on spines. As you can see, the Title Spine group doesn't fit within the spine area, so you need to transform the group.

9. **Scale the Title Spine layer group to 50% proportionally, and then drag the group until it is centered horizontally and vertically within the spine area.**

   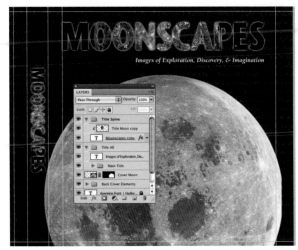

10. **In the Layers panel, expand the Title Spine group, and then expand the effects for the Moonscapes layer in that group.**

11. **Double-click the Outer Glow effect in the Layers panel.**

    As you can see in the Layer Style dialog box, the size is still 25 pixels — even though you scaled the layer to 50%. When you scale a layer with styles applied, the styles do not change in proportion to the layer. In the image window, you can see that the 25-pixel glow is too strong for the reduced title treatment.

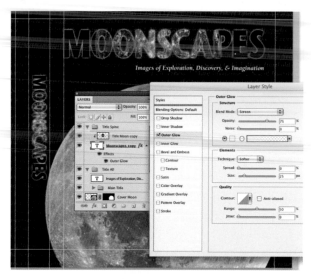

12. **Close the Layer Style dialog box.**

13. **In the Layers panel, select the Moonscapes layer in the Title Spine group. Choose Layer>Layer Style>Scale Effects.**

Note:

This is an easy way to edit the specific effects already applied.

14. **Change the Scale field to 50% (the same size you scaled the layer group) and click OK.**

    In this case, you had only one effect to scale, and you could have done so manually. But if you have a complex series of effects applied, this dialog box allows you to scale all of them at once.

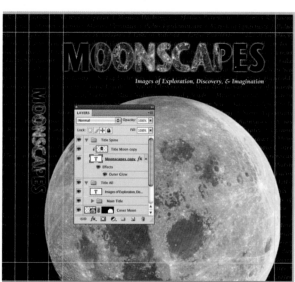

15. **Choose File>Save As. Save the file as moonscapes_final.psd in your WIP>Moon folder and continue to the final stage of the project.**

Photoshop offers 10 layer style options, which you can apply individually or in various combinations to create unique flat and dimensional effects for any layer.

Drop Shadow and Inner Shadow

Drop Shadow adds a shadow behind the layer; **Inner Shadow** adds a shadow inside the edges of the layer's content. For both types, you can define the blending mode, color, opacity, angle, distance, and size of the shadow.

- **Distance** is the offset of the shadow, or how far away the shadow will be from the original layer.
- **Spread** (for Drop Shadows) is the percentage the shadow expands beyond the original layer.
- **Choke** (for Inner Shadows) is the percentage the shadow shrinks into the original layer.
- **Size** is the blur amount applied to the shadow.

You can also adjust the Contour, Anti-aliasing, and Noise settings in the shadow effect. (See the Contour section later in this discussion for further explanation.)

The Layer Knocks Out Drop Shadow option for drop shadows allows you to knock out (remove) or maintain the shadow underneath the original layer area. This option is particularly important if you convert a shadow style to a separate layer that you move to a different position, or if the layer is semi-transparent above its shadow.

Global Light. The Use Global Light check box is available for Drop Shadow, Inner Shadow, and Bevel and Emboss styles. When this option is checked, the style is linked to the "master" light source angle for the entire file. Changing the global light setting affects any linked shadow or bevel style applied to any layer in the entire file. (You can change the Global Light settings in any of the Layer Style fields or by choosing Layer>Layer Style>Global Light.)

Outer Glow and Inner Glow

Outer Glow and **Inner Glow** styles add glow effects to the outside and inside edges (respectively) of the original layer. For either kind of glow, you can define the Blending Mode, Opacity, and Noise values, as well as whether to use a solid color or a gradient.

- For either kind of glow, you can define the **Technique** as Precise or Softer. **Precise** creates a glow at a specific distance; **Softer** creates a blurred glow and does not preserve detail as well as Precise.
- For Inner Glows, you can also define the **Source** of the glow (Center or Edge). **Center** applies a glow starting from the center of the layer; **Edge** applies the glow starting from the inside edges of the layer.
- The **Spread** and **Choke** sliders affect the percentages of the glow effects.
- The **Size** slider makes the effect smaller or larger.

Bevel and Emboss

This style has five variations: Outer Bevel, Inner Bevel, Emboss, Pillow Emboss, and Stroke Emboss:

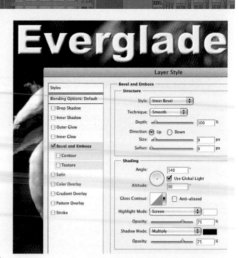

- **Inner Bevel** creates a bevel on the inside edges of the layer contents.
- **Outer Bevel** creates a bevel on the outside edges of the layer contents.
- **Emboss** creates the effect of embossing the layer contents against the underlying layers.
- **Pillow Emboss** creates the effect of stamping the edges of the layer into the underlying layers.
- **Stroke Emboss** applies an embossed effect to a stroke applied to the layer. (The Stroke Emboss effect is not available if you haven't applied a stroke to the layer.)

Any of these styles can be applied as **Smooth** (blurs the edges of the effect), **Chisel Hard** (creates a distinct edge to the effect), or **Chisel Soft** (creates a distinct but slightly blurred edge to the effect).

You can change the **Direction** of the bevel effect. **Up** creates the appearance of the layer coming out of the image; **Down** creates the appearance of something stamped into the image.

The **Size** slider makes the effect smaller or larger, and the **Soften** slider blurs the edges of the effect.

In the Shading area, you can control the light source **Angle** and **Altitude** (think of how shadows differ as the sun moves across the sky). You can also apply a **Gloss Contour** (see the following explanation of Contours). Finally, you can change the Blending Mode, Opacity, and Color settings of both highlights and shadows created in the Bevel or Emboss effect.

When a Bevel and Emboss style is applied, you can also apply Contour and Texture effects.

Contours

Contour options control the shape of the applied styles. Drop Shadow, Inner Shadow, Inner Glow, Outer Glow, Bevel and Emboss, and Satin styles all include Contour options. The default option for all but the Satin style is Linear, which applies a linear effect from solid to 100% transparent.

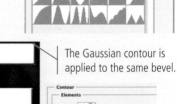

The easiest way to understand the Contour options is through examples. In the following series of images, the same Inner Bevel style was applied in all three examples. In the left image, you can clearly see the size and depth of the bevel. In the right images, the only difference is the applied contour. If you look carefully at the letter edge, you should be able to see how the applied contour shape maps to the beveled edge in the image.

The Gaussian contour is applied to the same bevel.

When you apply a contour, the **Range** slider controls which part of the glow is contoured. For Outer Glow or Inner Glow, you can add variation to the contour color and opacity using the **Jitter** slider.

The Linear contour is applied to the bevel.

The Cone contour is applied to the same bevel.

Satin

The Satin options apply interior shading to create a satiny appearance. You can change the Blending Mode, Color, and Opacity settings of the effect, as well as the Angle, Distance, and Size settings.

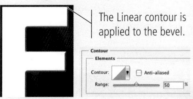

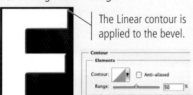

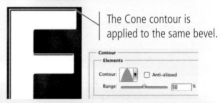

PHOTOSHOP FOUNDATIONS

Textures

The Textures options allow you to create texture effects using the same patterns you worked with in Project 2.

- The **Scale** slider varies the size of the applied pattern.
- The **Depth** slider varies the apparent depth of the applied pattern.
- The **Invert** option (as the name implies) inverts the applied pattern.
- If you check the **Link with Layer** option, the pattern's position is locked to the layer so you can move the two together. If this option is unchecked, different parts of the pattern are visible if you move the associated layer.
- When you create a texture, you can drag in the image window (behind the Layer Styles dialog box) to move the texture. When the Link with Layer option is checked, clicking the **Snap to Origin** button positions the pattern origin at the upper-left corner of the layer. If Link with Layers is unchecked, clicking the Snap to Origin button positions the pattern at the image origin point.

Color Overlay, Gradient Overlay, and Pattern Overlay

A **color overlay** is simply a solid color with specific Blending Mode and Opacity values applied. A color overlay can be used to change an entire layer to a solid color (with the Normal blending mode at 100% opacity), or to create unique effects using different Blending Mode and Opacity settings.

A **gradient overlay** is basically the same as a color overlay, except you use a gradient instead of a solid color. You can choose an existing gradient or define a new one (as you did in Project 2), change the Blending Mode and Opacity values of the gradient, apply any of the available gradient styles (Linear, Radial, etc.), and change the Angle and Scale values of the gradient.

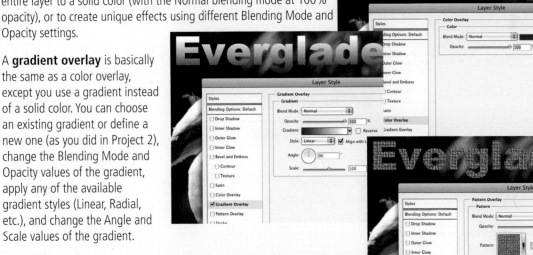

A **pattern overlay** is similar to the Texture options for a Bevel and Emboss style. You can choose a specific pattern, change the Blending Mode and Opacity values, and change the applied pattern scale. You can also link the pattern to the layer and snap the pattern to the layer or the file origin.

Stroke

The **Stroke** style adds an outline of a specific number of pixels to the layer. The Stroke effect can be added at the outside or inside of the layer edge, or it can be centered over the edge (half the stroke will be inside and half outside the actual layer edge). You can adjust the Blending Mode and Opacity settings of the stroke, and you can also define a specific color, gradient, or pattern to apply as the stroke.

Stage 4 Outputting Files

The last stage of most jobs — after the client has approved the work — is printing a proof. A printed proof is basically the output provider's roadmap of how the final job should look. As more processes move to all-digital workflows, a printed proof is not always required — especially if you're submitting files over a network, FTP site, or other method of digital transmission. But some output providers still require a printed proof, and you might want to print samples of your work at various stages of development.

PRINT THE COMPOSITE PROOF

1. **With moonscapes_final.psd open, choose File>Print.**

2. **In the Printer menu of the Print dialog box, choose the printer you're using (preferably one that can print tabloid-size paper).**

3. **If you have a tabloid-size printer, click the Page Setup button, make sure Tabloid is selected in the Paper Size menu, and then click OK to return to the Print dialog box.**

Note:

To output this file at 100%, you need a sheet at least 19" wide and 10" high. We're giving you the instructions to print to a tabloid-size sheet, which will require reducing the print percentage.

If you submit a scaled proof with a print job, make sure you note the scale percentage prominently on the proof.

4. **Regardless of the paper you are printing on, choose the Landscape Orientation option.**

   Ideally, you should always print proofs at 100%. If this is not possible, however, you can print a sample content proof by scaling the page to fit the available paper size.

5. **Check the Scale to Fit Media option.**

6. **Choose Color Management from the menu in the upper-right corner.**

Note:

Photoshop's Print dialog box (and many other dialog boxes, in fact) has a very useful feature in the Description area.

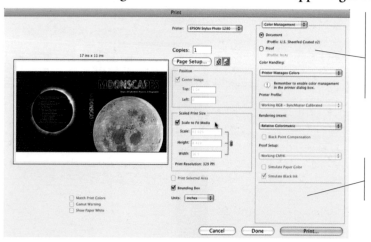

These settings are important if you are printing color-accurate proofs on high-end, managed proofing devices, or if you're printing a file directly to an output device (digital press or imagesetter).

Different descriptions appear when you roll over an option in the dialog box.

7. **Choose Output in the top-right menu and review the Output options.**

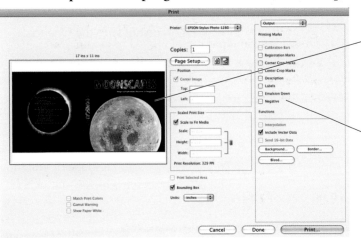

The preview dynamically changes to show the results of your choices in the dialog box.

Negative and Emulsion Down turn the image inside out optically and physically. Looking through conventional film provides the same display and final (film or digital plate) output.

8. **Click Print to output the file.**

9. **When the output process is complete, close the file.**

Print Output Options

PHOTOSHOP FOUNDATIONS

Use the following as a guide to help you decide which options to include in your output:

- **Calibration Bars** adds swatches of black in 10% increments (starting at 0% and ending at 100%).

- **Registration Marks** adds bulls-eye targets and star targets that are used to align color separations on a printing press. (Calibration bars and star target registration marks require a PostScript printer.)

- **Corner Crop Marks** adds crop marks to show the edges of the image (where it should be cut).

- **Center Crop Marks** adds a crop mark at the center of each edge of the image.

- **Description** adds description text (from the File>File Info dialog box) outside the trim area in 9-pt. Helvetica.

- **Labels** adds the file name above the image.

- **Emulsion Down** reverses the image on the output. This option is primarily used for output to a filmsetter or imagesetter.

- **Negative** inverts the color values of the entire output. This option is typically used if you are outputting directly to film, which will then be used to image a photo-sensitive printing plate (a slowly disappearing workflow).

- The **Background** option allows you to add a background color that will print outside the image area.

- The **Border** option adds a black border around an image. You can define a specific width (in points) for the border.

- The **Bleed** option moves crop marks inside the image by a specific measurement.

- The **Screen** option allows you to define the line screen, angle, and dot shape for each separation. If you're printing to a desktop printer, leave these options alone.

- The **Transfer** option allows you to adjust the transfer functions to compensate for dot gain. Transfer functions only work if you print to a PostScript printer. In addition, these functions have been known to cause output problems. It's better to adjust for dot gain in the CMYK Setup menu.

- The **Interpolation** option can help reduce the jagged appearance of low-resolution images by automatically resampling up when you print. This option is only available on PostScript Level 2 or 3 printers.

- The **Include Vector Data** option sends vector information in the output stream for a PostScript printer, so the vector data can be output at the highest possible resolution of the output device.

- The **Encoding** menu defines the format of data sent to the printer. Binary is the default setting for PostScript printers, but you can also choose JPEG, ASCII, or ASCII85 if you have a PostScript printer. JPEG encoding creates smaller files than binary, so they take less time to print; however, JPEG is a lossy compression scheme, so JPEG encoding decreases image quality. (JPEG encoding is not supported by PostScript Level 1.)

fill in the blank

1. _____ are the three primary colors in the additive color model.

2. _____ are the three primary colors in the subtractive color model.

3. A _____ describes the color characteristics of the device used to capture or create a digital image.

4. A _____ describes the color characteristics of a device that will be used to output a digital image.

5. The _____ menu command can be used to identify areas of potential color shift when an image is converted from one profile to another.

6. _____ is created by simply clicking (without dragging) with the Type tool.

7. _____ is the distance from one baseline to the next in a paragraph of type.

8. The _____ tools can be used to create selections in the shape of individual characters or entire words.

9. _____ describes the space between individual type characters (where the insertion point is placed).

10. _____ cannot be applied to type layers; you must first rasterize a type layer to apply them.

short answer

1. Briefly describe how color profiles are used in a color-managed workflow.

2. Briefly explain the difference between point type and area type.

3. Explain three different options for rasterizing type.

Portfolio Builder Project

Use what you learned in this project to complete the following freeform exercise.
Carefully read the art director and client comments, then create your design to meet the needs of the project.
Use the space below to sketch ideas; when finished, write a brief explanation of the reasoning behind your design.

art director comments

At a recent trade show for the book publishing industry, another publisher saw your work on the *Moonscapes* cover and wants to hire you to design covers for a new series of books that they will introduce for the next fall semester.

To complete this project, you should:

❑ Find or create a central image for the front cover of each book; use images that are somehow related to the topics of the books.

❑ Create each book cover to fit a 7 × 9.25″ final size, with a 0.375″ spine. The books will be soft cover, so they only need to incorporate 0.125″ bleeds beyond the trim.

Our company, Against The Clock, produces books that teach people how to use graphic design software like Adobe Photoshop and QuarkXPress. Our books take a step-by-step approach that walks students through specific exercises to teach the software skills they will need in their careers.

client comments

We're planning a new series that will complement the step-by-step books, called the Companion Series. These will cover the broader concepts and and issues that are important to successful graphic design, like color or basic design principles.

There will be four books in the series to begin (although we might add others later): Color, Type, Photography, and Writing. Each one will be titled The [Topic] Companion for Graphic Designers. This is a series, so all four covers should have the same general layout.

The title needs to appear on the front and back cover, as well as the spine. We've written the back cover copy for each book already, and provided it to you in the RF_Builders>Companions folder. You also need to include our logo on the front and back covers, and our name on the spine near the bottom.

We'd like to see some samples in about two weeks if that's possible.

project justification

_____

_____

_____

_____

_____

_____

_____

_____

_____

_____

_____

_____

213

Completing this project required a considerable amount of work with type, which can be either created from scratch or pasted from a text editor. Although not as robust as those in formal page-layout applications — which are specifically designed to create and control large blocks of text — the type controls in Photoshop are certainly useful for a range of different applications.

You learned about the options available in the Character and Paragraph panels, including anti-aliasing options for converting smooth-edge vector type to rasterized image elements. You also worked with a number of tools that create unique artistic effects from a Photoshop type layer — extracting image color to format type, applying styles to type layers, changing layer opacity and blending modes, and even creating a clipping mask from type.

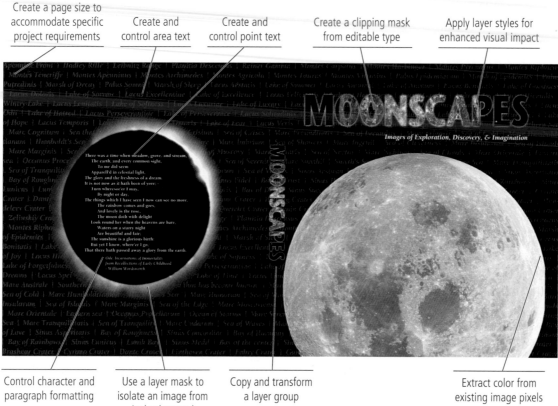

Create a page size to accommodate specific project requirements

Create and control area text

Create and control point text

Create a clipping mask from editable type

Apply layer styles for enhanced visual impact

Control character and paragraph formatting

Use a layer mask to isolate an image from its background

Copy and transform a layer group

Extract color from existing image pixels

Menu Image Correction

Your client is the owner of The Chateau, a five-star gourmet restaurant that has been operating in northern Los Angeles County for over five decades. The restaurant changes its menu frequently, so they currently use a chalkboard menu, presented on an easel at each table when guests are seated. The owner recently received a number of comments about the chalkboard menu being difficult to read, so he decided to create printed menus with the standard offerings and use the chalkboard to display the chef's daily specials.

This project incorporates the following skills:

❏ Evaluating images to determine the necessary corrections

❏ Repairing damaged images

❏ Understanding the relationship between tonal range and contrast

❏ Correcting image lighting and exposure problems

❏ Understanding how gray balance affects overall image color

❏ Correcting minor and severe image color problems

❏ Preparing corrected images for printing

Project Meeting

client comments

The Chateau is a unique destination restaurant that consistently wins awards from local and national food and wine reviewers. The restaurant was first opened in 1952 by Paul and Gina Roseman as a rest stop and diner for travelers along the Sierra Highway. While the restaurant remains in the family, it has evolved from home-style comfort food to more exotic fare such as wild game with a French twist.

The history of the restaurant is important to us. We have a Roseman family portrait — my great-grandparents — that we'd like to include on the back of the menu. The picture is a bit grainy and has some damage, though, and we'd like you to clean it up as much as possible. We also want to include a picture of the current executive chef, who is Paul and Gina's great-grandniece, in the same section. The only picture we have of her is very dark though, and we're hoping you can make it look better.

Otherwise, we've taken several pictures of different meals that Suzanne created. We want you to make sure they will look as good as possible when printed. You're the expert, so we trust that you know what needs to be done.

① Rosemans — touch up, fix damage
② Buffalo steak — fix brightness/contrast
③ Suzanne — lighten overall, add detail in shadows
④ Chicken — fix muddy/Exposure problem
⑤ Salmon — fix green cast throughout
⑥ Flan — fix red cast in plate
⑦ Pasta — bump contrast in midtones
⑧ Salad — correct color shift in reds/greens

art director comments

Digital images come from a wide variety of sources: scanned photographs and digital cameras are the two most common — as is the case in the client's images for this project. Some images can be used as is, or at least with only minor correction. Realistically, most professional photographers reshoot an image until they have one that doesn't need your help.

Unfortunately, however, not every project involves a professional photographer. Consumer-level cameras have come down in price and gone up in quality to the point where many non-professionals shoot their own photos without proper skill or knowledge. That means many of those images require a bit of help — and some require a lot.

Even when a professional photographer is involved, not every image comes from a perfectly lit studio. Location shots — where a subject is photographed in a "real-world" setting — can't always be captured perfectly. Those images usually need work as well. Fortunately, Photoshop provides a powerful toolset for solving most image problems, or at least improving the worst of them.

project objectives

To complete this project, you will:

- Remove grain with blur and sharpen techniques
- Heal severe scratches
- Clone out major damage
- Correct minor problems with the Brightness/Contrast adjustment
- Correct tonal range with the Levels adjustment
- Correct lighting problems with the Exposure adjustment
- Correct overall color problems with the Color Balance adjustment
- Correct precise color values with the Curves adjustment
- Correct an RGB image to CMYK gamut limits
- Embed color profile information in a file

Stage 1 **Retouching Damaged Images**

Image repair is the process of fixing scratches, removing dust, making tears disappear, and generally putting broken or damaged pictures back together again. **Retouching**, on the other hand, is the technique of changing an image by adding something that wasn't there or removing something that was there. Damage can come from a wide range of sources: creases, scratches from any number of abrasive objects, water spots, and tape marks to name just a few. Other image problems such as photographic grain are a natural part of photographs (especially old ones), and dust is common (if not inevitable) whenever photographs are scanned.

There are many different ways to approach image repairs. As you complete the exercises in this lesson, you'll use several tools — from basic to complex — to clean up damage in the client's family portrait from the early 1940s.

 ## REMOVE GRAIN WITH BLUR AND SHARPEN TECHNIQUES

Photographic film is made up of microscopic grains of light-sensitive material. These grains capture the image information, which is eventually processed into a print or transparency. While not usually apparent in a standard photographic print, the grain in a photograph can become pronounced when scanned with a high-resolution scanner. Enlarging an image during scanning further enhances any grain that already exists.

When grain is evident in a digital image, the grain pattern can destroy fine detail and create a mottled appearance in areas of solid color or subtle tone variation. Slower-rated film typically has the smallest and least-evident grain, while faster film can produce significant graininess.

Sharpening and blurring techniques are the best methods for removing photographic grain. The techniques you use in this exercise work for any image with grain. Older images — such as the one your client wants to use — almost always have obvious grain problems that can be fixed to some degree; antique images can be fixed only just so much. The techniques you learn in this project produce very good results if you need to remove grain from modern scanned images.

1. **On your desktop, copy the Menu folder from the WIP folder on your Resource CD into the WIP folder where you are saving your work.**

2. **Open the file rosemans.jpg from the RF_Photoshop>Menu folder.**

   As you can see, this image has some significant damage.

Obvious glue marks remain from the original photo mounting.

Scratches mar the image in important areas.

A sharp crease cuts into the Rosemans' daughter.

The corner has been torn off.

3. **Choose View>Actual Pixels to view the image at 100%.**

   When you zoom into the image, you can also see the photographic grain that was captured by the scanner.

Note:

Press Command-Opt-Zero/Control-Alt-Zero to view the image at 100%.

Grain is most obvious in large areas of solid (or nearly solid) color.

Grain in lighter areas can produce a sickly appearance in a person's face.

4. **Choose Filter>Blur>Gaussian Blur.**

   All Photoshop blur filters work essentially the same way: they average the brightness values of contiguous pixels to soften the image. Some filters, such as Gaussian Blur, simulate the effect of an unfocused camera lens; other blur filters are more useful for creating special effects.

5. **Make sure Preview is checked and change the Radius field to 1.5 pixels.**

   Using the Gaussian Blur filter, the Radius field defines (in pixels) the amount of blurring that will be applied. Photoshop uses this value to average the brightness of a pixel with that of the surrounding pixels. A radius value near 1 can soften an image and remove most photographic grain.

Note:

The Dust & Scratches filter (Filter>Noise>Dust & Scratches) can remove small amounts of noise and dust from images that are already very good; besides that, however, it is far inferior to the Gaussian and Smart Blur filters.

Note:

Using Gaussian Blur and Unsharp Masking in tandem is a common technique for cleaning up grainy images.

A small amount of Gaussian blur removes most of the photographic grain.

Areas of fine detail are also slightly blurred by the Gaussian Blur filter.

The Blur Filters

PHOTOSHOP FOUNDATIONS

The Filter>Blur menu includes a number of choices for applying corrective or artistic blurs to an image or selection.

Average finds the average color of an image or selection, and then fills the image or selection with the color to create a smooth appearance.

Blur and **Blur More** smooth transitions by averaging the pixels next to the hard edges of defined lines and shaded areas. When you apply these filters, you have no additional control: Blur is roughly equivalent to a 0.3-pixel radius blur, and Blur More uses approximately a 0.7-pixel radius.

Box Blur averages the color value of neighboring pixels. You can adjust the size of the area used to calculate the average value; a larger radius value results in more blurring.

Gaussian Blur blurs the selection by a specific amount.

Motion Blur includes an option for changing the blur angle, as well as a Distance value for the number of pixels to blur.

Radial Blur either spins the pixel around the center point of the image, or zooms the pixel around a center point based on the Amount setting. The farther the pixel is from the adjustable center point, the more the pixel is blurred. You can drag the Blur Center window to move the center point of the blur.

Shape Blur uses a specific shape (**kernel**) to create the blur. You can load different shape libraries by clicking the triangle and choosing from the list. Radius determines the size of the kernel; the larger the kernel, the greater the blur.

Smart Blur allows you to blur tones closely related in value without affecting the edge quality of an image. You can set a radius for blurring, just as you can with the Gaussian Blur filter. The Threshold setting allows you to determine how closely pixels must be related in tone before being blurred (from 0.01 to 100).

You can also specify a Quality level (High, Medium, or Low) or change the Mode setting. Using the Edge Only mode, edges are outlined in white, and the image is forced to black. Using the Overlay Edges mode, the color image is blurred, and the edges are outlined in white.

Surface Blur blurs an image while trying to preserve edges. The Radius option specifies the size of the blur in whole numbers. The Threshold option controls how much the tonal values of neighboring pixels must differ before being blurred. (You can only apply whole-number radius blurs.)

Lens Blur adds blur to an image to create the effect of a narrower depth of field so some objects in the image remain in focus, while others areas are blurred.

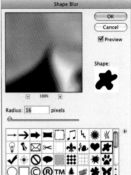

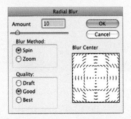

6. **Click OK to apply the Gaussian Blur to the image.**

   To remove the photographic grain, you had to blur the entire image; this means that areas of fine detail were also blurred. You can use a second technique — unsharp masking — to restore some of the lost edge detail.

7. **Choose Filter>Sharpen>Unsharp Mask and make sure the Preview check box is active in the dialog box.**

   Unsharp masking sharpens an image by increasing contrast along the edges in an image.

8. **Change the Amount to 150%, the Radius to 3.0 pixels, and the Threshold to 15 levels.**

Note:

The degree of sharpening applied to an image is often a matter of personal choice; however, oversharpening an image produces a halo effect around the edges.

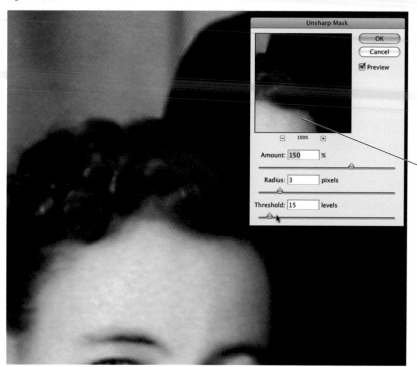

Drag here or click in the document window to change the visible area in the preview window.

The Amount option determines how much the contrast in edges will increase. Typically, 150–200% creates good results in high-resolution images.

The Radius option determines how many pixels will be included in the edge comparison; higher radius values result in more pronounced edge effects.

The Unsharp Mask filter locates pixels that differ in value from surrounding pixels by the threshold you specify; using a threshold of 15 means that colors must be more than 15 levels different before Photoshop identifies an edge. Using this higher value protects the smooth tones in the faces, while still allowing detail in the faces (the eyes, for example) to be sharpened.

Note:

The Sharpen, Sharpen More, and Sharpen Edges filters apply sharpening with no user control.

Note:

A majority of the images you work with benefit from sharpening if it's done correctly. On the other hand, too much sharpening can damage an image and make it appear artificial and harsh. Only experience and practice can teach you how much sharpening is too much, or when you haven't sharpened an image enough.

9. **Click OK to apply the Unsharp Mask filter.**

10. **Choose File>Save As. Save the file as `rosemans_working.psd` in your WIP>Menu folder using the Photoshop format. Continue to the next exercise.**

The Smart Sharpen Filter

The Smart Sharpen filter allows you to independently control the amount of sharpening that occurs in shadow and highlight areas. The Sharpen tab defines how much sharpening will be applied.

Amount and **Radius** have the same purpose as in the Unsharp Mask filter. A higher Amount increases contrast between edge pixels; a higher Radius value widens the effects applied to edges.

Remove defines the sharpening algorithm used to sharpen the image. Gaussian Blur is the method used by the Unsharp Mask filter. Lens Blur detects edges and detail in an image, and provides finer detail and fewer halos. Motion Blur tries to reduce the effects of blur due to movement.

Angle sets the direction of motion if you choose the Remove Motion Blur option.

The **More Accurate** check box processes the file more slowly for a more accurate blur removal.

Using the Shadow and Highlight tabs, you can adjust sharpening of dark and light areas. (If you don't see these tabs, make sure the Advanced radio button is selected.)

Fade Amount adjusts the amount of sharpening.

Tonal Width controls the range of tones in the shadows or highlights that are being modified. Smaller values restrict the adjustments to only darker regions for shadows and only lighter regions for highlights.

Radius defines the size of the area (in pixels) around each pixel used to determine whether a pixel is in the shadows or highlights.

Noise is defined as random pixels that stand out from the surrounding pixels, either hurting the overall appearance of the image (as in the case of visible grains in an old photograph) or helping to prevent printing problems (as in the case of a gradient that extends across a large area). Photoshop includes several filters (Filters>Noise) that can add or remove noise.

The **Add Noise filter** applies random pixels to the image. Uniform distributes color values of noise between 0 and the defined amount. Gaussian distributes color values of noise along a bell-shaped curve. Monochromatic adds random pixels without affecting the colors in the image.

The **Dust & Scratches filter** reduces noise by comparing the contrast of pixels within the defined radius; pixels outside the defined threshold are adjusted.

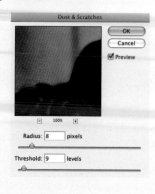

The **Median filter** reduces noise by blending the brightness of pixels within a selection. The filter compares the brightness of pixels within the defined radius, and replaces pixels that differ too much from surrounding pixels with the median brightness value of the compared pixels.

The final option for reducing noise is the **Reduce Noise** filter, which provides far greater control over different aspects of the noise correction. In Basic mode, you can remove luminance noise and color noise in the composite image. In Advanced mode, you can remove noise from individual color channels. (**Luminance noise**, also called grayscale noise, makes an image appear grainy; **color noise** usually appears as color artifacts in the image.)

- **Strength** controls the amount of luminance noise reduction.

- **Preserve Details** controls how carefully the filter compares the difference in luminance between adjacent pixels. Lower values remove more noise but result in less detail.

- **Reduce Color Noise** removes random color pixels from the image.

- **Sharpen Details** sharpens the image. Because the noise reduction process inherently blurs the image, this option applies the same kind of sharpening that is available in the Photoshop Sharpen filters.

- **Remove JPEG Artifacts** removes artifacts and halos caused by saving an image with a low JPEG quality setting (in other words, using a high lossy compression scheme).

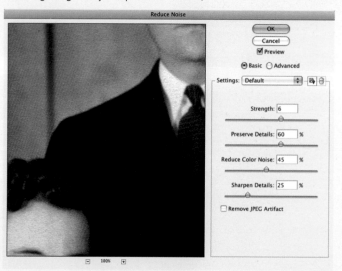

HEAL SEVERE SCRATCHES

The blur and sharpen routine from the previous exercise improved the client's image — the obvious grain is gone. Even though the edges are slightly less sharp than the original scan, they are sharp enough to produce good results when the image is printed. If you're working with images that aren't 90 years old, you'll be able to produce far sharper edges using these same techniques.

There are still a number of problems in the image that require intervention. Photoshop includes several tools for changing the pixels in an image — from painting with a brush to nudging selections on a layer to using repair tools specifically designed for adjusting pixels based on other pixels in the image.

Note:

Throughout this project, you are going to clean up blemishes on images and make other adjustments that require looking at very small areas. It can be very helpful to clean your monitor so you don't mistake on-screen dust and smudges with flaws in the images you are adjusting.

The **Spot Healing Brush tool** allows you to remove imperfections by blending the surrounding pixels. The **Healing Brush tool** has a similar function, except you can define the source pixels that will be used to heal a specific area. The **Patch tool** allows you to repair a selected area with pixels from another area of the image by dragging the selection area.

1. **With rosemans_working.psd open, make sure you are viewing the image at 100%, and then drag the image so you can see the lower half of the image.**

2. **Select the Spot Healing Brush tool in the Tools panel.**

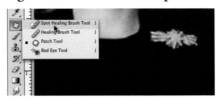

3. **In the Control panel, choose a 20-pixel hard-edge brush.**

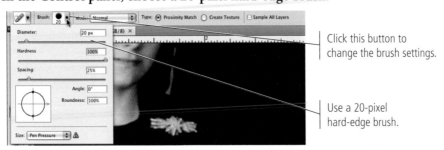

Click this button to change the brush settings.

Use a 20-pixel hard-edge brush.

Note:

You work extensively with brushes and brush settings in Project 7.

Note:

If you select Sample All Layers in the Control panel, the Spot Healing Brush tool pulls pixel data from all visible layers.

Proximity Match is the default setting; this method uses the pixels around the edge of the selection to find an image area to use as a patch for the selected area. Alternatively, you can use the **Create Texture** method, which uses all the pixels in the selection to create a texture for repairing the area.

4. **Place the cursor over the small white spot in the bottom-left corner of the image.**

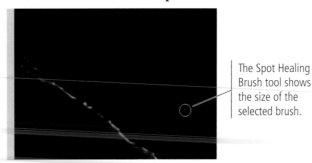

The Spot Healing Brush tool shows the size of the selected brush.

Note:

Press [to decrease the brush to the next preset size. Press] to increase the brush to the next preset size.

5. **Click immediately over the white spot to heal it.**

Don't worry about the crease yet; you fix that problem in the next exercise.

Note:

Because this image is very dark, it might be difficult to see the cursor over the black image areas. To check the size of the brush, try moving it outside the image area.

6. **Using the same technique, remove the remaining white spots from the dark area of the Rosemans' clothing.**

7. **Place the Spot Healing Brush cursor over the white spot on the younger woman's chin, and then click to heal the spot.**

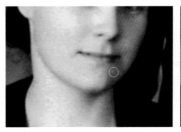 

The Spot Healing Brush tool is not effective in every situation. As you can see in this case, the tool actually makes the spot larger and more obvious instead of removing it.

Note:

You can place the cursor over the spot you want to correct and use the bracket keys to adjust the brush size until it's slightly larger than the spot you want to heal.

8. **Press Command/Control-Z to undo the previous step.**

9. **Choose the Healing Brush tool (nested under the Spot Healing Brush tool).**

10. **In the Control panel, choose a small brush size that's slightly larger than the white spot on the girl's chin (we used 9 pixels).**

When using the Healing Brush tool, the Mode menu in the Control panel determines the blending mode used to heal an area. The default option (Normal) samples the source color and transparency to blend the new pixels smoothly into the area being healed.

You can also change the source from Sampled (the pixels you defined by Option/Alt-clicking) to Pattern, which uses pixels from a defined pattern to heal the area. The Pattern option is a good choice for creating artistic effects, rather than healing blemishes in an existing photo.

Note:

The Replace mode preserves texture in the healed area when you used a soft-edge brush. Multiple, Screen, Darken, Lighten, Color, and Luminosity modes have the same function as the blending modes for specific layers and brushes (refer to Project 2 for an explanation of each blending mode).

11. Place the cursor directly below the spot you want to heal. Press Option/Alt and click to define the healing source.

Pressing Option/Alt with the Healing Brush tool allows you to select the source of the brush or the pixels that will be used to heal the spot where you next click.

Pressing Option/Alt allows you to define the source pixels that will be used to heal the next spot you click.

Note:

Using the Sample menu in the Control panel, you can sample source pixels from the current layer, from all layers including and below the current layer, or from all visible layers.

12. Place the cursor over the blemish on the girl's chin and click.

Unlike the Spot Healing Brush tool, the Healing Brush tool allows you to define the source of the healing. By choosing nearby pixels as the healing source, the blemish on the girl's chin disappears, and that spot blends nicely into the surrounding pixels.

The Healing Brush tool blends colors from the source pixels (which you defined in Step 11) with colors in the area where you click.

Note:

It might help to zoom in when you want to heal small areas such as this spot on the girl's chin. We are working at 200% in these screen shots.

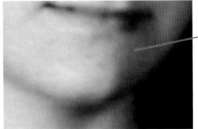

After clicking, the spot is healed using the source pixels.

13. Save the file and continue to the next exercise.

Aligning the Healing Source

PHOTOSHOP FOUNDATIONS

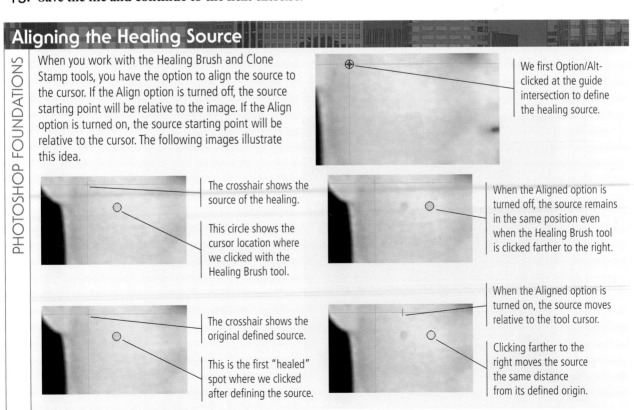

When you work with the Healing Brush and Clone Stamp tools, you have the option to align the source to the cursor. If the Align option is turned off, the source starting point will be relative to the image. If the Align option is turned on, the source starting point will be relative to the cursor. The following images illustrate this idea.

We first Option/Alt-clicked at the guide intersection to define the healing source.

The crosshair shows the source of the healing.

This circle shows the cursor location where we clicked with the Healing Brush tool.

When the Aligned option is turned off, the source remains in the same position even when the Healing Brush tool is clicked farther to the right.

The crosshair shows the original defined source.

This is the first "healed" spot where we clicked after defining the source.

When the Aligned option is turned on, the source moves relative to the tool cursor.

Clicking farther to the right moves the source the same distance from its defined origin.

CLONE OUT MAJOR DAMAGE

The client's image has definitely been improved by removing the grain and healing the small blemishes, but four major areas of damage still need to be fixed. These larger areas require more control over the healing process, which the Clone Stamp tool provides.

Original scan  Repaired image so far

The Clone Stamp tool paints one part of an image over another part, which is useful for duplicating objects or removing defects in an image. As with the Healing Brush tool, you can define the source that will be cloned when you click with the tool; the difference is that whole pixels are copied, not just their color value. Be careful when you use the Clone Stamp tool, however, because depending on the brush you choose, you can actually create more damage than you fix.

1. **With the file rosemans_working.psd open, zoom into the bottom-left corner (where the crease marks the image) and select the Clone Stamp tool.**

2. **In the Control panel, choose a soft-edge brush large enough to cover the crease line.**

   Using the Clone Stamp tool, the Control panel combines brush options (brush size, blending mode, opacity, and flow) with healing options (alignment and sample source, which you used in the previous exercise).

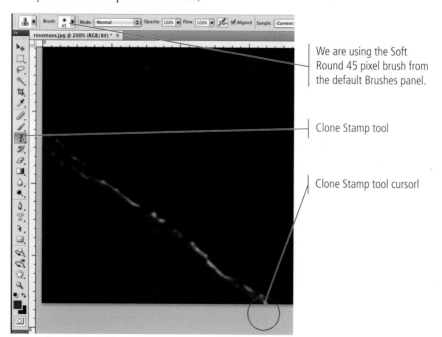

We are using the Soft Round 45 pixel brush from the default Brushes panel.

Clone Stamp tool

Clone Stamp tool cursorl

<!-- Note blocks in margin -->*Note:*

You can choose any brush available to Photoshop, just as you can when you use the Brush tool. Hard-edge brushes can result in harsh lines where you clone pixels; soft-edge brushes can help prevent harsh lines from appearing.

Note:

As with any brush tool, you can use the bracket keys to enlarge or reduce the Clone Stamp brush size.

3. **In the Control panel, make sure the Align option is turned on.**

In this case, you want the cloning source to remain relative to the cursor, even if you stop and start several times. If you clone a large area relative to the same source origin (in other words, with the Align option turned off), you could end up with an unwanted pattern in the area you clone.

4. **Place the cursor directly above and to the right of the crease. Option/Alt-click to define the cloning source.**

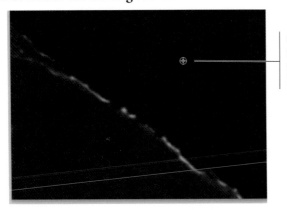

Option/Alt-click to define the cloning source, just as you did with the Healing Brush tool.

5. **Click over an area of the crease and drag to clone out the crease.**

As you drag, notice that the source crosshairs move in relation to the Clone Stamp cursor. Because you turned on the Align option in Step 3, you can stop and restart cloning, and the source retains the same relative position to the tool cursor.

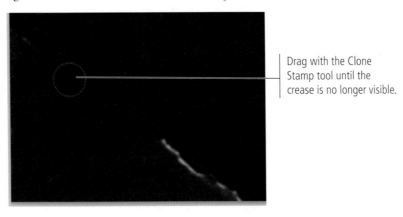

Drag with the Clone Stamp tool until the crease is no longer visible.

Note:

If you had used a hard-edge brush, the subtle tone variation in the image might have resulted in a visible (although slight) hard edge that would have caused as much damage as it fixed.

6. **Use the same process to fill in the torn area in the bottom-right corner of the image.**

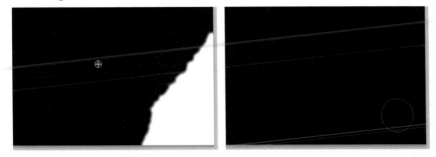

7. **Zoom into the scratch on the man's left shoulder.**

Cloning out damage in areas of solid color is fairly simple. This area presents a more difficult problem since the area you need to fix has an edge that must be maintained.

Note:

When you are cloning — especially large areas — it's usually a good idea to clone in small strokes or even single clicks. This method can help you avoid cloning in patterns or "railroad tracks" that do as much damage as good. When cloning large areas, it's also a good idea to frequently resample the clone source to avoid cloning the same pixels into a new noticeable pattern.

8. **In the Control panel, select a brush that just barely covers the edge of the man's jacket, and make sure the Align option is off.**

To prevent cloning a hard edge, we used a 30-pixel brush with a 50% Hardness value.

9. **Place the cursor over the edge you want to reproduce and Option/Alt-click to define the source.**

Because the Align option is turned off, each successive click uses the same source point.

Option/Alt-click to define the clone source.

10. **Place the cursor over the right-most area of the scratch.**

As you move the Clone Stamp tool cursor, the source pixels move along with the tool cursor to give you a preview of what will happen when you click.

11. **Click without dragging when the cloned pixels appear to align properly with the area behind the scratch.**

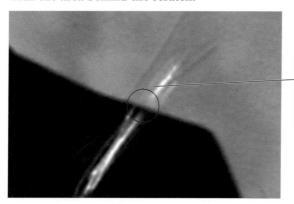

Clicking without dragging clones a 30-pixel area. Because the brush we chose has 50% hardness, the center (where the shoulder edge is) is clear, but the outside parts of the brush are feathered into the surrounding area.

12. **Move the cursor slightly to the left, again centering the cursor preview over the would-be edge, and click without dragging.**

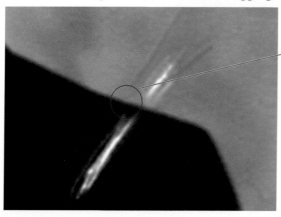

With the Align option turned off, you again clone from the same source point.

13. Repeat this process as necessary to clone out the remaining scratch along the man's shoulder.

We clicked two more times to completely remove the scratch along the shoulder line. If you're unsatisfied with the result of a clone, simply undo the action (Command/Control-Z) and try again. Cloning — and especially cloning edges — often takes more than one try to achieve the desired result.

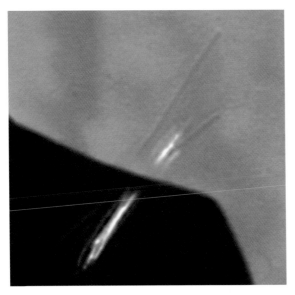

14. Using the Clone Stamp tool, clean up the rest of the scratch around the man's shoulder.

We used a 30-pixel brush size with a 25% Hardness value. In the area of the backdrop, we defined an aligned source that was very close to the scratched areas. By clicking and dragging in small swaths, and by clicking numerous times without dragging, we were able to maintain the mottled appearance of the backdrop without creating pattern-like railroad tracks with the cloning tool.

Note:

As we stated earlier, it's also a good idea to frequently resample the clone source to avoid cloning in unwanted patterns.

15. Using any method you prefer, clean up the scratches and glue residue on the left side of the photo.

As with the mottled background above the man's shoulder, it's best to use a small, soft-edge brush and clone out the damage in short strokes or single clicks. Experiment with frequently moving the clone source so you can avoid creating an unwanted pattern while removing the damage.

16. Choose File>Save As and choose TIFF in the Format/Save As Type menu. Change the file name to `rosemans_fixed.tif` and save it with the default TIFF options in your WIP>Menu folder.

The Clone Source Panel

PHOTOSHOP FOUNDATIONS

The Clone Source panel (Window>Clone Source) allows you to store up to five sources for the Clone Stamp or Healing Brush tool. These sources can be from any layer of any open image, which allows you to create unique blended effects by combining pixels from multiple layers or multiple files.

> Store and access up to five sources from any layer of any open image.
>
> Transform the offset, size, and angle of the clone source.

The Show Overlay options allow you to show (at the defined opacity) the source pixels on top of the area where you are cloning. For example, let's say you want to clone the gorilla into the giraffe photo. You would first define a clone source in the gorilla image, and then make the giraffe image active.

With the Show Overlay option checked, placing the Clone Stamp cursor over the giraffe image shows the gorilla on top of the giraffe. When you click in the giraffe image with the Clone Stamp tool, that area of the gorilla image will be cloned into the giraffe image; the overlay allows you to preview the areas of the source that will be cloned into the giraffe image.

If the Auto Hide option is checked, the overlay is only visible when the mouse button is not clicked. The Invert option reverses the overlay into a negative representation of the source image. You can also change the blending mode of the overlay from the default Normal to Darken, Lighten, or Difference.

We defined a clone source here.

When the Clipped option is checked, the clone source appears within the tool cursor area.

Using the overlay, you can see the Clone Stamp cursor in relation to the clone source. Clicking will clone this spot from the gorilla image into the giraffe image.

We defined a clone source here.

Stage 2 Correcting Lighting Problems

Before you start correcting problems with lighting and color, you should understand the different parts of an image, as well as the terms used to describe these areas.

- **Highlights** are defined as the lightest areas of the image that include detail. Direct sources of light such as a light bulb or reflected sunlight on water are called **specular highlights;** they should not be considered the highlights of an image.

- **Shadows** are the darkest areas of the image that still contain some detail; areas of solid black are not considered shadow tones.

- The shades between the highlights and shadows are the **midtones** (or **gamma**) of the image.

Contrast and saturation play an integral role in reproducing high-quality images. **Contrast** refers to the tonal variation within an image; an image primarily composed of highlights and shadows is a high-contrast image, while an image with more detail in the midtones is a low-contrast image.

Contrast is closely linked to **saturation**, which refers to the intensity of a color or its variation away from gray. The saturation of individual colors in an image, and the correct saturation of different colors in relation to one another, affects the overall contrast of the image. If an image is under- or oversaturated, the contrast suffers — detail is lost and colors appear either muted or too bright.

Note:

Image adjustments can be applied directly to the image pixels or as non-destructive adjustment layers using the Adjustments panel. In this project, you edit the actual image pixels; you use the adjustment layer method in Project 6.

CORRECT PROBLEMS WITH BRIGHTNESS/CONTRAST

Depending on the image, several tools are available for correcting problems related to overly dark or overly light images. The most basic adjustment option — Brightness/Contrast — can fix images that need overall adjustment to brightness, contrast, or both. If an image requires more sophisticated adjustment, you should use one of the other adjustment options.

1. **Open the file buffalo.jpg from the RF_Photoshop>Menu folder.**

   This image has an overall dark feel, probably caused by poor lighting or underexposure. The Brightness/Contrast adjustment can correct this problem.

2. **Choose Image>Adjustments>Brightness/Contrast and make sure the Preview option is checked.**

3. Drag the Brightness slider to +50.

Increasing the overall brightness creates an immediate improvement in this image, although some areas of detail are still muddy.

4. Drag the Contrast slider to +15.

Increasing the contrast brings out more detail in the food texture (pay particular attention to the meat), which is the focal point of the image.

5. Click OK to apply the change.

6. Use any of the techniques you learned earlier to fix the white spot in the front edge of the steak.

We used the Spot Healing Brush tool to remove the white spot.

7. Save the file in your WIP>Menu folder as a TIFF file named buffalo_fixed.tif.

8. Close the file and continue to the next exercise.

Note:

Remember, you have to choose File> Save As to save the file with a different name or format.

CORRECT CONTRAST AND TONAL RANGE WITH LEVELS

While the Brightness/Contrast option is a good choice for making basic adjustments, the Levels adjustment is the best approach for correcting contrast — which in turn enables you to enhance image detail throughout the entire tonal range. Using Levels, adjusting contrast is a three-step process:

- Determine the image's highlight areas (the lightest areas that contain detail).

- Determine the image's shadow areas (the darkest areas that contain detail).

- Adjust the gamma (the contrast in midtones of an image) to determine the proportion of darker tones to lighter tones.

1. **Open the file `chef.jpg` from the RF_Photoshop>Menu folder.**

   This image is extremely dark, with very little detail in the shadow area. The overall Brightness/Contrast adjustments could not correct this image since you need to change the position of points along the tonal range.

2. **Display the Histogram panel (Window>Histogram), and then choose Expanded View from the panel Options menu.**

   The Histogram panel can help you identify problems that need to be corrected. When you first display the panel, it probably appears in Compact view, which shows only the graphs for the individual color channels and the composite image.

3. **In the Histogram panel, change the Channel menu to RGB.**

   The histogram — the chart that shows the distribution of tones — can display a single graph for the entire composite image (all channels combined) or for individual channels.

   In Expanded view, the panel shows the distribution of pixels from the darkest to the lightest portion of the image, for the entire image or for individual color channels.

Choose from this menu to view and modify the histogram for individual channels.

These shadow values are pushing out of the histogram "container," which shows that there is a problem in the shadow tones.

The white space to the left of the histogram indicates that some tones in the available range are not being used.

4. **Click the Warning icon in the upper-right corner of the panel to reset the cache.**

Every time you zoom in or out of an image, Photoshop stores the results of the display in a **cache** (a drive location that keeps track of what you're doing). The image you're looking at on the Histogram often doesn't match the results on the drive. The Warning icon shows there's a problem; clicking the icon resets the image and rereads the cache.

Note:

If you see the Warning icon in the Histogram panel, click the icon to match the disk cache with what's happening in the live image.

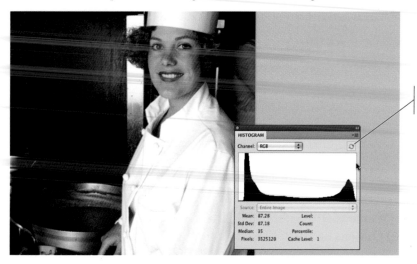

Clicking the Warning icon resets the cache.

Histogram Statistics

The histogram shows the distribution of pixels — or more accurately the tonal values of those pixels — from the darkest to the lightest portions of an image, for the entire image or for individual color channels. The Histogram panel can help identify problems that need to be corrected, while also showing you the overall effect of a potential correction you might be considering.

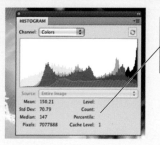

Expanded view of the Histogram panel shows detailed statistics about pixels on all or individual channels.

In Expanded view, you can see more information about how pixels are distributed in the image (from shadows on the left to midtones in the center to highlights on the right).

- The **Mean** value is an average point of the brightness values. A Mean of 128 usually identifies a well-balanced image. Images with a Mean of 170 to 255 are light; images with a Mean lower than 90 are very dark. (As you can see, the image you're working with in this exercise is relatively dark — a Mean of 87.50.)

- The **Standard Deviation** (Std Dev) value represents how widely the brightness values vary.

- The **Median** value shows the middle value in the range of color values.

- The **Pixels** value displays the total number of pixels used for the graphic displayed on the histogram.

- The **Level** statistic displays the intensity level of the pixels below the mouse cursor.

- **Count** is the same as pixels – but *only* for the area below the cursor (the Pixels value shows the total number for the histogram).

- Values displayed as a **Percentile** represent the percentage of pixels **below or to the left** of the cursor location. Zero represents the left edge of the image and 100% is the right edge.

- The **Cache Level** is determined by the Performance preferences (Preferences>Performance) and is related to the Cache Refresh icon (and Warning icon). The larger your cache, the more you can do before the image and the disk cache don't match. On the other hand, a larger cache requires more RAM for the application to run smoothly.

5. **Choose Image>Adjustments>Levels and make sure Preview is checked.**

The Levels dialog box shows a histogram like what you saw in the Histogram panel.

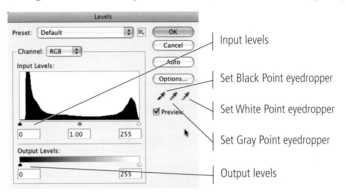

Input levels

Set Black Point eyedropper

Set White Point eyedropper

Set Gray Point eyedropper

Output levels

Note:

You can change input and output levels by moving the sliders, entering actual values in the boxes above the slider sets, or by using the eyedroppers to select the brightest and darkest points in the image.

The Levels dialog box has two sets of sliders to control input levels and output levels. Each set has a black slider for adjusting the shadows in an image and a white slider to adjust highlights. The Input Levels slider also has a gray triangle in the center of the slider bar for adjusting gamma or midtones.

The **tonal range** of an image is the amount of variation between the lightest highlight and the darkest shadow in a particular image. A grayscale image can contain 256 possible shades of gray. Each channel of a color image can also contain 256 possible shades of gray. To achieve the best contrast in an image, the tonal range of the image should include as many levels of gray as are available.

Note:

The Input sliders in the Levels dialog box correspond to the tonal range of the image.

6. **Move the Input Shadow slider to the right until it touches the left edge of the curve.**

This simple adjustment extends the colors in the image to take advantage of all 256 possible tones. This adjustment has a small effect on the shadow area of the image, but the majority of the colors in the image are still clustered near the shadow point (as you can see by the spike in the histogram).

Note:

Any pixels that exist to the left of the Input Shadow slider are reproduced as solid black, and they have no detail; any pixels that exist to the right of the Input Highlight slider are reproduced as pure white.

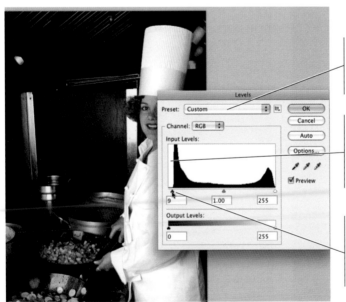

Choose from this menu to view and modify the histogram for an individual channel.

The white space to the left of the histogram indicates that some of the tones in the available range are not being used.

Dragging the Shadow Input slider to the left edge of the histogram extends the shadows into the full tonal range.

Note:

To decrease contrast in an image, you can adjust the Output sliders. This method effectively compresses the range of possible tones that can be reproduced, forcing all areas of the image into a smaller tonal range. Areas originally set to 0 are reproduced at the value of the Output Shadow slider; areas originally set to 255 are output at the value of the Output Highlight slider.

7. **Move the Input Gamma slider to the left until the middle box below the slider shows 2.0.**

   The Input Gamma slider allows you to control the proportion of darker tones to lighter tones in the midtones of an image.

   If you drag the slider to the left (increasing gamma), you increase the proportion of lighter grays in the image. This change effectively increases the contrast in lighter shades, but also lightens the entire image and decreases contrast in the darker areas.

   If you drag the slider to the right (decreasing gamma), you extend the tonal range of the darker grays; this method allows those areas of the image to be reproduced with a larger range of shades, which increases the contrast in the darker shades.

Note:

The entire image is lightened by increasing gamma.

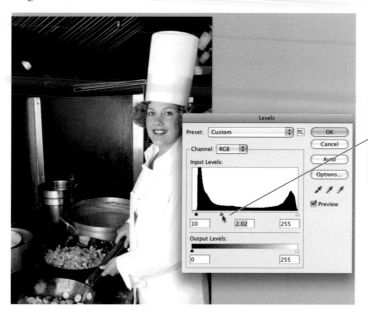

Dragging the Gamma Input slider extends the range between the midtone and the highlights, creating greater contrast and showing more detail throughout the image.

8. **Click OK to close the Levels dialog box.**

9. **Save the file in your WIP>Menu folder as a TIFF file named chef_fixed.tif and close the file.**

10. **Continue to the next exercise.**

Identifying Shadows and Highlights

As you moved the Shadow and Highlight sliders in the previous exercise, you changed the **black point** and **white point** of the image — the points at which pixels become black or white. The goal is to find highlight and shadow points that maintain detail. Choosing a point that has no detail causes the area to turn totally white (highlight) or black (shadow) with no detail reproduced. In some images, it can be difficult to visually identify the black and white points in an image; in these cases you can use the Levels dialog box to help you find those areas.

If you press Option/Alt while dragging the Input Shadow or Input Highlight slider, the image turns entirely white or black (respectively). As you drag, the first pixels that become visible are the darkest shadow and the lightest highlight.

Option/Alt dragging the Input Shadow slider turns the entire image white.

As you drag right, the first pixels that become visible in the image are the darkest shadows in the image.

Option/Alt clicking the Input Highlight slider turns the entire image black.

As you drag left, the first pixels that become visible represent the lightest highlight in the image.

These tiny specs might not be noticeable unless you look very carefully (and you have a dust-free monitor).

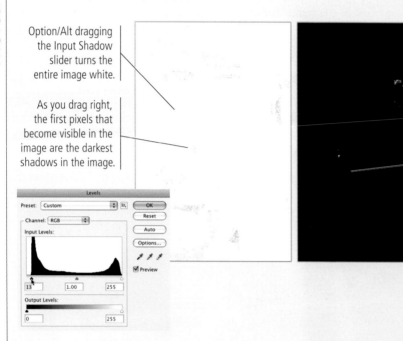

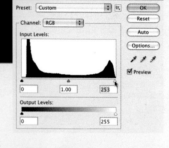

Once you have identified the highlight and shadow points in the image, select the White Point eyedropper and click the highlight, and then select the Black Point eyedropper and click the shadow to define those two areas of the image.

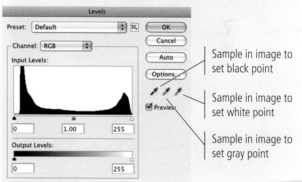

Sample in image to set black point

Sample in image to set white point

Sample in image to set gray point

CORRECT LIGHTING PROBLEMS WITH THE EXPOSURE ADJUSTMENT

Many images are either overexposed or underexposed when photographed. If an image is underexposed, the image appears dark and lacks detail in the shadows. If an image is overexposed, the image appears too light and lacks detail in the highlights. You can use the Exposure adjustment to correct the exposure — and thus, the overall detail and contrast in the image.

Keep in mind: Photoshop cannot create information that doesn't exist. If you have an underexposed image with no detail in the shadow areas, Photoshop cannot generate that detail for you. Some problems are simply beyond fixing.

The Exposure dialog box is designed to make tonal adjustments to 32-bit HDR (high dynamic range) images, but it also works with 8-bit and 16-bit images. The Exposure Adjustment works by performing calculations in a linear color space (gamma 1.0) rather than the image's current color space.

Note:

Note: HDR stands for high-density range (32-bit) images.

The Gradient Map Adjustment

PHOTOSHOP FOUNDATIONS

The **Gradient Map adjustment** (Image>Adjustments>Gradient Map) enables you to create interesting artistic effects by mapping the tones of an image to the shades in a defined gradient.

In the Gradient Map dialog box, you can apply any defined gradient by clicking the arrow to the right of the gradient sample and choosing from the pop-up menu, or you can edit the selected gradient by clicking the sample gradient ramp. The **Dither** option adds random noise to the effect. If you check the **Reverse** option, image highlights map to the left end of the gradient, and image shadows map to the right end of the gradient, effectively reversing the gradient map.

The composite histogram of an RGB image starts at the darkest point and ends at the lightest point with 256 total possible tonal values. If you think of the gradient as having 256 steps from one end to the other, then you can see how the shades of the selected gradient map to the tones of the original image.

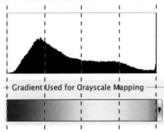

1. **Open chicken.jpg from the RF_Photoshop>Menu folder.**

2. **Choose Image>Adjustments>Exposure and make sure Preview is checked.**

3. **Click the White Point eyedropper, and then click the white area on the top edge of the plate.**

   The eyedroppers in the Exposure dialog box adjust the image's luminance (or the degree of lightness, from white to black). By adjusting the luminance only, you can change the lightness of the image without affecting the color.

   - Clicking with the Black Point eyedropper shifts the point you click to black (0 luminance).
   - Clicking with the White Point eyedropper shifts the point you click to white (100 luminance).
   - Clicking with the Gray Point eyedropper shifts the point you click to gray (50 luminance).

   Note:

   The White Point and Gray Point eyedroppers affect the Exposure value. The Black Point eyedropper affects the Offset value.

Click here with the White Point eyedropper to define the white area of the image.

Clicking with the White Point eyedropper changes the Exposure setting.

White Point eyedropper
Gray Point eyedropper
Black Point eyedropper

4. **Drag the Gamma Correction slider left to extend the midtone range, which increases contrast and brings out detail in the image. (We used a setting of 1.25.)**

The Gamma slider adjusts the image midtones. Dragging the slider left lightens the image, improving contrast and detail in the midtones and highlights. Dragging the slider right darkens the image, extending the range and increasing detail in the shadows.

Extending the Gamma Correction value into the shadow range brings out more detail in the midtones.

5. **Click OK to finalize the adjustment.**

6. **Save the file as a TIFF file named** `chicken_fixed.tif` **in your WIP>Menu folder.**

7. **Close the file and continue to the next stage of the project.**

Note:

The Offset slider lightens (dragged to the right) or darkens (dragged to the left) the shadows and midtones of the image. The white point (highlight) remains unaffected, but all other pixels are affected.

Stage 3 **Correcting Color Problems**

Before starting to color-correct an image, you need to understand how different colors interact with one another. Remember from Project 3: Two primary color models — RGB and CMYK — are used to output digital images. (Other models such as LAB and HSL have their own purposes in color conversion and correction, but they are not typically output models.)

Although the RGB and CMYK models handle color in different ways, these two color models are definitely linked. RGB colors are directly inverse (opposite) to CMY colors, referring to the position of each color on a color wheel. The relationship between primary colors is the basis for all color correction.

Referencing a basic color wheel can help you understand how RGB colors relate to CMY colors. If you center an equilateral triangle over the color wheel, the points of the triangle touch either the RGB primaries or the CMY primaries. Adding together two points of the triangle results in the color between the two points. Red and blue combine to form magenta, yellow and cyan combine to form green, and so on.

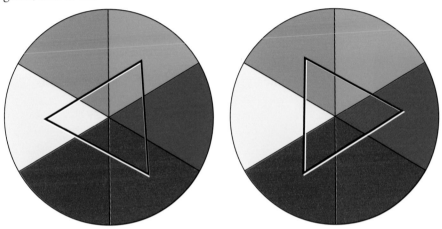

Opposite colors on the color wheel are called **color complements**. Using subtractive color theory, a color's complement absorbs or subtracts that color from visible white light. For example, cyan is opposite red on the color wheel; cyan absorbs red light and reflects green and blue. Because you know green and blue light combine to create cyan, you can begin to understand how the two theories are related.

How does all this apply to color correction?

If you want to add a specific color to an image, you have three options: add the color, add equal parts of its constituent colors, or remove some of its complement color. For example, to add red to an image, you can add red, add yellow and magenta, or remove cyan. Conversely, this means that to remove a color from an image, you can remove the color itself, remove equal parts of its constituents, or add its complement. To remove cyan from an image, for example, you can remove cyan, remove blue and green, or add red.

Make sure you understand the relationships between complementary colors:

- To add red, add yellow and magenta or remove cyan.

- To add blue, add cyan and magenta or remove yellow.

- To add green, add cyan and yellow or remove magenta.

- To remove cyan, remove blue and green or add red.

- To remove yellow, remove green and red or add blue.

- To remove magenta, remove blue and red or add green.

Note:

While it might seem easiest to simply add or subtract the color in question, a better result might be achieved by adding one color and subtracting another. For example, if an image needs less blue, simply removing cyan can cause reds to appear pink or cyan to appear green. Adding magenta and yellow to balance the existing cyan creates a better result than simply removing cyan.

Note:

An important point to remember is that any color correction requires compromise. If you add or remove a color to correct a certain area, you also affect other areas of the image.

Many vague and technical-sounding terms are mentioned when discussing color. Is hue the same as color? The same as value? As tone? What's the difference between lightness and brightness? What is chroma? And where does saturation fit in?

This problem has resulted in several attempts to normalize color communication. A number of systems have been developed to define color according to specific criteria, including Hue, Saturation, and Brightness (HSB); Hue, Saturation, and Lightness (HSL); Hue, Saturation, and Value (HSV); and Lightness, Chroma, and Hue (LCH). Each of these models or systems plots color on a three-dimensional diagram, based on the elements of human color perception — hue, colorfulness, and brightness.

Hue is what most people think of as color — red, green, purple, and so on. Hue is defined according to a color's position on a color wheel, beginning from red (0°) and traveling counterclockwise around the wheel.

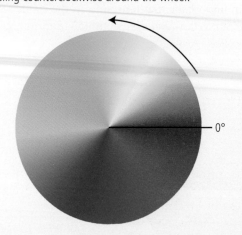

Saturation (also called "intensity") refers to the color's difference from neutral gray. Highly saturated colors are more vivid than those with low saturation. Saturation is plotted from the center of the color wheel. Color at the center is neutral gray and has a saturation value of 0; color at the edge of the wheel is the most intense value of the corresponding hue and has a saturation value of 100.

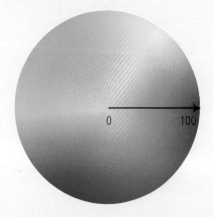

If you bisect the color wheel with a straight line, the line creates a saturation axis for two complementary colors. A color is dulled by the introduction of its complement. Red, for example, is neutralized by the addition of cyan (blue and green). Near the center of the axis, the result is neutral gray.

Chroma is similar to saturation, but chroma factors in a reference white. In any viewing situation, colors appear less vivid as the light source dims. The process of chromatic adaptation, however, allows the human visual system to adjust to changes in light and still differentiate colors according to the relative saturation.

Brightness is the amount of light reflected off an object. As an element of color reproduction, brightness is typically judged by comparing the color to the lightest nearby object (such as an unprinted area of white paper).

Lightness is the amount of white or black added to the pure color. Lightness (also called "luminance" or "value") is the relative brightness based purely on the black-white value of a color. A lightness value of 0 means there is no addition of white or black. Lightness of +100 is pure white; lightness of −100 is pure black.

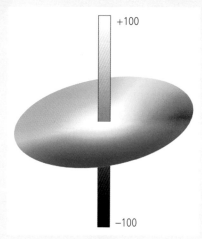

All hues are affected equally by changes in lightness.

Understanding Gray Balance

Understanding the concept of neutral gray is fundamental to effective color correction. Once you correct the contrast (tonal range) of an image, many of the remaining problems can be at least partially (if not entirely) corrected by correcting the **gray balance**, or the component elements of neutral grays within an image.

In the RGB color model, equal parts of red, green, and blue combine to create a shade of gray that is equal to the percentage of each component — R=0 G=0 B=0 creates pure black, while R=255 G=255 B=255 creates pure white. The RGB model uses light to create color, so equal percentages of red, green, and blue combine to create an equal, neutral shade of gray. To correct an image in RGB mode, you should evaluate and correct the neutral grays so they contain equal percentages of the three primary colors.

Using the CMYK color model, equal percentages of cyan, magenta, and yellow theoretically combine to produce an equal shade of gray — C=0 M=0 Y=0 creates pure white, while C=100 M=100 Y=100 theoretically creates pure black. As you learned earlier, however, the impurities of inks pigments — specifically cyan — do not live up to this theory. When you print an area of equal parts cyan, magenta, and yellow, the result is a muddy brown because the cyan pigments are impure. To compensate for the impurities of cyan, neutral grays must be adjusted to contain equal parts of magenta and yellow, and a slightly higher percentage of cyan.

Note:

The following exercise relies purely on numbers to correct gray balance. To see an accurate preview of image color on screen, you should calibrate your monitor and create a monitor profile that you can load into Photoshop.

CORRECT COLOR CAST WITH THE COLOR BALANCE ADJUSTMENT

Color cast is the result of improper gray balance, when one channel is significantly stronger or weaker than the others. An image with improper gray balance has an overall predominance of one color, which is most visible in the highlight areas. The image you correct in this exercise has a strong green cast, which needs to be removed.

1. **Open the file salmon.jpg from the RF_Photoshop>Menu folder.**

2. **Display the Info panel (Window>Info).**

   The Info panel displays color information for the current location of the cursor. You can view color values in both RGB and CMYK for the same pixel.

3. **Choose the Color Sampler tool (nested under the Eyedropper tool) in the Tools panel.**

Note:

If you don't see both color modes, choose Panel Options in the panel Options menu. You can change the color mode for each sample.

Color Sampler tool

The Color Sampler tool can place up to four sample points in the image.

Color values for the current cursor location, in both RGB and CMYK modes.

4. In the Control panel, choose 3 by 3 Average in the Sample Size menu.

Instead of correcting based on individual pixel values, you can average a group of contiguous pixels as the sample value. Doing so prevents accidentally correcting an image based on a single anomalous pixel (a dust spot, for example).

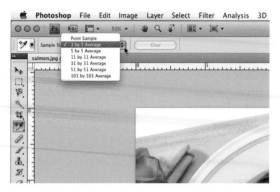

Note:

Some people find it helpful to work in Full Screen mode when correcting color to eliminate distracting color from other windows or applications that are open behind Photoshop.

5. Click the cursor on the lower-left plate lip to place a color sample.

6. Click to add a second sample point to the top-right plate lip.

The two samples show a strong predominance of green; these numbers reflect the visible color cast in the image.

Sample points are numbered in order of creation.

This is the color sample we placed in Step 5.

The Info panel now shows the values associated with each of the two sample points you created.

7. Choose Image>Adjustments>Color Balance.

Color Balance is a basic correction tool that can effectively remove overall color cast. The Color Balance dialog box presents three sliders for each pair of complementary colors. You can adjust the highlights, shadows, or midtones of an image by selecting the appropriate radio button; the Preserve Luminosity check box ensures that only the colors shift, leaving the tonal balance of the image unchanged.

Note:

Delete an existing sample point by Option/Alt-clicking the point.

8. Click the Highlights radio button in the Tone Balance section.

The focal point of this image is green spinach, which you don't want to affect. Instead, you need to remove the green cast from the highlight, where it is most obvious.

9. **Drag the Magenta/Green slider left until the middle field shows −10.**

   Remember, adding a color's complement is one method for neutralizing that color. Increasing magenta in the highlight areas neutralizes the green color cast.

You'll see the color correct as you move the slider; but always double check statistical values through the use of the Info, Histogram, and other related panels.

These fields correspond to the three color sliders. The middle field shows the Magenta/Green adjustment.

The values after the "/" show the result of the dialog box changes, which will be the actual sample values if you click OK in the Color Balance dialog box.

Changing the color balance brings the three values much closer to equal (called "in balance").

10. **Click OK to apply the adjustment.**

11. **Save the file in your WIP>Menu folder as a TIFF file named** `salmon_fixed.tif`.

12. **Close the file and continue to the next exercise.**

The Variations Adjustment

PHOTOSHOP FOUNDATIONS

The Variations adjustment allows you to make adjustments based strictly on visible information. You can see a preview of the original image compared to the result of any changes you make. The lower-left area of the window shows the result of adding any single primary color to the part of the image selected with the radio buttons (Shadows, Midtones, Highlights, or Saturation). You can also darken or lighten the image by clicking an option in the right column of the window. The Variations adjustment is a quick and easy technique, but it lacks the fine control of other correction methods.

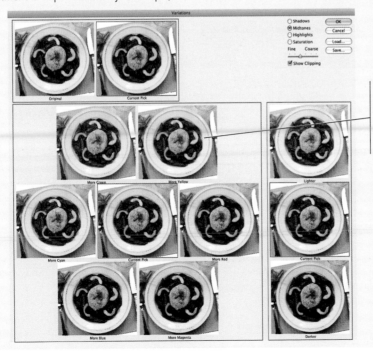

The Variations dialog box is conveniently arranged in the same order as the basic color wheel; the additive primaries are in between the correct subtractive primary pairs.

CORRECT GRAY BALANCE WITH CURVES

The diagram in the Curves dialog box is the heart of the Curves adjustment. When you open the Curves dialog box, a straight diagonal line in the graph represents the existing color in the image.

Note:

The Curves adjustment is the most powerful color-correction tool in Photoshop. If you understand the ideas behind curves, you can use this tool to remove color cast, enhance overall contrast, and even modify color values in individual channels.

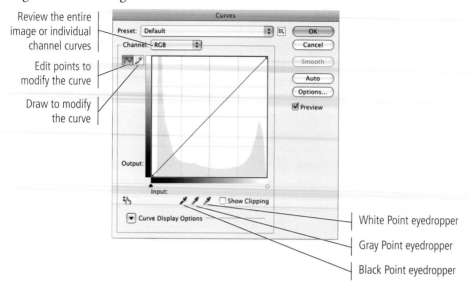

Review the entire image or individual channel curves

Edit points to modify the curve

Draw to modify the curve

White Point eyedropper

Gray Point eyedropper

Black Point eyedropper

The horizontal axis represents the input color value, and the vertical axis represents the output color value. The upper-right point is the maximum value for that color mode (255 for RGB images and 100 for CMYK images). The bottom-left corner of the curves grid is the zero point.

The color mode of the image determines the direction of the input and output scales. In both CMYK and RGB, 0 means "none of that color." However, remember the difference between the two different color modes:

- The additive RGB color model starts at black and adds values of each channel to produce different colors, so 0, 0, 0 in RGB equals black.

- The subtractive CMYK model starts with white (paper) and adds percentages of each ink (channel) to produce different colors, so 0, 0, 0, 0 in CMYK equals white.

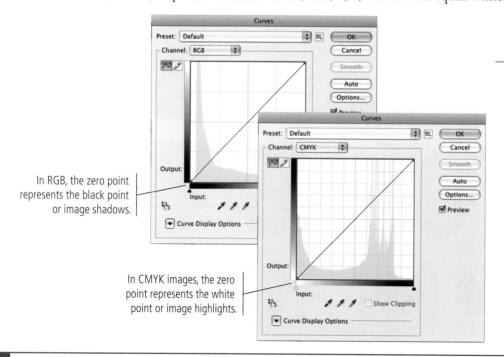

In RGB, the zero point represents the black point or image shadows.

In CMYK images, the zero point represents the white point or image highlights.

Note:

Remember, the additive colors (RGB) at full strength combine to create pure white, while the subtractive colors (CMYK) at full strength combine to create pure black.

Every curve is automatically anchored by a black point and a white point. (For RGB, the black point is at the bottom left and the white point is at the top right.) You can add points along the curve by simply clicking the curve. You can also move any point on the curve by clicking and dragging.

When you move points on the curve of an image (whether for the whole image or for an individual channel), you are telling Photoshop to, "Map every pixel that was [this] input value to [that] output value." In other words, using the following image as an example, a pixel that was 128 (the input value) will now be 114 (the output value). Because curves are just that — curves, and not individual points — adjusting one point on a curve changes the shape of the curve as necessary.

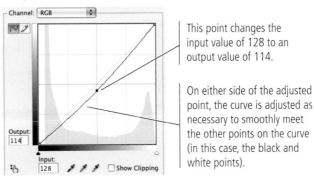

This point changes the input value of 128 to an output value of 114.

On either side of the adjusted point, the curve is adjusted as necessary to smoothly meet the other points on the curve (in this case, the black and white points).

1. **Open the file flan.jpg from the RF_Photoshop>Menu folder.**

2. **Using the Color Sampler tool, place a sample point on the left plate lip.**

   This image has a strong red cast, which needs to be neutralized. You can correct cast by removing the cast color or adding the other two primaries; the goal is equal (or nearly equal) parts of red, green, and blue in the neutral areas such as the plate lip.

The sample shows a strong red cast in what should be neutral areas.

Note:

Easily recognizable "neutral" areas — such as the white plate in this image — are the best places to look for global color problems; fixing these will also fix many problem areas you can't immediately recognize.

Note:

Your sample might be in a slightly different place, showing slightly different values. Use the values you see on your screen, rather than the numbers in our screen shots, to complete the following steps.

   In the Info panel, the sample values show that the red channel has a value of 232, the blue channel has a value of 214, and the green channel has a value of 215. To fix the cast in this image, you will use the middle of these values (the green channel) as the target and adjust the other two curves.

3. **Choose Image>Adjustments>Curves and make sure the Preview option is checked in the Curves dialog box.**

4. **Choose Red in the Channel menu to display the curve for only the Red channel, and then click the line on the graph to place a point near the three-quarter grid intersection.**

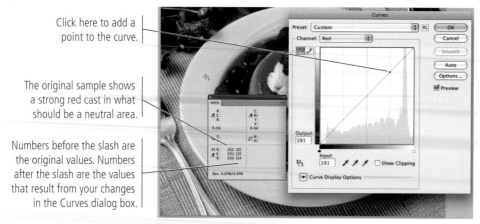

Click here to add a point to the curve.

The original sample shows a strong red cast in what should be a neutral area.

Numbers before the slash are the original values. Numbers after the slash are the values that result from your changes in the Curves dialog box.

5. **With the new point selected on the curve, type the original Red value in the Input field (ours is 232).**

6. **Type the original Green value in the Output field (ours is 215).**

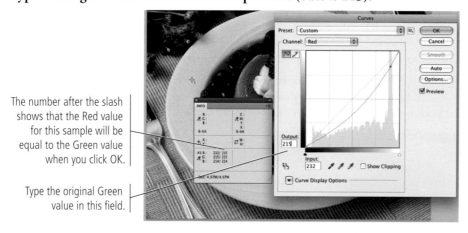

The number after the slash shows that the Red value for this sample will be equal to the Green value when you click OK.

Type the original Green value in this field.

7. **Choose Blue in the Channel menu.**

8. **Add a point to the curve, and then adjust the input value to match your target output value (the original Green value). Using our sample point, we adjusted the 214 Input value to a 215 Output value.**

You can add the point anywhere along the curve; when you change the Input value to 214, the point automatically moves to that location along the curve.

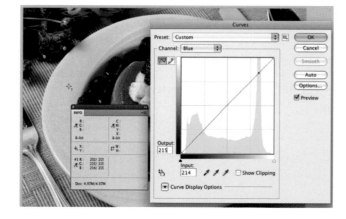

Curve Display Options

The Curve Display options allow you to control what is visible in the graph. (If you can't see the Curve Display options, click the button to the left of the heading.) The Show Amount Of radio buttons reverse the input and output tone scales. Light is the default setting for RGB images; Pigment/Ink % is the default setting for CMYK images.

The On-Image adjustment tool lets you click and/or drag directly on an image to determine where the point should appear on the curve. You can add 14 points on a curve, and delete points by pressing Command/Control-delete.

Click this button to show or hide the Curve Display options.

By default, the lightest point for an RGB image is in the top right.

The darkest point for an RGB image is in the bottom left.

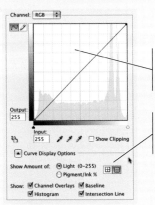

Gridlines in the graph can help you more precisely position curve points.

Use these buttons to show a four-by-four grid or a ten-by-ten grid.

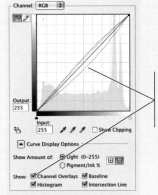

By choosing Show Amount of Pigment/Ink %, the tone scales are reversed. For this RGB image, the lightest point moves to the bottom left and darkest point moves to the top right.

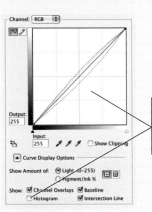

When the Histogram option is turned off, the graph does not show the representative histogram.

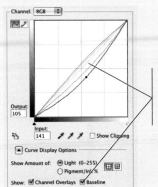

When the Channel Overlays option is checked, each channel is represented on the graph by a separate line.

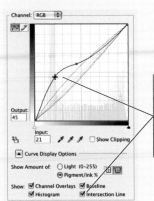

When the Intersection Line option is active, crosshairs appear when you drag a point in the graph, which can help you more precisely adjust curve points.

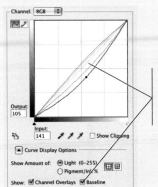

When the Baseline option is active, the original curve is represented by a gray line.

9. **Click OK to apply the change and close the Curves dialog box.**

You can see how simply correcting gray balance has a significant impact on the image.

10. **Save the file in your WIP>Menu folder as a TIFF file named flan_fixed.tif.**

11. **Close the file and continue to the next exercise.**

Adjusting Curves On-Screen

The On Image Adjustment tool in the Curves dialog box allows you to make curve adjustments by interacting directly with the image (behind the dialog box). When the On Image Adjustment tool is active, clicking in the image places a point on the curve based on the pixel data where you clicked; you can then drag up or down within the image area to move that point of the curve (in other words, to change the output value of the selected input value).

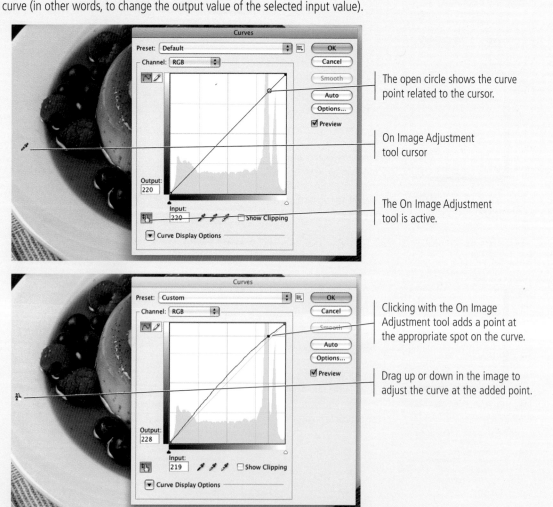

The open circle shows the curve point related to the cursor.

On Image Adjustment tool cursor

The On Image Adjustment tool is active.

Clicking with the On Image Adjustment tool adds a point at the appropriate spot on the curve.

Drag up or down in the image to adjust the curve at the added point.

CORRECT CONTRAST WITH CURVES

Remember, contrast is essentially the difference between values in an image. By adjusting the points on the curve, you increase the tonal range between those points — which means you also increase the contrast in that same range.

In the following image, Point A has an Input value of 167 and an Output value of 182. Point B has an Input value of 87 and an Output value of 62. Mathematically:

- Original tonal range (Input values): 167 to 87 = 80 available tones

- New tonal range (Output values): 182 to 62 = 120 available tones

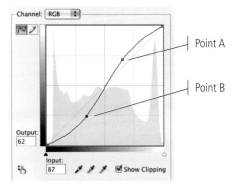

By making these two curve adjustments, we significantly increased the tonal range available for the image's midtones, which means we also significantly increased the contrast in the midtones. A steeper curve indicates increased tonal range and increased contrast. Notice, however, that the curves before Point B and after Point A are much shallower than the original curves, which means this change also significantly reduced the contrast in the shadow and highlight areas.

Points to Remember about Curves

Curves are very powerful tools, and they can be intimidating. To simplify the process and make it less daunting, keep these points in mind:

- Aim for neutral grays.

- You can adjust the curve for an entire image, or you can adjust the individual curve for each channel of the image.

- The bottom tone scale shows the Input value, and the left tone scale shows the Output value.

- Changes made to one area of a curve affect all other areas of the image.

- The steeper the curve, the greater the contrast.

- Increasing contrast in one area inherently decreases the contrast in other areas of the image.

1. **Open the file pasta.jpg from the RF_Photoshop>Menu folder.**

   This image lacks contrast, which makes the colors appear flat and washed out.

2. **Choose Image>Adjustments>Curves and make sure Preview is checked.**

As with Levels, the empty area at the left of the histogram shows that the image does not use the entire available tonal range.

3. **Activate the Show Clipping option, click the black point on the bottom-left corner of the graph, and then drag until some pixels start to appear in the image (behind the dialog box).**

   We dragged the Input Black point just past the point where the histogram shows the darkest shadows in the image. (You performed this same action in the Levels dialog box when you adjusted the Input Shadow slider.) The Input and Output fields show that any pixels with an Input value of 13 will be output as 0; anything with an Input value lower than 13 will be clipped to solid black.

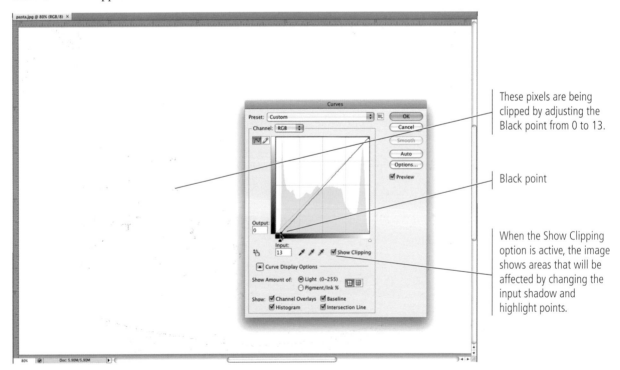

These pixels are being clipped by adjusting the Black point from 0 to 13.

Black point

When the Show Clipping option is active, the image shows areas that will be affected by changing the input shadow and highlight points.

4. **Repeat Step 3, dragging the White point left until the lightest areas of the image start to appear behind the dialog box.**

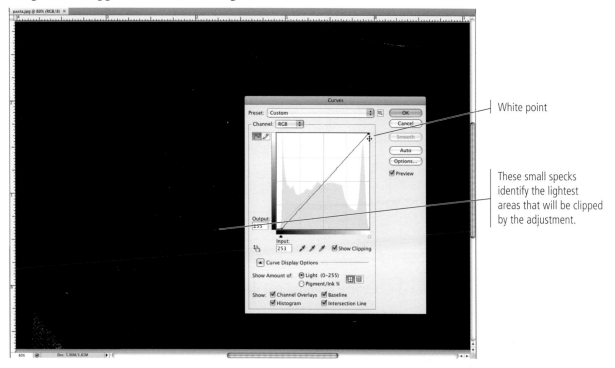

White point

These small specks identify the lightest areas that will be clipped by the adjustment.

5. **Turn off the Show Clipping option so you can see the actual image behind the dialog box.**

Even this small change improved the image, but the midtones — especially in the pasta, which is the focal area of the image — need some additional contrast. To accomplish that change, you need to steepen the curve in the middle of the graph.

6. **Click the curve to create a point at the quartertone gridline and drag it slightly to the right.**

We adjusted the curve point from an Input value of 81 to an Output value of 62.

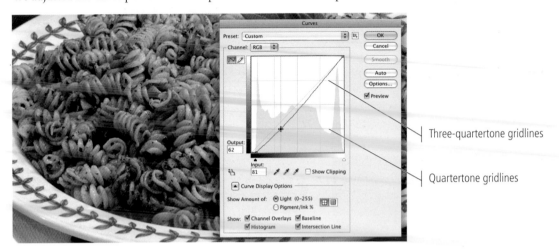

Three-quartertone gridlines

Quartertone gridlines

7. **Click the curve at the three-quartertone gridline and drag the point to the left.**

We adjusted the 175 Input value to a 190 Output value.

The adjusted points steepen the curve, increasing contrast between the two points.

8. **Click OK to apply the changes and close the dialog box.**

Adjusting the contrast with curves improved the detail in the image and enhanced the overall image color.

9. **Save the file in your WIP>Menu folder as a TIFF file named pasta_fixed.tif.**

10. **Close the file and continue to the next stage of the project.**

Note:

Contrast adjustments can have a major impact on color as well as on sharpness. Take particular note of the green basil leaves; no direct color adjustment was done to these two images, but the leaves are noticeably greener and brighter after you adjust the curves.

Stage 4 **Preparing Images for Print**

You might have noticed that all the images for this project are in the RGB color mode. Printing, however, relies on the CMYK mode to output color images. And as you might remember from Project 3, the CMYK mode has a much smaller gamut than the RGB mode — which means some colors might be lost when RGB values are converted to CMYK values for output (called **color compression** or **color shift**).

This problem leads to two different schools of thought about when to correct colors — in the original RGB image (before converting to CMYK) or in the converted CMYK image (after color shift has already occurred). Most experts lean toward the first option since images are often used for multiple media, some of which require the RGB model. By correcting in RGB, you can do your color corrections once and use the same corrected file for different types of output.

When you correct images that will be printed, however, remember that colors outside the CMYK gamut will shift based on the selected rendering intent (refer to the discussion of color management in Project 3). It simply doesn't make sense to blindly allow Photoshop to shift the colors you so painstakingly corrected.

CORRECT OUT-OF-GAMUT COLOR WITH CURVES

Fortunately, Photoshop contains the necessary tools for previewing out-of-gamut colors, which means you can correct colors *before* converting an image. If you have no out-of-gamut colors, then there is nothing to shift, and you can be fairly confident that your color images will be reproduced as you intended.

1. **Open the file salad.jpg from the RF_Photoshop>Menu folder.**

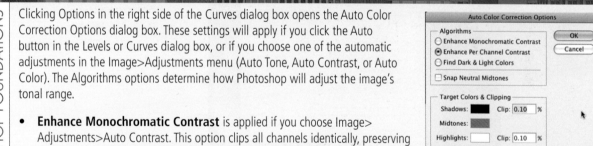

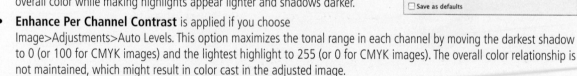

Automatic Color Correction

PHOTOSHOP FOUNDATIONS

Clicking Options in the right side of the Curves dialog box opens the Auto Color Correction Options dialog box. These settings will apply if you click the Auto button in the Levels or Curves dialog box, or if you choose one of the automatic adjustments in the Image>Adjustments menu (Auto Tone, Auto Contrast, or Auto Color). The Algorithms options determine how Photoshop will adjust the image's tonal range.

- **Enhance Monochromatic Contrast** is applied if you choose Image> Adjustments>Auto Contrast. This option clips all channels identically, preserving overall color while making highlights appear lighter and shadows darker.

- **Enhance Per Channel Contrast** is applied if you choose Image>Adjustments>Auto Levels. This option maximizes the tonal range in each channel by moving the darkest shadow to 0 (or 100 for CMYK images) and the lightest highlight to 255 (or 0 for CMYK images). The overall color relationship is not maintained, which might result in color cast in the adjusted image.

- **Find Dark & Light Colors** is applied if you choose Image>Adjustments>Auto Color. This option uses the average lightest and darkest pixels in an image to maximize contrast while minimizing clipping.

- **Snap Neutral Midtones** is also applied if you choose Image>Adjustments>Auto Color. This option finds an average neutral color in an image, and then adjusts the midtone (gamma) values to make the color neutral.

In the Target Areas & Clipping options, you can define the target shadow, midtone, and highlight values by clicking the appropriate color swatch. The Clip fields determine how much of the darkest shadow and lightest highlight will be clipped (ignored) when you apply an automatic adjustment. In other words, a Shadow Clip setting of 1% means Photoshop will ignore the first 1% of the darkest pixels when adjusting the image.

If you change the Target Areas & Clipping settings, you can save those settings as the defaults by checking the Save As Defaults option. You can then apply those settings by clicking the Auto button in the Levels or Curves dialog box.

2. Choose Edit>Assign Profile.

You can use this dialog box to change the profile you're using for this image. If an image has an embedded profile, the third radio button is selected and the embedded profile appears in the list. You can choose to not color manage the image, change to your working profile, or choose any other available profile from the Profile menu.

This image uses the Adobe RGB (1998) profile.

3. Click OK to close the Assign Profile dialog box.

Remember, color management relies on profiles to accurately translate color from one model to another. This dialog box shows you the starting point — the embedded image profile.

4. Choose Edit>Color Settings. In the Color Settings dialog box, make sure U.S. Sheetfed Coated v2 is selected in the Working Spaces CMYK menu, and then click OK.

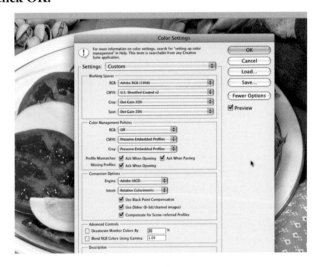

Note:

Photoshop CS4 ships with a large collection of common profiles, which are meant to meet the needs of diverse manufacturing environments in which Photoshop is used for what's commonly called **prepress** *(the process of getting images ready to print).*

5. Choose View>Proof Colors.

This toggle provides a quick preview of what will happen when the image is converted to the CMYK working-space profile — without affecting the actual file data.

Note:

We assume this restaurant menu will be printed on a sheetfed press. However, always ask your output provider what profile to use for a specific job.

View>Proof Colors shows that converting this image will result in a dramatic shift in the red areas of the image.

6. **Choose View>Proof Colors again to display the actual RGB image.**

The Proof Colors and Gamut Warning displays are toggles; when you select them, they turn on if they were off or turn off if they were on.

7. **Choose View>Gamut Warning.**

The areas that shifted are now highlighted with a gray overlay. This overlay shows you exactly what you need to correct; when this image is printed on a commercial sheetfed press, those regions will not reproduce as expected.

Note:

Command/Control-Y toggles the Proof Colors view on or off.

Shift-Command/Control-Y toggles the Gamut Warning View.

Note:

If you continued to this project directly from Project 3, the Gamut Warning might appear as a red overlay (which you defined in Project 3). You can change it back to gray in the Transparency & Gamut pane of the Preferences dialog box.

8. **Save the file as salad.psd, and continue to the next exercise.**

ADJUST HIGHLIGHT AND SHADOW POINTS FOR PRINT

For images that will be commercially printed, some allowance must be made in the highlight and shadow areas for the mechanics of the printing process. In CMYK images, shades of gray are reproduced using combinations of four printing inks. In theory, a solid black would be printed as 100% of all four inks, and pure white would be 0% of all four inks. This, however, does not take into consideration the limitations of mechanical printing.

To accurately reproduce highlights and shadows on a commercial printing press, you need to understand the concept of minimum printable dot and maximum printable dot.

Images are printed as a pattern of closely spaced dots called a **halftone**. When viewed on the page, the dots create the illusion of continuous color. Different sizes of dots create different shades of color — larger dots create darker shades and smaller dots create lighter shades.

There is a limit to the smallest size dot that can be faithfully and consistently reproduced. A 1% dot is so small that the mechanical aspect of the printing process causes anything specified as a 1% dot to drop out, resulting in highlights that lack detail and contrast. The **minimum printable dot**, then, is the smallest printable dot, and should be specified for highlights in a CMYK image. There is some debate over the appropriate highlight setting because different presses and imaging equipment have varying capabilities. To be sure your highlights will work on most printing equipment, you should define the highlight as C=5 M=3 Y=3 K=0.

Maximum printable dot is the opposite of minimum printable dot. The paper's absorption rate, speed of the printing press, and other mechanical factors limit the amount of ink that can be placed on the same area of a page. If too much ink is printed, the result is a dark blob with no visible detail; heavy layers of ink also result in drying problems, smearing, and a number of other issues.

Total ink coverage is the largest percentage of ink that can be safely printed on a single area, and therefore dictates the shadow dot you define in Photoshop. This number, similar to minimum printable dot, varies according to the ink/paper/press combination being used for a given job. The Specifications for Web Offset Publications (SWOP, www.swop.org) indicates a 300% maximum value. Many sheetfed printers require 280% maximum, while the number for newspapers is usually around 240% because the lower-quality paper absorbs more ink.

Unless your images will be printed in a newspaper, 290% is an acceptable shadow for most applications. You can safely define shadows as C=80 M=70 Y=70 K=70. If you need to adjust a lower or higher number for specific projects, you can do so at any time.

1. **With salad.psd open and the gamut warning visible, choose Image>Adjustments>Curves.**

2. **Double-click the White Point eyedropper.**

3. **In the Select Target Highlight Color dialog box, change the CMYK values to C=5 M=3 Y=3 K=0 and click OK.**

Note:

Even though you are working on an RGB image, you can still correct it to target CMYK white and black values.

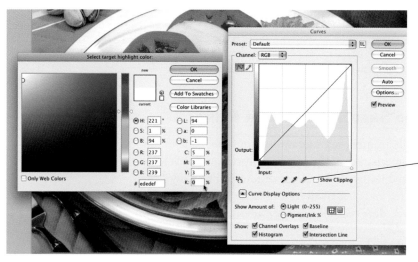

Double-click the White Point eyedropper to open the Select Target Highlight Color dialog box.

4. **With the White Point eyedropper selected, click the lightest highlight in the image where you want to maintain detail.**

We used this plate edge as the white point.

5. **Double-click the Black Point eyedropper. Change the target CMYK values to C=80 M=70 Y=70 K=70, and then click OK.**

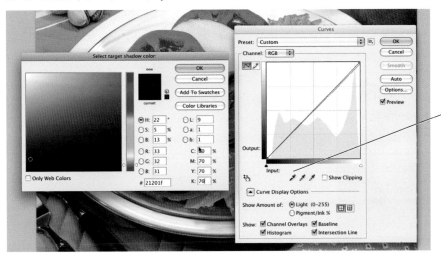

Double-click the Black Point eyedropper to open the Select Target Shadow Color dialog box.

6. **With the Black Point eyedropper selected, click the darkest area of the image where you want to maintain shadow detail.**

By defining the target highlight and shadow points in the image, you can see that the gray gamut warning is nearly gone from the green areas, and it's significantly reduced in the red areas.

We used this shadow as the black point.

7. **Display the curve for the Red channel only.**

8. **Add a point near the midpoint, and then drag the point down to steepen the overall Red curve.**

Just a slight adjustment, from 146 Input to 116 Output, removes nearly all the gamut warning from the image.

9. **Display the curve for the Green channel and make adjustments until most or all of the gamut warning is gone.**

Experiment with points along the curve until you are satisfied that the gamut warning has been removed.

10. **Click OK to apply your changes.**

11. **Click No in the warning message.**

If you change the target Black Point, Gray Point, or White Point eyedropper values, Photoshop asks if you want to save the new target values as the default settings when you click OK to close the Curves dialog box.

Note:

You can turn the gamut warning off and on while the Curves dialog box is open. Simply choose the option from the View menu and toggle the gray overlay off and on.

12. Save the file and continue to the next exercise.

Because the RGB gamut is so much larger than the CMYK gamut, you can expect colors to be far less brilliant (especially in the outer ranges of saturation) when corrected to the CMYK gamut. It's better to know this will happen and control it, rather than simply allow the color management engine to shift colors where it deems best.

CONVERTING IMAGE COLOR MODES

Although many modern workflows convert RGB images to CMYK during the output process (called "on-the-fly" or "in-RIP conversion"), there are times when you need to manually convert RGB images to CMYK. This is a fairly simple process, especially if you have corrected your images to meet the requirements of the printing process.

1. With the corrected salad image open from the previous exercise, choose Image>Mode>CMYK.

This menu option converts the image to the CMYK color mode using the current working space profile. Since you intentionally defined the working profile and corrected the image to that profile, you can safely use this menu option to convert the RGB image to CMYK.

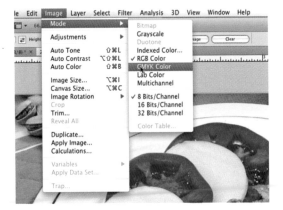

2. Click OK in the resulting warning dialog box.

If you had not completed the process in the previous series of exercises, you shouldn't convert the image color mode. Color mode is not something that should be simply switched on a whim, but is rather the final stage of a specific process.

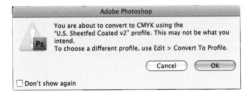

If you didn't precisely follow this workflow, but you are certain the image colors are correct, you can convert an image to a different model by choosing Edit>Convert to Profile and choosing any available profile in the Destination Space Profile menu.

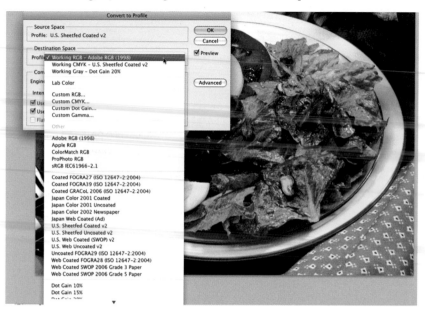

3. **Choose File>Save As and navigate to your WIP>Menu folder as the target.**

4. **Change the Format/Save As Type menu to TIFF, and then add _CMYK to the end of the existing file name (before the extension).**

5. **Macintosh users: In the bottom half of the Save As dialog box, make sure the Embed Color Profile:U.S. Sheetfed Coated v2 option is checked.**

   Windows users: In the bottom half of the Save As dialog box, make sure the ICC Profile: U.S. Sheetfed Coated v2 option is checked.

   This image has been corrected and converted to the U.S. Sheetfed Coated v2 color profile. By embedding the profile into the TIFF file, other applications and devices with color management capabilities will be able to correctly process the image color data in the file, based on the embedded profile.

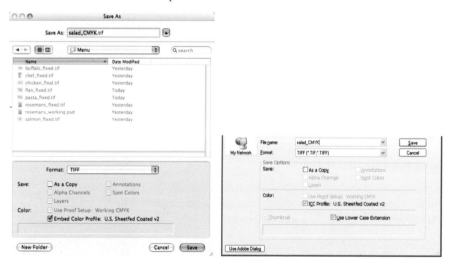

6. **Click Save, and then click OK to accept the default TIFF options.**

7. **Close the file.**

Converting Images to Grayscale

PHOTOSHOP FOUNDATIONS

An RGB image has three channels and a CMYK image has four channels; each channel is a grayscale representation of the tones of that color throughout the image. A grayscale image has only one channel; the grayscale tones in that channel are the tones in the entire image. Choosing Image>Mode>Grayscale simply flattens the component color channels, throwing away the color information to create the gray channel.

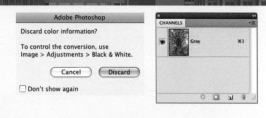

The Desaturate adjustment (Image>Adjustments>Desaturate) has a similar effect, but maintains the same number of channels as the original image. This adjustment averages the individual channel values for each pixel and applies the average value in each channel. (Remember, equal values of red, green, and blue combine to create a neutral gray value.)

If you need to convert a color image to grayscale, you might want to carefully consider which data to use for generating the gray channel. The Black & White adjustment (Image>Adjustments>Black & White) enables you to control the conversion process. In the Black and White dialog box, you can either choose one of the built-in presets, or you can drag the individual color sliders to determine how dark that color component will be in the resulting image.

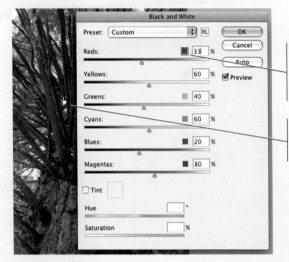

When you move the mouse cursor over the image, it changes to an eyedropper icon. You can click an area in the image to highlight the predominant color in that area. Click within the image and drag to dynamically change the slider associated with that area of the image.

The Reds slider is highlighted, indicating that red is the predominant color where you clicked in the image.

Clicking here and dragging left or right changes the associated Reds slider.

Remember, equals parts red, green and blue combine to create a neutral gray. Applying the Black & White filter maintains the existing color channels, with the exact same data in all three channels. Because the adjusted image is still technically in a color mode (not Grayscale), you can also use the Tint options in the Black & White dialog box to apply a hue or saturation tint to the grayscale image. After using the Black & White dialog box to control the conversion of colors to grayscale, you can safely discard the color data by choosing Image>Mode>Grayscale.

Red channel   Green channel   Blue channel

Original channel data

Channel data after Black & White adjustment

The Channel Mixer Adjustment

You can use the Channel Mixer adjustment to change the values of individual channels in an image, affecting overall color balance and contrast. The Output Channel menu determines which channel you are changing; the Source Channel sliders determine how much of the original channels will be used to create the new output channel values.

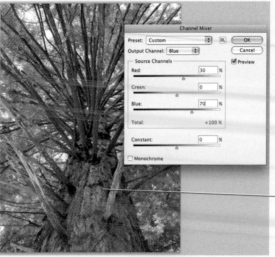

Replacing 30% of the Blue channel with information from the Red channel significantly affects the overall color and contrast in the image.

The Constant slider adjusts the overall grayscale value of the output channel. Negative values add more black to the channel (reducing the target color in the overall image), and positive values add more white to the channel (increasing the target color in the overall image).

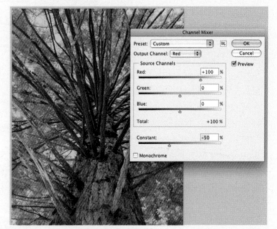

You can also use the Channel Mixer to control the conversion to grayscale. If you check the Monochrome option, the output channel automatically changes to gray.

When the Monochrome option is checked, you can change the percentage of each component channel that will be used to generate the grayscale values. If the combined channel values are higher than 100%, Photoshop displays a warning icon next to the total.

The "Output Channel:Gray" option is deceptive, since there is no Gray channel in either an RGB or CMYK image. As with the Black and White adjustment, the Channel Mixer results in a color image with the same color channels that it had before you applied the adjustment. All the color channels have equal data, however, so you can safely discard color data by choosing Image>Mode>Grayscale.

The Match Color Adjustment

The Match Color adjustment (Image>Adjustments>Match Color) allows you to match colors between multiple RGB images, layers, or selections. In the Match Color dialog box, the Target shows the image, layer, or selection you are modifying. The changes are based on values from the source image and layer selected in the Image Statistics area. You can change the luminance or color intensity of the target image, fade the adjustment, and neutralize color cast caused by the adjustment.

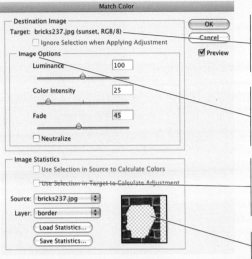

The Destination Image Target is the active image (and selected layer, if applicable) when you open the adjustment dialog box.

If the target image has an active selection area, click this check box to apply the change to the entire target image instead of the selected area only.

If the target or source image has an active selection area, click these check boxes to apply changes based on the selected area only.

Choose the source image and layer to which the target will be matched.

- The **Luminance** slider affects the brightness in the target image; higher values lighten the image.
- The **Color Intensity** slider adjusts the color saturation in the target image; higher values increase the color saturation.
- The **Fade** slider changes the amount of adjustment applied to the target image; higher values (i.e., more fade) reduce the amount of the adjustment.
- The **Neutralize** check box automatically removes color cast in the target image.

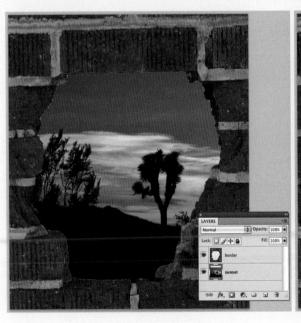

Project Review

fill in the blank

1. The _____ filter locates pixels that differ in value from surrounding pixels by the threshold you specify; it sharpens an image by increasing contrast along the edges in an image.

2. _____ is defined as random pixels that stand out from the surrounding pixels.

3. The _____ blends colors from user-defined source pixels with colors in the area where you click.

4. The _____ paints one part of an image over another part, which is useful for duplicating specific objects or removing defects in an image.

5. _____ are direct sources of light such as a light bulb or reflected sunlight on water; they should not be considered the highlights of an image.

6. _____ refers to the tonal variation within an image.

7. A _____ is a visual depiction of the distribution of colors in an image.

8. _____ is defined according to a color's position on a color wheel, beginning from red (0°) and traveling counterclockwise around the wheel.

9. _____ (also called "intensity") refers to the color's difference from neutral gray.

10. _____ (also called "luminance" or "value") is the amount of white or black added to the pure color.

short answer

1. Explain the concept of neutral gray.

2. List three important points to remember when working with curves.

3. Briefly explain the concepts of minimum printable dot and maximum ink coverage.

Portfolio Builder Project

Use what you learned in this project to complete the following freeform exercise.
Carefully read the art director and client comments, then create your design to meet the needs of the project.
Use the space below to sketch ideas; when finished, write a brief explanation of the reasoning behind your design.

art director comments

The tourism board director dined at The Chateau recently. In a conversation with the restaurant owner, he mentioned a new project about local architecture. Mr. Roseman, pleased with your work on the menu images, recommended you for the job.

To complete this project, you should:

❏ Find at least 10 photos of different architectural styles throughout the Los Angeles metropolitan area.

❏ Use photo retouching techniques to clean up any graffiti and trash that is visible in the images.

❏ Use correction techniques to adjust the tonal range and gray balance of the images.

❏ Correct and convert all images based on the U.S. Sheetfed Coated v2 CMYK destination profile.

client comments

Over the next year, we're planning on publishing a series of promotional booklets to show tourists that L.A. is more than just Hollywood.

Each booklet in the series will focus on an 'interest area' such as fine art or — for the first one — architecture. The city has a diverse architectural mix, from eighteenth-century Spanish missions to 1920s bungalows to the Walt Disney Concert Hall designed by Frank Gehry in the 1990s.

We'd like at least ten pictures of different landmarks or architectural styles, corrected and optimized for printing on a sheetfed press. If possible, we'd also like some historical images to include in a 'building a metropolis' section on the first couple of pages.

Of course, Los Angeles is a large city, and cities have their problems — not the least of which is graffiti and garbage. We are trying to attract tourists, not turn them away. Make sure none of the images show any graffiti or blatant litter; if any shows in the images you select, give them a good digital cleaning.

project justification

_____
_____
_____
_____
_____
_____
_____
_____
_____
_____
_____
_____
_____

As with many other skills, it takes time and practice to master image correction techniques. Understanding the relationship between brightness and contrast, and how these two values affect the quality of reproduction in digital images, is the first and possibly most critical factor in creating a high-quality image. An image that has too much contrast (a "sharp" image) or not enough contrast (a "flat" image) translates to an unsatisfactory print.

A basic understanding of color theory (specifically complementary color) is the foundation of accurate color correction. Effective color correction relies on the numbers, rather than what you think you see on your monitor. As you gain experience in correcting images, you will be better able to predict the corrections required to achieve the best possible output.

Remove photographic grain with blur and sharpen techniques

Use the Healing Brush and Spot Healing Brush tools to correct scratches

Use the Clone Stamp tool to remove major damage

Correct contrast and tonal range using the Levels adjustment

Correct minor color problems using the Brightness/Contrast adjustment

Correct gray balance using the Curves adjustment

Correct lighting problems with the Exposure adjustment

Correct overall color cast using the Color Balance adjustment

Correct contrast with the Curves adjustment

Correct and convert the image using the defined destination CMYK profile

Catalog Cover

Your client is a mail-order children's clothing company that sends monthly catalogs to a large mailing list throughout the United States. July is their biggest sales months since parents are buying their children new clothes for the start of the school year. The company hired your agency to create the new fall catalog, which will be mailed in mid-June. Your job is to build the catalog cover.

This project incorporates the following skills:

❏ Using filters and adjustments to identify edges in a complex image

❏ Creating a complex mask by adjusting an Alpha channel

❏ Painting directly on an Alpha channel

❏ Compositing a background image with special effects

❏ Adding layer effects to spot-color objects

❏ Building a spot channel for a special ink color

❏ Creating warped and spot-color type

client comments

We don't have a physical store front, so we depend on mail-order for our business. Although many sales come from our Web site, other customers prefer printed catalogs. And since we get so many orders from those catalogs, we print and mail thousands of every issue.

Each catalog cover features a child wearing an item from our new product line. Our photographer did a great job for this year's back-to-school issue. The model's name is Stephanie and we love her photo. We'd like you to put some kind of image behind the picture of Stephanie that says "school" without being overwhelming or taking too much attention away from the girl's face.

Our catalog covers are printed on a six-color press. Each issue uses a different spot color for our company name and some kind of banner, as well as a flood varnish on the sixth press unit. You can pick the spot color to match an item on the cover.

art director comments

The clients were fairly specific about what they want. Since this is the back-to-school issue, I found a good picture of a school bus that will work well as the background image.

The hardest part of this job is going to be isolating Stephanie from her background so you can put the bus behind her. Any time you have a person in a photo, you have to deal with hair — and little wisps can be extremely difficult to isolate in a selection. Photoshop has some good tools for making this task a bit easier, but it still requires manual intervention.

The catalog is 9.75 × 7.75″ trimmed, so you need to build the final file to that size with 1/8″ bleeds. The job will be printed on a Web press because of the high volume.

For the fifth color, use a yellow similar to the bus. Yellow is blue's complement — the yellow type, banner, and bus will work very well as a visual foil for the blue in Stephanie's shirt. Be aware that using spot colors in Photoshop requires a few tricks and workarounds that are different from what you do when you work with regular image channels.

project objectives

To complete this project, you will:

- ❑ Duplicate an image channel to create an Alpha channel mask

- ❑ Use effects filters and Levels adjustments to isolate edges in an Alpha channel

- ❑ Posterize an Alpha channel to remove shading

- ❑ Use the Brush and Eraser tools to complete a complex mask

- ❑ Composite a complex image onto a different background image

- ❑ Edit a background image for visual impact

- ❑ Create a spot channel for a fifth ink separation, and add design elements to the spot channel

- ❑ Save the file in the DCS format to preserve spot-color information

Stage 1 Creating a Complex Selection

You've already learned a number of different ways to make selections, from basic shape selections with a marquee to color-based selections using the Color Range options. There are some images, however, that defy these tools. Specifically, images with various colors with thin lines and complex edges can be difficult to isolate. The girl's picture for this project is a perfect example.

You need to isolate the girl from the gray background.

These thin wisps of hair can be very difficult to cleanly separate from a background.

The foreground has too many different hues to allow a color-based selection.

 EVALUATE AND DUPLICATE AN EXISTING IMAGE CHANNEL

An Alpha channel based on existing image data is the best option for creating this type of complex mask. Creating that channel is a multi-step process, beginning with evaluating the individual image channels to find the one with the most contrast.

1. **On your desktop, copy the Catalog folder from the WIP folder on your Resource CD to the WIP folder where you're saving your work.**

   Use your WIP>Catalog folder to save files for this project.

2. **Open the file kid.jpg from the RF_Photoshop>Catalog folder and display the Channels panel.**

3. **Open the Channels panel Options menu and choose Panel Options. In the resulting dialog box, select the large thumbnail, and then click OK.**

   When working with channels, the larger thumbnail can be helpful.

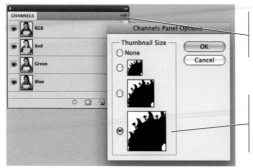

Click here to access the Channels panel Options menu.

The largest thumbnail provides more information directly within the Channels panel.

Every RGB has image a composite channel and three color channels (one for each primary color), and every CMYK image has a composite channel and four color channels.

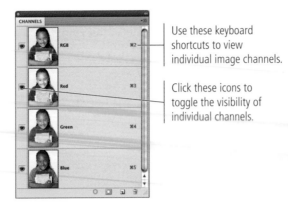

Use these keyboard shortcuts to view individual image channels.

Click these icons to toggle the visibility of individual channels.

4. **Click the Red channel in the panel to view only that channel in the image window.**

Each pixel in an RGB image has a value of 0 to 255 for each of three channels. When you look at individual channels, you see the grayscale representation of tones for that color channel.

Note:

In the Interface pane of the Preferences dialog box, you can check the Show Channels in Color option to show individual channels in color instead of grayscale.

5. **Click the Green channel in the panel to view only that channel in the image window.**

6. **Click the Blue channel in the panel to view only that channel in the image window.**

    This channel has the greatest edge contrast; you'll use it to build your Alpha channel.

7. **Click the Blue channel in the panel and drag it to the Create New Channel button at the bottom of the panel.**

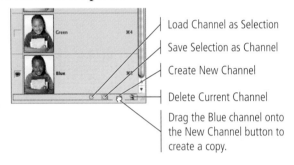

Load Channel as Selection

Save Selection as Channel

Create New Channel

Delete Current Channel

Drag the Blue channel onto the New Channel button to create a copy.

    Dragging an existing channel onto the Create New Channel button creates an exact copy of the channel.

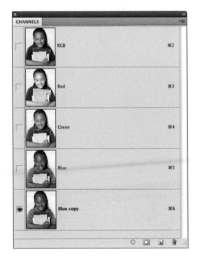

8. In the Channels panel, click the empty space to the left of the RGB composite channel to make the composite image visible behind the Blue copy Alpha channel.

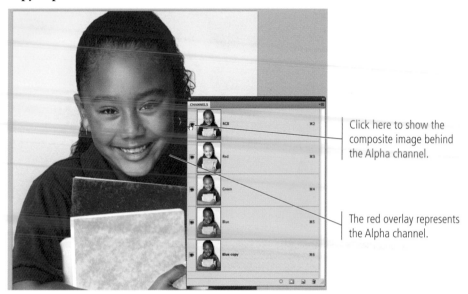

Click here to show the composite image behind the Alpha channel.

The red overlay represents the Alpha channel.

9. With the Blue copy channel still selected, choose Channel Options from the Channels panel Options menu.

10. Change the channel name to Girl Mask and change the Opacity field to 100%.

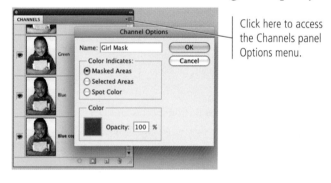

Click here to access the Channels panel Options menu.

11. Click OK to change the channel options.

When you're finished with this stage of the project, the 100% opaque mask will entirely obscure the girl, and the background will have no red overlay.

12. Save the file in your WIP>Catalog folder as a native Photoshop file named `kid_working.psd`.

You can't save an Alpha channel in a JPEG image, so you should use the native Photoshop format.

13. Continue to the next exercise.

 ## FIND AND ISOLATE EDGES IN THE ALPHA CHANNEL

There are several ways to find the edges in an image, using either image adjustments or filters. The specific image might determine which option is best. In many cases — including this project — the best approach is a combination of two or more methods.

1. With `kid_working.psd` open from your WIP>Catalog folder, hide all but the Girl Mask channel.

This channel already has fairly good edge contrast. However, the channel still shows a large range of shades, when the channel mask ultimately needs only two shades — masked (black) and not masked (white).

2. With the Girl Mask channel selected, choose Filter>Other>High Pass.

The High Pass filter maintains edge details and turns non-edges gray. The Radius value determines the difference in pixels required to define an edge. Lower Radius values result in more edges and less transition detail between the edges and non-edges; higher Radius values result in fewer edges and a pronounced halo effect between edges and non-edges.

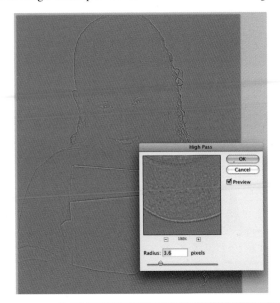

3. **Drag the Radius slider right until you see a strong halo around the girl's outline (we used a 40.6-pixel radius).**

This process could work with a very small Radius value, but the halo effect of the higher radius is important here. The white areas behind the wispy hair will become white areas in the Alpha channel mask — eliminating the need to later manually edit out the areas between individual wisps of hair.

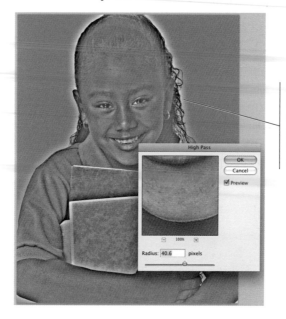

The high Radius value adds a halo large enough to surround the girl's hair, which will become an important part of the Alpha channel mask.

4. **Click OK to apply the filter and return to the image window.**

The next step is to increase the contrast between the edges and the non-edges so you can easily fill in and erase as necessary to create the mask — in essence, you want to turn this Alpha channel into a coloring book that is easy to fill in between the lines. As you learned in Project 4, using Levels is one of the easiest ways to increase contrast.

5. **With the Girl Mask channel still selected in the Channels panel, choose Image>Adjustments>Levels.**

The histogram in the Levels dialog box reflects the distribution of pixels across the available tonal range in the selected channel only. The High Pass filter produced a lot of middle grays, with black edges and white halos.

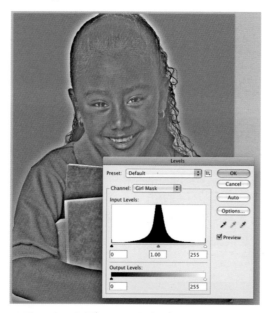

6. **Drag the Input Shadow slider right until the Input Shadow field shows 120.**

7. **Drag the Input Highlight slider left until the associated field shows 136.**

   Remember, when you move the Input sliders in the Levels dialog box, you define the available tonal range. Using these settings in the Levels dialog box, you define a tonal range of only 17 possible values. The image shows the result of the settings — most pixels have been pushed to either pure black or pure white; the edges are very pronounced, even in the areas with the wispy hair.

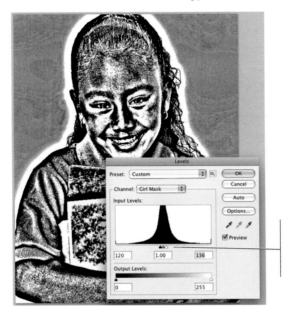

The adjusted Input and Output sliders limit the tonal range to only 17 possible values.

8. **Click OK to close the Levels dialog box and make the RGB composite channel visible behind the Alpha channel.**

   Because you had the Girl Mask channel selected when you made the High Pass and Levels changes, you did not affect the actual image pixels. It's important to remember that you are only editing the mask channel in this stage of the project.

Click here to make the composite image visible behind the mask channel.

9. **Save the file and continue to the next exercise.**

The Filter>Other submenu includes four options in addition to the High Pass filter. This miscellany of filters really doesn't fit anywhere else, so the filters are lumped together under "Other."

Custom allows you to change the Brightness values of each pixel in the image based on a mathematical operation known as convolution. Each pixel is reassigned a value based on the values of surrounding pixels. You can click Save in this dialog box to save your settings as a custom filter, which you can then reload for any other image.

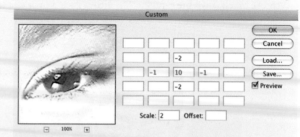

The Custom dialog box displays a grid of fields. The center field represents the pixel being evaluated; each surrounding field represents the pixel in the same position around the pixel being evaluated. The numbers in each field determine how much the brightness of each pixel is being multiplied (from −999 to +999); you don't have to enter values in all the text boxes. The value in the Scale field divides the sum of the Brightness values of the pixels included in the calculation. The value in the Offset field is added to the result of the scale calculation.

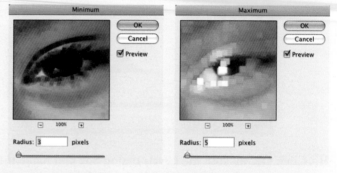

The **Maximum** filter has the effect of expanding white areas and shrinking black areas (called a **choke**). The **Minimum** filter has the opposite effect, expanding black areas and shrinking white areas (called a **spread**). These filters replace a pixel's Brightness value with the highest (Maximum) or lowest (Minimum) Brightness value of surrounding pixels within the defined radius.

Offset moves a selection a specified horizontal or vertical amount. (The Offset filter can be applied to any selection — part of a layer, an entire layer, an entire channel, or an entire image.) Moving a selection results in empty areas where the original pixels used to reside; the Undefined Areas options define how those areas will be filled.

- **Set to Background** fills those areas with the current background color.
- **Repeat Edge Pixels** creates a streak-like effect from the pixels at the edge of the moved selection.
- **Wrap Around** creates a tiled effect by filling the empty area with pixels from the moved selection.

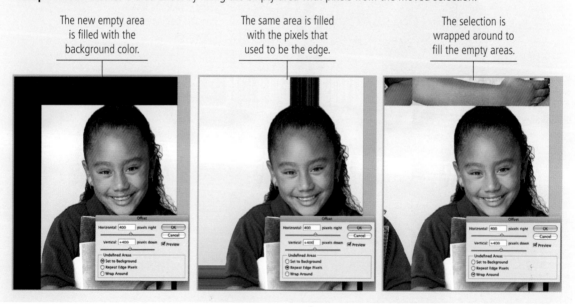

| The new empty area is filled with the background color. | The same area is filled with the pixels that used to be the edge. | The selection is wrapped around to fill the empty areas. |

REMOVE SHADING FROM THE ALPHA CHANNEL

When you adjusted the levels of the Girl Mask channel, you reduced the tonal range to 17 possible tones. In Project 2, however, we explained that the values in an Alpha channel are actually degrees of transparency (see page 111). When you view the composite image behind the Alpha channel, you can still see through some of the red mask to the actual image pixels. The complete mask, however, requires pixels to be either solid black (masked) or solid white (not masked) — in other words, the mask channel should have only two tones or levels.

1. **With kid_working.psd open, hide the composite RGB channel and make sure the Girl Mask channel is selected.**

2. **Choose Image>Adjustments>Posterize.**

    The word "posterize" means to reduce an image to only a few different shades — which is exactly what you need to do in this step.

3. **In the Posterize dialog box, drag the Levels slider all the way to the left until the field shows that the mask channel uses only 2 levels.**

4. **Click OK in the Posterize dialog box to apply the adjustment, and then make the RGB composite visible behind the Alpha channel.**

Although there are still unfilled areas on the mask, there are no longer any semi-transparent red areas.

5. **Save the file and continue to the next exercise.**

PHOTOSHOP FOUNDATIONS

Special Effects Adjustments

In addition to Posterize, several other options in the Image>Adjustments submenu are used to create special effects that mimic photographic techniques that predate digital image manipulation.

The **Invert** adjustment reverses the color values of the image, creating the effect of a photographic negative.

The **Equalize** adjustment extends the Brightness values of an image so they occupy the entire range of available brightness levels (from 1 to 99%). The lightest part of the image is mapped to full brightness and the darkest part of the image is mapped to black. Although this might sound very similar to extending the tonal range with Levels, the Equalize adjustment typically produces choppy results; it is best used when you want to create special effects rather than fine color adjustments.

Invert

The **Threshold** adjustment converts images to high-contrast bitmap images. Pixels in the resulting image are either black or white; there are no intermediate shades of gray. Any pixels with a value lower than the defined Threshold Level are black; pixels with a value higher than the defined Threshold Level are white.

Equalize

Threshold

ERASE AND PAINT THE ALPHA CHANNEL

Your mask channel still needs a bit of clean-up work to fill in some areas (where the girl is still visible) and remove unwanted parts (in the background area). Combining the High Pass filter with an extreme Levels adjustment will create a fairly clear set of edges that will make the clean-up easier.

1. With **kid_working.psd** open, hide the composite RGB channel and make sure the Girl Mask channel is selected.

2. In the Tools panel, click the button to restore the default foreground and background colors to black and white (respectively).

3. Click the Switch Foreground and Background Colors button to set the foreground to white and the background to black.

   When you work on an Alpha channel, the default foreground and background colors are opposite of what they are when you work on a regular layer or color channel.

   To fill the solid black areas, you can either use the default foreground and background colors and use the Brush, or you can reverse the default foreground and background colors and use the Eraser tool.

4. Select the Eraser tool in the Tools panel.

Note:

Be very careful when you paint directly on an Alpha channel.

Eraser tool

Click this button to restore the default foreground and background colors.

Click this button to reverse the default foreground and background colors.

These areas need to be removed from the mask (white).

The area inside the heavy black edges needs to be entirely filled with black.

5. In the Control panel, choose Brush from the Mode menu.

   You can use the Eraser tool as a solid square block, using the same settings as the Pencil tool or Brush tool.

6. **Choose a large, round brush with 100% hardness, 100% opacity, and 100% flow.**

Since the areas you need to fill are fairly well defined, you can start with a large brush size, and then use smaller brush sizes when you need to work on more detailed areas.

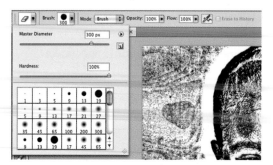

7. **Click with the Eraser tool to fill in areas of solid black on the mask channel, avoiding any area of fine detail (especially around the girl's ears and neck).**

The following image shows how far we got with the 300-pixel brush. We zoomed in closely to the edges so we could see exactly where the lines appeared. Around the edges, we used individual clicks of the Eraser tool rather than dragging strokes.

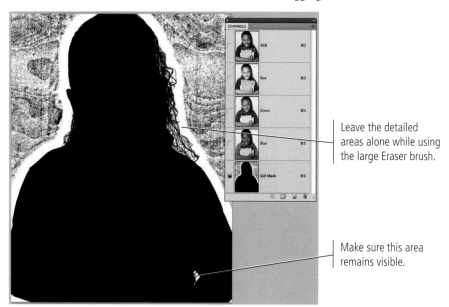

Leave the detailed areas alone while using the large Eraser brush.

Make sure this area remains visible.

8. **Switch the background and foreground colors, and then use the same large-brush Eraser tool to remove the gray areas from the image background. If necessary, use the bracket keys to reduce ([ ) or enlarge ( ]) the brush size so you can remove most of the pixels from the background area. Again, ignore the hair areas for now.**

Because the background color is now white, using the Eraser tool "paints" white in place of the gray background pixels. You can achieve the same result using the Brush tool with the foreground color set to white.

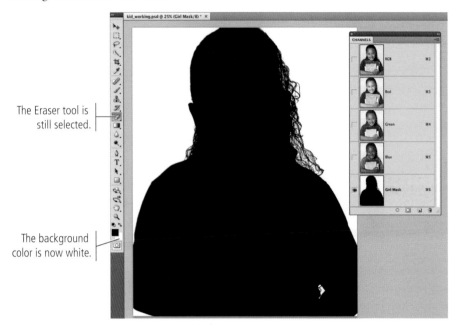

The Eraser tool is still selected.

The background color is now white.

9. **Make the RGB composite channel visible behind the mask channel.**

Viewing both the composite and Alpha channels, you can now clearly see what still needs to be filled.

When viewing only the Alpha channel, it was difficult to tell exactly what needed to be masked.

10. **Zoom in to the girl's face.**

11. **Use either the Brush tool with a black foreground color or the Eraser tool with a black background color to fill in the detailed areas of the mask.**

12. **Adjust the brush size as necessary to be as accurate as possible in the detail areas.**

The Photoshop tools make this process easier, but some amount of manual work will always be necessary to clean up a complex, fine-detailed mask such as this one.

13. **When you are satisfied with your mask, save the file as** `girl_masked.psd` **in your WIP>Catalog folder, and then continue to the next stage of the project.**

Stage 2 Compositing Complex Selections

The main goal of this project is to create a catalog cover that's a composite of two images, several type layers, and a banner shape on a spot channel. The best approach for creating this composite piece is to build a new file where you can place all the pieces.

DEFINE THE COMPOSITE FILE

Because this catalog cover is being designed for print, you should build the main file using the CMYK color mode. The two images you will composite into the cover are in the RGB mode, however, which means you need to evaluate the potential for color shift when you copy the two images into your composite file.

Keep the following job requirements in mind as you complete this exercise:

- Trim size: 7.75″ × 9.75″

- Bleeds: 0.125″ on all four sides

- Printing method: Web press

1. **Create a new file (File>New) named** catalog **that is 8″ wide by 10″ high, set to 300 pixels per inch, using the CMYK color mode and a white background. In the Advanced options, choose U.S. Web Coated (SWOP) v2 as the color profile.**

2. **Click OK to create the new file.**

3. **Place a guide at 0.125″ (1/8″) in from each file edge.**

These guides mark the trim size of the piece.

Drag from the rulers to add a guide at 1/8″ from each side of the image.

Note:

Zoom in if necessary so you can place the guides precisely.

4. **Save the file as catalog_working.psd in your WIP>Catalog folder, and continue to the next exercise.**

VERIFY COLOR IN THE COMPONENT IMAGES

As we stated in the previous exercise, the two images for this cover are currently in the RGB color mode. When you paste the images into the composite file, they will be converted to the working space of the composite file (U.S. Web Coated (SWOP) v2). Rather than leaving color issues to chance, you should check for potential problem areas in the two images before pasting them into the main file.

1. **Open the file girl_masked.psd from your WIP>Catalog folder. Make sure the Girl Mask channel is hidden and the composite RGB image is visible.**

2. **Choose View>Proof Setup>Custom.**

By choosing Custom in the View>Proof Setup submenu, you can proof to any destination profile without changing your default working space.

3. **In the Customize Proof Condition dialog box, choose U.S. Sheetfed Coated v2 in the Device to Simulate menu.**

This is the working profile of the composite file you created in the previous exercise, so you should use this profile for proofing colors.

Note:

If you continued to this project from Project 4, your defined CMYK working space will be U.S. Sheetfed Coated v2.

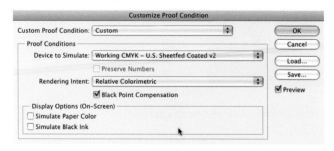

4. **Click OK to close the dialog box.**

5. **Choose View>Gamut Warning.**

   You might remember from Project 4 that out-of-gamut colors are highlighted with a gray overlay. With the gamut warning turned on, it appears that all colors in this image are within the U.S. Sheetfed Coated v2 gamut.

6. **Open the file bus.jpg from the RF_Photoshop>Catalog folder.**

7. **Choose View>Gamut Warning.**

   The Proof Setup menu remembers your previous choice, so you don't need to re-establish the destination profile to simulate.

   The gamut warning shows a small area of color that will shift when the file is copied into the composite file. However, you are ultimately going to blur this image as part of the composite background; you are using the image to suggest a theme, not show an exact representation. So in this case, you can accept the small amount of color shift.

You can see areas of this image that are out of gamut, but they'll be fixed in the composite catalog cover.

8. **Leave the girl and bus files open and continue to the next exercise.**

COMPOSITE THE COMPONENT IMAGES

You already know how to move pixels from one file to another. You can copy (or simply drag) an entire layer or even a specific selection using the Move tool. Once the two component images are composited into the catalog file, you can start to make adjustments so the two images work together in a single composition.

1. **With all three images open, (bus.jpg, girl_masked.psd, and catalog_working.psd), arrange the document window so you can see all three open files at the same time.**

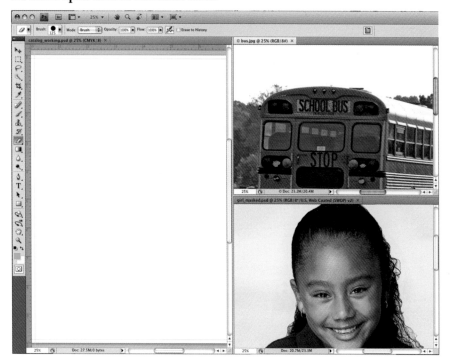

2. **Display the Layers panel.**

3. **Using the Move tool, drag the image layer from the bus file into the catalog_working file.**

4. **Close the bus file.**

5. **Make girl_masked.psd the active file.**

6. **Choose Select>Load Selection.**

   One advantage of using Alpha channels is that they can be loaded at any time.

   In the Load Selection dialog box, the document menu automatically shows the active document, and the Channel menu defaults to the only available Alpha channel. If you have more than one Alpha channel, you can use this menu to determine which selection you want to make.

Note:

You can also select an Alpha channel in the Channels panel and click the Load Channel as Selection button at the bottom of the panel.

7. **Activate the Invert check box.**

   A mask protects the areas it covers. When you load this Alpha channel as a selection, you are actually selecting anything that is not red when the channel is visible. In this case, you want to select the area that is red (the girl), so you must invert the selection.

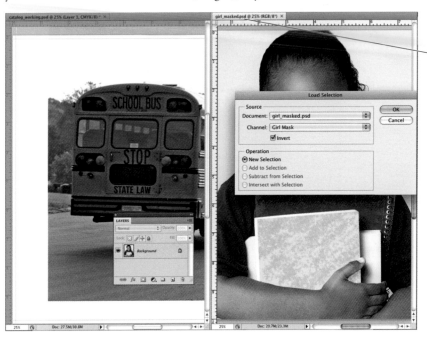

The girl_masked file is active.

8. **Click OK to create the selection.**

   This type of complex selection often results in halos around fine edges. Modifying the selection slightly will prevent the halo effect from occurring without destroying the edge detail.

9. **Choose Select>Modify>Feather.**

10. **In the Feather Selection dialog box, change the Feather Radius field to 1.5 pixels and click OK.**

11. **In the Channels panel, make sure the RGB composite channel — not the Girl Mask channel — is selected.**

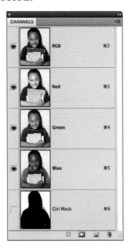

12. **Choose Edit>Copy, and then close the girl_masked file.**

13. **With the catalog_working file active, choose Edit>Paste.**

   The original photo was captured at the appropriate size for the catalog cover, so when you paste the photo, it perfectly matches the catalog_working file size.

Using Edit>Paste, the girl is pasted into the center of the catalog_working file.

14. **Save catalog_working.psd. Click OK if you see a warning about maximizing compatibility, and continue to the next exercise.**

Now that the two images are in the main file, you can position and manipulate them to create a unified design. Each image occupies its own layer, making it easy to control the various pieces.

1. **With catalog_working.psd open from your WIP>Catalog folder, rename Layer 1 as bus and rename Layer 2 as girl.**

   Meaningful layer names are always a good idea, even if the file has only a few layers.

2. **Select the girl layer. Using the Move tool, drag right until her head occupies only the right half of the page.**

   It might be helpful if you place a guide to mark the horizontal center of the page.

Note:

You might want to press Shift to constrain the movement to be exactly horizontal.

This positioning leaves the cut-off portion of the girl's arm visible. You'll use the spot-color banner to hide that flaw in the original photo.

3. **With the bus layer selected, enter Free Transform mode (Edit>Free Transform or Command/Control-T) and scale the layer to about 85% proportionally.**

4. **Using the Move tool, drag the bus layer so the back end of the bus is directly inside the left trim guide, and the top edge of the bus is about 2.5″ from the top of the image.**

The bus image is still very strong, and it takes too much attention away from the girl.

Resizing the picture leaves an empty space at the top and the bottom, which needs to be fixed.

5. Use the Clone Stamp tool to fill in pavement in the bottom-left corner of the bus layer.

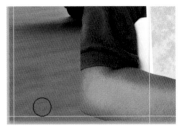

6. With the bus layer selected, choose Filter>Blur>Motion Blur.

7. Apply a blur to the bus so the image becomes less prominent.

We applied a 70-pixel blur with a –9° angle.

The filter is applied to the selected layer only.

8. Place (File>Place) the file **logotype.ai** from the RF_Photoshop>Catalog folder into the catalog_working file. In the Place dialog box, use the default Crop To option.

9. Position the logotype in the empty white space in the upper-left corner of the image.

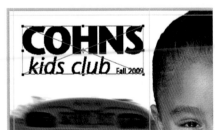

10. **When you're satisfied with the position of the logo, press Return/Enter to finalize the placement. Move the logotype to the top of the layer stack.**

The client provided this logotype, with the season added in the appropriate location. Remember, though, that the company name (COHNS) needs to be set in the fifth color; you'll manage that process in the next stage of this project.

11. **Save the file and continue to the next exercise.**

 ## CREATE A SHAPE LAYER AND WARPED TEXT

The only piece of the cover left to create is the banner, which will ultimately be placed on a spot channel. Working with spot channels is one of the few areas of weakness in Photoshop, so the best option is to create the objects as regular layers, and then copy the relevant bits to a spot channel later.

1. **With catalog_working.psd open, choose the logotype layer to make it the active layer.**

You want the shape layer to appear at the top of the layer stack. By first selecting the logotype layer, the new shape layer you are about to create will automatically appear directly above the logotype layer — at the top of the layer stack.

2. **Choose the Custom Shape tool (nested under the Rectangle tool).**

3. **In the Control panel, make sure the Shape Layers option is selected.**

4. **Click the arrow button to the right of the Shape menu to open the Custom Shape panel, and then show the Custom Shape panel Options menu.**

The options in this menu should be familiar — you saw similar options in Project 2 when you worked with styles, gradients, and patterns. You can change the display of the shapes in the panel, load shapes from external files, and access a number of built-in shape libraries.

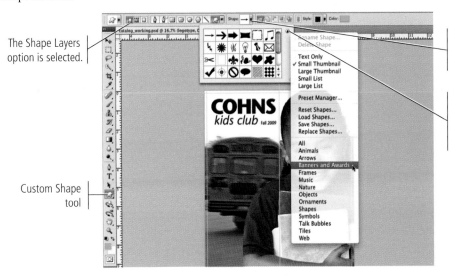

The Shape Layers option is selected.

Custom Shape tool

Click here to open the Custom Shape panel.

Click here to access the Options menu for the Custom Shape panel.

Note:

You can choose from a large number of common and special shapes from the built-in shape libraries when you use the Custom Shape tool.

5. **Choose Banners and Awards in the panel Options menu. Click OK when asked if you want to replace the current shapes with the new set.**

6. **In the Custom Shape panel (on the Control panel), choose the Flag shape.**

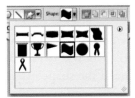

Note:

Extensions on files are normally hidden by operating system preferences. However, there are times you see them anyway. Here you see the ".csh" extension, which is used for custom shape sets.

7. **Open the Styles panel (from the Control panel), and then open the Styles panel Options menu. Choose No Style from the Options menu.**

Click here to open the Style panel.

Click here to open the panel Options menu and access the No Style option.

8. **Click the Color swatch in the Control panel to open the Color Picker. Move the cursor over the image and click to select a yellow color as the shape layer color.**

Ultimately, the shape you are creating will be moved to a spot channel to reproduce the banner in a specific color of ink, so it really doesn't matter what color you use in this step. We're working with a representative yellow so you can get a feel for the composition before you add the spot channel information.

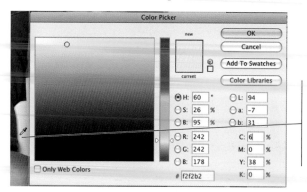

We chose a yellow from the girl's notebook. The color you pick doesn't need to exactly match ours; you will ultimately replace this color with a spot color.

9. **Draw the custom shape in the bottom-left corner of the image, wide enough to fill the left half of the file and about 3″ high.**

The Custom Shape tool creates a vector path based on the specific shape you select. Because you chose the Shape Layer option, the new shape layer is added to the Layers panel.

Make sure the Shape 1 layer is at the top of the stack, or the girl will cover half of it.

10. **Using the Direct Selection tool, adjust the anchor points of the flag shape until the banner covers the flat area where the girl's arm was cut off by the edge of the original photo. Make sure the left edge of the shape extends to the left edge of the image.**

You already know how to edit vector paths, so we won't tell you exactly what to move where. Our solution is shown in the following image. The most important thing is that the flat part of the girl's arm needs to be covered.

The left edge of the shape should meet the left edge of the image.

The shape should hide areas where the girl's arm is cut off.

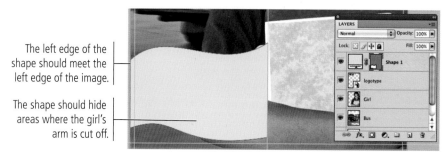

11. **Add a drop shadow to the shape layer using the following settings:**

Blend mode:	Multiply Black	Distance:	15 px
Opacity:	75%	Spread:	10%
Angle:	120°	Size:	40 px

Note:

Apply the drop shadow by choosing Layer>Layer Style>Drop Shadow, or by clicking the fx button at the bottom of the Layers panel and choosing Drop Shadow from the menu.

12. **In the Tools panel, choose the Type tool, and then click the Default Foreground and Background Colors button.**

13. **Click in the image window to create a type layer with a point-type object, and then type:**
    Back to
    School
    Savings!

14. **Format the type as 60-pt. ATC Oak Bold with 48-pt leading.**

15. **Using the Move tool, move the type layer so the text is over the banner shape.**

16. **Select the Type tool again and click inside the existing type to place the insertion point. Click the Create Warped Text button in the Control panel.**

Create Warped Text button

17. **In the Warp Text dialog box, choose Flag from the Style menu.**

   As long as text remains editable, your warping options are limited to this list of predefined shapes. When you work with rasterized text (or any other pixel-based selection), you can also create custom warps, which you do in Project 6.

18. **Adjust the Bend settings until you're satisfied with the warped text in relation to your banner shape.**

   We changed the Bend setting to –10% and the Horizontal Distortion setting to +10% to match our banner shape.

19. **Click OK to close the Warp Text dialog box.**

20. **Use the Move tool to adjust the position of the type layer (if necessary).**

21. **Save the file and continue to the final stage of the project.**

PHOTOSHOP FOUNDATIONS

Warp Options

Photoshop includes 15 built-in warp styles. The icon next to each style name suggests the result of applying that style. Use the following as a visual guide when you want to experiment with these warp style options.

Arc	Arc Lower	Arc Upper	
KID	KID	KID	
Arch	Bulge	Shell Lower	Shell Upper
KID	KID	KID	KID
Flag	Wave	Fish	Rise
KID	KID	KID	KID
Fisheye	Inflate	Squeeze	Twist
KID	KID	KID	KID

Stage 3 Working with Spot Channels

Spot colors are frequently used to produce a special look, to match an exact color, or to highlight a certain aspect of a job (for example, with varnish or other special coating). Spot-color inks are opaque, so they produce the desired result with a single printing unit instead of by combining varying percentages of the four process inks. If you want to create a certain look, or if a color must be the same on every printed job, a spot color is usually the best choice. Remember, however, that adding spot color to a process job adds to the cost, and budgets are usually a consideration when designing a print project.

Although Photoshop includes a number of built-in spot-color libraries, spot colors are typically selected from printed swatch books that show the exact color of the ink. Don't rely on the on-screen previews when you select a spot color.

Every designer should also have a set of spot-color guides, such as the ones produced by Pantone. (Pantone is the most common spot-color system in the United States, but ask your printer which one they use before building spot colors in any design job.) These printed spot-color guides usually show coated and uncoated samples. Some also show the process color combination that produces the closest possible match to the spot ink. If you want to approximate a special ink color, you can use those ink percentages to designate the process color in a layout or illustration program.

 ## Define a New Spot Channel

To work with spot colors in Photoshop, you have to create a new channel to include the information for that ink. Anything printed in the spot color needs to be placed or copied onto the spot channel.

1. With **catalog_working.psd** open, display the Channels panel.

2. Open the Channels panel Options menu and choose New Spot Channel.

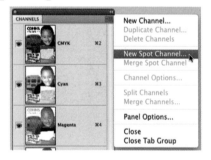

3. In the New Spot Channel dialog box, click the Color swatch to open the Select Spot Color dialog box.

Click this swatch to open the Select Spot Color dialog box.

4. **Click the Color Libraries button to access the built-in spot-color libraries.**

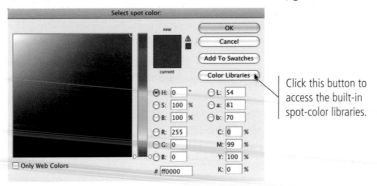

Click this button to access the built-in spot-color libraries.

5. **In the Book menu, choose Pantone Solid Coated.**

6. **Type 810 to scroll quickly to the color that was selected for this job.**

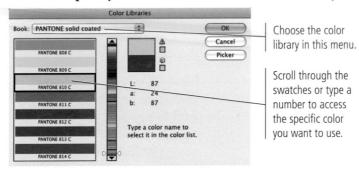

Choose the color library in this menu.

Scroll through the swatches or type a number to access the specific color you want to use.

7. **Click OK to return to the New Spot Channel dialog box.**

8. **Make sure the Solidity option is set to 100%.**

Solidity for a spot channel is similar to layer opacity. If the ink channel is not entirely opaque (with a 100% Solidity value), CMYK elements under the spot areas will be visible through the spot ink. In this case, you want the spot-ink areas to completely obscure underlying CMYK elements, so you have to use a 100% Solidity value.

Note:

Double-clicking a spot-color channel on the Channels panel opens the same dialog box you see when you first create a new spot channel.

9. **Click OK to add the new spot channel to the file.**

The newly added Pantone spot-color channel doesn't contain anything yet.

10. **Save the file and continue to the next exercise.**

Understanding Duotones

Spot colors are sometimes used to print monotone, duotone, tritone, and quadtone images. **Monotones** are grayscale images printed with one ink (typically not black). **Duotones**, **tritones**, and **quadtones** are grayscale images printed with two, three, and four inks (respectively).

Of the four types of images, duotones are the most common. In many cases, duotones are printed with black ink for the shadows and midtones and one other color for the highlights. This technique produces an image with a slight tint that adds visual interest to images in a two-color print job. In Photoshop, duotones are treated as single-channel, 8-bit grayscale images. You can convert any 8-bit grayscale image by choosing Image>Mode>Duotone.

Choose Monotone, Duotone, Tritone, or Quadtone in this menu.

Click these icons to change the curve associated with each ink.

Click these swatches to change the colors of the duotone.

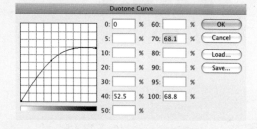

In a duotone image, you can't access the individual ink channels in the Channels panel. You can, however, manipulate the channels through the curves in the Duotone Options dialog box.

You can't use the Channels panel to access the individual inks in a duotone image.

Each ink has a curve that specifies how the color is distributed across shadows and highlights. This curve maps each grayscale value in the original image to a specific ink percentage. The default curve (a straight diagonal line) indicates that the grayscale values in the original image map to an equal percentage of ink. For example, a 50% midtone pixel becomes a 50% tint of the ink.

If you need direct access to the individual channels in a duotone, you can convert it to Multichannel mode (Image>Mode>Multichannel).

After converting to Multichannel mode, the individual ink separations are available in the Channels panel.

There are certain limitations to working with spot colors in Photoshop. You can't apply effects to a spot channel (such as the drop shadow behind the banner on the catalog cover). You also can't store vector information on a spot channel, which means vector shape and type layers will be rasterized if you move that content to a spot channel.

1. **With `catalog_working.psd` open, Control/right-click the logotype layer and choose Rasterize Layer from the contextual menu.**

   When you placed the logotype file, it was placed as a Smart Object. To move part of this object to the spot-color channel, you first have to rasterize the Smart Object.

2. **With the logotype layer selected, use the Rectangle Marquee tool to draw a marquee around the word "COHNS".**

   Be careful to select no part of the words "kids club."

3. **Make sure the CMYK composite channel is selected in the Channels panel and the logotype layer is selected in the Layers panel.**

   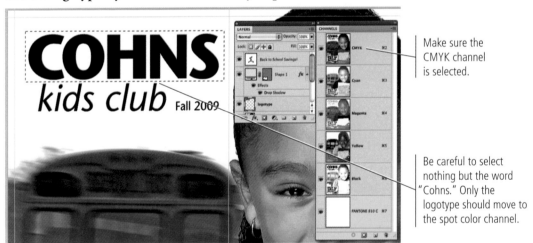

   Make sure the CMYK channel is selected.

   Be careful to select nothing but the word "Cohns." Only the logotype should move to the spot color channel.

4. **Choose Edit>Cut.**

5. **Select the Pantone 810 C channel in the Channels panel and choose Edit>Paste.**

6. **Using the Move tool, drag the pasted content into place above the "kids club" text.**

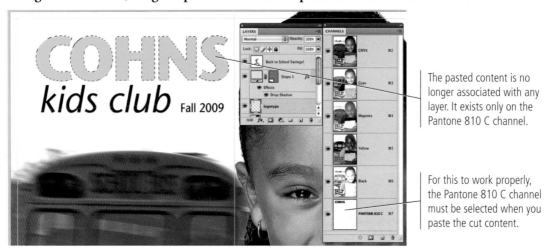

The pasted content is no longer associated with any layer. It exists only on the Pantone 810 C channel.

For this to work properly, the Pantone 810 C channel must be selected when you paste the cut content.

7. **Control/right-click the Shape 1 layer in the Layers panel and choose Rasterize Layer from the contextual menu.**

8. **Control/right-click the Back to School Savings type layer and choose Create Work Path from the contextual menu.**

Rather than leaving plain black text, you're going to use this path to remove (knock out) the letter shapes from the banner.

9. **In the Paths panel, Control/right-click Work Path and choose Make Selection from the contextual menu.**

10. **Click OK in the resulting Make Selection dialog box to accept the default settings.**

   This dialog box allows you to feather the resulting selection without the need to use the Select>Modify menu.

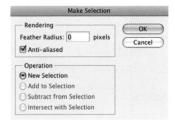

11. **Hide the Back to School Savings type layer.**

12. **In the Layers panel, select the rasterized Shape 1 layer and press Delete/Backspace.**

   Pressing the Delete button erases the selection area from the selected layer.
   You can now see the drop shadow in the knocked out areas of the letter shapes.

Select the Shape 1 layer to delete the selection from the shape area.

13. **Expand the effects for the Shape 1 layer. In the Layers panel, Control/right-click the Drop Shadow effect and choose Create Layer from the contextual menu.**

As we stated at the beginning of this exercise, you can't apply effects to spot channel content. To maintain the drop shadow after the banner has been moved to the spot channel, you have to create an independent layer from the drop shadow effect.

Control/right-click the Drop Shadow effect to access the contextual menu.

14. **If you see a warning about effects not being reproduced by layers, click OK.**

Drop shadows can be reproduced with layers, so you can dismiss the warning.

15. **Deselect the active selection.**

16. **Save the file and continue to the next exercise.**

MOVE LAYER CONTENT TO A SPOT CHANNEL

Unfortunately, there is no easy way to map specific layer content to a specific spot channel. To ensure that specific objects print in a spot color, you have to manually cut the content from its layer and paste the content directly onto the appropriate spot-color channel.

1. **With catalog_working.psd open, draw a rectangular selection marquee around the banner shape.**

2. **Make sure the CMYK composite channel is selected in the Channels panel and the Shape 1 layer is selected in the Layers panel.**

3. **Choose Edit>Cut.**

4. **Select the Pantone 810 C channel in the Channels panel and choose Edit>Paste.**

   The pasted content is not at full strength because the original yellow color maps to a light gray tone on the new channel.

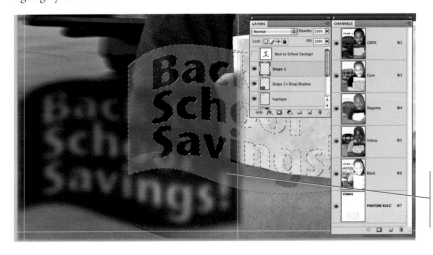

The pasted content is automatically pasted in the middle of the document window.

5. **Using the Move tool, drag the pasted content into place over the drop shadow.**

6. **With the marching ants still showing around the selection, choose Edit>Fill.**

7. **Choose Black in the Use menu, make sure the Mode is set to Normal, set the Opacity to 100%, and then click OK.**

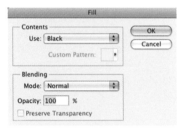

Remember, each channel is a grayscale representation of one color separation. When you pasted the yellow banner onto the channel, the yellow was converted to a shade of gray as part of that channel data. For the banner to be at full strength of the spot color, it must be filled with solid black on the channel.

8. **Save the file as `catalog_final.psd` in your WIP>Catalog folder and continue to the final exercise.**

SAVE THE FILE WITH SPOT COLOR INFORMATION

When you use spot colors, you have to use a file format that can store the spot channel information. The native Photoshop format (PSD) obviously stores the spot channels, but not all applications can work with native Photoshop files.

You can also use the DCS (Desktop Color Separation) 2.0 format, which is an extension of the EPS (Encapsulated PostScript) format. DCS is a pre-separated format that can be saved as a single file, or with each separation saved in an individual file, and then all files are combined at the output stage of a job.

1. **With `catalog_final.psd` open, choose File>Save As.**

2. **Choose Photoshop DCS 2.0 in the Format/Save As Type menu.**

Choosing Photoshop DCS 2.0 in the Format/Save As Type menu changes the extension to ".eps."

3. **Click Save.**

4. **In the DCS 2.0 Format dialog box, choose TIFF (8 bits/pixel) in the Preview menu.**

The Macintosh options (on Macintosh computers) can't be used on Windows computers. The TIFF preview option can be viewed on any computer. It's always a good idea to be inclusive (when you have the option), so use the preview that can be viewed on both platforms.

5. **In the DCS menu, choose Single File with Color Composite (72 pixel/inch).**

The "72 pixel/inch" refers to the preview only; when the file is printed, the full resolution (300 pixels/inch) will be output.

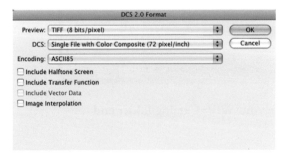

6. **Click OK to save the file.**

7. **When the Save process is complete, close the file.**

Note:

The resulting DCS file is flattened; the DCS format does not support multiple layers.

Project Review

fill in the blank

1. Duplicating one of the existing color channels results in a _____.

2. The _____ filter maintains edge details and turns non-edges gray.

3. The _____ adjustment reduces images to only a defined number of shades of gray.

4. The _____ adjustment converts images to high-contrast bitmap images; pixels in the resulting image are either black or white.

5. Individual channels are actually _____ representations of the amount of a primary color in different areas of the image.

6. The Custom Shape tool can be used to create _____ from built-in or external libraries.

7. _____ are special inks used to print specific colors, often those that are outside the CMYK gamut.

8. A _____ is an image with only two channels, typically black and one other spot color.

9. Spot color information is stored in a _____; it is not associated with any Photoshop layer.

10. Images with spot colors must be saved in the _____ or _____ format.

short answer

1. Briefly describe the characteristics of an Alpha channel.

2. Briefly explain the process of painting directly on a channel.

3. Briefly explain why spot colors are used in commercial graphic design.

Use what you learned in this project to complete the following freeform exercise.
Carefully read the art director and client comments, then create your design to meet the needs of the project.
Use the space below to sketch ideas; when finished, write a brief explanation of the reasoning behind your design.

art director comments

The Cohn's marketing director is very pleased with the completed back-to-school catalog cover, and would like your agency to take over the ongoing catalog project. The Spring catalog, which will be mailed in early February, is the next issue to design.

To complete this project, you should:

❏ Isolate the child in the client's photograph from her background.

❏ Find an appropriate background image for the "Spring" theme of the catalog.

❏ Composite the different cover elements into a cohesive design.

❏ Build a spot channel with the company name and some kind of banner.

client comments

When the weather starts to get warmer, parents need to buy new clothes to replace the ones their kids grew out of since the previous year. The Spring catalog is our second biggest seller.

We have an adorable picture of Andrea for the catalog cover. Her shirt is from our new Sweet Sherbet collection, which will include a lot of pastel shades and light cotton fabrics. (We sent the photograph and the logotype for this issue in the RF_Builders>Catalog folder.)

For this issue's spot color, we were thinking something in a blue shade. We haven't used a blue color for a while, and a blue would contrast well with the peach shirt — in fact, that's one of the reason's we picked this picture for the cover.

Like the Fall catalog, Andrea should fill most of the catalog cover. Find something 'spring-y' to put in the background, but make sure it's subtle.

Use a different shape for the banner this time, with the words 'Spring into Savings!'.

project justification

_____
_____
_____
_____
_____
_____
_____
_____
_____
_____
_____
_____
_____
_____

Project Summary

This project highlighted a number of aesthetic and technical issues of building a unified composition from a set of disparate elements. Many on-the-job projects include complex selections such as the one you created in this project. And although the tools available in Photoshop make the process far easier than painting every pixel by hand, you should be prepared to do some amount of manual clean-up to perfect the fine details of a selection mask. Patience and attention to detail separate great work from average work.

In addition to creating and refining a mask to remove the girl from her background, you had to work around the problem of close framing by the original photograph. Although the photo was created to the correct size, moving the girl off center in the final composition left an unnatural edge. Painting the missing part of the girl's arm would be possible for an accomplished artist, but hiding the problem with other design elements is far easier (and more common) for a Photoshop artist.

Use existing channel information to create a complex selection

Save a complex selection as an alpha channel

Use a complex selection to isolate a complex image from its photographic background

Create and warp a type layer

Use the type layer to select and remove pixels from another layer

Rasterize effects and shape layers

Copy elements from regular layers to a spot color channel

Advertising Samples

You are the in-house designer for a printing company, so your client is the new accounts manager, who is pitching your company's new large-format printing services to a potential customer. She asked you to morph an existing sample ad onto a number of different photos to help promote the company's new "Advertise Anywhere!" services.

This project incorporates the following skills:

❏ Patching a photo to remove unwanted elements

❏ Replacing specific colors in a photo to change the appearance of an object

❏ Using adjustment layers to change hue and saturation values for specific objects in a photo

❏ Adjusting an image's shadows and highlights to correct bad lighting

❏ Applying lighting effects to unify composite images

❏ Wrapping a layer around irregular, non-flat surfaces

❏ Transforming a layer using one- and two-point perspectives

❏ Using 3D functions to wrap artwork around an object

Project Meeting

client comments

Our new "Advertise Anywhere!" campaign is designed to help our clients promote their products by placing large ads in unusual places — on a bench, on the paint strips in parking lots, wrapped around a city bus, and in other non-traditional locations. The producer of *Nighttime News 6* is very interested, but wants to see some samples. He asked me to do a presentation in two weeks for his superiors, including several network executives. If they like what they see, this contract could evolve into a bigger contract with the entire network.

We already created a sample ad for the news program, and I asked my assistant to gather some photos to use in the presentation. We have pictures of the client's office building, as well as the building where their new production studio will be located — we want to personalize the presentation. We also want to show the client two unusual examples, so we chose pictures of a large water tank by the freeway and a hot air balloon.

art director comments

Since the "Advertise Anywhere!" program is new for our company, the owner is excited about presenting to the first potential client. All the pictures they want to use need some help to make them as attractive as possible.

In the fuel tank photo, there's a bunch of litter in the foreground that I want you to clean up.

The bright yellow in the balloon is going to detract attention from the sample ad. Remove the yellow from the balloon body and mute the other colors a bit so the sample ad stands out.

The studio photo isn't bad, but it's been painted since we took the photo. To personalize the presentation, convert the brown front façade to dark red and clean up any marks.

If you place the ad onto the office building as it is now, most of the ad will end up in dark shadows. Adjust the photo's overall lighting before you wrap the ad around the building.

Finally, I want you to create something to show off our "wrap" creating abilities. Take the ad and wrap it around a can to show what an object might look like in three dimensions.

project objectives

To complete this project, you will:

❏ Use the Patch tool to replace one area of an image with pixels from another area

❏ Use adjustment layers to apply color changes to specific areas of an image

❏ Use the Replace Color adjustment to change selective colors in an image

❏ Use the Perspective transformation to match a layer to the perspective in the background image

❏ Use the Shadow/Highlight adjustment to correct an underexposed image

❏ Use the Vanishing Point filter to wrap a layer in perspective around a sharp corner

❏ Use the Lighting Effects filter to unify composited images

❏ Create a custom warp transformation to morph a sample ad onto a round shape

❏ Use 3D functions to wrap an image around an object

Stage 1 Clean and Adjust Images

Photoshop includes a number of tools for creating irregular composite images — such as wrapping a flat ad around the shape of a fuel tank along the desert highway, or placing an ad on a hot air balloon floating in the distance. Before you composite the images for this project, however, you need to do some clean-up work on the background photos. The best approach is to fix the images first, and then morph the ad onto the corrected files.

Use the Patch Tool

In Project 5, you learned a number of techniques for retouching damaged images. The Spot Healing tools are excellent choices for cleaning up marks and blemishes, and the Clone Stamp tool can effectively copy pixels from one location to another. The Patch tool is another option for repairing and retouching images, specifically when you need to replace larger areas of unwanted pixels.

1. **On your desktop, copy the Outdoors folder from the WIP folder on your Resource CD to the WIP folder where you're saving your work.**

   Use your WIP>Outdoors folder to save all files for this project.

2. **In Photoshop, open tanks.jpg from the RF_Photoshop>Outdoors folder.**

This image will make a better client sample without the annoying litter along the edge of the road.

Note:

If you repaired the antique image in Project 4, you're already familiar with the healing tools. While the Healing Brush tool is well suited to correct external damage (such as the scratch in the portrait), the Patch tool is the best choice for removing static objects that are actually part of the image.

3. **Choose the Patch tool in the Tools panel (nested under the Healing Brush or Spot Healing Brush tool).**

   The Patch tool allows you to repair a selected area with pixels from another area or a pattern. It matches texture, lighting, and shading of the sampled pixels to the source (selected) pixels.

4. **Zoom in to the large white object in the bottom center of the image.**

5. **Using the Patch tool, draw a selection marquee that entirely surrounds the piece of trash.**

Because of the texture and detail in the surrounding area, the other repair tools are not the best choices for removing this object from the roadside. The Patch tool, on the other hand, allows you to sample pixels from other areas of the image and blend them smoothly over the selected area.

Patch tool — Unwanted image area

Selection marquee

Patch tool cursor

6. **In the Control panel, make sure the Source option is selected and the Transparent option is not checked.**

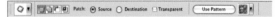

The Source and Destination options define what the selection marquee represents.

- If Source is selected, the original marquee represents the area that will be patched.

- If Destination is selected, the original selection marquee represents the pixels that will be copied to another area.

7. **Place the Patch tool cursor inside the selection marquee, and then click and drag to the left.**

The pixels inside the second marquee (where you drag to) will be used to fill the original marquee location. This tool shows a dynamic preview; as you drag the marquee, the original selection changes to show the result that will be created when you release the mouse button.

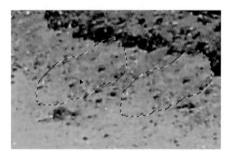

8. **When you are satisfied with the preview of new pixels, release the mouse button.**

The Patch tool blends the selection edge smoothly into the surrounded area, preventing unwanted harsh edges around the patch.

9. **Press Command/Control-D to turn off the selection marquee so you can review your results.**

If you aren't satisfied, undo the patch selection and try again.

Note:

Deselection is considered a step, so you can't use the one-process Undo command. You have to use the History panel to go back two steps and restore the original pixels, or use the Step Backward command (Command-Option-Z/Control-Alt-Z).

Note:

Make sure you deselect the marquee between each patch.

10. **Using the same technique, remove the rest of the litter from the foreground of this image.**

The mechanics of the Patch tool are simple and effective. The most difficult part of this process is determining what to select and what to use as replacement pixels. Keep the following tips in mind when you clean up the rest of the roadside trash from this photo:

- The Source option is best if you want to remove something from an image. The Destination option is best if you want to add or make copies of specific image areas.

- It helps to work at 100% view when you use the Patch tool.

- Use the smallest selection area possible to achieve the best results.

- Choose replacement pixels from an area near the pixels you want to replace. This helps avoid obvious difference in color or lighting in the patched area.

- Areas of high contrast outside the selection edge produce a soft blended effect that won't be apparent until you release the mouse button. This might cause more damage than it fixes.

Replacement pixels   Original selection

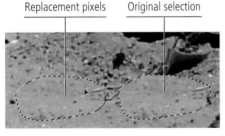

After releasing the mouse button, the unselected part of the litter blends into the original selection area.

- If you want to patch an edge, choose a similar edge as the replacement pixels.

- When you choose the replacement pixels, be careful to avoid creating unwanted patterns or obvious (but unwanted) copies of image elements.

Replacement pixels

These exact spots now appear twice in close proximity, which is simply not natural.

11. Save the file as a native Photoshop file named `tanks_clean.psd` **in your WIP>Outdoors folder, and then close the file.**

12. Continue to the next exercise.

REPLACE COLORS IN PARTS OF AN IMAGE

The Replace Color adjustment allows you to select and replace a specific range of colors in an image. This adjustment option is a simple method for making overall changes to hue, saturation, or lightness in selected areas without having to experiment with layer blending modes.

1. Open the file `studio.jpg` **from the RF_Photoshop>Outdoors folder.**

On the actual building, this façade has been repainted a deep red.

The fresh paint removed these white streaks.

2. **Choose Image>Adjustments>Replace Color.**

3. **Using the Eyedropper tool from the Replace Color dialog box, click in the image (behind the dialog box) to select the brown stucco façade of the building.**

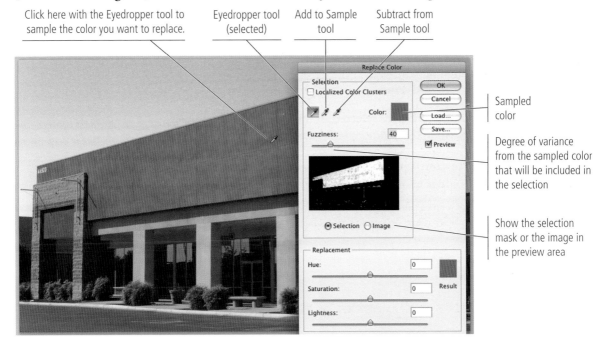

Click here with the Eyedropper tool to sample the color you want to replace.

Eyedropper tool (selected)

Add to Sample tool

Subtract from Sample tool

Sampled color

Degree of variance from the sampled color that will be included in the selection

Show the selection mask or the image in the preview area

4. **Drag the Fuzziness slider right to increase the selection tolerance.**

   As you increase the fuzziness, you can see other areas of the image being added to the selection. Various areas in this image share many of the same earth tones, which means you can't select the façade color without affecting some other areas of the image — or at least, not without a couple of extra steps.

Increasing fuzziness adds more areas to the selection.

5. **Click Cancel to close the Replace Color dialog box.**

6. In the Layers panel, Control/right-click the Background layer and choose Duplicate Layer from the contextual menu. Click OK to accept the default layer name.

Note:

When you Control/right-click a layer and select Duplicate Layer, you can use the Destination options to place the duplicate layer in the stack for the current (open) image, any open image, or a new image.

7. With the Background Copy layer selected in the Layers panel, choose Image>Adjustments>Replace Color.

8. Click in the image to sample the same brown as the selection color, and then move the Fuzziness slider all the way to the right.

   The preview shows that a large portion of the image is selected, including areas that you don't want to change. That's okay, since you'll use a layer mask to eliminate those areas from the duplicate layer.

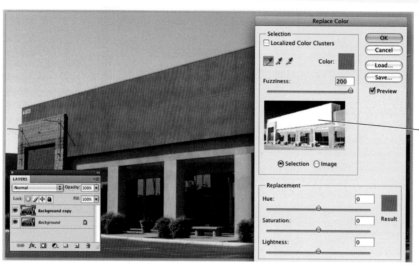

Much of the building has some shade of brown, so full Fuzziness selects most of the building face.

9. In the Replacement area, experiment with the Hue, Saturation, and Lightness sliders until you find a dark red color.

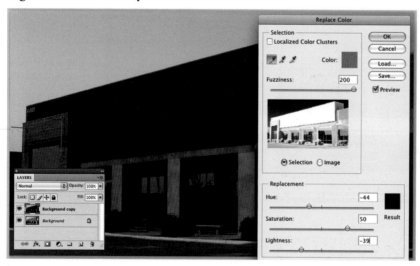

Note:

You can also click the Result color swatch and define a replacement color in the Color Picker dialog box.

Note:

It's important to understand that image adjustments apply to the selected area or layer only. These adjustments do not apply to all layers in an image.

10. Click OK to apply the change to the selected layer.

11. **Using any method you prefer, draw a selection marquee around the edges of the façade.**

Since this selection has straight edges, the Polygonal Lasso tool will do a fine job of creating the selection. You could also draw a work path with the Pen tool, and then make a selection based on the work path.

12. **With the selection active (you can see the marching ants), click the Add Layer Mask button at the bottom of the Layers panel.**

When you add a layer mask with an active selection, the areas outside the selection are automatically masked.

Add Layer Mask button

13. **Zoom in to the edges of the façade and make sure the mask covers exactly what you want it to cover. Use the Brush tool to clean up the mask edges if necessary, especially around the brick edges in the left side of the image.**

Remember, when you paint on a mask, black adds to the mask and white removes areas from the mask. You should also make sure to select the mask in the Layers panel (instead of the actual layer) before painting on the mask.

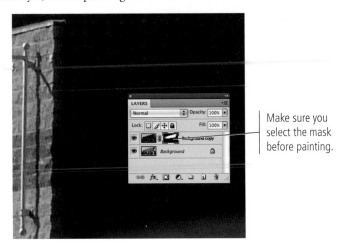

Make sure you select the mask before painting.

14. **With the Background Copy layer selected, choose Merge Down from the Layer panel Options menu.**

Merge Down combines the selected layer with the next layer down in the Layers panel. **Merge Visible** combines all visible layers into a single layer. **Flatten Image** combines all layers into the Background layer, giving you the option to discard hidden layers.

Note:

You can also Control/ right-click the layer name and choose Merge Down from the layer's contextual menu.

Because the next layer down is the Background layer, merging the selected layer down combines the Background Copy layer into the Background layer.

15. **Use any technique you prefer to remove the white streaks from the building's façade.**

We used a combination of the Spot Healing tool to clean up the spots on the face and the Clone Stamp and Patch tools to clean up the edges.

16. **Save the file as a native Photoshop file named `studio_clean.psd` in your WIP>Outdoors folder, and then close the file.**

17. **Continue to the next exercise.**

Selective Color Adjustment

The **Selective Color adjustment** (Image>Adjustment>Selective Color) allows you to change the ink values in specific primary colors or neutrals without affecting other colors.

For example, if water looks too yellow, you should remove yellow to produce a more inviting blue color. If you reduce the overall amount of yellow, however, you might affect other areas such as the pier and island in the image shown below. The Selective Color option allows you to adjust the yellow component of only blues and greens, so you can fix the water without affecting the pier and island.

The Relative method changes the existing amount of cyan, magenta, yellow, or black by its percentage of the total. For example, if you start with a pixel that is 70% yellow and remove 10%, 7% is removed from the yellow (10% of 70% = 7%).

The Absolute method adjusts the color in absolute values. If you start with a pixel that is 70% yellow and remove 10%, the yellow pixel is set to 60%.

Water in the original image
has a strong yellow cast.

Adjusting ink percentages of only the greens
and blues makes the water more inviting
without affecting the pilings in the foreground.

ADJUST HUE AND SATURATION WITH AN ADJUSTMENT LAYER

Correcting the previous image highlighted one of the potential drawbacks of using image adjustments: You might change areas you don't want to change, requiring a workaround (in this case, a duplicate layer with a mask) to achieve the effect you want.

The process you used in the previous exercise is very common — so much so that Photoshop includes built-in options for creating adjustment layers, which effectively achieve the same result you accomplished manually. An adjustment layer is an empty layer containing an adjustment (such as a Levels or Curves adjustment) that modifies the layers below it.

1. **Open the file balloon.jpg from the RF_Photoshop>Outdoors folder.**

   The Hue/Saturation adjustment, which allows you to change the Hue, Saturation, and Lightness values of specific primary colors, is perfectly suited for changing this yellow balloon to white.

The art director wants this yellow balloon to be white so it doesn't distract from the sample ad.

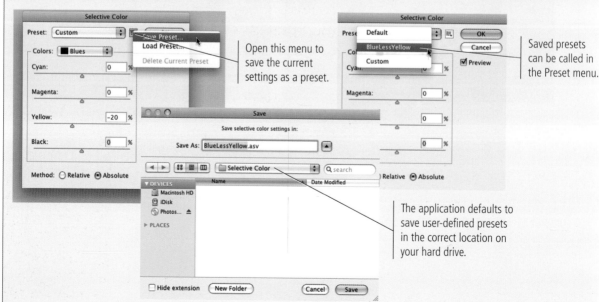

Using Adjustment Presets

The Preset menu at the top of the Selective Color dialog box is useful if you need to make the same adjustment to multiple images — for example, you know photos from a particular digital camera always have a yellow cast in the blue areas. (The same Preset options are available in all adjustments dialog boxes.)

Open this menu to save the current settings as a preset.

Saved presets can be called in the Preset menu.

The application defaults to save user-defined presets in the correct location on your hard drive.

PHOTOSHOP FOUNDATIONS

PHOTOSHOP FOUNDATIONS

In addition to the tools you have used throughout this book, a number of tools in the Tools panel can be used to make basic corrections.

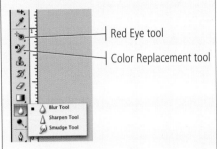

Red Eye tool

Color Replacement tool

The **Red Eye tool** removes the red-eye effect caused by flash photography.

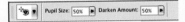

In the Control panel, the Pupil Size menu controls the size of the area affected by the tool. The Darken Amount option sets the darkness of the correction.

The **Blur tool** softens hard edges and reduces detail.

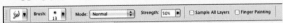

The **Sharpen tool** increases contrast at edges to increase apparent sharpness.

The **Smudge tool** allows you to push pixels around in an image, as if you were dragging your finger across wet (digital) paint.

All three of these tools use a selected brush preset to affect the image. You can choose a specific blending mode, as well as the strength of the effect as you paint a brush stroke. Multiple brush strokes increases the tool's effect.

If the Sample All Layers option is checked, you can affect the selected layer using data from all layers in the file. For the Smudge tool, the Finger Painting option adds the foreground color to the beginning of the brush stroke.

Original Image · Blurred · Sharpened · Smudged

The **Color Replacement tool** attempts to simplify replacement of specific colors in your image. You can define the brush you want to use, and then paint over a targeted color to replace it with the foreground color.

You can replace the color, or you can choose Hue, Saturation, or Luminosity in the Mode menu. The sampling options determine how color will be replaced:

- **Continuous** samples colors as you drag.
- **Once** replaces color only in areas of the color you first click.
- **Background Swatch** replaces only areas of the current background color.

The Limits menu determines how the tool's effect can be constrained:

- **Discontiguous** replaces the sampled color under the brush tip.
- **Contiguous** replaces color contiguous with the color under the brush tip.
- **Find Edges** replaces connected areas of the sampled color, attempting to preserve the sharpness of shape edges.

Tolerance defines how much variance from the sample will be affected. The **Anti-alias** option smoothes edges of the affected areas.

The Color Replacement tool works best for images with high-contrast edges.

Using the Adjustments Panel

PHOTOSHOP FOUNDATIONS

Adjustment layers provide another way to apply many of the same adjustments that are available in the Image>Adjustments menu. The difference is that adjustment layers are non-destructive; rather than permanently affecting the pixels in your image, adjustment layers store the adjustment settings in a special layer so you can change the settings or toggle the adjustment on or off at any point in your workflow.

The Adjustments panel offers most of the same options that are available in the Add a New Fill or Adjustment Layer button at the bottom of the Layers panel. (The lower half of the Adjustments panel includes a number of defined presets, which ship with the application. You can expand any of these folders and simply click a specific preset to apply the related settings.)

Clicking one of the adjustment buttons in the top half of the Adjustments panel adds an adjustment layer above the currently selected layer; while the adjustment layer is selected in the Layers panel, the Adjustments panel displays the settings for the selected adjustment.

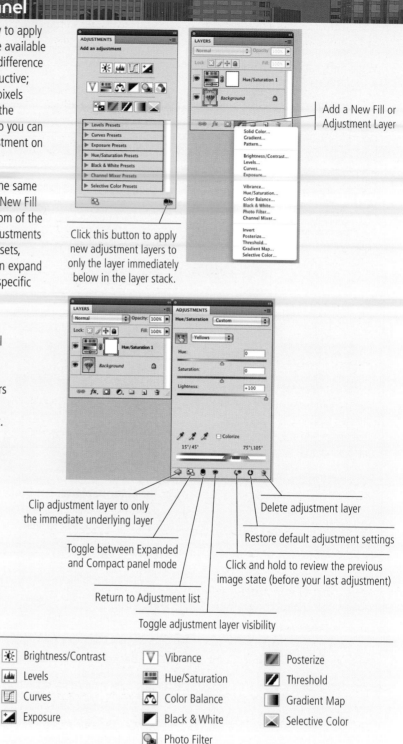

Add a New Fill or Adjustment Layer

Click this button to apply new adjustment layers to only the layer immediately below in the layer stack.

Clip adjustment layer to only the immediate underlying layer

Delete adjustment layer

Restore default adjustment settings

Toggle between Expanded and Compact panel mode

Click and hold to review the previous image state (before your last adjustment)

Return to Adjustment list

Toggle adjustment layer visibility

The top half of the Adjustments panel includes icons for each of the available adjustments.

Brightness/Contrast	Vibrance	Posterize
Levels	Hue/Saturation	Threshold
Curves	Color Balance	Gradient Map
Exposure	Black & White	Selective Color
	Photo Filter	
	Channel Mixer	
	Invert	

2. Activate the Adjustments panel and click the Hue/Saturation button.

The Hue/Saturation adjustment can be extremely useful for shifting the Hue, Saturation, or Lightness value of an entire image or for selected primary colors.

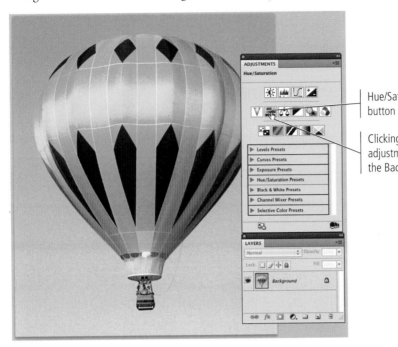

Hue/Saturation button

Clicking creates a new adjustment layer above the Background layer.

Note:

You can use adjustment layers for most of the adjustments available in the Image>Adjustments menu. (For some reason, a few adjustments — including the Replace Color adjustment you used in the previous exercise — have been left out of this panel.)

Adding an adjustment layer creates a new layer on top of the currently selected layer (in this case, the Background layer). This allows you to easily show or hide the adjustment, apply multiple adjustments to the same layer, or even delete an adjustment from the file without permanently changing the pixels on the original layer.

Note:

You can add adjustment layers using either the Adjustments panel or the menu at the bottom of the Layers panel.

The adjustment layer is identified by an icon that matches the Hue/Saturation icon in the Adjustments panel.

3. **In the Adjustments panel, choose Yellows in the Edit menu and drag the Lightness slider all the way to the right.**

If you remember from Project 4, lightness is the position of a color along the black/white scale. Lightness of 0 adds no white or black to the hue. Lightness of −100 is solid black (obscuring all other color). Lightness of +100 is pure white (removing all color).

Choose from this Edit menu to adjust the entire image, or individual additive or subtractive primary colors.

Since the balloon was pure yellow, changing the yellow lightness to +100 converts the yellow parts of the balloon to pure white.

4. **Review the Layers panel.**

Adjustment layers automatically include a layer mask, which allows you to isolate portions of an image for correction. Adjustment layers are also helpful for experimenting with corrections without permanently affecting the underlying layer.

Hide or show the adjustment by clicking the visibility icon for the layer.

Select the adjustment layer in the Layers panel to show the related settings in the Adjustments panel.

Adjustment layers automatically include an empty layer mask, which you can edit to protect areas of the underlying layers.

5. **In the Layers panel, click the Adjustment Layer Mask icon to select it.**

6. **Using a large brush with a black foreground color, paint over the area of the basket to protect that area from the increased Lightness setting for yellows.**

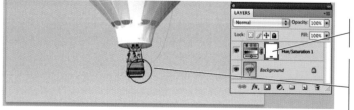

The adjustment layer mask is selected.

Painting on the mask restores the color in the balloon basket and passengers.

Note:

The adjustment from an adjustment layer is not permanent unless you flatten the image.

Note:

Adjustment layers affect all underlying layers. If you want an adjustment layer to affect only the next layer down, Control/right-click the adjustment layer and choose Create Clipping Mask from the contextual menu.

7. **With the adjustment layer selected, choose Merge Down in the Layers panel Options menu.**

Note:

Another advantage of using adjustment layers is that you can change the opacity, order, or blending mode of an adjustment layer, just as you can with a regular layer.

8. **Save the file as `balloon_clean.psd` in your WIP>Outdoors folder.**

9. **Close the file and continue to the next exercise.**

The Photo Filter Adjustment

The Photo Filter adjustment (Image>Adjustments>Photo Filter, or accessed in the Adjustments panel) creates the effect of taking a photo through colored filters to adjust color balance or create an artistic effect.

You can choose one of the defined filters in the Filter menu, or you can apply a custom color filter by clicking the Color swatch and choosing from the Color Picker dialog box. For example, you can choose a specific filter from the Filter menu to create a specific mood (such as a Sepia or Underwater filter), or apply a custom magenta filter to remove a green color cast.

The Density slider adjusts the amount of color applied to the image (higher density means more color). If the Preserve Luminosity option is checked, the color adjustment has no effect on the overall lightness/darkness of the image.

The original image

The image after applying the Cooling Filter (80)

PHOTOSHOP FOUNDATIONS

ADJUST IMAGE SHADOWS AND HIGHLIGHTS

The Shadows/Highlights adjustment is well suited for correcting highlight and shadow areas of an image. (Photoshop calculates the changes based on the values of surrounding pixels.) Using the basic settings, you can adjust the values of shadows and highlights independently. If the Show More Options box is checked, you can also exercise finer control over each area.

1. **Open the file office.jpg from the RF_Photoshop>Outdoors folder.**

This overall image is extremely dark; most of the building is in shadows.

PHOTOSHOP FOUNDATIONS

Extended Control for Shadows/Highlights Adjustments

When the Show More Options box is checked in the Shadows/Highlights dialog box, you can fine-tune the adjustments for both highlights and shadows, as well as modify the options for color correction and midtone contrast.

Tonal Width defines the part of the tonal range that will be modified by the adjustment. If you set the Tonal Width value to 100%, the adjustment will be applied to half of the entire tonal range. Smaller values restrict the adjustment to smaller regions of the related area (shadows or highlights).

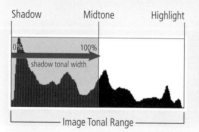

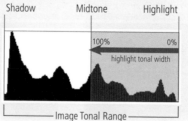

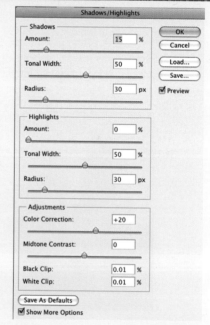

Radius controls the size of the area around each pixel that is used to determine whether a pixel is in the shadows or highlights.

Color Correction finetunes the colors in areas that are changed by your choices in the Shadows and Highlights sections of the dialog box. Higher Color Correction values tend to produce more saturated colors.

Midtone Contrast adjusts the contrast in the midtones, similar to the Input Gamma slider in the Levels dialog box.

Black Clip and **White Clip** determine how much of the extreme shadows and highlights are clipped, just as with the Clip options in the Auto Color Correction Options dialog box.

2. **Choose Image>Adjustments>Shadow/Highlight.**

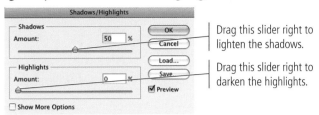

Drag this slider right to lighten the shadows.

Drag this slider right to darken the highlights.

3. **Reduce the Shadow Amount value to 15% to lighten the shadows in the image.**

   An Amount value of 0% means no change will be applied to that area; larger values result in lighter shadows or darker highlights.

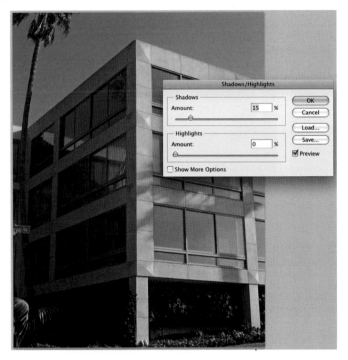

4. **Click OK to apply the change.**

5. **Save the file as a native Photoshop file named `office_clean.psd` in your WIP>Outdoors folder, and then close the file.**

6. **Continue to the next stage of the project.**

Painting Image Exposure and Saturation

The Dodge and Burn tools are used to lighten or darken areas of an image (respectively). These tools are based on traditional photographic techniques for exposing specific areas of a print. Photographers hold back light to lighten an area on the print (**dodging**) or increase the exposure to darken areas on a print (**burning**).

When using the Dodge or Burn tool, you can define a brush tip in the Options bar, as well as the image range you want to affect (highlights, midtones, or shadows) and the degree of exposure.

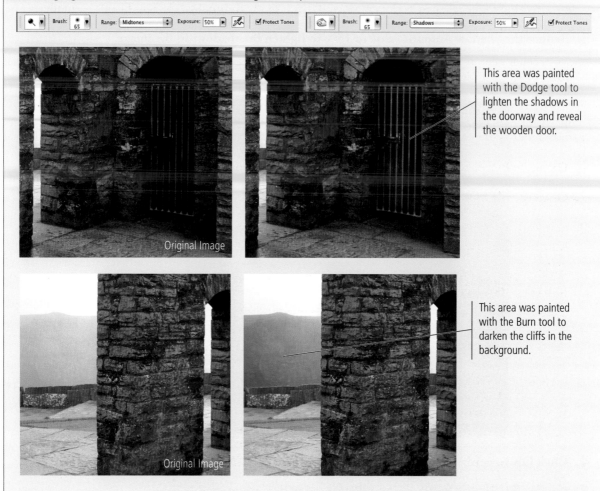

This area was painted with the Dodge tool to lighten the shadows in the doorway and reveal the wooden door.

Original Image

This area was painted with the Burn tool to darken the cliffs in the background.

Original Image

The Sponge tool changes the color saturation of an area. As with the Dodge and Burn tools, you can define a specific brush to use. You can also define the mode of the Sponge tool — Saturate or Desaturate — and the flow rate for the tool's effect.

This wall was painted with the Sponge tool in Saturation mode to enhance the green shades in the moss.

Original Image

Stage 2 Working in Perspective

Many compositing jobs will be straightforward copy-and-paste jobs — putting multiple images together, possibly adjusting size, clipping edges, or blending edges into other elements — such as the work you completed in the earlier projects of this book.

Other jobs are more complex, especially jobs that require you to make one object appear to be a seamless part of another image. When your goal is to merge one element with another existing image, pay close attention to details such as size, angle, and depth so the composited element blends naturally with the background image.

TRANSFORM THE PERSPECTIVE OF A LAYER

Basic transformations such as scale, rotation, skew, and perspective can all be accomplished in Free Transform mode. For skewing a flat ad onto a flat surface, Free Transform mode is the simplest choice.

1. **Open the file `studio_clean.psd` from your WIP>Outdoors folder.**

2. **Open the file `banner.tif` from the RF_Photoshop>Outdoors folder.**

3. **Select the entire banner file (Select>All or Command/Control-A), copy it, and then paste it into the studio_clean file.**

4. **With Layer 1 (of the studio_clean file) selected in the Layers panel, choose Edit>Free Transform.**

When you choose one of the Transform options, handles appear around the selection or layer so you can control the transformation.

5. **Using the Control panel, scale the layer to 73% proportionally, and then drag the banner so the top-right corner of the banner is near the top-right corner of the studio façade.**

Use the W and H fields to resize the banner graphic to 73% of its original size.

Free Transform Options

You can transform any layer or selection using the options in the Edit>Transform menu or by choosing Edit>Free Transform. (Most of the options in the Edit>Transform submenu — Scale, Rotate, Skew, and Distort — can actually be applied using the Free Transform option, making these choices redundant.)

When you choose Edit>Free Transform, the selection is surrounded by handles that allow you to control the transformation. Use the following images as a guide for controlling your transformations.

Click a center handle to stretch or shrink the selection in one direction.

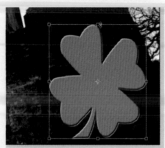

Command/Control-click a center handle to skew the selection.

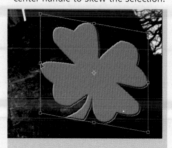

Click slightly outside a corner handle to rotate the selection.

Click a corner handle to stretch or shrink the selection horizontally and vertically at the same time.

Command/Control-click a corner handle to distort the selection.

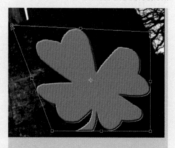

Press Option/Alt while making any free transformation to apply it equally on both sides of the selection center.

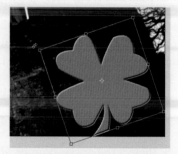

Pressing Shift with any of the transformations constrains the transformation to 45-degree increments. For example, if you press Shift while skewing a selection, the skew will be constrained to exactly horizontal or vertical.

If you choose Edit>Transform>Perspective, dragging a corner handle has the same effect as pressing Command-Option-Shift/Control-Alt-Shift when working in Free Transform mode. Dragging a side handle has the same effect as pressing Command/Control-Shift when in Free Transform mode.

The advantage to Perspective transformation mode is that you don't have to use the modifier keys. The disadvantage is that you can't change anything other than the horizontal or vertical skew and the reflective horizontal or vertical distortion of the selection.

When you choose Edit>Transform>Perspective, drag a corner handle to shrink or expand that side of the selection around the center point.

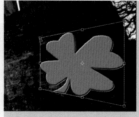

In Free Transform mode, press Command/Control and drag a side handle to skew the selection at any angle.

When you choose Edit>Transform>Perspective, drag a center handle to skew the selection.

Press Command/Control-Shift and drag a side handle to skew the selection exactly vertical or horizontal.

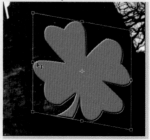

6. **Command/Control-click the center-left transformation handle and drag down to skew the layer.**

   Simply dragging a center handle stretches or shrinks the selection. Pressing the Command/Control key allows you to skew a selection instead of changing its horizontal or vertical size.

Press Command/Control and drag the center handle to skew the selection.

Note:

Press Shift while Command/Control-dragging to skew the object exactly vertical or exactly horizontal.

7. **Command/Control-click the top-left transformation handle and drag down to distort the perspective of the layer.**

   Simply dragging a corner handle stretches or shrinks the selection. Pressing the Command/Control key allows you to distort the image's shape, which affects perspective when you drag straight corners in this manner.

Press Command/Control and drag the corner handle to alter the perspective of the selection.

Note:

Press Shift while Command/Control-dragging to constrain the movement of the transformation handle to 45° angles.

8. **Adjust the bottom corner handles so the banner fits entirely within the front of the façade.**

9. **When you're satisfied with the position, size, and perspective of the banner, press Return/Enter to finalize the transformation.**

10. **Apply a slight drop shadow to the ad layer. We used the following settings:**

Blend Mode:	Multiply Black	**Opacity:**	75%
Angle:	125°	**Distance:**	10
Spread:	0	**Size:**	5

Note:

We used the 125° angle for the drop shadow to approximate the angle of shadows that already exist in the image.

11. **Save the file as studio_ad.psd in your WIP>Outdoors folder, close the file, and continue to the next exercise.**

Content-Aware Scaling

As you have seen, dragging the side handles of a selection can distort important objects — especially if you don't press Shift to constrain the selection while you scale it. There are times, however, when you might need to scale something in only one direction, but you don't want the distortion that might result. In this case, content-aware scaling might be your solution.

Dragging the side handle in Free Transform mode significantly distorts the image detail.

Content-Aware Scaling identifies and tries to protect areas of detail when you scale the image. In some cases, however, the image focus might have little or no detail within the shape areas (for example, the white bird in the following image). In this case, you can identify a specific mask area to protect when you use Content-Aware Scaling.

Choosing Edit>Content-Aware Scale shows the same transformation handles you see when you choose Edit>Free Transform.

Use this menu to protect a specific mask area.

Click this button to protect skin tones from scaling.

Dragging the side handle in Content-Aware Scale mode maintains as much of the original detail and proportions as possible.

Original image

Image scaled using Content-Aware Scale mode

Image scaled using Content-Aware Scale mode, but with the bird area protected by a mask.

USE THE VANISHING POINT FILTER

The previous exercise used **one-point perspective** — an artistic principle in which all lines in an image ultimately meet at a single invisible vanishing point outside the edges of the image. To effectively merge one image into another, the new image must be adjusted to use the same vanishing point as the original. The Free Transform option is usually enough to combine images in one-point perspective.

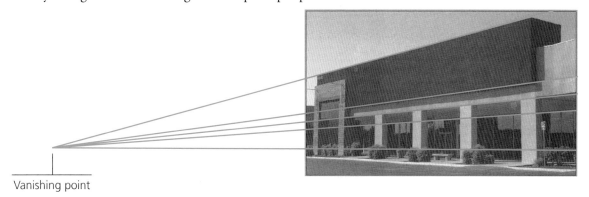

Vanishing point

Many images have more than one side (or plane), where lines go off in two different directions. This type of image has **two-point perspective** because there are two different vanishing points. Combining images in two-point perspective (such as wrapping a selection around a corner) is a bit more difficult to manage using the Free Transform option. Fortunately, the Vanishing Point filter makes the process relatively easy — once you understand how it works.

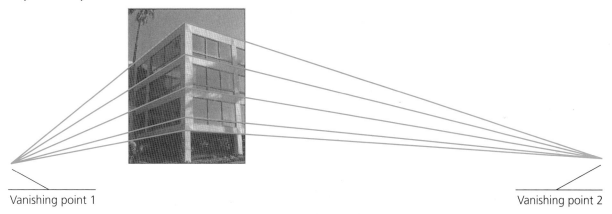

Vanishing point 1   Vanishing point 2

1. Open the file **office_clean.psd** from your **WIP>Outdoors** folder.

2. Add a new empty layer to the file and make sure it is selected in the Layers panel.

    The results of the Vanishing Point filter will become part of the selected layer. If you don't add a new layer before using the filter, the sample ad will be automatically flattened into the background.

3. **Select the entire banner file and copy it to the Clipboard.**

   The object — whether from the active file or any other file — that you want to put into perspective needs to be copied before you open the Vanishing Point filter.

4. **With the office_clean file active, choose Filter>Vanishing Point.**

   The Vanishing Point filter has its own interface, where you can define the perspective in an image and place other selections into those planes.

5. **With the Create Plane tool selected (it is by default), set the Grid Size to 200 pixels.**

6. **Click at the top corner where the two sides of the building meet.**

7. **Use the lines in the image to draw a perspective plane around the first section of windows on the right face of the building.**

   The Create Plane tool defines the first perspective plane of the image. When you define the perspective plane, make sure you follow the path of lines in the image so the vanishing point of your plane matches the vanishing point in the image.

Note:

When you define the third corner of the plane, lines automatically connect the first and third points with the mouse cursor. Simply click to anchor the fourth corner point.

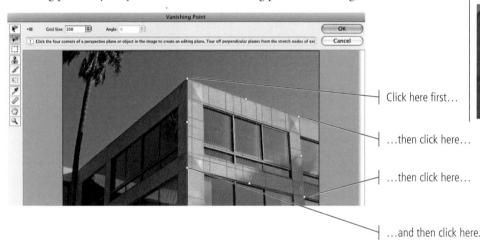

Click here first…

…then click here…

…then click here…

…and then click here.

8. **With the Edit Plane tool selected, drag the top-, bottom-, and right-center handles in toward the center of the first section of windows, so the plane edges are about halfway between the surrounding windows. (Leave the left edge at the building corner.)**

Drag the top, right, and bottom handles in toward the center of the concrete blocks surrounding the first bank of windows.

9. **Press Command/Control, click the left-center handle, and then drag left to create a secondary plane that's perpendicular to the first plane.**

   If you click the handle before pressing Command/Control, this step won't work. Make sure you press the modifier key before you click and drag the handle.

Press Command/ Control, and then drag this handle to add a secondary plane.

10. **Drag the top- and bottom-corner handles on the left side of the secondary plane until the plane more closely matches the perspective of lines on the left face of the building.**

Drag these handles up or down to adjust the perspective of the secondary plane.

11. **Press Command/Control-V to paste the copied pixels from the Clipboard (the banner file you copied in Step 3).**

    The pasted pixels appear in the top-left corner of the preview, surrounded by a selection marquee.

12. **Click inside the selection marquee and drag onto any part of the perspective plane.**

The selection is dropped into the perspective plane, cleanly wrapped around both sides of the building.

13. **Drag the selection inside the plane until the ad fills the entire defined plane area.**

14. **Select the Transform tool in the left side of the Vanishing Point filter dialog box.**

15. **In the Vanishing Point filter Options menu, turn off the Clip Operations to Surface Edges option.**

Transform tool

This option should be unchecked (turned off).

When the Clip option is off, you can see the entire selection, including areas outside the defined perspective plane.

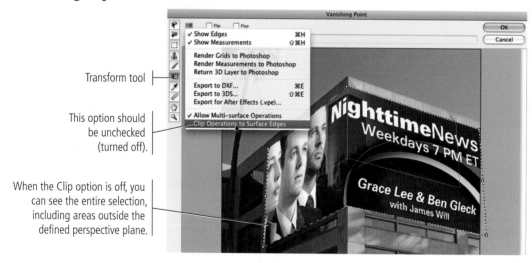

16. **Drag the side handles of the selection until all of the banner text fits within the plane edge.**

    The perspective planes still produce a very good result, even though you are scaling out of proportion to fit the banner within the allowed space.

17. **Reactivate the Clip Operations to Surface Edges option, and then click OK to apply the Vanishing Point filter.**

18. **Apply a drop shadow using the following settings:**

Blend mode:	Multiply Black		Opacity:	75%
Angle:	40°		Distance:	5
Spread:	0		Size:	10

Note:

The 40-degree angle helps match the drop shadow angle to the apparent light source in the office image.

19. **Save the file as office_ad.psd in your WIP>Outdoors folder, close the file, and then continue to the next exercise.**

Vanishing Point Controls

The Vanishing Point dialog box might seem intimidating at first, but it's fairly easy to use once you understand the tools. Most of these tools perform the same functions as in the main Photoshop interface; the Marquee tool, however, is the most notable difference.

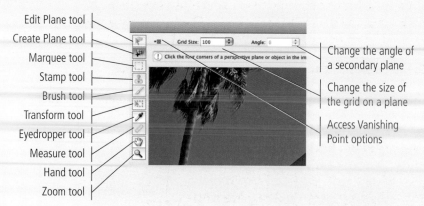

- Edit Plane tool
- Create Plane tool
- Marquee tool
- Stamp tool
- Brush tool
- Transform tool
- Eyedropper tool
- Measure tool
- Hand tool
- Zoom tool

Change the angle of a secondary plane

Change the size of the grid on a plane

Access Vanishing Point options

In addition to pasting a selection from the Clipboard, you can use the Marquee tool to make selections within the perspective planes in the Vanishing Point dialog box. Once you've drawn a selection, a number of options become available above the preview.

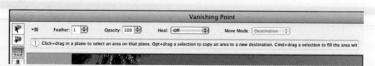

- The **Feather** option defines how many pixels at the selection edges are blurred to help smooth the transition from the copied pixels to the original pixels.

- The **Opacity** option allows you to adjust the opacity of moved pixels, which is useful if you aren't building the filter onto a new layer.

- The **Heal** menu defines the blending mode for moved pixels, which is also useful if you aren't building the filter onto a new layer.

- The **Move Mode** menu is similar to the Patch tool Source and Destination options.

  - If Destination is selected, clicking inside a selection marquee and dragging moves the marquee to a new position, maintaining the same perspective defined in the plane. (You can press Command/Control and drag from inside a Destination mode marquee to fill the selection with pixels from another area.)

  - If Source is selected, clicking inside a selection marquee and dragging fills the marquee with pixels from the destination area.

- Once you have moved pixels into a selection, you can use the Transform tool to rotate or scale the selection, as well as flip it horizontally or vertically using the check boxes that appear over the preview image.

Defined perspective plane

Using the Marquee tool, we defined the original selection to be large enough to copy the entire shutter.

With the marquee set to Destination Move mode, we clicked inside the original marquee and dragged to the place we wanted to create a new shutter. (Notice the size and shape of the marquee, which is altered to match the defined perspective plane.)

We then switched to Source Move mode and dragged back over the original selection to create a second shutter.

WARP THE SAMPLE AD

Linear perspective, such as the two examples you just created, is fairly easy to adjust (especially using the Vanishing Point filter). However, the world is not entirely linear; objects with curves also have depth and perspective. Compositing onto rounded objects is slightly more complicated than linear perspective, but you can accomplish the task with patience and attention to detail.

1. **Open the file `tanks_clean.psd` from your WIP>Outdoors folder.**

2. **Select the entire banner file, copy it, and then paste it into the tanks_clean file.**

3. **Scale the placed ad to 35% and position it in the center of the front fuel tank (above the top of the fence).**

4. **Choose Edit>Transform>Warp.**

   This is the same option you used in Project 5 to warp text. However, when you warp anything other than text, you have more options and better control over the warp.

Click here to finalize the transformation.

Click here to cancel the transformation.

Custom is automatically selected in the Warp type menu.

When transforming anything other than text, a grid and handles appear for controlling the warp.

5. **In the Control panel, choose Arc Upper from the Warp menu.**

As for warping text, the same predefined warp options are available for warping an object.

The background image — the fuel tank — is only slightly curved. A minor Arc Upper warp should be enough to add perspective to the ad layer.

The default Bend value (50%) is obviously too much for this compositing job.

6. **Experiment with Bend values until you're satisfied with the result. (We used a 4% bend.)**

The Bend value changes only the edges affected by the warp you apply; in the case of Arc Upper, only the top edge changes when you modify the Bend value.

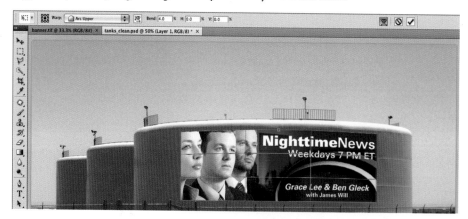

7. **In the Control panel, click the Commit button to finalize the transformation.**

8. **Apply a drop shadow to the layer using the following settings:**

Blend mode:	Multiply Black	Opacity:	75%
Angle:	90°	Distance:	2
Spread:	0	Size:	5

Note:

The 90° angle helps match the drop shadow angle to the apparent light source in the tanks image.

9. **Save the file as** `tanks_ad.psd` **in your WIP>Outdoors folder and close the file.**

10. **Continue to the next exercise.**

 ## APPLY A CUSTOM WARP

In some cases, the predefined warp styles are adequate. In other cases — such as warping the ad around the balloon in this exercise — the existing styles simply do not work.

1. **Open the file** `balloon_clean.psd` **from your WIP>Outdoors folder.**

2. **Select the entire banner file, copy it, and then paste it into the balloon_clean file.**

3. **Scale the ad layer to 40% proportionally and position it as shown in the following image:**

4. **Choose Edit>Transform>Warp. Apply the Arch warp to the ad layer with a 12% bend.**

5. **Choose Custom in the Warp menu on the Control panel.**

These handles control the warp curves between points on the grid.

Beginning from the Arch warp style gives you a better starting point than simply starting from the basic Custom warp.

6. **Drag the corner points on the warp grid to be directly inside the second seam line on the balloon.**

Position the two left corner points directly inside this seam line.

7. **Drag the handles on the left side of the grid to bloat the left side of the layer.**

   Handles on a warp grid are just like handles on a vector path (the ones you create with the Pen tool). Curves follow the direction you drag the connected handles.

Drag these two handles left so the left edge of the ad follows the line of the seam.

8. Repeat Steps 6–7 for the right side of the ad.

9. Adjust the top and bottom handles to fit the edges vertically within the area between the color patches.

Use this seam to align the ad's top edge.

Use this seam to align the ad's right edge.

Use this seam to align the ad's bottom edge.

10. Finalize the transformation, and then apply a drop shadow using the following settings:

Blend mode:	Multiply Black	Opacity:	75%
Angle:	120°	Distance:	3
Spread:	0	Size:	5

Note:

The 120° angle helps match the drop shadow angle to the apparent light source in the balloon image.

11. Save the file as **balloon_ad.psd** in your WIP>Outdoors folder, and then close the file.

12. Close the banner file.

13. Continue to the next stage of the project.

Stage 3 Working with Lighting

Photoshop provides extremely powerful tools for creating one composite image from a number of separate components. And although the tools and techniques for doing this type of work are fairly mechanical, some degree of human judgment is required to ensure the separate pieces blend together seamlessly.

We've seen extreme cases of mismatched lighting, where one person in a photo was squinting into the bright sunlight when everyone else was in cooler shadows. Of course, not all lighting problems are this obvious, but even subtle differences can make good technical composites appear "off" to the casual observer. Whenever you composite images, you need to be careful that the lighting is consistent across the entire composition.

The lighting in the original photo is evenly lighting the surface, so the composited ad is fine as is.

The shadows on this side of the building should also affect the composited ad.

The bright sun glare on this spot of the balloon should also affect the composited ad.

This ad is too bright for the apparent position of the sun (directly overhead).

Lighting Effects in Depth

The **Lighting Effects filter** (Filter>Render>Lighting Effects) allows you to create different lighting effects in RGB images. You can apply several different lighting types:

- **Omni** shines light in all directions from directly above the image. You can drag the center handle (the focus point, where the light is pointing) to change the position of the light, and you can drag the handles on the circle to change the size of the light. Making the light smaller effectively makes the light seem farther away. (Think about how much light a small 5-watt bulb casts, compared to a full-size 60-watt bulb; the light of the larger bulb extends much farther than the light of the smaller bulb.)

 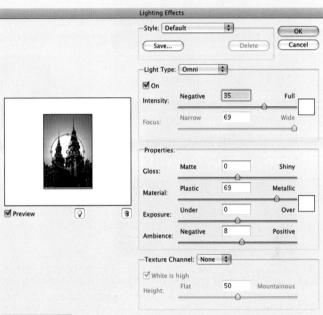

- **Directional** shines light from far away so the light angle doesn't change. You can drag the white handle to change the focus point of the light source. The black handle is the hot spot, or where the most light hits the image; drag this point to change the direction and length of the light source. A shorter line produces more light; a longer line produces less light.

 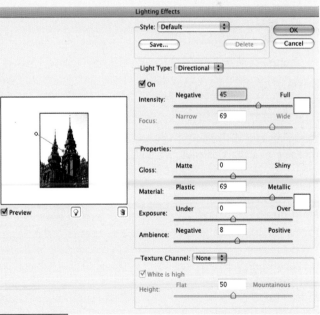

- **Spotlight** casts an elliptical beam of light. The line in the preview window defines the light direction and angle, and the handles define the edges of the ellipse. You can change the position of the light source by dragging the center handle (the focus point); change the light angle by dragging the black handle (the light source or hot spot) at the end of the line; and change the size and shape of the light by dragging the other three handles around the circle edge.

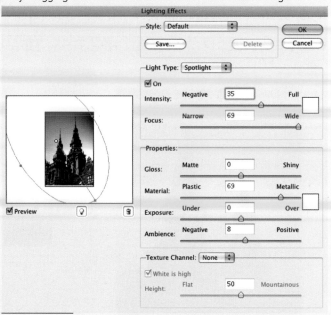

For all three types of lighting, the Intensity slider determines how bright the light appears; full intensity (100) is the brightest light, while negative intensity (down to −100) removes light. You can also change the color of any light source by clicking the swatch to the right of the Intensity slider and choosing a light color in the Color Picker dialog box.

For the Spotlight lighting type, you can also define the focus, or how much of the spotlight ellipse is filled with light.

In addition to the light type, you can define different properties for the light source:

- **Gloss** simulates the effect of different photographic finishes, from low reflectance (Matte) to high reflectance (Shiny).
- **Material** determines which is more reflective, the light (Plastic) or the object on which the light is cast (Metallic).
- **Exposure** decreases (Under) or increases (Over) the lighting effect.
- **Ambience** adds the effect of a second diffuse light source (such as sunlight) that evenly affects the entire image. You can define the color of the ambient light by clicking the color swatch in the Properties section. Positive Ambience values (up to 100) tint the entire image with the ambient light color; negative values (to −100) remove the ambient light color from the image.

You can add up to 16 different light sources to a single image by dragging the light bulb icon onto the preview image. Each light source can have different type and property settings. You can also turn specific light sources on or off by selecting a specific source and toggling the On check box in the Light Type area of the dialog box. If you want to delete a specific light source, select it on the preview and click the Delete button below the preview.

Lighting Effects Styles

Photoshop includes 17 default lighting styles (accessed in the dialog box Style menu), which you can apply to any image. You can also save your own lighting styles by clicking Save in the Style area of the dialog box; all defined light sources (and their properties) will be saved in the style so you can call it again later for another image.

Texture Channels

The **Texture Channel** option allows you to create unique effects based on an existing channel. When the White is High option is checked, white areas in the selected Alpha channel are raised (like an embossing effect), based on the Height setting from Flat (0) to Mountainous (100). When you uncheck the White is High option, black areas of the Alpha channel are raised.

APPLY AN OMNI LIGHTING EFFECT

Omni light shines in all directions from a source point. Omni light is a good option when you want to place a highlight point and blend the shadow away from that spot — as in the case of the balloon ad.

1. Open **balloon_ad.psd** from your WIP>Outdoors folder.

2. With Layer 1 selected in the Layers panel, choose Filter>Render> Lighting Effects.

3. Choose Omni in the Light Type menu.

4. In the preview image, click the white circle (the light source) and drag it to the bottom-left corner of the ad preview.

   If you look at the original image, you'll see the bottom-left corner is the brightest point in the image — where the sun directly strikes the balloon.

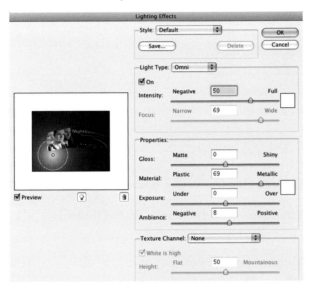

5. Click the black handle on the outside of the light source and drag out to enlarge the light.

   The preview shows the extremely bright result of this light.

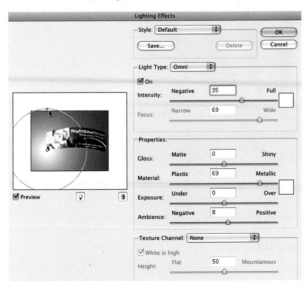

6. **Reduce the Intensity value to 15.**

The reduced Intensity value creates a better effect on the left side of the ad, but the entire right side is now very dark. A second smaller light source will solve this problem.

7. **Click the light bulb icon and drag it to the bottom center of the preview image to add a second light source.**

8. **Change the second light source type to Omni with an Intensity value of 30. Leave the light at the default size.**

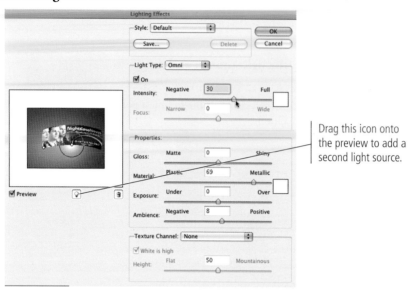

Drag this icon onto the preview to add a second light source.

9. **Click OK to apply the lighting effect and close the dialog box.**

10. **Flatten the file, and then save it as `balloon_final.tif` in your WIP>Outdoors folder.**

11. **Close the file and continue to the next exercise.**

APPLY A DIRECTIONAL LIGHTING EFFECT

Directional light shines from far away, so the overall light angle remains the same across an image. The Directional Light effect is a perfect correction for the fuel tanks image, which is lit from directly above the tank but very far away (the sun is about 92 million miles away, in fact). You want to apply a light source to the ad layer that makes the ad appear to be in the same shadows as the side of the tank.

1. Open the file **tanks_ad.psd** from your **WIP>Outdoors folder.**

2. Make sure Layer 1 is selected in the Layers panel and choose **Filter>Render>Lighting Effects.**

3. **If more than one light source appears in the preview area, click the focus point of one of the light sources and drag it to the trashcan icon below the preview.**

4. **Click the remaining focus point in the preview to select it, and change the Light Type menu to Directional.**

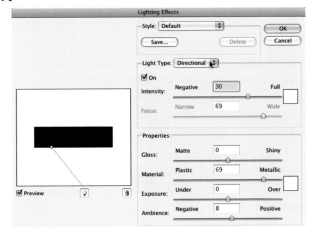

5. **Reduce the Intensity value to 10.**

   You don't want to create a bright light. In fact, in this case you are actually using the lighting effect to create a shadow over the entire ad, since the side of the tank is in shadow.

6. **Drag the selected focus point to the center of the ad. Drag the black handle to directly above the white handle, and make the line very short.**

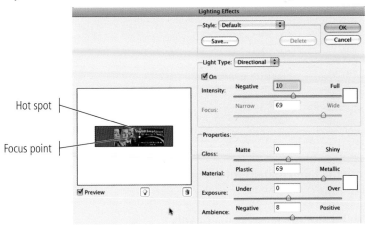

7. **Click OK to apply the effect and close the dialog box.**

8. **Flatten the file, save it as** `tanks_final.tif` **in your WIP>Outdoors folder, and then close the file.**

9. **Continue to the next exercise.**

APPLY A SPOTLIGHT LIGHTING EFFECT

Spotlight casts an elliptical beam of light from a specific direction. This type of light is a good choice for lighting the right half of the office building ad, while leaving the left half of the ad in shadow.

1. **Open the file** `office_ad.psd` **from your WIP>Outdoors folder.**

2. **Make sure Layer 1 is selected in the Layers panel and choose Filter>Render>Lighting Effects.**

3. **Change the Light Type menu to Spotlight.**

This line determines the length of the light source.

4. **Drag the white center point to the immediate right of the center of the ad (where it folds around the building).**

5. **Change the Intensity value to 30 and the Focus value to 100.**

6. **Drag the light source handle to be horizontally aligned to the center point, and enlarge the ellipse so the entire right side of the ad is within the light source.**

This position for the light source roughly matches the direction of the light source in the original building image.

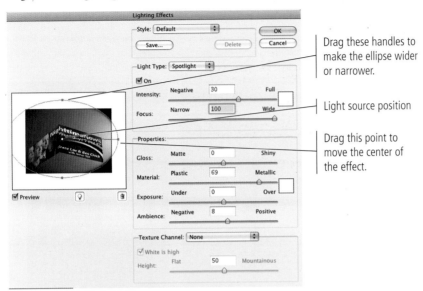

Drag these handles to make the ellipse wider or narrower.

Light source position

Drag this point to move the center of the effect.

7. **Click OK to apply the lighting effect and close the dialog box.**

8. **Flatten the file, save it as `office_final.tif` in your WIP>Outdoors folder, and then close the file.**

9. **Open the file `studio_ad.psd` from your WIP>Outdoors folder.**

This file does not need a lighting adjustment, so you can simply finalize the file at this point.

10. **Flatten the file, save it as `studio_final.tif` in your WIP>Outdoors folder, and then close the file.**

11. **Continue to the next stage of the project.**

The Rendering Filters

The **Clouds** filter (Filters>Render>Clouds) fills the currently selected layer with a random cloud-like pattern that varies between the foreground and background colors. The **Difference Clouds** filter (Filters>Render>Difference Clouds) does the same thing but returns a cloud pattern that looks as though it were affected by the Difference blending mode. Because these filters replace the content of the current layer, they are best applied on a separate layer that you can mask and blend to create the look you want.

The original image has a flat, dull sky.

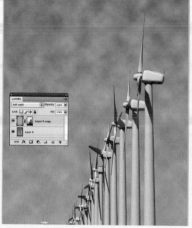

The Clouds filter applied to a new layer, on which the foreground and turbines have been masked. The Soft Light blending mode produces a less stark effect.

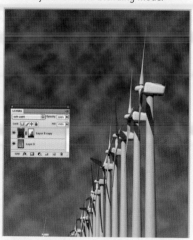

The Difference Clouds filter applied to the same layer, with the same layer mask and blending mode.

The **Fibers** filter (Filters>Render>Fibers) fills the currently selected layer with a pattern that looks like woven fibers of the foreground and background colors. The Variance option controls how the colors vary (a low value produces long streaks of color, and a high value results in very short fibers). The Strength option controls how each fiber looks; low strength produces a loose weave, and high strength produces a tighter weave. The Randomize button changes the pattern randomly; you can keep clicking the button to generate new patterns until you find one that you like.

The **Lens Flare** filter (Filters>Render>Lens Flare) simulates the refraction caused by shining a bright light into a camera lens. You can drag the crosshair in the small preview image to change the position of the flare center, change the brightness of the flare, and define the type of lens to simulate.

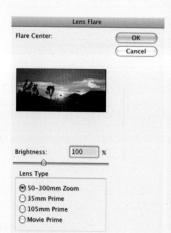

Stage 4 Working in Three Dimensions

Photoshop CS4 Extended includes the ability to create real-time, three-dimensional artwork, whether from scratch or by importing wire frames and rendered artwork from industry-standard 3D applications such as Maya or 3D Studio Max.

The following is a brief introduction to Photoshop's 3D functionality. If you have never worked in real three dimensions before, you will almost certainly have to spend some extra time learning the related terminology. We also encourage you to experiment with the various 3D tools until you are comfortable manipulating objects in digital space.

You should already be familiar with the concept of the X and Y axes. When you work with 3D files, you also need to understand the concept of the Z axis, which creates depth.

Note:

You must have Photoshop Extended to complete the exercises in this stage of the project.

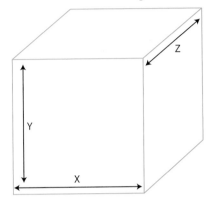

Note:

*In 3D terminology, moving an object in 3D space (near to far) is called a **translation**; rotating an object in 3D space is called a **transformation**.*

- **Meshes** (sometimes called **wireframes**) are the basic skeletons of three-dimensional objects. The mesh defines the underlying shape of the 3D object.

- **Materials** refer to the physical surface of an object (for example, the aluminum of a soda can or the felt of a fedora hat). Photoshop uses a number of texture-map characteristics to create the material appearance of a 3D object; you can also define existing two-dimensional Photoshop layers as the material for a mesh.

- **Lighting** affects the way highlights and shadows are created on and by a 3D object. Photoshop supports three different types of lighting (infinite, spot, and point) to create different lighting effects.

- **Camera position** refers to the point of view relative to the object. Photoshop includes the ability to move the camera around an object on all three axes.

To understand digital 3D modeling, you should try to think about the way you interact with the world at large. When you walk around a car, for example, you are able to see the different sides of the car; the front, back, and sides all have different appearances.

You should also understand that what you see depends not only on your position relative to an object, but also on the position of the object. For example, if you stand still but someone backs a car into a parking space, you see a different aspect of the same car.

Finally, what you see on a 3D object also depends on the position of the light. When the garage light shines behind you, for example, you might see your own reflection in the car's window. When the interior lights are on, you see more of the car's interior than your reflection.

It's important to keep these overall concepts in mind: 3D modeling considers the physical shape and position of an object, your position relative to the object, and the position of light sources relative to the object.

The exercises in this stage of the project were designed to introduce you to the 3D possibilities available in Photoshop CS4 Extended. If you are interested in this field of work, we encourage you to continue your 3D education in formal modeling and rendering, as well as advanced software techniques for both Photoshop and dedicated 3D applications such as 3D Studio Max or Maya.

As one of the sponsors of a local 5K charity walk, your client plans to give cans of energy drinks to participants. They heard about your company's new equipment for creating custom wraps, and they asked if you could wrap their ad around the cans. You are going to use the 3D functions in Photoshop to create a sample to show the client what the finished cans might look like.

Photoshop can open existing 3D files created in other applications and import 3D objects as new 3D Photoshop layers. You can also use built-in functionality to create some 3D objects from scratch. In this case, you're going to create a new 3D object from a built-in shape preset.

1. **Open the Performance pane of the Preferences dialog box. Make sure the Enable OpenGL Drawing option is checked and click OK.**

   OpenGL is a hardware function that makes it possible to work with complex files such as 3D. If this option is not available (grayed out) on your computer, your video card and/or driver does not support OpenGL.

   If you cannot use OpenGL, your 3D options and functionality will be very limited and very slow; all processes will be performed (if possible) by the Photoshop application instead of the video card in your computer.

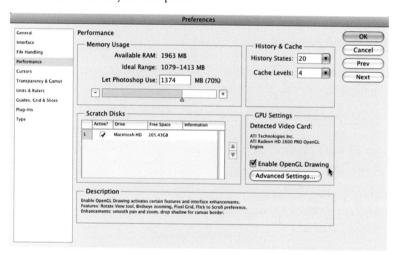

2. **Create a new file that is 6 × 6 inches, 150 ppi, using the RGB color mode.**

   3D layers can add significantly to file size, which will in turn significantly increase the amount of processing time required to complete different tasks within the file. You are creating a sample image that will be printed on your local desktop printer; the settings we specified should be sufficient to produce a good-quality sample print.

3. Choose 3D>New Shape from Layer>Soda Can.

The new 3D shape appears in the document window; the Layers panel shows that the default Layer 1 has been converted to a 3D layer. If Layer 1 had any content before you created the 3D shape, that content would have been applied as the material for the shape (more on materials in the next exercise).

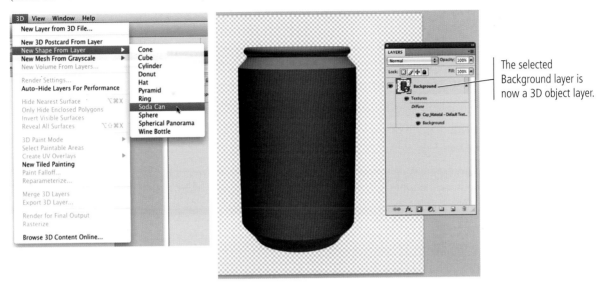

The selected Background layer is now a 3D object layer.

4. Choose Window>3D to open the 3D panel.

The 3D panel can be used to review, edit, and manage all the various aspects of the 3D layer. The Scene tab shows a summary of the meshes, materials, and lighting that affect the 3D object.

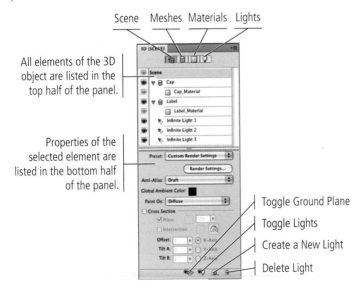

Scene   Meshes   Materials   Lights

All elements of the 3D object are listed in the top half of the panel.

Properties of the selected element are listed in the bottom half of the panel.

Toggle Ground Plane
Toggle Lights
Create a New Light
Delete Light

5. **Click the Toggle Ground Plane button at the bottom of the 3D panel.**

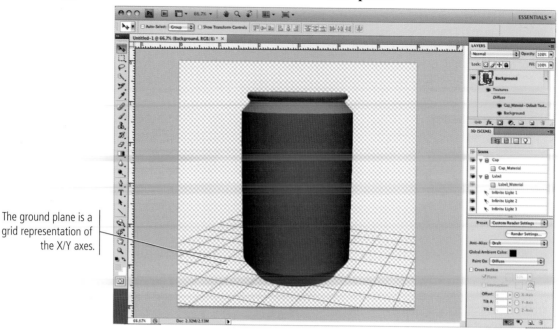

The ground plane is a grid representation of the X/Y axes.

6. **Choose the 3D Rotate tool in the Tools panel.**

When you select one of the 3D tools, the 3D Axis appears in the top-left corner of the document window. The 3D Axis shows the current X-, Y-, and Z-axis orientation of the 3D object. Although it might seem intimidating at first, it will make more sense after you have clicked around a bit and experimented with the various options.

Note:

If your computer does not have OpenGL support, the 3D Axis will not be available.

Return to Initial Object Position

Use these buttons to access the nested 3D Object tools.

Use this menu to display specific saved views (top, bottom, etc.) of the selected object.

Use these fields to define specific numeric positions for the object.

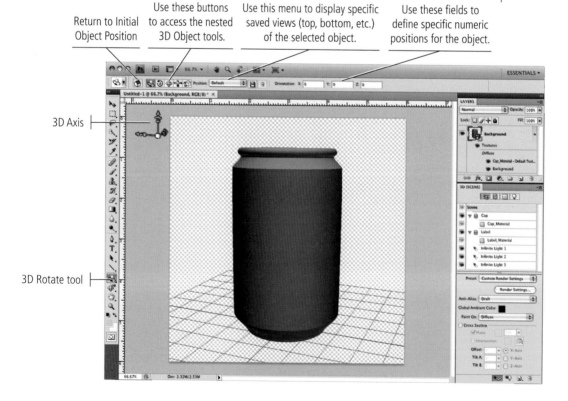

3D Axis

3D Rotate tool

7. **Place the cursor over the 3D Axis until a dark gray bar appears above the graphic.**

8. **Click the zoom icon and drag right to enlarge the 3D Axis graphic.**

   You can apply virtually any changes to the object position using the 3D Axis graphic. Making it larger makes it easier to see the available controls.

Note:

Choose View>Show>3D Axis to toggle this icon on and off.

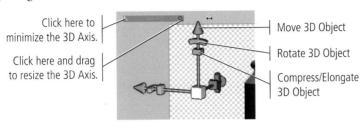

Click here to minimize the 3D Axis. | Move 3D Object
Click here and drag to resize the 3D Axis. | Rotate 3D Object
Compress/Elongate 3D Object

Note:

In the 3D Axis, the X axis is green, the Y axis is red, and the Z axis is blue.

Each axis in the graphic has three different controls:

- **Move 3D Object** changes the position of the object along the selected plane.
- **Rotate 3D Object** changes the rotation of the object along the selected plane.
- **Compress/Elongate 3D Object** changes the size of the object along the selected plane.

Other options are available when you place the cursor over the intersection of the 3 axes.

9. **Click the Compress/Elongate control for the Z axis and drag down.**

   As you drag, the can gets shorter because you are shortening the Z axis of the object.

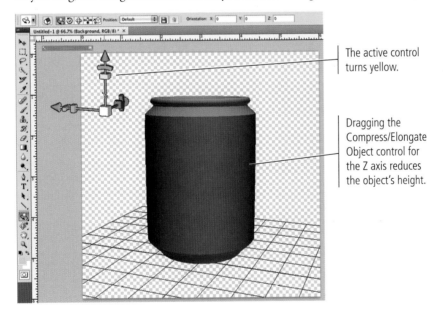

The active control turns yellow.

Dragging the Compress/Elongate Object control for the Z axis reduces the object's height.

10. Click the Rotate control for the X axis and drag up.

The 3D Axis shows the angle of rotation as you drag.

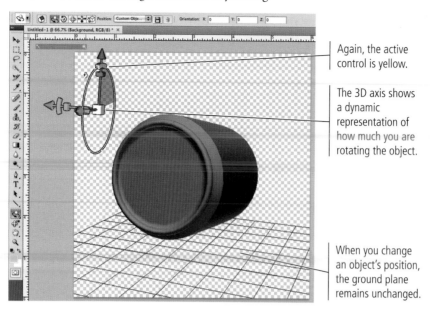

Again, the active control is yellow.

The 3D axis shows a dynamic representation of how much you are rotating the object.

When you change an object's position, the ground plane remains unchanged.

11. Click the Move control for the Y axis and drag around.

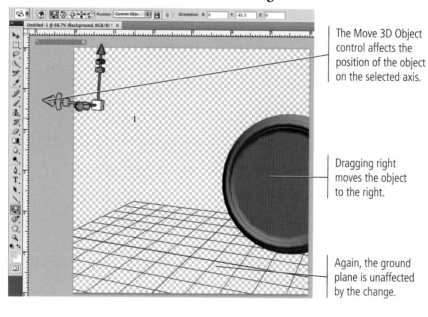

The Move 3D Object control affects the position of the object on the selected axis.

Dragging right moves the object to the right.

Again, the ground plane is unaffected by the change.

Note:

The precise position and appearance of the cursor in relation to the 3D Axis graphic provides considerable feedback about what will happen when you click and drag.

12. Place the cursor over the intersection of the three axes. When the center cube appears, click and drag out to resize the object.

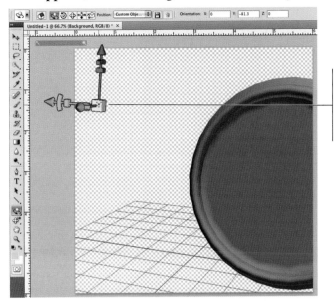

Three arrows in the cursor show that clicking and dragging will resize the object in all three directions.

Note:

When you see a flat plane appear at the edge of the graphics cube, click and drag around to move an object along two axes at once.

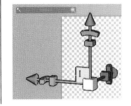

13. In the Control panel, click the house icon to return the object to its initial position.

In the Control panel for any of the 3D tools, clicking the Home button resets the object or camera position to its default starting point. This is an important distinction because — like so many of Photoshop's functionalities — the 3D capabilities are non-destructive. Nothing is permanent until you flatten the file into a single two-dimensional layer.

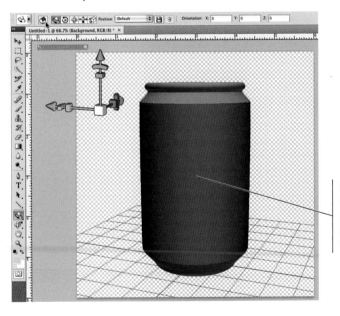

Changing the object position is non-destructive. You can always restore the object to its original position.

14. **Choose the 3D Orbit tool in the Tools panel. Drag around the screen and watch the effect on the ground plane.**

Return to Initial
Camera Position

Use these buttons
to access the nested
3D camera tools.

The 3D Axis changes
to reflect the new
point of view.

3D Orbit tool

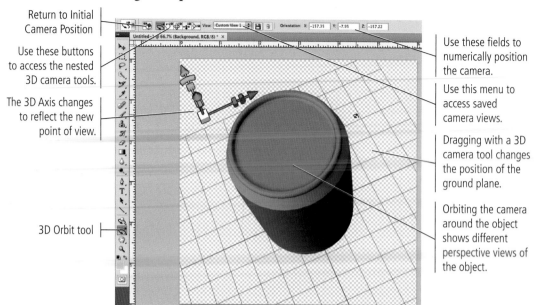

Use these fields to
numerically position
the camera.

Use this menu to
access saved
camera views.

Dragging with a 3D
camera tool changes
the position of the
ground plane.

Orbiting the camera
around the object
shows different
perspective views of
the object.

15. **In the Control panel, click the house icon to return the object to its initial position.**

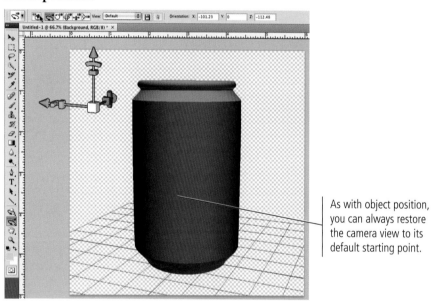

As with object position,
you can always restore
the camera view to its
default starting point.

16. **Save the file as `can_working.psd` in your WIP>Outdoors folder, and continue to the next exercise.**

PHOTOSHOP FOUNDATIONS

The Tools panel includes two sets of tools for working in three dimensions. You can access the different tools in the Tools panel nested toolsets, or you can choose the primary tool in the Tools panel and access the variant in the Control panel.

The 3D object tools, defaulting to the 3D Rotate tool, affect the position of the actual 3D object. (These tools duplicate functions that can be applied using the 3D Axis graphic.)

- **3D Rotate tool**.
  Drag up-down to rotate
  the object around the X axis, or left-right to rotate
  around the Y axis. Press Option/Alt to rotate the
  object around the Z axis.

- **3D Roll tool**. Drag left-right to rotate the object
  around the Z axis.

- **3D Pan tool**. (In the Control panel, the tool tip for
  this variant says "Drag" instead of "Pan".) Drag left-
  right to move the object horizontally, or up-down to
  move the object vertically, without affecting its depth or
  rotation. Press Option/Alt and drag up-down to move
  the object along the X/Z axis (horizontally far to near).

- **3D Slide tool**. Drag left-right to move the object
  horizontally, or up-down to move the object on the
  X/Z axis (horizontally far to near). Press Option/Alt and
  drag up/down to move the object along the X/Y and
  axes simultaneously.

- **3D Scale tool**. Drag up-down to make the object
  proportionally larger or smaller. Press Option/Alt
  to scale the object along the Z axis only.

The 3D camera tools, defaulting to the 3D Orbit tool, affects the **scene** or your view of the object (in other words, where the "camera" is located relative to the object).

- **3D Orbit tool**.
  Drag up-down to move the
  camera around the X axis, or left-right to move the
  camera around the Y axis. Press Option/Alt and drag
  left-right to move the camera around the Z axis. (Think
  of this as holding the camera on the object while you
  move around the object.)

- **3D Roll View tool**. Drag left-right to move the
  camera around the Z axis. Press Option/Alt and drag
  left-right to move the camera around the Y axis, or press
  Option/Alt and drag up-down to move the camera
  around the X axis.

- **3D Pan View tool**. Drag left-right or up-down to move
  the camera in a specific direction. (Think of this as if the
  camera was mounted to a tripod, and you swing it back
  and forth, up and down.) Press Option/Alt and drag up-
  down to to pan in the x or z direction.

- **3D Walk View tool**. Drag to move the camera both
  around the Y axis and along the Z axis (near to far)
  at once. Press Option/Alt as you drag to walk in the
  X/Z direction.

- **3D Zoom tool**. Drag up-down to move the camera
  closer or farther away from the object, without affecting
  any axis of the view.

In film-studio terminology, "zooming" refers to changing the
camera lens settings, while "walking the camera" physically
moves the camera in relation to the subject being filmed.

ADJUST MATERIALS FOR THE 3D OBJECT

As we mentioned in the introduction to this stage of the project, the material is the surface of a 3D object. You can use the 3D panel to create a new file or load an existing 2D file to use as the material (called a **texture map**) for a specific mesh.

1. **With `can_working.psd` open, display the Mesh tab of the 3D panel.**

   The soda can shape is comprised of two separate meshes — one for the top and bottom of the can (the cap) and one for the flat area (the label). You can use the tools in this section of the panel to move the selected mesh independently, just as you use the primary 3D object tools (in the Tools panel) to move the entire 3D object.

   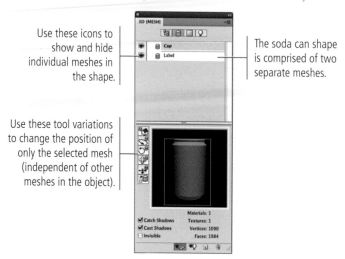

   Use these icons to show and hide individual meshes in the shape.

   The soda can shape is comprised of two separate meshes.

   Use these tool variations to change the position of only the selected mesh (independent of other meshes in the object).

2. **Display the Materials tab of the 3D panel, and make sure the Label_Material option is selected in the top half of the panel.**

   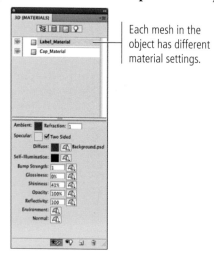

   Each mesh in the object has different material settings.

3. **Click the Texture Map Menu button for the Diffuse option, and choose Load Texture from the menu.**

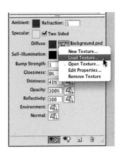

The Diffuse setting defines the color of the material if you don't apply a specific texture map; you can also use this option to load a specific 2D file that will conform to the surface of the object — as in the label of the can, which is perfect for this application.

The Self-Illumination setting is similar to the Diffuse option; it also defines the color, texture, or 2D layer that conforms to the mesh surface. However, this option simulates the effect of an object being lit from within, such as a backlit sign in a restaurant.

4. **Navigate to the file `banner.tif` in the RF_Photoshop>Outdoors folder and click Open.**

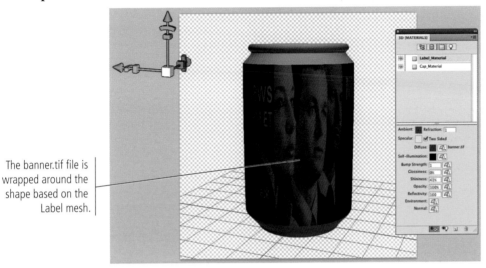

The banner.tif file is wrapped around the shape based on the Label mesh.

5. **Choose the 3D Rotate tool in the Tools panel.**

6. **Click in the document window and drag left or right until you can see all three faces on the can label.**

Rotating the object shows different areas of the applied label file.

7. **Save the file and continue to the next exercise.**

Working with 3D Materials

In addition to loading existing files for different material maps, you can also create new files from directly within the 3D panel.

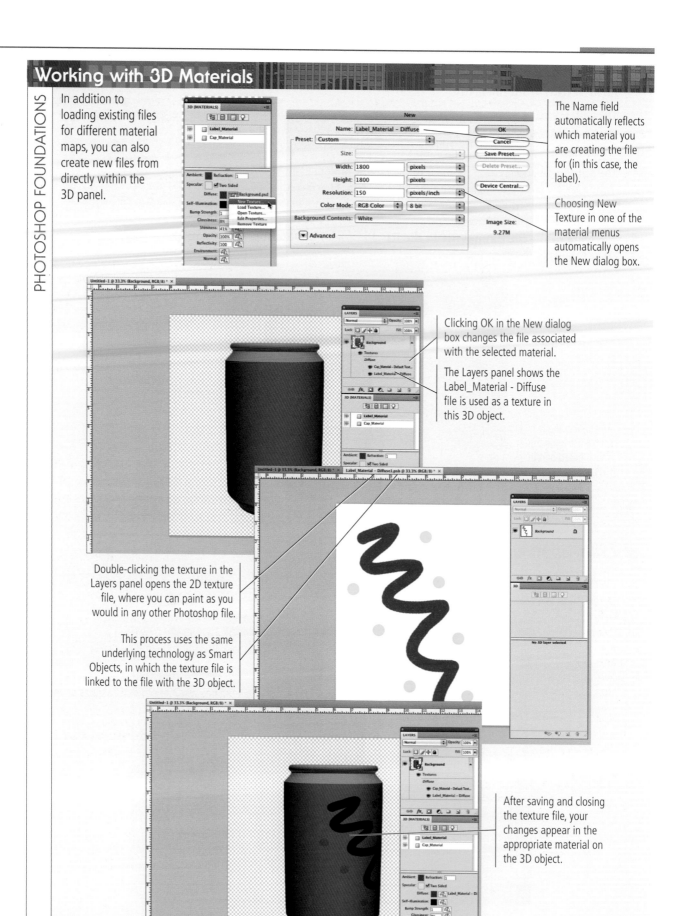

The Name field automatically reflects which material you are creating the file for (in this case, the label).

Choosing New Texture in one of the material menus automatically opens the New dialog box.

Clicking OK in the New dialog box changes the file associated with the selected material.

The Layers panel shows the Label_Material - Diffuse file is used as a texture in this 3D object.

Double-clicking the texture in the Layers panel opens the 2D texture file, where you can paint as you would in any other Photoshop file.

This process uses the same underlying technology as Smart Objects, in which the texture file is linked to the file with the 3D object.

After saving and closing the texture file, your changes appear in the appropriate material on the 3D object.

You can also use the Edit Properties option to change the size of the material file and create a repeating pattern. The **Target** menu determines whether changes apply to a specific layer or to the composite image. The **U Scale** and **V Scale** resize the texture; the **U Offset** and **V Offset** values reposition the texture.

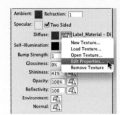

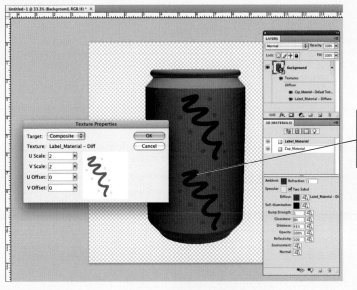

Increasing the U Scale and V Scale values creates a repeating pattern on the object.

3D Material Options

Ambient defines the color of ambient light that's visible on reflective surfaces.

Refraction is the change in light direction that occurs when light strikes a surface (think of the classic "bent pencil in a glass of water" example).

Specular defines the color of specular highlights (i.e., areas where the light is 100% reflected).

Diffuse is the color of the surface material, or the 2D map (file) that makes up the reflective surface of the object.

Self-illumination is the color or map (file) of the surface material; this setting results in the effect of interior lighting, such as a painting on a light bulb.

Bump Strength adds bumps in the material surface without altering the actual object mesh. In a defined bump map file, lighter gray values create raised areas, and darker gray values create flatter areas. (The numeric field only applies if you have defined a bump map file.)

Glossiness controls the amount of light that reflects off the object's surface. You can also define a glossiness map file, in which the intensity of colors controls the material gloss; black areas create full glossiness, and white areas remove all glossiness.

Shininess defines the dispersion of reflected light. Low values result in more apparent light, and high values result in less apparent light and cleaner highlights.

Opacity determines the transparency of the surface material. If you define a map file for this setting, lighter areas in the map are less transparent, and darker areas are more transparent.

Reflectivity determines whether other 3D objects (if any) are reflected in the material surface.

Environment stores an image of the environment around the object, which can be seen in reflective areas of the object.

Normal is similar to the Bump Strength/Map option, but can use an RGB image as the map file.

ADJUST LIGHT SOURCES

As you can see in the current file, the overall object is very dark; the existing light sources do not sufficiently highlight your work. Fortunately, Photoshop includes a number of options to edit existing light sources and create new ones to show an object to its best advantage.

1. **With can_working.psd open, display the Lights tab of the 3D panel.**

    Each existing light source is listed in the top half of the panel, divided into three categories:

    -   **Point lights** shine in all directions, such as light that emanates from a light bulb.
    -   **Spot lights** shine relatively narrow beams of light on specific spots of the object.
    -   **Infinite lights** shine in a single direction from a seemingly far distance (such as the sun).

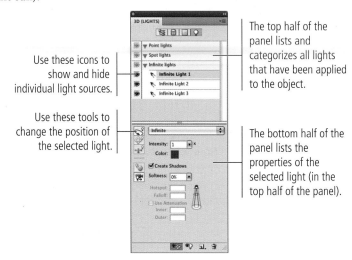

Use these icons to show and hide individual light sources.

Use these tools to change the position of the selected light.

The top half of the panel lists and categorizes all lights that have been applied to the object.

The bottom half of the panel lists the properties of the selected light (in the top half of the panel).

2. **Click the Toggle Lights button at the bottom of the panel to show the three lights in the document window.**

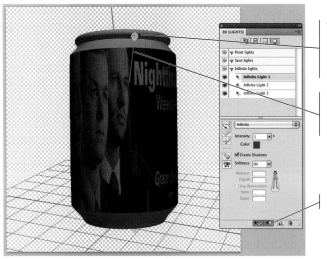

When lights are toggled on, they appear in the document window as light blue orbs.

Infinite Lights appear as a small blue sphere with a single projecting line.

Toggle Lights button

Note:

Different types of light have different appearances, indicative of the ways each one casts light.

3. **Select Infinite Light 1 in the 3D panel and click the panel's Delete button.**

Infinite Light 1 was shining from the back of the object; in this case, you're creating a sample that will ultimately be a flat print, so the back light is unnecessary.

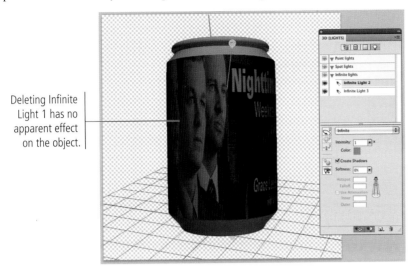

Deleting Infinite Light 1 has no apparent effect on the object.

Note:

If you use the 3D object tools to reposition the object, the lights do not move relative to the object.

If you use the 3D camera tools to change the point of view, the lights move in relation to the object (just as the ground plane moves when you change the camera).

4. **Select Infinite Light 2 in the 3D panel and click the Color swatch in the lower half of the panel.**

Creating 3D Postcards from 2D Layers

PHOTOSHOP FOUNDATIONS

In addition to importing existing 3D files or using the built-in 3D shapes, you can also convert 2D layers into 3D "postcards" that can be manipulated just as would a 3D shape. When you choose 3D>New 3D Postcard from Layer, the selected layer is converted to a piece of virtual transparent plastic. The content of the selected layer is attached to the "front" of the postcard and appears in reverse on the "back" of the postcard.

Like a regular postcard, you can move and rotate the 3D postcard object to view it at different angles.

You can drag the axes to view the back of the postcard, which is the reverse of the front.

5. **In the resulting Color Picker, choose a very light blue color and click OK.**

The color of the light source can significantly affect the overall appearance of the object. We're using blue to unify the light source with the blue in the banner ad. Different modeling projects, however, might include an actual visible light source; in that case you should try to avoid casting a light of a color other than the visible one.

Changing the color of the light source has a significant effect on the appearance of the object.

6. **Click the Rotate the Light button in the bottom half of the panel.**

Lighting Options

Photoshop supports three types of lights: point, spot, and infinite. Each type has a unique appearance in the document window, showing how each type casts light on the surface of an object.

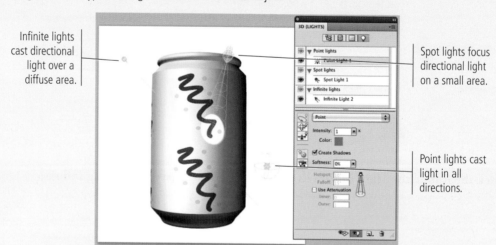

Infinite lights cast directional light over a diffuse area.

Spot lights focus directional light on a small area.

Point lights cast light in all directions.

Intensity adjusts the brightness of the light; you can also use the Color swatch to change the color of the selected light. If Create Shadows is checked, different mesh surfaces will create shadows on other areas of the mesh or on other mesh objects; the Softness value blurs the edges of the resulting shadows.

For spot lights, the hotspot defines the width of the brightest light (the "spot"). The Falloff value defines the outermost width of the light, including the area in which the brightest part fades to no light.

If Use Attenuation is checked for spot or point lights, the Inner and Outer values essentially define the length of the light source and the distance between the light's full strength (Inner), and the distance at which no light from the source will reach the object (Outer).

PHOTOSHOP FOUNDATIONS

7. **Click in the document window and drag to move the light source to directly outside the left edge of the object, shining at approximately 30°.**

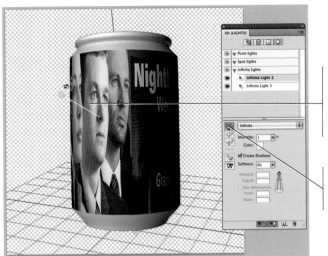

Moving the light to the left lightens the left side of the object, just as you would expect if the sun were shining on that side of the can.

This tool allows you to rotate the light around the object.

8. **Select the Infinite Light 3 in the top half of the panel, and then click the Move to Current View button.**

This option changes the selected light source to shine onto the front-center of the object.

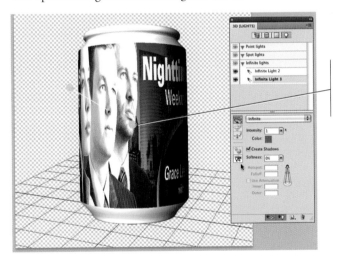

Move to Current View moves the light to shine directly onto the center of the object view.

9. **Click the Rotate the Light button in the lower half of the panel, and drag Infinite Light 3 to shine at approximately 45° from near the right edge of the image.**

Casting the light from the right but farther away lightens the side of the object without creating an overwhelming "two suns" effect.

10. Click the **Toggle Ground Plane** and **Toggle Lights** buttons at the bottom of the 3D panel to turn off those options.

If left turned on in the document window, the lights and ground plane will appear in the final print.

Note:

This is far from a complete dissertation on all 3D options available in Photoshop CS4. Our goal was to introduce these tools and show how they might be useful for visual artists who want to add depth to their work. If you plan to pursue a career in 3D art and animation, we encourage you to expand on this basic introduction with classes or books on dedicated animation software and techniques.

11. Save the file as `can_final.psd`.

12. Print the file to your local color printer, and then close the file.

fill in the blank

1. When using the Patch tool, choose the _____ option to select an area that will be copied to another area (where you drag the marquee).

2. The _____ adjustment allows you to change the ink values in specific primary colors or neutrals without affecting other colors.

3. The _____ adjustment allows you to change the Hue, Saturation, and Lightness values of specific primary colors.

4. The _____ tool attempts to simplify replacement of specific colors in your image; you can paint over a targeted color to replace it with the foreground color.

5. The _____ tool mimics a process used in traditional photo development, and is used to lighten an area of a photograph.

6. _____ identifies areas of detail in an image and tries to maintain those areas while scaling areas with less detail.

7. In _____, all lines in an image move toward a single location on the horizon.

8. The _____ provides an easy interface for transforming layer content onto a perspective plane.

9. The _____ transformation can be used to distort a flat rectangular object into a custom shape, such as around the side of a balloon.

10. A(n) _____ light source shines light in all directions from directly above the image.

short answer

1. Briefly explain the advantages to using Adjustment Layers rather than applying adjustments to regular layers from the Image>Adjustments menu.

2. Briefly explain the difference between destructive and non-destructive image editing.

3. Briefly explain the three types of lighting that can be created using the Lighting Effects filter.

Use what you learned in this project to complete the following freeform exercise.
Carefully read the art director and client comments, then create your own design to meet the needs of the project.
Use the space below to sketch ideas; when finished, write a brief explanation of your reasoning behind your final design.

art director comments

Your company's sales manager has another potential client for the Advertise Anywhere! program, and would like to build a personalized presentation similar to the one you did for the Nighttime News show.

To complete this project, you should:

❑ Build a sample ad for the Go Green clean energy initiative.

❑ Find background images on which you can composite the sample ad.

❑ Clean up or adjust the background images as necessary to create the best possible samples.

❑ Composite the sample ad onto the different backgrounds; adjust perspective and lighting as necessary to make the samples appear as natural as possible.

client comments

The director of the Go Green clean energy initiative saw the Nighttime News ads that we placed around the city, and called the show's marketing director to find out where they were created. I just got off the phone with her, and we have a meeting scheduled next week to present some ideas for advertising the Go Green 2009 campaign.

I need you to create a sample ad at the same size as the news show sample. It should include imagery that supports the idea of clean energy — hydroelectricity, windmills, or whatever. The only text for the ad should be the words 'Go Green!', and the Web site address (www.ggenergy.org).

For the background images, find a variety of different types of images. Methods of public transportation, buildings, and large outdoor signs are all good options, but we also want to highlight the 'anywhere' part of Advertise Anywhere! services. Get creative with these sample backgrounds — think up unusual locations where ads might be seen by large numbers of people.

project justification

_____
_____
_____
_____
_____
_____
_____
_____
_____
_____
_____
_____
_____

Compositing images such as the ones in this project is part skill (applying necessary corrections), part judgment (determining the perspective and light source in the background images), and part experimentation (exploring the transformation and filter options to find the best possible solution to the specific problem). Some jobs — like this one — require all these skills. Individually, the correction and transformation tools you used to create these samples will be invaluable during your graphic design career.

Composite the ad layer with a built-in Warp transformation

Composite the ad layer with the Vanishing Point filter

Use the Patch tool to clean up digital garbage

Apply a Directional lighting effect to unify the layers

Correct lighting with the Shadow/Highlight adjustment

Apply a Spotlight lighting effect to unify the layers

Use a Hue/Saturation adjustment layer to change the balloon color

Apply an Omni lighting effect to unify the layers

Use the Replace Color adjustment to apply a fresh coat of paint

Composite the ad layer in Free Transform mode

Wrap the sample ad around a 3D object

Composite the ad layer with a custom warp tranformations

House Painting

Your client, a real estate developer, is planning a new pre-sales campaign for the company's latest master plan community. He has line-art sketches of the completed houses, but he wants color "paintings" to show prospective buyers what the finished houses might look like. You were hired to create a full-color digital rendering based on one of the artist's black-and-white sketches.

This project incorporates the following skills:

❏ Converting an image from bitmap to RGB color mode

❏ Loading a custom swatch panel to access approved colors

❏ Using fill and stroke techniques to create the basic shapes in the artwork

❏ Using hard and soft brushes to create detail in the painting

❏ Using brush blending modes to achieve special effects such as deep shadows

❏ Creating and applying custom patterns to create large areas of consistent texture

❏ Setting brush options to randomize brush strokes and paint "natural" scenes

In three months we break ground on a new master plan community targeted for middle-income families. We are installing an on-site sales office soon so we can start preselling, and we want to be able to show potential buyers what finished houses will look like.

Our architect gave us pen-and-ink renderings, but we want something more realistic — like a painting — in color. If you can create a painting, we can print several copies to frame and hang around the office. When we get closer to building the houses, we might also launch a direct mail sales campaign and do some other print advertising. It depends on how many plots we can presell.

We've worked with an environmental designer to create the community master plan, and we've finalized everything from the site map to the stucco and trim colors that will be used for the finished houses. I showed your art director swatches of the paint chips, and we're hoping you can use those to create the actual painting.

Most people in our field will tell you that high-quality art is part creativity and part technique. Your role in this project is to provide technique, since the actual artwork was already drawn by the architect.

The client isn't sure what he's going to do with the final artwork. He knows it's going to be printed, definitely as a framed print in the sales office, possibly in brochures and newspapers, and probably on his Web site as well.

With all these possible uses, you need to produce a versatile file that can support many file formats. The RGB color space is larger than CMYK, so create the painting in RGB and start with high enough resolution for print.

The large-format output company has switched to an all-PDF workflow for output. They don't accept any native application files, so you'll have to save the final painting as a high-resolution PDF file. The service rep also said their output devices convert color on the fly, and they get better results from RGB images than images already converted to CMYK.

To complete this project, you will:

- ❏ Convert a bitmap image to RGB
- ❏ Import custom swatches
- ❏ Create fill shapes
- ❏ Fill areas with the Paint Bucket tool
- ❏ Use hard- and soft-edge brushes
- ❏ Clone repeating drawing elements
- ❏ Create texture with a faux-finish brush
- ❏ Use opacity and blending modes to create deep shadows
- ❏ Define and save a custom pattern
- ❏ Change brush settings to paint random elements
- ❏ Create and save a brush preset
- ❏ Export a PDF file for print

Stage 1   Preparing the Workspace

This project differs from the ones you've completed so far. In this project, you use Photoshop to create original artwork — that is, rather than compositing images and text to create a finished job, you use Photoshop tools to create the actual pixels that make up the finished artwork.

Some of the skills you learn in this project (including mixing colors and painting with brushes) are normally used by creative designers to develop original, one-of-a-kind digital artwork — starting with nothing other than an idea. By starting with an existing line art drawing, however, you can use the same tools and techniques to build full-color artistic renderings, even if you don't have the natural painting ability of da Vinci or Picasso.

CONVERT A BITMAP TO RGB

The provided sketch is a bitmap (or line art) image, which you learned about in Project 1. It contains only two tonal values — black and white. Any apparent shading was created using traditional artistic techniques such as crosshatching and pointillism.

Line art images are typically scanned between 1200 and 2400 pixels per inch to provide enough data for cleanly outputting the images on a high-resolution output device. The first task in creating a color image from a line art drawing is converting the scanned bitmap image to RGB, which actually requires two separate steps.

1. **On your desktop, copy the Realty folder from the WIP folder on your Resource CD to the WIP folder where you're saving your work.**

2. **Open the file house.tif from the RF_Photoshop>Realty folder.**

3. **Choose Image>Mode>Grayscale.**

   You can't convert a bitmap image directly to RGB because the bitmap mode has only two possible tonal values (black and white). You have to first convert the image to grayscale, and then convert it to RGB so you can paint it in full color.

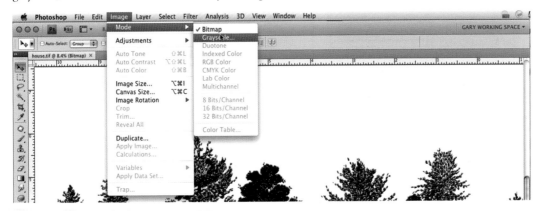

4. **In the Grayscale dialog box, enter 1 in the Size Ratio field and click OK.**

   Because bitmap images are typically at much higher resolution than necessary for grayscale or color images, you can scale the image at the same time as you convert it to grayscale. The Size Ratio option is the factor for scaling down the bitmap image (for example, a Size Ratio value of 2 reduces the grayscale image by 50%). We prefer to convert using a 1-to-1 ratio, and then manually resize or resample the image using the Image Size dialog box.

Note:

After you click OK, the conversion process might take a few minutes to complete, depending on the speed of your computer. Photoshop has to calculate a lot of pixel data to turn this bitmap image into a grayscale image.

5. Choose Image>Image Size.

The original image was scanned at 1200 pixels per inch, which is appropriate for bitmap images. As you can see, converting the bitmap image to grayscale at a 1-to-1 ratio resulted in 136.6 megabytes — a huge size that might be unmanageable, depending on your computer.

For grayscale and RGB, you need only 300 pixels per inch. You can simply resample the file to discard the unnecessary resolution.

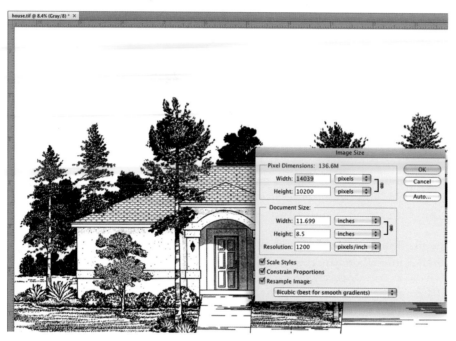

6. With the Resample Image option checked, type 300 in the Resolution field, leave the units set to pixels/inch, and then click OK.

At 300 ppi, you can see the dramatic reduction in file size — down to 8.54 megabytes.

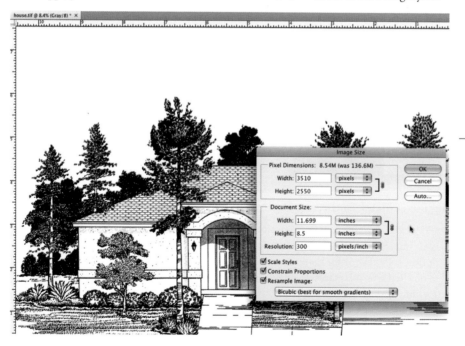

Note:

When you click OK, the change in resolution dramatically reduces the view of the image in the document window.

7. **Choose Image>Mode>RGB Color.**

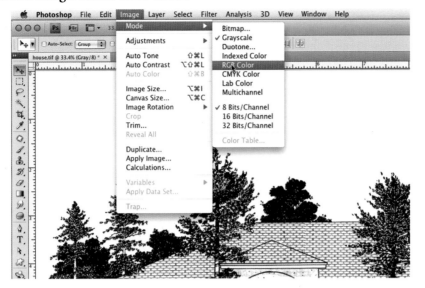

After the conversion is complete, the file is around 25 megabytes — large, but workable.

Note:

You could have converted to RGB before resampling the image, but you would have been working with a file of about 400 megabytes before resampling. By resampling first, you have a more manageable file size to convert to RGB.

8. **Resize the image to fit in the document window.**

9. **Rename the Background layer Sketch and lock the layer.**

You're going to use this layer as a template for your painting. Locking the layer prevents you from accidentally moving or altering the original artwork.

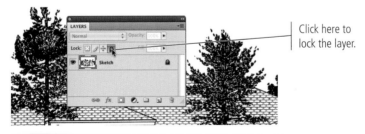

Click here to lock the layer.

10. **Save the file as house_working.psd in your WIP>Realty folder and continue to the next exercise.**

IMPORT CUSTOM SWATCHES

The Swatches panel stores colors you use frequently; you can access them by simply clicking a swatch in the panel. You can use swatches from a number of built-in libraries commonly used in the graphics industry, or you can create custom swatch libraries that can be shared with other applications in the Adobe Creative Suite.

Rather than randomly picking colors for the various elements of the house, you will use a set of custom swatches based on the color scheme defined in the community master plan.

1. **With house_working.psd open, open the Swatches panel (Window>Swatches).**

   Photoshop includes a default set of swatches chosen from the various built-in swatch libraries.

2. **In the Swatches panel Options menu, choose Replace Swatches.**

   The options in this menu are similar to the ones you used for patterns, gradients, and styles in Project 2. You can create a new swatch, change the panel view, manage visible swatch sets, or open built-in swatch libraries.

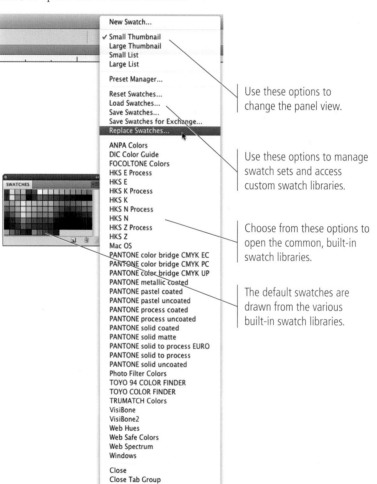

Use these options to change the panel view.

Use these options to manage swatch sets and access custom swatch libraries.

Choose from these options to open the common, built-in swatch libraries.

The default swatches are drawn from the various built-in swatch libraries.

Note:

If you have Adobe Illustrator, that application includes a number of thematic swatch libraries, such as Earthtone, Foliage, and Skintones. You can import these swatch libraries, which have been saved in the Adobe Swatch Exchange (.ase) format, from the Adobe Illustrator>Presets folder into the Photoshop Swatches panel.

You can save custom swatch sets from Photoshop to be used in other Adobe applications by choosing Save Swatches for Exchange in the Swatches panel Options menu. (To save a swatch library for only Photoshop, you can use the Save Swatches command to save the swatch library with the ".aco" extension.)

3. Navigate to the file **home color.ase** in the RF_Photoshop>Realty folder and click Load.

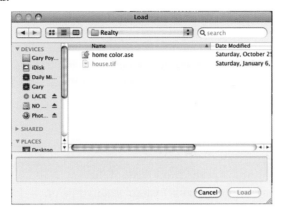

Note:

Note for Creative Suite users: If you are sharing swatches between applications, Photoshop doesn't recognize pattern swatches, gradient swatches, or the Registration swatch from Illustrator or InDesign, nor does Photoshop transfer "book color" references such as HSB, XYZ, duotone, Monitor RGB, opacity, totally ink, or webRGB from within the application.

4. **Using the Swatches panel Options menu, change the panel to Small List view.**

Because you chose Replace Swatches in the panel Options menu in Step 2, the new panel contains only the swatches from the ASE file. These swatches were created specifically for this project, using basic names that will make it easier to complete the house painting.

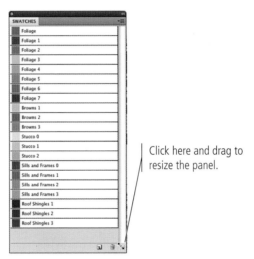

Click here and drag to resize the panel.

5. **Continue to the next stage of the project.**

Stage 2 **Filling Solid Areas**

The easiest way to start a painting such as this one is to create the basic shapes that make up the object you are painting. You can make a basic selection and simply fill it with a color (Edit>Fill), use the Paint Bucket tool to fill areas of similar color, or use brushes and painting techniques to paint specific areas. When you combine these techniques with Photoshop layers, you can also use transparency and blending modes to create digital images that appear as though they were painted with a traditional easel, canvas, and brushes.

CREATE FILL SHAPES

In this exercise, you use standard selection tools to paint the front walls of the house — large and relatively simple areas that you can fill with "stucco" colored paint.

1. **With house_working.psd open, create a new layer named Walls.**

2. **With the Walls layer selected, use the Rectangular Marquee tool to draw a selection around the front of the garage face (including the pillars to the left and right of the garage door).**

   Don't worry if your selection covers parts of the bushes and doesn't include the pieces that stick out from the basic rectangular shape. You refine the selection in the following steps, and you paint the bushes on higher layers later in this project.

Rectangular selection marquee

3. **In the Control panel, choose the Add to Selection option.**

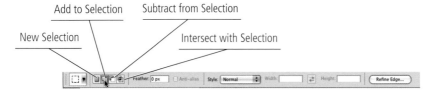

4. **Draw additional selection marquees to select the entire face of the house.**

   Zooming in might make it easier to refine the selection, especially in the smaller areas where the house shape extends slightly.

5. **If necessary, use the Subtract from Selection option to remove unwanted areas from the selection.**

We outlined the selection area in bright yellow to make it easy to see in this screen capture. Your selection will be visible as "marching ants."

6. **Click the Stucco 1 swatch in the Swatches panel to define that swatch as the foreground color.**

7. **Choose Edit>Fill.**

8. **Choose Foreground Color in the Use menu of the Fill dialog box.**

You can fill a selection with a number of different options:

- Choose the defined foreground or background color
- Choose Color to define a specific color in the Color Picker dialog box
- Choose Pattern, and then choose a specific pattern in the pop-up menu
- Choose History to fill the object with a specific history state (if possible)
- Choose Black, 50% Gray, or White

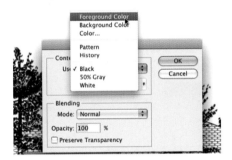

You can also define a specific blending mode and opacity for the filled pixels. Using layers for different elements, however, is typically a better option than changing the fill transparency settings because you can adjust the layer blending mode and opacity as often as necessary.

9. **Click OK to fill the wall selection.**

Note:

Press Shift-F5 to open the Fill dialog box.

Note:

You can also define a specific blending mode and opacity for the filled pixels. Using layers for different elements, however, is typically a better option than changing the fill transparency settings because you can adjust the layer blending mode and opacity as often as necessary.

Note:

Press Command-Delete/ Control-Backspace to fill the selection with the current background color. Press Option-Delete/ Alt-Backspace to fill the selection with the current foreground color. Press Command-Option- Delete/Control-Alt- Delete to fill the selection with the selected state in the History panel.

10. **With the Walls layer selected in the Layers panel, change the Opacity setting to 50%.**

Semi-transparent fills make it possible to continue painting the elements that comprise the original artwork. When you're finished, you can return this layer to 100% opacity. If you had changed the fill opacity to 50% in the Fill dialog box, you would be unable to change it back to 100%.

Note:

Transparency is the amount of light that shows through an object. Photoshop (and most other graphics applications) recreates this visual phenomenon by adjusting the Opacity value of a layer or object.

You can drag the slider or type a value directly in the Opacity field.

You can now see the original drawing (the Sketch layer at 100% opacity) and the semi-transparent fill on the Walls layer.

11. **Turn off the current selection (Select>Deselect), save the file, and then continue to the next exercise.**

Note:

In this case, the finished artwork will be at full opacity. While you're working, however, it helps to see through various layers.

FILL AREAS WITH THE PAINT BUCKET TOOL

The Paint Bucket tool has the same basic functionality as the Fill dialog box — you click the tool cursor to fill an area with the current foreground color. In the Control panel, you can choose the color, blending mode, and opacity of the fill.

1. **With house_working.psd open, hide the Walls layer and add a new layer named Front Trim at the top of the layer stack.**

2. **Choose the Paint Bucket tool (nested under the Gradient tool) in the Tools panel. In the Control panel, type 30 in the Tolerance field and activate the All Layers option.**

Unlike the Fill dialog box, the Paint Bucket tool creates fills based on the defined sample tolerance (which is similar to the settings used to create a selection based on a color range).

In addition to the fill color, blending mode, and opacity, the Control panel includes settings for tool tolerance and anti-aliasing, as well as whether to fill only contiguous pixels within the defined tolerance. The All Layers option allows you to sample pixels from all visible layers instead of only the selected layer.

Use these settings to determine the sensitivity of the Paint Bucket tool cursor.

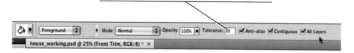

3. Change the foreground color to the Browns 1 swatch.

4. Click the Paint Bucket tool cursor inside each of the trim (not wall) areas in the front of the house. (Use the following image as a guide for the areas you should fill.)

Make sure you click on both sides of the trees. In some segments, you might need to click several times to fill the primary shapes.

Some areas of the selection are outside the tool's tolerance; those areas are not filled.

5. Hide the Sketch layer.

Because of the points used to create texture in the sketch, the Paint Bucket tool did not fill all the shapes. That's okay, though, because you can use the empty spots to create texture of your own.

Don't worry about the areas where trees and bushes cover the house. You're going to include the trees in your painting, so your trees will cover those areas.

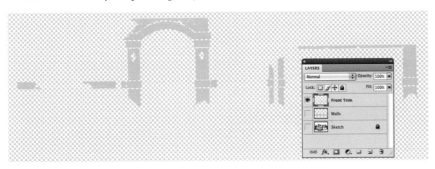

6. Show the Sketch layer and create another new layer named Fascia.

7. Using the Paint Bucket tool, fill the lower part of the fascia boards with the Browns 2 swatch.

8. Fill the upper part of the fascia boards with the Browns 3 swatch.

These are the fascia boards.

9. Save the file and continue to the next stage of the project.

Stage 3 Painting with Brushes

Filling a selection area is one of the more basic aspects of painting in Photoshop. To create complex custom artwork, you can use Photoshop brushes in the digital workspace just as you would use traditional brushes on canvas. The built-in brushes come in hundreds of shapes and sizes; combining these brushes with options such as opacity, flow, and blending mode provides an almost infinite array of choices for painting pixels in a Photoshop layout.

If you completed Project 2, you should be familiar with using Photoshop brushes to paint and erase areas of a layer mask — but there is far more to using brushes than what you learned in that project. Painting the house in this project requires several different types of brushes, as well as controlling the brush options to complete various areas of the painting.

When you choose the Brush tool, you must first select a specific brush. You can choose one of the built-in brush presets from the Control panel, or you can define your own brush by changing the Master Diameter and Hardness settings. You can also use the Control panel to change the blending mode, opacity, and flow of the current brush, as well as work in Airbrush mode.

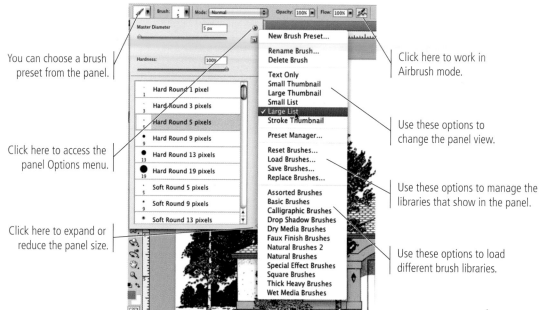

You can choose a brush preset from the panel.

Click here to access the panel Options menu.

Click here to expand or reduce the panel size.

Click here to work in Airbrush mode.

Use these options to change the panel view.

Use these options to manage the libraries that show in the panel.

Use these options to load different brush libraries.

You learned about blending modes and opacity in an earlier project. The other brush options require a little bit of explanation.

- **Master diameter** is the size of the brush tip, measured in pixels.

- **Hardness** is the percentage of the brush diameter that's completely opaque. For example, a Hardness setting of 50% for a brush with a 10-pixel diameter means that 5 pixels in the brush center are hard, and the remaining diameter has a feathered edge.

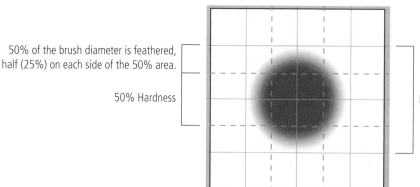

50% of the brush diameter is feathered, half (25%) on each side of the 50% area.

50% Hardness

Master diameter

Note:

Pressure sensitivity becomes an issue when you use a drawing tablet. The harder you press, the more "paint" is applied. Many of the painting tools in Photoshop — including the Brush tool — include options to allow pressure sensitivity while you paint.

- **Flow** sets the rate at which color is applied as you paint repeatedly over the same area. As you continue painting over the same area (while holding down the mouse button), the amount of color "builds up."

In the following example, we set the brush color to C=100 M=50, with a Flow setting of 50%. Each successive click moved the color values 50% closer to the brush color.

Contrary to what many people think, the Flow setting does not apply hard percentages of the brush color. The first click resulted in 25% magenta, or 50% of the brush color value. The second click produced 38% magenta, which is the result of adding 50% of the difference between the first click (25% magenta) and the brush color (50% magenta) — or one half of the difference between 25 and 50 (25 / 2 = 12.5).

For the third click, 50% of the difference between 38 (the previous value) and 50 (the brush value) is added: 50 – 38 = 12 / 2 = 6 + 38 = 44

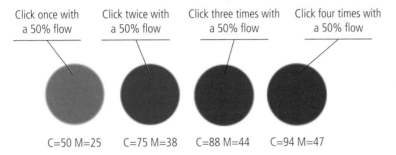

| Click once with a 50% flow | Click twice with a 50% flow | Click three times with a 50% flow | Click four times with a 50% flow |

C=50 M=25   C=75 M=38   C=88 M=44   C=94 M=47

- **Airbrush mode** simulates painting with an airbrush. If you hold down the mouse button or move the cursor back and forth over the same area, more color builds up in the same location. (Brush hardness, opacity, and flow options control how fast and how much "paint" is applied.)

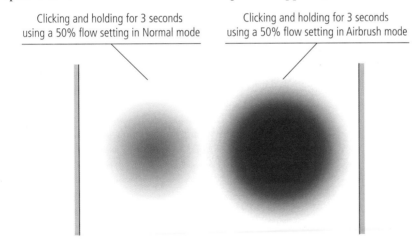

Clicking and holding for 3 seconds using a 50% flow setting in Normal mode

Clicking and holding for 3 seconds using a 50% flow setting in Airbrush mode

Note:

Press the Left Bracket key ([ ) or Right Bracket key ( ]) to decrease or increase (respectively) the current brush diameter to the next predetermined size.

Press Shift-[to decrease brush hardness, and press Shift-] to increase the brush hardness.

Note:

Color values are always whole numbers, which is why the magenta value is rounded to 38 instead of the mathematical 50% value of 37.5.

Note:

Press a number key to define the brush opacity setting in increments of 10% (e.g., pressing 6 sets the opacity to 60%).

Note:

Press Shift and a number key to define the brush flow setting in increments of 10% (e.g., pressing Shift-6 sets the flow to 60%).

USE HARD BRUSHES

The brush Hardness setting allows you to paint sharp lines or soft, feathered edges. Both of these possibilities are important when creating different kinds of artwork. Most painting projects — including this one — require a combination of hard- and soft-edge brushes.

1. **With** house_working.psd **open, hide the Front Trim and Fascia layers. Create two new layers at the top of the layer stack — one named** Garage Door **and one named** GD Panels.

   The Garage Door layer will hold the overall door area; the GD Panels layer will hold the painted lines that form the shapes on the raised panels within the garage door.

2. **Draw a rectangular selection around the garage door. Make sure all door edges are included in the selection.**

   Make sure you select the entire garage door. Some of the area above the door on the left will be within the selection rectangle.

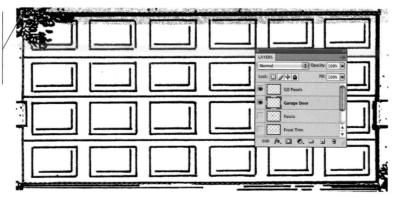

3. **With the Garage Door layer selected, change the foreground color to the Sills and Frames 1 swatch.**

4. **Choose the Paint Bucket tool in the Tools panel. Make sure the All Layers option is turned off in the Control panel.**

   If the All Layers option is selected, clicking with the Paint Bucket tool would sample from the Sketch layer, and some of the selected area wouldn't be entirely filled.

5. **Click the Paint Bucket tool inside the selection marquee.**

   Since the active layer (Garage Door) has no current content, the Tolerance setting is irrelevant. The entire selection area fills with the Sills and Frames 1 color.

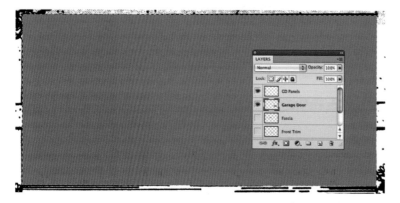

Note:

As hard as we tried to get this image exactly square on the scanner bed, no scans are perfect. There's a chance that the straight lines, paths, and guides you create in Photoshop will not exactly match the horizontal, vertical, or angled lines in your scans. A very slight difference is nothing to worry about. The finished product will look fine because the original scan will ultimately be deleted.

6. **Turn off the selection marquee. Change the Garage Door layer Opacity value to 50% so you can see the underlying sketch.**

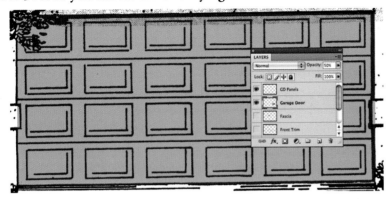

7. **Choose the Brush tool in the Tools panel. In the Control panel, click the Brush button to open the Brushes panel and select the Hard Round 13 pixels brush.**

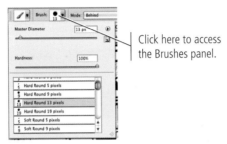

Click here to access the Brushes panel.

Note:

If you don't see the brush names, choose Large List or Small List from the panel Options menu.

8. **Place the brush cursor over one of the panel edges in the top row of the garage door.**

The default brush cursor shows the size of the selected brush tip. In this case, the 13-pixel brush is clearly wider than the line you want to paint.

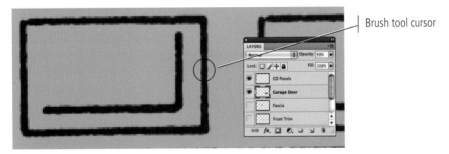

Brush tool cursor

9. **In the Brushes panel, choose the Hard Round 5 pixels brush. Place the cursor over one of the panel edges.**

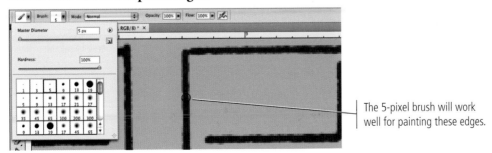

The 5-pixel brush will work well for painting these edges.

10. **Make the GD Panels layer active. Change the foreground color to the Sills and Frames 0 swatch.**

11. **Click at the top of one of the panel insets (the backwards "L" shapes), press Shift, and then click at the lower-right corner of the panel inset.**

12. **Press Shift and click at the lower-left corner of the panel inset.**

Pressing Shift and then clicking again connects the first and second points with a straight line of the brush color. You can also press Shift while dragging to paint a perfectly horizontal or vertical line.

Note:

Zooming in helps when you're working on the smaller details of a painting (such as the garage door panels).

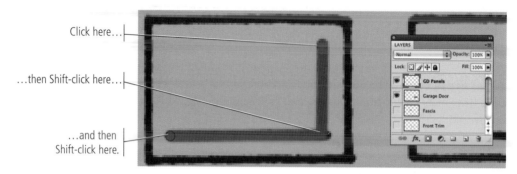

Click here…

…then Shift-click here…

…and then Shift-click here.

13. **Save the file and continue to the next exercise.**

The Pencil Tool

PHOTOSHOP FOUNDATIONS

The Pencil tool (nested under the Brush tool) is very similar to the Brush tool. However, like a physical pencil, the Pencil tool draws hard-edge lines instead of brush strokes. In the Control panel, you can select a brush preset from any of the available hard-edge brushes. You can also define the blending mode and opacity to use for the pencil stroke.

If the **Auto Erase** option is checked, the Pencil tool paints based on the defined foreground and background colors in the Tools panel, as compared to the color of pixels under the tool cursor. If you draw over an area that contains the foreground color, that area is erased to the background color. If you draw over an area that does not include the foreground color, the Pencil tool simply applies the foreground color.

In the following image, we sampled a color from the snail's head as the foreground color, and we used a bright magenta as the background color.

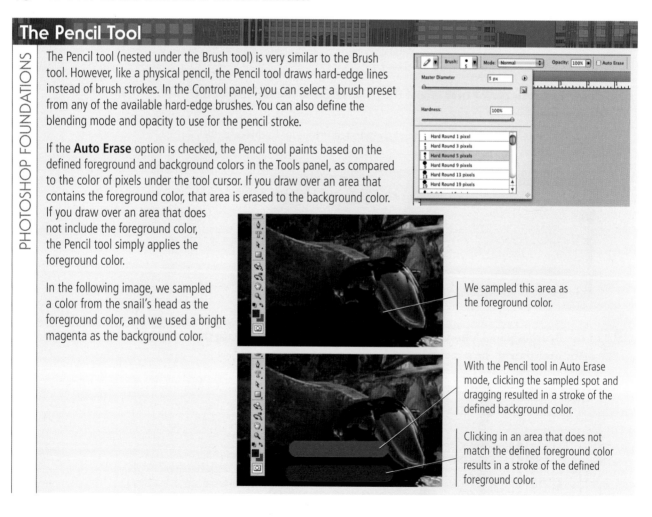

We sampled this area as the foreground color.

With the Pencil tool in Auto Erase mode, clicking the sampled spot and dragging resulted in a stroke of the defined background color.

Clicking in an area that does not match the defined foreground color results in a stroke of the defined foreground color.

USE SOFT BRUSHES

Painting with a hard brush results in colored pixels edged by white pixels. In the real world, however, there are very few perfectly hard edges with no variation in shades. Soft-edge brushes are far more useful for creating artwork that includes the subtle color variations found in a real object.

1. **With house_working.psd open, zoom in to the garage door panel where you already created the inset. Make sure the GD Panels layer is selected.**

2. **Open the Cursors pane of the Preferences dialog box (in the Photoshop menu on Macintosh or the Edit menu on Windows).**

3. **In the Painting Cursors area, make sure the Full Size Brush Tip and Show Crosshair in Brush Tip options are turned on. Click OK to apply the change.**

   The Full Size Brush Tip option changes the cursor to include the entire brush area, including the feathered part of soft-edge brushes.

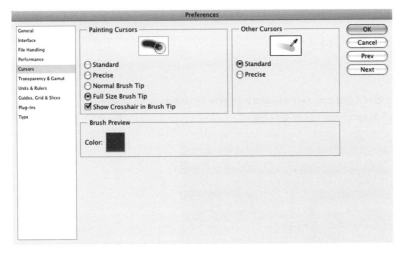

4. **Draw a rectangular selection marquee around the garage door panel where you painted the inset.**

5. **With the Brush tool active, place the cursor so the crosshairs are exactly on top of the selection marquee.**

6. **Press the Right Bracket key ( ]) to enlarge the brush until half the cursor covers the panel edge in the sketch.**

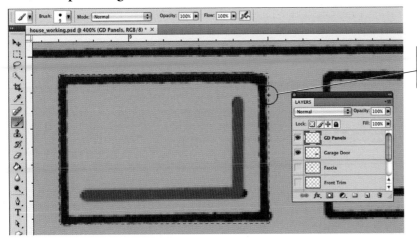

We enlarged the brush size to 9 pixels so half the cursor covers the panel edge.

7. **Click at the top-right corner of the selection marquee, press Shift, and drag down to paint the panel's right edge.**

Even though half the cursor is outside the selection marquee, areas outside the marquee are not painted. Always remember that when you have an active selection, you can only affect the area inside the selection.

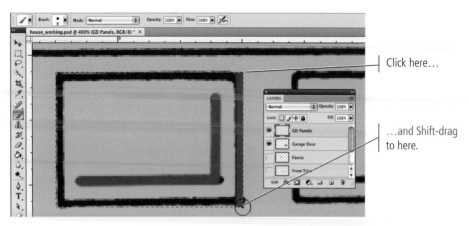

Click here...

...and Shift-drag to here.

8. **Undo the last brush stroke (Edit>Undo).**

The hard-edge brush results are a bit too hard to create the effect of a realistic shadow.

9. **Using the Brushes panel in the Control panel, change the brush size (Master Diameter) to 15 px and the Hardness value to 0%.**

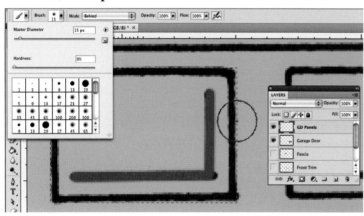

10. **Click at the top-right corner of the selection marquee and Shift-drag down to paint the right edge of the panel.**

Even though these screen shots show the art at 400%, which naturally causes the edges to appear soft even though we used a hard brush, you should be able to see the difference between the hard-edge line and the soft-edge line.

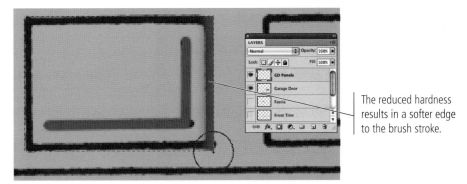

The reduced hardness results in a softer edge to the brush stroke.

11. **Using the same technique, paint the stroke that makes up the top edge of the panel.**

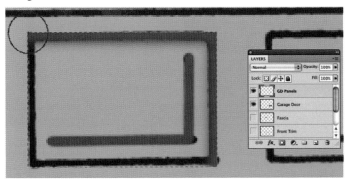

12. **Change the foreground color to Sills and Frames 3, and reduce the size of the brush to 10 px. Paint the left and bottom sides of the panel.**

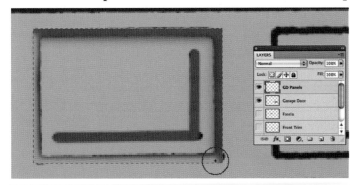

13. **Turn off the active selection, save the file, and continue to the next exercise.**

PHOTOSHOP FOUNDATIONS

The **Eraser tool** removes pixels where you click. If you erase from the Background layer or in a regular layer with transparency locked, the background color shows through where you erased.

- The default Block mode simply erases the area under the square cursor; you can't control the size, shape, opacity, or flow of the tool. When using the Eraser tool, the opacity setting determines the strength of the tool; 100% opacity entirely erases pixels.

- If you choose Brush mode, you can define the specific brush preset, opacity, and flow, as well as use the Eraser brush in Airbrush mode.

If the **Erase to History** option is checked, dragging with the Eraser tool (in any mode) reveals the selected state in the History palette.

- If you choose Pencil mode, you can define the specific brush and opacity; Pencil mode does not offer flow control or Airbrush mode.

The **Magic Eraser tool** works on the same principle as the Magic Wand tool. Clicking with the tool erases all pixels within the defined tolerance.

Clicking with the Magic Eraser tool removes all pixels within the defined tolerance.

The **Background Eraser tool** (nested under the Eraser tool) erases pixels while attempting to maintain the edges of an object in the foreground. The Background Eraser samples color at the brush center, and deletes that color where it appears inside the brush. In the Options bar, you can define the brush size and settings. You can also specify different sampling and tolerance options to control the range of pixels that are affected.

The sampling options determine how color will be replaced:

- **Continuous** samples colors as you drag.
- **Once** erases color only in areas containing the color you first click.
- **Background Swatch** erases only areas containing the current background color.

The Limits menu constrains the tool's effect:

- **Discontiguous** erases the sampled color where it occurs under the brush.
- **Contiguous** erases colors that are contiguous with the color immediately under the brush tip.
- **Find Edges** erases connected areas of the sampled color, attempting to preserve edge sharpness.

Tolerance defines how much variance from the sample will be affected. The **Anti-alias** option smoothes edges of the affected areas. If the **Protect Foreground Color** option is checked, pixels of the defined foreground color in the Tools palette will be protected from erasure.

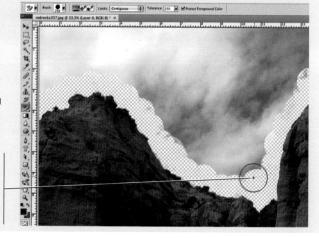

Clicking and dragging with the Background Eraser tool removes pixels within the defined tolerance; the high-contrast edge of the foreground object (the rocks) remains unaffected.

DUPLICATE REPEATING ELEMENTS

When working on a project that requires you to paint a number of objects that look exactly the same, you could paint each one individually. Another option is to complete one of the objects, and then duplicate it to create the others. While each job determines which method is best, in this case, copying the completed panel is a perfectly reasonable way to create the repeated elements.

1. **With house_working.psd open, make sure the GD Panels layer is selected.**

2. **With the Move tool active, press Option/Alt-Shift, and then click-drag down.**

   This method of copying a selection (or layer, if there is no specific selection marquee) is called **cloning**.

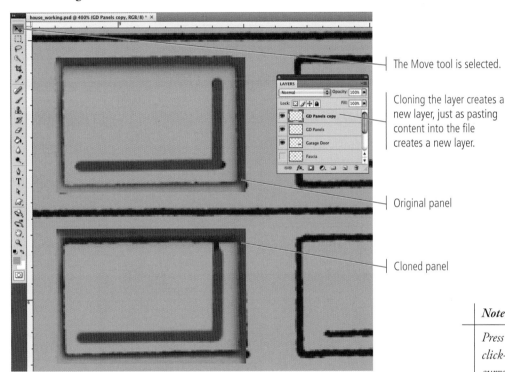

The Move tool is selected.

Cloning the layer creates a new layer, just as pasting content into the file creates a new layer.

Original panel

Cloned panel

3. **Drag a horizontal ruler guide to the top edge of each row of door panels.**

4. **Drag a vertical ruler guide to the left edge of each column of door panels.**

Note:

Press Option/Alt and click-drag to clone the current selection.

Press Shift to constrain movement to 45° increments.

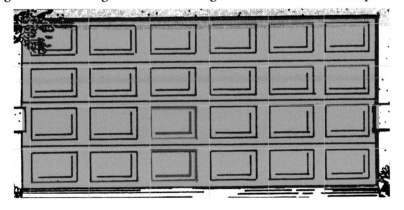

5. **Clone the panel painting enough times to create all the panels from the original artwork. Use the guides to position the copies.**

   You can minimize work by cloning more than one layer at a time. For example, you could clone enough copies for the top row of panels, merge those six layers, and clone the merged layer three more times. As you become more familiar with Photoshop, you'll develop your own shortcuts to improve productivity and streamline your workflow.

6. **In the Layers panel, select all 24 copies of the GD Panel layer and choose Merge Layers from the panel Options menu.**

Note:

You could accomplish the same general effect using the Align options in the Control panel. We find it easier to use guides to place each clone as we create it.

7. **Change the Garage Door layer opacity to 80%.**

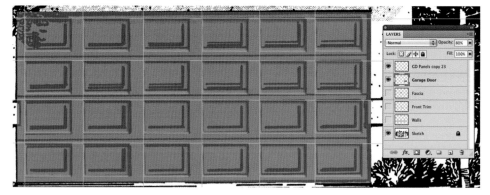

8. **Merge the GD Panel copy layer with the Garage Door layer.**

The merged layer adopts the attributes (name, opacity, etc.) of the topmost layer included in the merge.

9. **Rename the newly merged layer** `Garage Door`.

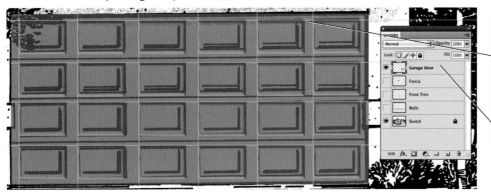

The main garage door area, which was 80% opaque, is still semi-opaque, but you can no longer independently change the opacity of this area.

The merged layer adopts the opacity of the topmost layer.

10. **Remove the page guides (View>Clear Guides), save the file, and continue to the next exercise.**

Painting Back in Time

PHOTOSHOP FOUNDATIONS

The **History Brush tool** allows you to restore specific areas of an image back to a previous state. In the Control panel, you can choose the brush preset and brush settings that you want to use. When you paint with the History Brush tool, areas where you paint return to the target state or snapshot in the History panel. (The same effect can be achieved using any of the regular Eraser tools with the Erase to History option active.)

In the images shown here, we opened a file and made a Levels adjustment to lighten the image. We then applied some painting and touch-ups, as well as a filter to make the image look like a line-art drawing. In the final step, we selected the adjusted, unfiltered state and used the History Brush tool to restore only the clock tower back to the photographic pixels.

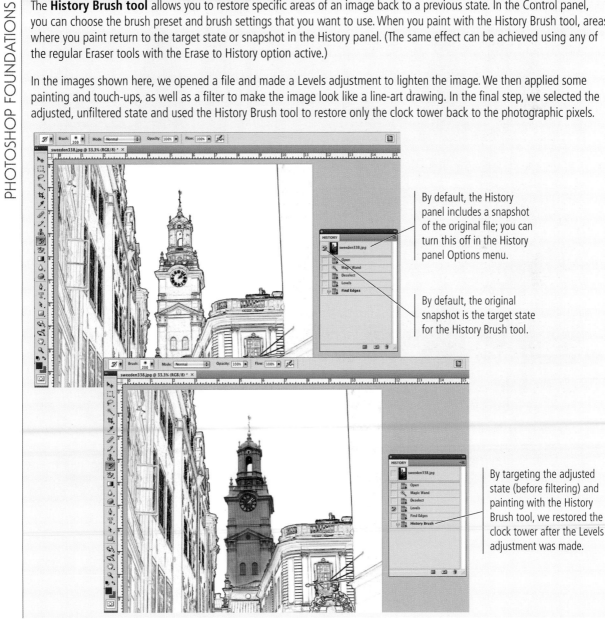

By default, the History panel includes a snapshot of the original file; you can turn this off in the History panel Options menu.

By default, the original snapshot is the target state for the History Brush tool.

By targeting the adjusted state (before filtering) and painting with the History Brush tool, we restored the clock tower after the Levels adjustment was made.

PHOTOSHOP FOUNDATIONS

The **Art History Brush tool** paints with stylized strokes, using the targeted history state (or snapshot) as the source data for the painting. (We can't say the tool "restores" the data, because results from the artistic style of the brush could hardly be called "restorative.")

In the Control panel, you can define the brush preset, blending mode, and opacity, as well as a specific style that will be used for the brush marks. The Area option defines the area that will be covered with the brush marks; larger area values result in a greater area covered, as well as more brush marks created by the stroke. Tolerance limits the area where brush strokes can be applied; higher tolerance values limit painting to areas that significantly differ from colors in the targeted state of the snapshot.

In the following series of images, we targeted the original image snapshot in the History panel, and then restored the clock tower by using the Art History Brush with different style settings.

Restored with the Tight Short style

Restored with the Loose Medium style

Restored with the Dab style

Restored with the Tight Curl style

When you're painting something like this house, you start with spaces defined by sharp, black lines drawn on white paper. In the case of the bitmap scan provided by your client, there are plenty of lines to define the objects in the drawing. But as we stated in the previous exercise, real-world objects rarely contain sharp black lines.

Fortunately, the same techniques you used to draw the Garage Door layer — using relatively hard and fairly soft brushes in combination, as well as using selection marquees — can be used to draw almost everything else in this painting. (The only exceptions are the plants and the roof, which require different techniques.)

1. **With house_working.psd open, make sure the Garage Door layer is selected.**

2. **Choose the Magic Wand tool and make sure the Sample All Layers option is turned off in the Control panel.**

   As with the Paint Bucket tool, you can use the Magic Wand tool to create a selection based on the content of all visible layers in the file. In this case, you want to base your selection on the Garage Door layer only, so the Sample All Layers option needs to be turned off.

3. **Click anywhere outside the filled door.**

   Because the door is the only object on the layer, the only area that gets selected is the empty portion of the layer.

Marching ants surround the entire image…

…and the painted garage door area.

Everything but the painted garage door is selected.

4. **Choose Select>Inverse to select only the filled area of the layer (the door).**

5. **Change the foreground color to the Sills and Frames 0 swatch.**

6. **Create a new layer above the Garage Door layer named Shadows.**

7. **With the Shadows layer active, choose Edit>Stroke.**

   The Stroke dialog box is similar to the Fill dialog box, except you use this dialog to define the stroke for the current selection.

Note:

Press Command/ Control-Shift-I to invert a selection.

8. **In the Stroke dialog box, set the Width value to 5 px and the Location value to Center. Click OK to apply the stroke.**

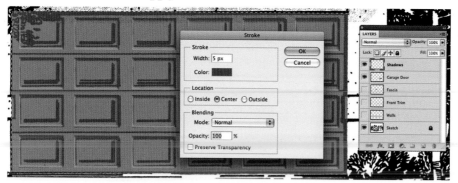

9. **With the selection marquee still active, use the same soft-brush technique you used for the panels to create a soft shadow on the top edge of the door.**

   We used a 25-pixel brush with a 25% Hardness setting.

10. **Hide the Sketch layer and review your work.**

Note:

The Location value of the stroke determines the placement of the stroke width in relation to the selection marquee.

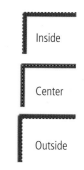

Inside

Center

Outside

11. **Using any method you prefer, paint three horizontal lines to separate the four sections of the garage door.**

   We used the 3-pixel hard-edge brush and the click-Shift-click method to connect the end points of each line.

Note:

Painting is always a subjective assignment. The result from each designer will almost always appear slightly different.

12. **Merge the Shadows and Garage Door layers and rename the merged layer Garage Door.**

13. **Turn off the active selection and show the Sketch layer.**

14. **Save the file and continue to the next exercise.**

PAINT BEHIND EXISTING COLOR

The Behind blending mode is only available when you are creating pixels (painting, adding a fill or stroke to a selection, and so on). This blending mode adds new pixels behind the existing pixels; any existing pixels that are fully opaque will entirely hide the new pixels. This technique is extremely useful for filling spaces and lining edges of existing areas.

1. With `house_working.psd` open, show the Front Trim and Fascia layers.

2. Drag the Garage Door layer below the Front Trim layer.

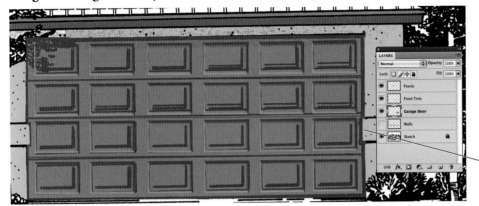

The Front Trim layer needs to be above the Garage Door layer for these elements to appear in front of the door.

3. Hide the Garage Door layer, and then select the Front Trim layer as the active layer.

4. Change the foreground color to the Sills and Frames 0 swatch.

5. Choose the Brush tool and select the Soft Round 17 pixels brush preset.

6. In the Control panel, set the Blending Mode menu to Behind.

7. Place the brush cursor so the crosshairs are slightly inside the filled area of the trim, and then drag down to create a soft edge behind the existing fill.

8. **Hide the Sketch layer, show the Garage Door layer, and review the results.**

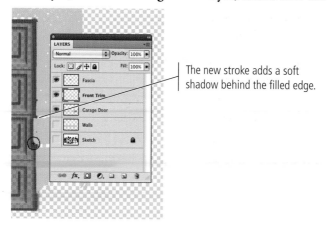

The new stroke adds a soft shadow behind the filled edge.

9. **Continue with the same brush to line the edge of the entire inside column.**

10. **Choose a larger, hard brush and paint the unfilled areas of the front trim around the garage.**

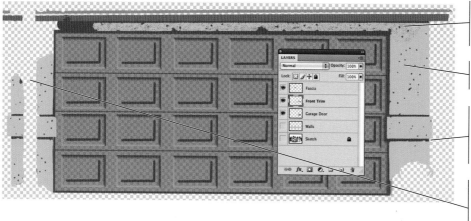

Using the Behind blending mode, only the gaps in the existing color are filled.

We used a 20-pixel brush with 100% hardness.

Be careful around the edges. Don't extend the painting beyond the outsides of the right column.

Don't worry about filling in the area of the trees. You'll cover that later with a tree painting.

11. **Using a small, soft-edge brush, add a small, soft edge on the outside edge of the columns.**

We chose a 7-pixel brush with 0% hardness, and used the click-Shift-click method with the cursor crosshair slightly inside the existing fill area.

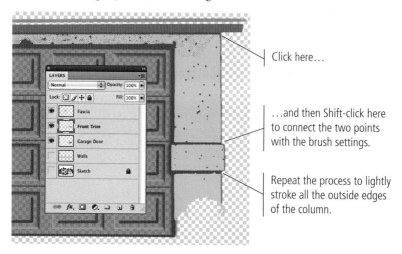

Click here…

…and then Shift-click here to connect the two points with the brush settings.

Repeat the process to lightly stroke all the outside edges of the column.

12. Use the same basic techniques to fill the empty areas of all the face trim:

- Toggle the Sketch layer on and off as necessary to review where trees will obscure the house. Don't worry about perfectly filling those areas.

- Use a soft-edge brush to edge the existing fills, and use a hard-edge brush to fill the gaps left by the Paint Bucket tool.

- Review the sketch to determine the direction of shadows. Apply slightly larger edges to the sides where shadows fall in the sketch.

- On the Fascia layer, fill the empty areas of the fascia boards, and add an edge to those elements. Apply a larger, soft edge along the bottom edge of the fascia boards, and use a smaller, hard edge along the top and sides of the boards.

Note:

The document tab displays the name of the active layer. This tab can be very helpful when you're working on complex files with multiple layers.

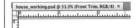

13. Show the Sketch layer and review your work. Make any necessary adjustments.

14. Save your work and continue to the next exercise.

 ## CREATE TEXTURE WITH A FAUX FINISH BRUSH

Textures can be sampled from other images, copied and pasted into place, and created from scratch using combinations of brush styles and options. In this exercise, you use a textured brush to turn what are now simple brown walls into realistic-looking stone.

1. With **house_working.psd** open, hide all but the Walls layer. Set the Walls layer opacity to 80%.

2. Make a selection area that includes only the filled area of the Walls layer.

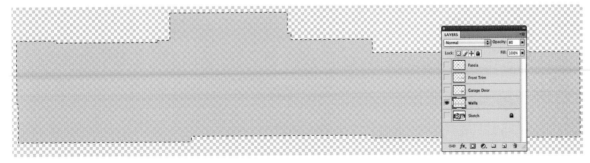

3. Choose the Brush tool. In the Control panel, make sure the brush blending mode is set to Normal.

4. **Display the Brushes panel from the Control panel, and then choose Faux Finish Brushes in the panel Options menu.**

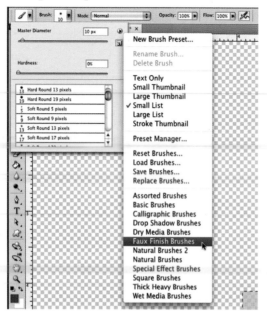

5. **In the warning message dialog box, click OK to replace the current brushes with the new set.**

6. **Select the Stencil Sponge – Wet preset. Make the brush size large enough to cover the highest part of the fill in the Walls layer.**

A 695-pixel brush is large enough to cover the entire area in one brush stroke.

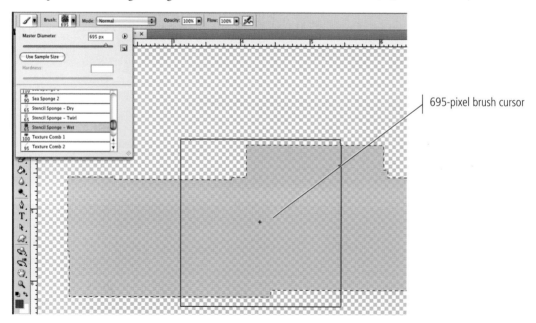

695-pixel brush cursor

7. Change the foreground color to the Stucco 2 swatch, and then click and drag from left to right to paint the texture into the selection area.

The added texture is very subtle because the layer is partly transparent.

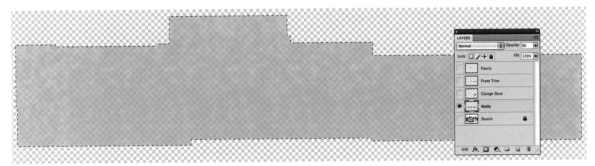

8. Change the Walls layer Opacity value to 100%.

9. Turn off the active selection, save the file, and continue to the next exercise.

USE OPACITY AND BLENDING MODES TO CREATE DEEP SHADOWS

In many cases, it's a better idea to paint on a separate layer and adjust the layer's blend options (blending mode and opacity). In other cases, however, adjusting the settings for the specific brush makes it easier to create subtle elements such as the shadows on the front of the house.

1. With **house_working.psd** open, make all layers visible, and then create a new layer named **House Shadows** at the top of the layer stack.

2. Set the foreground color to Sills and Frames 1. Reduce the Walls layer Opacity value to 50% so you can see the sketch through the walls.

3. In the Control panel, use the Brushes panel Options menu to reset the brushes, replacing (not appending) the existing brushes.

Note:

Because this is such a large project, we include Steps 2 and 3 to ensure you are at the same point we are. In your real-world workflow, you will frequently lock and unlock layers — especially for a complex painting project such as this one.

4. **Choose the Airbrush Soft Round 100 brush. In the Control panel, change the brush Opacity value to 25% and the Blending Mode menu to Multiply.**

5. **Use the shadows in the Sketch layer as a guide to paint the shadow strokes on the House Shadows layer.**

   Because you are using Airbrush mode, each successive brush stroke applies more color. Use multiple strokes to build darker shadows near the house edges that cast the shadows.

   Using reduced brush opacity and the Multiply blending mode, you can build darker shadows onto the Walls layer without completely obscuring the color and texture of the wall — just as actual shadows appear in real life.

6. **Move the Front Trim and Fascia layers above the House Shadows layer.**

The shadows on the Sketch layer define where you need to paint shadows on the House Shadows layer.

7. **Return the Walls layer opacity to 100%.**

8. **Use the Eraser tool to remove any of the painted shadow from the pillars on either side of the garage door.**

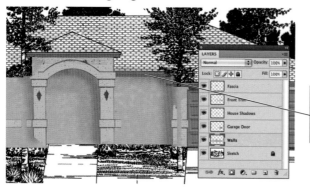

Erase any shadows that extend beyond the fascia boards or into other areas where they don't belong.

9. Hide everything except the Sketch layer.

10. Create two new layers named FD Panels and Front Door. Arrange the new layers directly below the Front Trim layer in the layer stack.

11. Make the Front Door layer active.

12. Paint the front door, using the same method you used to paint the garage door:

    - Create a selection marquee and fill it with a color for the main door shape. We used the Sills and Frames 2 swatch.

    - Create one of the panels by making a selection marquee, and then use a soft round brush in Normal mode at 100% opacity to paint a dark color on the top and right edges, and a light color on the bottom and left edges. We used Roof Shingles 1 for the shadows and Stucco 0 for the highlights.

    - Duplicate the panel five times, reducing the height of the two top panels after you clone them.

    - Use the Paint Behind mode to add a soft shadow behind the door edges. We used the Roof Shingles 1 swatch for all shadows.

    - Paint a shadow around the door frame area, with a hard edge on the outside and a soft edge on the inside. Use a selection marquee to create the hard edge.

    - Paint a solid, hard-edge line across the front of the door jamb. We used the Sills and Frames 0 swatch.

    - Use a small, hard brush to paint the door handle in black.

    - Merge all layers that comprise the door into a single layer named Front Door.

13. Save the file and continue to the next exercise.

APPLY STROKES TO CLOSED PATHS

The window on the front of the house requires a bit more detail than most other elements in this painting. To create this detail, you use a combination of methods to add strokes to both closed and open paths.

1. With **house_working.psd** open, make sure the Walls layer is hidden, and then create a new layer named **Windows**.

2. Use the Pen tool in Path mode to draw the top curved portion of the window.

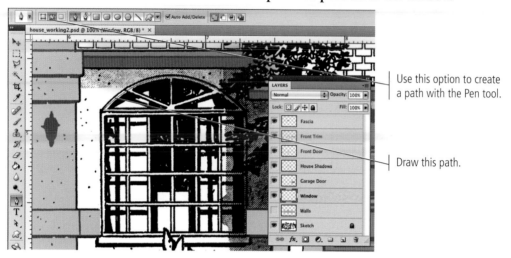

Use this option to create a path with the Pen tool.

Draw this path.

3. In the Paths panel, right-click the work path and choose Make Selection from the contextual menu. In the resulting Make Selection dialog box, set the Feather Radius value to **0** and click OK.

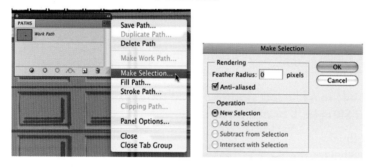

4. Choose Edit>Stroke. Apply a 6-pixel black stroke centered on the selection marquee and click OK.

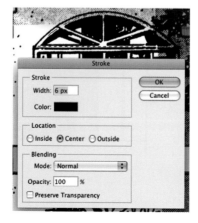

5. Immediately choose Edit>Stroke again, and apply a 3-pixel white stroke centered on the selection marquee.

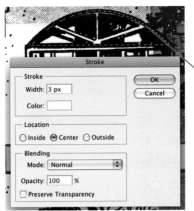

It is largely obscured by the sketch, but the selection marquee has been outlined with a 6-pixel black stroke.

6. Hide the Sketch layer and review your work.

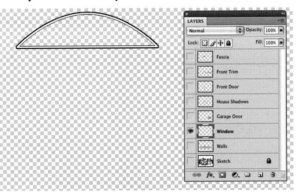

7. Show the Sketch layer, and then use the same 6-pixel-black/3-pixel-white sequence of strokes to create the outer frame of the square window.

8. Hide the Sketch layer and review your work.

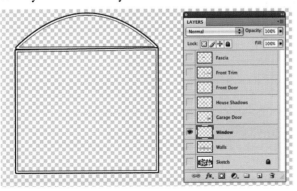

9. Show the Sketch layer, save the file, and continue to the next exercise.

APPLY STROKES TO OPEN PATHS

The rest of the lines in the window are basically straight lines. The easiest way to create them is to use simple, straight lines. However, these straight lines do not create closed shapes from which you can make a selection, so you need a slightly different method to create the inner lines of the window.

1. **With house_working.psd open, show the Sketch layer, and then create a new layer immediately above the Window layer.**

   You will use this layer as a temporary workspace, so it isn't necessary to name it.

2. **Use the Pen tool to draw a vertical line that represents the middle division of the window.**

   Because this is an open path (i.e., it doesn't create an actual shape), creating the black-and-white effect for this vertical path requires a slightly different method.

3. **Choose the Pencil tool (nested under the Brush tool) in the Tools panel, and then reset the default foreground and background colors.**

4. **In the Control panel, choose the Hard Round 5 pixels brush from the Brushes panel.**

   The Pencil tool is very similar to the Brush tool, except it only creates hard edges (just like an actual pencil). In this case, you use the Pencil tool characteristics to stroke the open path you created in Step 2.

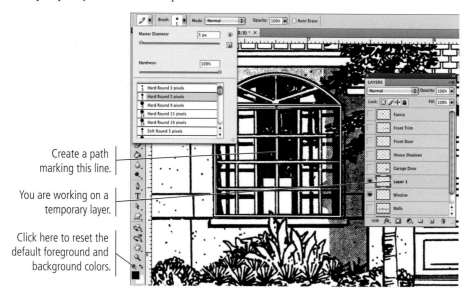

Create a path marking this line.

You are working on a temporary layer.

Click here to reset the default foreground and background colors.

5. **With the work path selected in the Paths panel, choose Stroke Path from the panel Options menu.**

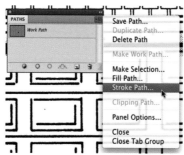

6. **In the resulting Stroke Path dialog box, choose Pencil, and then click OK.**

Using this method, you can define a specific tool to use for the stroke. The current characteristics of the selected tool will be applied, which is why you set the Pencil tool options in Steps 4 and 5.

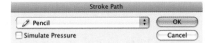

7. **With the Pencil tool still selected, choose the Hard Round 3 pixels brush in the Control panel, and then swap the foreground and background colors.**

8. **With the work path still selected in the Paths panel, choose Stroke Path from the panel Options menu.**

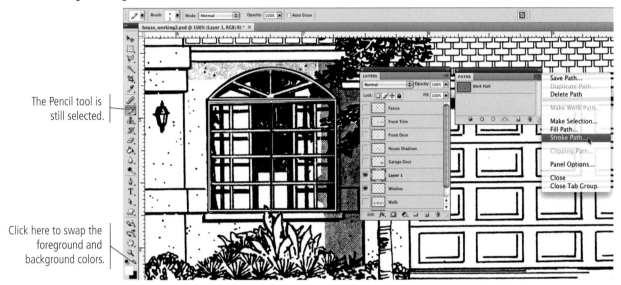

The Pencil tool is still selected.

Click here to swap the foreground and background colors.

9. **Choose Pencil in the resulting dialog box and click OK. Hide the Sketch layer and review your work.**

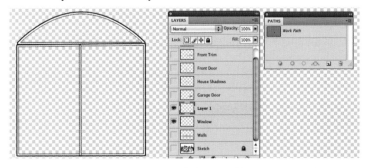

10. **Select the Move tool. Press Option/Alt, and then click and drag left to clone the layer containing the vertical line.**

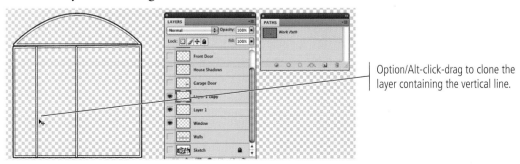

Option/Alt-click-drag to clone the layer containing the vertical line.

11. **Repeat Step 10 three times to create the three remaining vertical lines.**

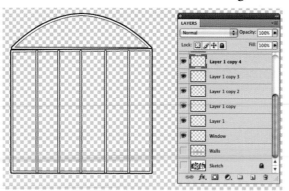

12. **Repeat the process from this exercise to create the remaining horizontal lines of the window.**

13. **Select all temporary layers and the Window layer and merge them. Rename the new merged layer Window.**

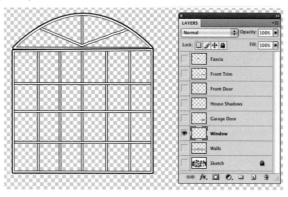

14. **Save the file and continue to the next exercise.**

 ## PAINT WINDOW SHADOWS TO ADD DEPTH

The rest of the window area — the windowsill and the interior shadows cast by the window lines — requires more of the same techniques you learned earlier.

1. **With house_working.psd open, show all layers and review your work.**

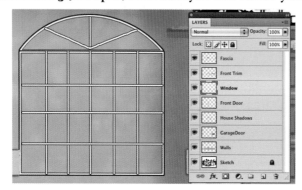

2. Set the Walls layer to 50% opacity so you can see the underlying sketch. Create a new layer named **Window Trim** above the Window layer. Draw the windowsill and remaining piece of front trim, using solid fills and soft-edge shadows (as you did for the front trim elements).

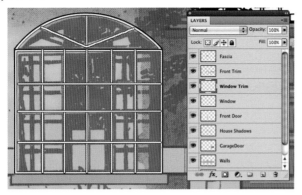

3. Create another new layer named **Window Inside** below the Window layer. Fill the window area with black at 20% opacity.

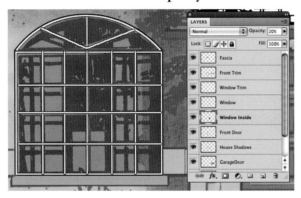

4. Create another new layer named **Window Shadows** below the Window layer but above the Window Inside layer. Use a soft brush with a low brush Flow setting, and use black as the foreground color to paint the shadows that fall inside the house. Change the brush size, flow, and opacity as necessary to create the various shadow areas.

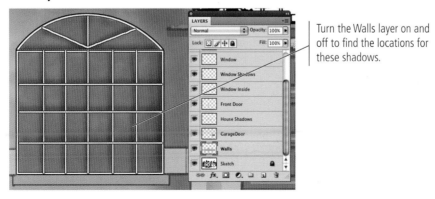

Turn the Walls layer on and off to find the locations for these shadows.

5. Group the four window component layers into a single layer group (folder) named **Window**.

6. **Create the lights on a layer named Lights that sits anywhere above the Front Trim layer.**

   We used a small, hard brush (changing from 3 to 5 pixels, as necessary) with black as the foreground color and simply traced the shapes on the Sketch layer.

7. **Show all layers.**

8. **Drag the Front Door layer and Window layer set below the House Shadows layer so those elements are correctly affected by the shadows.**

9. **Save the file and continue to the next stage of the project.**

Stage 4 Working with Patterns

The only element of the house left to paint is the roof. Manually drawing every shingle would take hours, and it would be difficult (if not impossible) to create the uniformity that is an actual part of real roofing shingles. A better solution is to use a pattern fill. Unfortunately, the built-in Photoshop pattern sets do not include a roof tile pattern, so in this exercise, you create your own.

CREATE A NEW PATTERN

You can create a pattern from anything you can paint. The trick to creating a good repeating pattern is placing elements such that, when the section you create is repeated in the pattern fill, any apparent edges align properly.

1. **Create a new file that is 1″ by 1″ at 300 pixels/inch in the RGB color space.**

   You're creating a **pattern tile**, or the basic painting that repeats when you use this pattern to create a fill. A 1″ by 1″ square is an easy size to divide, so it's a good basis for creating the pattern.

2. **Drag guides to split the file into four equal rows and four equal columns.**

   Use the 1/4″ marks on the horizontal and vertical rulers to place the guides.

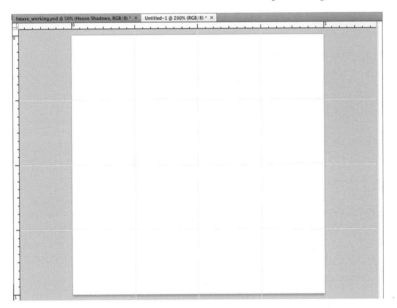

3. **Fill the entire image with the Roof Shingles 2 swatch.**

   Swatches are not specific to a single file. Even though you imported the swatches with the house file open, you can use the custom swatches when you work in other files.

4. **Expand the document window so you can see at least an inch of the gray area around the image canvas.**

5. **Using the Rectangular Marquee tool, create a rectangular selection that covers the lower three-quarters of the canvas.**

6. **Change the foreground color to the Roof Shingles 1 swatch.**

7. **Choose the Brush tool and select the Soft Round 13 pixels brush from the default brush set.**

8. **Place the cursor so the crosshair is exactly on the first horizontal guide, slightly outside the left edge of the canvas.**

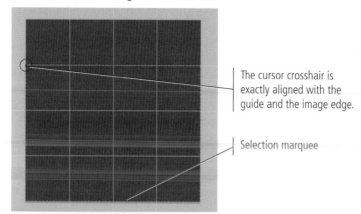

The cursor crosshair is exactly aligned with the guide and the image edge.

Selection marquee

9. **Press Shift, and then click and drag right to create the edge of the first horizontal tile.**

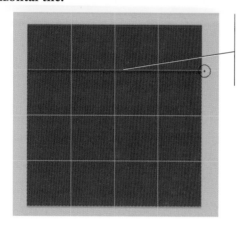

The selection marquee and the placement of the brush cursor create a hard edge on the top of the stroke and a soft edge on the bottom.

10. **Turn off any active selection (Select>Deselect).**

11. **Use the same technique to create the other two horizontal lines in the middle of the file.**

12. **Place the cursor with the crosshair at the exact top-left corner of the file. Shift-click and drag right to create the top horizontal line.**

In this case, you don't need to create a selection marquee; the image boundary serves the same purpose as the marquees you used to create the lines in the middle of the image.

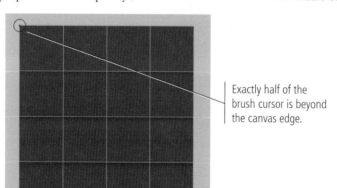

Exactly half of the brush cursor is beyond the canvas edge.

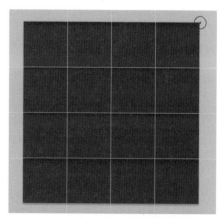

Note:

Pressing Shift constrains the stroke to perfectly horizontal or vertical.

13. **Place the cursor over the exact intersection of the top and left guides. Shift-click and drag up to create the first vertical tile edge.**

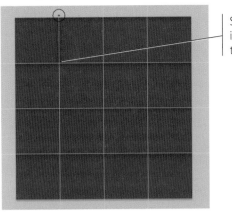

Start with the cursor crosshair in the exact location where the two guides meet.

14. **Create the remaining interior vertical lines, starting each time at the exact intersection of two guides. (Use the following image as a guide for placing the vertical lines.)**

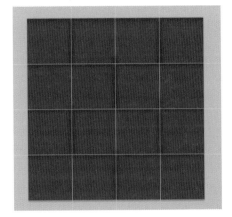

15. **Place the cursor crosshair exactly on the second horizontal guide at the edge of the canvas. Shift-click and drag up to the first horizontal guide.**

By placing the cursor crosshair on the edge of the canvas, exactly half of the brush stroke is on the left edge and half is on the right edge. When this tile is repeated in a pattern, the two half-strokes will stitch together seamlessly.

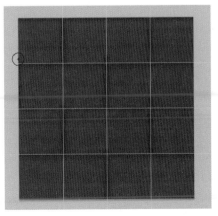

16. **Repeat the process on the right side of the canvas, between the first and second horizontal guides.**

17. **Create the remaining vertical strokes on the left and right edges for the fourth row of tiles.**

18. **Hide the guides (View>Show>Guides) and review your progress.**

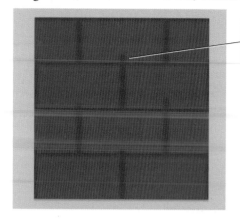

The vertical lines should not extend above the horizontal lines.

Note:

When guides are visible, it's easy to draw a selection marquee that snaps to the guides.

19. **Show the guides (View>Show>Guides), and then draw a selection marquee around only the top quarter of the canvas.**

20. **Set the background color to the Roof Shingles 2 swatch.**

21. **Use the Eraser tool in Block mode to erase the vertical line that extends into the first row of shingles.**

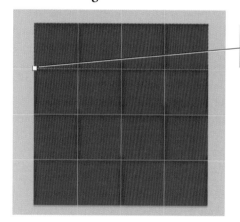

You don't need to be precise with the eraser; only the part inside the selection marquee will be erased.

22. **Repeat the process to erase the top ends from the vertical lines as necessary.**

The erased areas show the background color — which is set to the same color you originally used to fill the canvas.

23. **Save the file as tiles.psd in your WIP>Realty folder and continue to the next exercise.**

DEFINE A NEW PATTERN

As you saw in the previous exercise, defining a pattern tile is the most complicated part of creating a pattern — carefully aligning elements so any edges form a seamless pattern instead of a seemingly meaningless mess. Once you have defined the tile, creating and applying the pattern is fairly easy.

1. **With `tiles.psd` open, choose Edit>Define Pattern.**

2. **In the Pattern Name dialog box, type `Shingles` and click OK.**

3. **Make the `house_working.psd` file active in the document window.**

4. **Create a new layer named `Roof 1` at the top of the layer stack.**

5. **Using the Polygonal Lasso tool, draw a selection around the main roof area.**

   You might have to make some assumptions in the top corners, where the sketched trees obscure the roof corners.

Don't worry if the selection covers some of the house. You'll rearrange layers to fix any potential problems.

6. **Choose Edit>Fill, and choose Pattern in the Use menu.**

7. **Click the Custom Pattern menu and choose Shingles from the bottom of the list.**

   This is the pattern you created in the previous exercise. It was added to the existing patterns available in the Patterns panel.

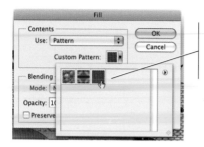

Don't worry if your list includes more patterns. In this project, you only use the patterns you create from scratch.

8. **Click OK to fill the selection area with the pattern.**

   As you can see, lines you painted on the pattern tile align seamlessly when you create the pattern fill, but the 1″ square pattern tile is far too large for this image.

9. **Make the tiles.psd file active in the document window and open the Image Size dialog box (Image>Image Size).**

10. **With the Resample Image option turned on, resample the image to 0.25″ by 0.25″ and click OK.**

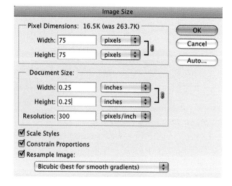

11. **Choose Edit>Define Pattern. Name the new pattern Small Shingles and click OK.**

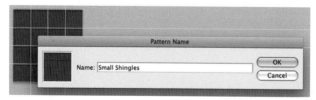

12. Save the adjusted tiles image as `tiles_small.psd` in your WIP>Realty folder and close it.

13. With the main roof area still selected in the house_working file, fill the selection with the new Small Shingles pattern.

Use this menu to change the view to Small List so you can distinguish between the two shingles patterns.

14. Hide the Roof 1 layer.

15. Use the same process to create the two remaining sections of the roof, each on its own layer. Name the new layers `Roof 2` and `Roof 3`.

16. Show the Roof 1 layer.

With all three roof sections showing, you can now see two problems. First, the main roof is obscuring the porch covering and fascia. Second, all three pieces of the roof were created with the same pattern, so all three pieces merge seamlessly together.

17. **Drag the Lights, Fascia, and Front Trim layers to the top of the layer stack. Delete the section of roof tile that falls below the porch archway.**

18. **Use the Paint Behind method with the Roof Shingles 1 swatch to add hard and soft edges around the roof sections, filling in gaps between the roof sections and fascia boards.**

19. **Group the three roof sections into a layer folder named Roof, save the file, and continue to the next exercise.**

 ## SAVE CUSTOM PATTERNS

You never know when a particular pattern or other asset might be useful. By default, when you quit Photoshop you lose any custom assets unless you intentionally save them. Since you've taken the time to create the pattern for a tiled roof, it's a good idea to save it so you can use it again later.

1. **With house_working.psd open, choose Edit>Preset Manager.**

   You can use the Preset Manager dialog box to control built-in and custom assets, including brushes, swatches, gradients, styles, patterns, contours, custom shapes, and tools.

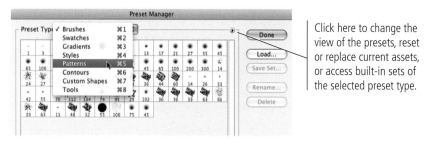

Click here to change the view of the presets, reset or replace current assets, or access built-in sets of the selected preset type.

2. **Choose Patterns in the Preset Type menu.**

3. **Shift-click to select all patterns except the two custom patterns you created.**

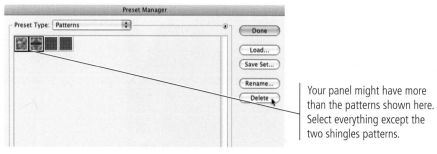

Your panel might have more than the patterns shown here. Select everything except the two shingles patterns.

4. **Click Delete to remove the selected patterns from the dialog box.**

   You're deleting these patterns from the panel only. Because these patterns are part of one of the built-in sets (in this case, the Patterns 2 set), you can always load them again by choosing that set in the Patterns panel Options menu.

5. **Select the two remaining pattern swatches and click the Save Set button.**

6. **In the Save dialog box, name the set `Portfolio Patterns.pat` and click Save.**

   When you save a custom pattern set, the Save dialog box defaults to the Presets>Patterns folder in the Photoshop CS4 application folder. The extension (".pat") is automatically added for you. All you need to do is type the name.

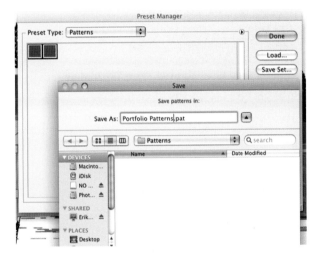

   After the pattern set has been saved, you can access those patterns again by clicking the Load button in the Presets Manager or by opening the Patterns panel Options menu.

7. **Click Done to close the Preset Manager, and then continue to the next stage of the project.**

The Pattern Stamp Tool

PHOTOSHOP FOUNDATIONS

The Pattern Stamp tool (nested under the Clone Stamp tool) is used to paint patterns onto selected areas of an image. In the Control panel, you can define the specific brush preset and brush settings, as well as the pattern you want to apply.

The Impressionist option creates an artistic interpretation of the pattern; you have no control over the results, other than the specific brush and options being used.

If the Aligned option is checked, the pattern is basically locked to the layer; clicking and dragging reveals the part of the pattern that exists where you drag. Think of the Aligned option this way: The entire layer is theoretically "filled" with the selected pattern; when you paint with the Pattern Stamp tool, the pattern fill is revealed in those areas where you paint — in other words, the pattern is aligned in each successive stroke.

When the Aligned option is not checked, each stroke of the Pattern Stamp tool paints the pattern onto the selected layer. The pattern is not aligned from one stroke to the next.

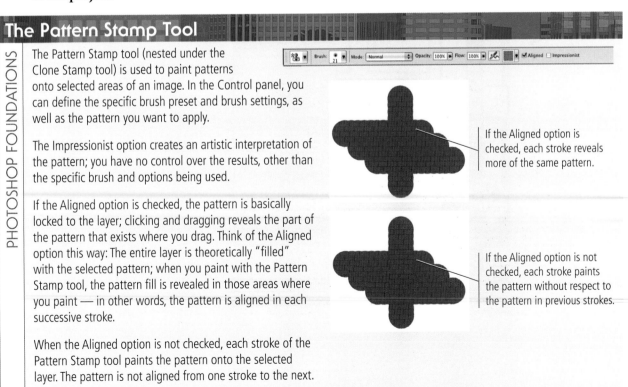

If the Aligned option is checked, each stroke reveals more of the same pattern.

If the Aligned option is not checked, each stroke paints the pattern without respect to the pattern in previous strokes.

Stage 5 Painting Nature

Some elements of this painting are far less structured than the house. The trees, bushes, grass, and other natural elements can't be created by filling and painting with basic brushes — or at least, you can't make them look natural with the tools you've learned so far. These elements should be painted more randomly so they look as natural as possible.

PAINT SHADES OF NATURE

When it comes to painting the landscaping, it helps to have an eye for art in general (more so than for any other component of this project). That's not to say, however, that you need to be Michelangelo to finish this project. The best place to start is creating the "solid" elements such as the tree trunks and sidewalks, using skills that you learned in earlier exercises.

1. **With house_working.psd open, create a new layer named Tree Trunks at the top of the layer stack. Hide all other layers except the Sketch layer.**

   You're going to use a series of different layers to create the various landscaping elements. Doing so will allow you to control the different pieces, including rearranging or merging them together as necessary to create the best possible result. These layers should be on top of the layer stack because most of the trees and bushes are in the sketch foreground (i.e., in front of the house).

2. **Select the Paint Bucket tool and choose Browns 1 as the foreground color.**

3. **In the Control panel, use a Tolerance setting of 30 and make sure the Contiguous and All Layers options are active.**

4. **Click the white areas of the tree trunk to fill them with the foreground color.**

   If you click the wrong area, you might fill most of the sketch with the foreground color. If this happens, simply undo the last click (Edit>Undo) and try again.

> **Note:**
>
> *As we have mentioned, it's common to lock, hide, and move layers as necessary when working on a complex assignment like this one. At times, the position of specific layers becomes critical; so, too, does making sure you're working on the correct layer. When you work on a complex file, plan your work and then carefully follow those plans.*

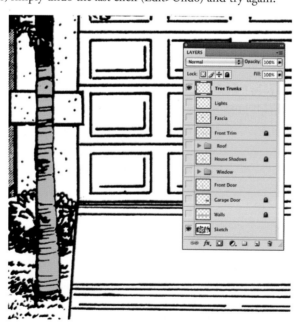

5. **Choose the Brush tool. Use a small, hard brush (we used 9 pixels) with the Blending Mode menu set to Behind. Change the foreground color to Browns 3 and paint some of the black areas on the right side of the tree trunk.**

We painted the right half of the trunk (behind the existing fills) with the Browns 3 color. In the next step we'll use the darker Browns 2 to paint the left half of the trunk, creating a three-dimensional feeling.

Keep in mind that the edges of your painting don't have to perfectly match the sketch. Try to avoid straight lines, however, since very few (if any) real trees have perfectly straight edges.

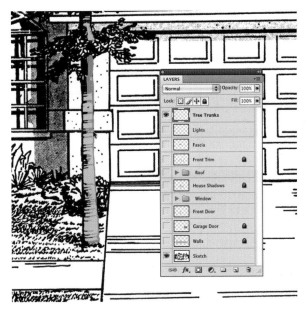

6. **Change the foreground color to Browns 2 and paint the left side of the trunk using the same Behind blending mode.**

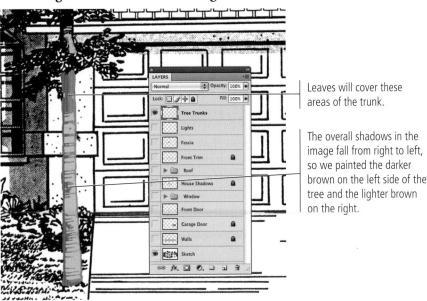

Leaves will cover these areas of the trunk.

The overall shadows in the image fall from right to left, so we painted the darker brown on the left side of the tree and the lighter brown on the right.

7. **Use the same process to paint the remaining tree trunks.**

8. **Create a new layer named** Sidewalks **at the top of the layer stack. Fill the sidewalk and driveway sections with 10% black and use darker shades of gray to create the shadows in the concrete.**

In the sketch, the driveway area doesn't have a solid edge, so simply clicking with the Paint Bucket tool would fill most of the layer with gray. Instead, use the Polygon Lasso tool to draw a marquee around the driveway areas, and then click inside the marquee with the Paint Bucket tool.

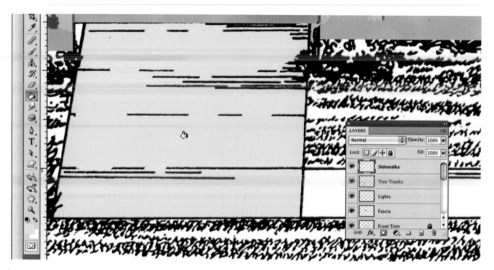

Sidewalks and driveways have straight edges; we used the click-Shift-click method to create the straight-line shadows around the edges of the driveway area.

9. **Save the file and continue to the next exercise.**

CHANGE BRUSH SETTINGS TO PAINT RANDOM ELEMENTS

The randomness of shapes, colors, and textures that occurs in nature simply cannot be painted using basic lines — regardless of the brush size, flow, opacity, and other options. So for this exercise, we can't provide specific step-by-step instructions to create every required brush stroke. Every person will end up with different results.

To create the leaves, shrubs, and grass, we can only provide advice on how to select the best tool settings for the job. You should experiment with the different brush settings as you paint these elements. Use layers liberally as you create the various elements so you can easily turn off or delete objects and try again.

1. **With house_working.psd open, create a new layer named Leaves directly above the Tree Trunks layer.**

2. **Select the Brush tool. Set the foreground color to the Foliage 5 swatch and the background color to the Foliage 7 swatch.**

    We will explain the method we used to create the first tree, then you can experiment with different brushes and settings to create the rest of the foliage.

3. **Open the Brushes panel (Window>Brushes).**

    The freestanding Brushes panel shows the same brushes that are available in the Control panel.

4. **Open the Brushes panel Options menu and choose Expanded View.**

    In Expanded view, you can control a number of options for the selected brush; these settings are not available in the Control panel.

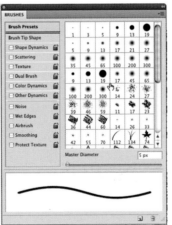

5. **Using the Brushes panel Options menu, load the Natural Brushes 2 set (replacing the existing set) and display the panel in Large List view.**

Note:

As you paint, don't forget about the History panel. You can step back up to 20 brush strokes, or you can create new History snapshots at regular intervals so you can return to earlier stages of your work.

Using the Brushes panel in Extended view, you can control an extensive array of brush settings. Clicking an option in the left side of the panel shows the related options. The bottom area of the panel shows a dynamic preview of your choices in the various options.

Brush Tip Shape

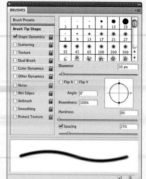

Diameter controls the size (in pixels) of the brush.

Use Sample Size resets a brush to its original diameter. (This is available only if the brush was created by selecting pixels in an image and choosing Edit>Define Brush.)

Flip X and **Flip Y** change the direction of a brush tip on the X (horizontal) or Y (vertical) axis.

Angle defines the angle for an elliptical brush.

Roundness controls the ratio between the short and long axes of the brush; 100% creates a round brush, 0% creates a linear brush, and middle values create elliptical brushes.

Hardness controls the size of the brush's hard center. (This is the same as the Hardness setting in the Options bar.)

Spacing controls the distance between brush marks in a stroke. The spacing is a percentage of the brush diameter.

Scattering

Scatter controls how brush marks are distributed in a stroke, based on the maximum percentage defined here. If Both Axes is active, brush marks are distributed radially; if Both Axes is not active, brush marks are distributed perpendicular to the stroke path.

Count defines the number of brush marks applied at each spacing interval.

Count Jitter varies the number of brush marks for each spacing interval, based on the maximum percentage defined here.

Shape Dynamics

Size Jitter varies the size of brush marks in a stroke, based on the maximum percentage defined here. You can also use the Control menu to vary the size of brush marks:

- Off provides no control over the variation.

- Fade varies the size of brush marks between the initial diameter and the minimum diameter in a specified number of steps (from 1 to 9999).

- Pen Pressure, Pen Tilt, and Stylus Wheel vary the size of brush marks, based on the pen pressure, tilt, or position of the pen thumbwheel (if you have a drawing tablet).

Minimum Diameter defines the minimum brush (as a percentage of brush diameter) when Size Jitter is used.

Tilt Scale specifies the scale factor for brush height when Pen Tilt is active in the Control menu.

Angle Jitter varies the angle of brush marks in a stroke (as a percentage of 360°). The Control menu specifies how you control the angle variance of brush marks:

- Off, Fade, Pen Pressure, Pen Tilt, and Stylus Wheel have the same meanings as for Size Jitter (above).

- Initial Direction bases the angle of brush marks on the initial direction of the brush stroke.

- Direction bases the angle of brush marks on the overall direction of the brush stroke.

Roundness Jitter varies the roundness of brush marks in a stroke (as a percentage of the ratio between the brush height and width).

Minimum Roundness specifies the minimum roundness for brush marks when Roundness Jitter is enabled.

Texture

Textured brushes use patterns to make strokes look as though they were painted on paper or canvas. After you choose a pattern from the palette, you can set many of the same options that are available when applying a texture effect to a layer.

Invert reverses the high (light) and low (dark) points in the texture; when Invert is selected, the lightest areas are the low points and the darkest areas are the high points.

Scale defines the size of the pattern texture as a percentage of the pattern size.

Texture Each Tip applies the selected texture to each brush mark, rather than to the brush stroke as a whole.

Mode defines the blending mode that combines the brush and the pattern.

Depth defines how deeply color affects the texture. At 0%, all points receive the same amount of color, which obscures the texture; at 100%, low points are not painted.

Minimum Depth specifies the minimum depth to which color can penetrate.

Depth Jitter varies the depth (when Texture Each Tip is selected), based on the maximum percentage defined here.

Dual Brushes

A dual brush combines two brush tips. The second brush texture is applied within the brush stroke of the primary brush; only the areas where both brushstrokes intersect are painted.

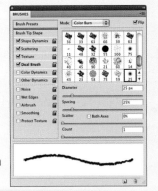

Mode defines the blending mode that will combine brush marks from the two brushes.

Diameter defines the size of the dual tip (in pixels).

Spacing defines the distance between the dual-tip brush marks in a stroke, as a percentage of the brush diameter.

Scatter determines how dual-tip brush marks are distributed in a stroke, based on the maximum percentage defined here. If Both Axes is active, dual-tip brush marks are distributed radially; if Both Axes is not checked, dual-tip brush marks are distributed perpendicular to the stroke path.

Count defines the number of dual-tip brush marks at each spacing interval.

Color Dynamics

Color dynamics determine how the color of paint changes over the course of a stroke.

Foreground/Background Jitter varies between the foreground and background colors, based on the percentage of allowable variation defined here.

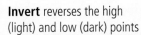

Hue Jitter varies the hue in the brush stroke; lower percentages in this setting create less hue variation across the stroke.

Saturation Jitter varies the saturation in a brush stroke; lower percentages in this setting create less saturation variation across the stroke.

Brightness Jitter varies the brightness in a brush stroke; lower percentages in this setting create less brightness variation across the stroke.

Purity increases or decreases the saturation of the color, between –100% and 100%. (At –100%, the color is fully desaturated; at 100%, the color is fully saturated.)

Other Dynamics

Opacity Jitter varies the opacity of color in a brush stroke, up to the opacity value defined in the Options bar.

Flow Jitter varies the flow of color in a brush stroke, up to the flow value defined in the Options bar.

Other Brush Options

Noise adds randomness to brush tips that contain shades of gray (e.g., soft tips).

Wet Edges causes paint to build up along the edges of the brush stroke, creating a watercolor effect.

Airbrush applies gradual tones to an image, simulating traditional airbrush techniques (this is the same as the Airbrush button in the Options bar).

Smoothing, which creates smoother curves in brush strokes, is most useful if you are using a drawing tablet.

Protect Texture applies the same pattern and scale to all textured brushes to simulate a consistent canvas texture throughout the entire image.

6. **With Brush Presets selected in the Brushes panel, choose Wet Brush 60 pixels in the list.**

This will be the starting point; you'll change the settings based on this selected brush preset.

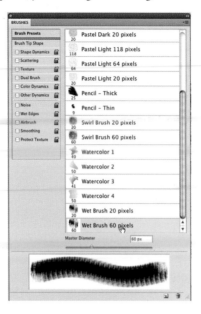

7. **Choose Brush Tip Shape in the list of options. Change the Angle to −30°.**

Leaves are rarely straight up and down, so your brush strokes shouldn't be either.

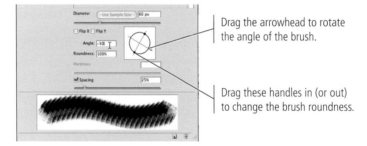

Drag the arrowhead to rotate the angle of the brush.

Drag these handles in (or out) to change the brush roundness.

8. **Select Shape Dynamics in the list on the left. Change all the Jitter sliders to values near the middle of the scale, and then set all the Control menus to Off.**

Real leaves come in many different shapes and sizes. By jittering all these settings, you allow Photoshop to randomize the brush marks that will create the leaves.

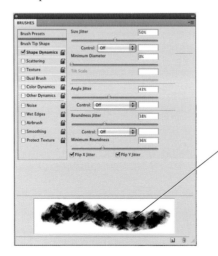

Notice the new preview, which dynamically shows the results of your settings.

9. **In the Scattering options, allow Photoshop to scatter the marks along both axes using a low setting (we used 250).**

   By scattering along both axes, you get a more random result than if brush marks only move perpendicularly from the brush stroke. Watch the preview to evaluate the results of different scatter values.

10. **Set the Count value to 2 to prevent overloading the brush marks in any particular area.**

   You can use multiple brush strokes to build up more marks in the same space.

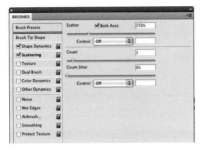

11. **In the Color Dynamics options, apply a high Foreground/Background Jitter setting.**

   You could manually vary the colors by frequently switching the foreground color, but this option speeds the process by varying the colors in a single brush stroke without choosing new paint colors.

12. **In the Other Dynamics options, apply a small amount of opacity jitter.**

   A slight variation in the stroke opacity will further increase the randomness of the brush marks. Because some marks will be semi-transparent, overlapping areas will produce an even broader range of color without manually changing the brush color.

13. Click with the brush and drag around the leafy area of the tree to the left of the garage door.

14. Hide the Sketch layer and review your work.

The settings you applied created a random set of brush marks, differing in size, angle, roundness, position, color, and opacity.

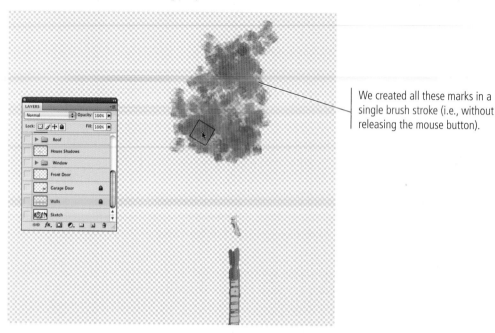

We created all these marks in a single brush stroke (i.e., without releasing the mouse button).

15. Show the Sketch layer again and continue painting the leaves. To further increase variation, change the brush size a few times.

16. Change to a smaller brush size (around 35 pixels) and change the foreground color to Foliage 3. Paint some lighter spots throughout the trees to add depth.

17. **Show all other layers. Paint leaves over any areas where the house is not perfectly painted.**

18. **Save the file and continue immediately to the next exercise.**

 ## CREATE A BRUSH PRESET

As with custom patterns, you must save custom brush presets if you want to be able to use them again later (after quitting and relaunching Photoshop). You have a lot of leaves to paint in this image, so it's a good idea to save the brush you defined in the previous exercise.

1. **With house_working.psd open, access the Brushes panel Options menu and choose New Brush Preset.**

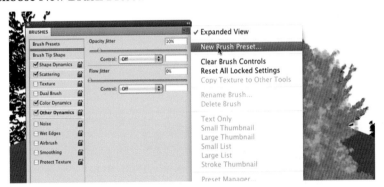

Note:

If you changed your Brushes panel or quit Photoshop since the previous exercise, you might have to go back and re-create the Leafy Scatter brush for this exercise to work properly.

2. **In the Brush Name dialog box, name the new preset Leafy Scatter.**

3. **Choose Edit>Preset Manager.**

4. **With Brushes showing in Small List view, select everything other than the Leafy Scatter brush you created in Step 2, and then click Delete.**

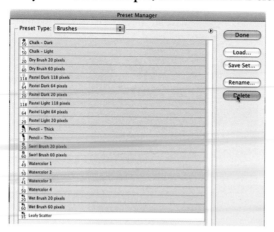

5. **Select the remaining brush and click Save Set.**

6. **In the Save dialog box, name the new set** `Portfolio Brushes.abr` **and click Save.**

   New brush sets are saved by default in the Presets>Brushes folder in your Photoshop application folder. The extension ".abr" is automatically added, so you only need to type the file name.

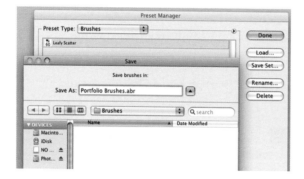

7. **Click Done to close the Preset Manager, and then continue to the next exercise.**

 ## FINISH THE PAINTING

Using the skills and techniques you just learned, paint the rest of the landscaping in the image. Keep the following tips in mind as you paint these elements.

1. **Create, rearrange, and merge layers as necessary to produce the best result.**

2. **Grass — especially new sod — has far less randomness than leaves.**
   - **Choose foreground and background colors that are only slightly different (try Foliage 6 and Foliage 7).**
   - **Start with a brush preset that looks like a blade of grass (try one of the veining brushes in the Faux Finish Brushes set).**
   - **Use a small brush size with a small amount of size and angle jitter, and allow the marks to flip horizontally (Flip X Jitter option).**
   - **Experiment with different settings for foreground/background and opacity jitter.**

Creating Sampled Brushes

In addition to defining brush presets by adjusting built-in brush settings, you can create new brushes from existing image information. When you choose Edit>Define Brush Preset, the new brush will be created based on the current selection area. If nothing is currently selected, all visible layers will be combined to create the brush preset.

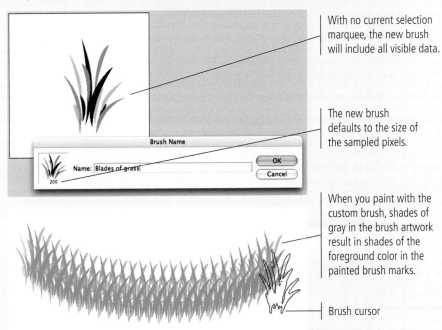

With no current selection marquee, the new brush will include all visible data.

The new brush defaults to the size of the sampled pixels.

When you paint with the custom brush, shades of gray in the brush artwork result in shades of the foreground color in the painted brush marks.

Brush cursor

It's important to note that brushes are always grayscale, even when you sample a color image to create the brush.

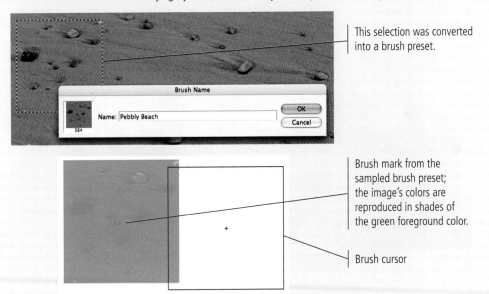

This selection was converted into a brush preset.

Brush mark from the sampled brush preset; the image's colors are reproduced in shades of the green foreground color.

Brush cursor

3. As with the tree leaves, the bushes also need variation.

   - Try the Stencil Sponge–Twirl brush from the Faux Finish Brushes set, using the Foliage 2 and Foliage 3 swatches as the foreground and background colors.

   - Use a small brush size with relatively low roundness.

   - Apply a small amount of size and angle jitter, and a medium-to-high roundness jitter.

   - Scatter the marks along both axes at a lower percentage, and increase the count to add more brush marks in the same space.

   - Use medium jitter between the foreground and background colors, as well as the color brightness.

4. The flat-leaf plants have far less variation than any other foliage element. You could manually draw the leaf shapes, or you could use random brushes to create a similar effect.

   - Try starting with the Veining Feather 1 brush from the Faux Finish Brushes set.

   - Use a large brush size with a small amount of size and angle jitter.

   - Allow 100% jitter between the foreground and background colors, and allow the opacity to jitter around 50%.

5. When you're finished, fill the Sketch layer with white. Save the file as house_final.psd in your WIP>Realty folder and continue to the final stage of the project.

The Tool Presets Panel

Just as saving a custom brush preset allows you to access that brush again later, tool presets allow you to save and reuse settings for any Photoshop tool. Tool presets can be accessed in the Control panel or in the Tool Presets panel (Window>Tool Presets). The structure of the panel Options menu offers the same options as other asset panels — control what is visible in the panel, load and save custom sets of tool presets, and access built-in sets of tool presets.

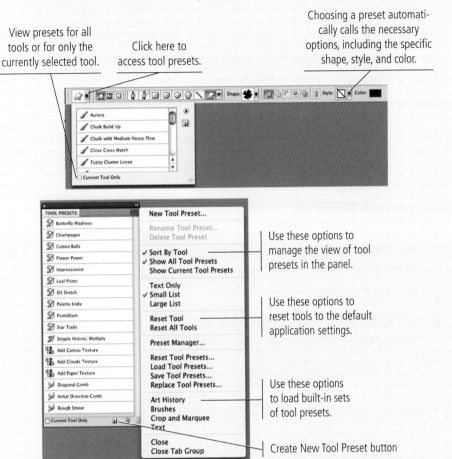

View presets for all tools or for only the currently selected tool.

Click here to access tool presets.

Choosing a preset automatically calls the necessary options, including the specific shape, style, and color.

Use these options to manage the view of tool presets in the panel.

Use these options to reset tools to the default application settings.

Use these options to load built-in sets of tool presets.

Create New Tool Preset button

To save your own tool presets, simply choose New Tool Preset from the panel Options menu or click the Create New Tool Preset button at the bottom of the panel. The new tool preset will include whatever tool and options are currently selected.

Stage 6 Publishing the Project

The Portable Document Format (PDF) was created by Adobe to facilitate cross-platform transportation of documents, independent of the fonts used, linked files, or even the originating application. The format offers a number of advantages:

- PDF files can contain all the information needed to successfully output a job.

- Data in a PDF file can be high or low resolution, and it can be compressed to reduce file size.

- PDF files are device-independent, which means you don't need the originating application or the same platform to open and print the file.

- PDF files are also page-independent, which means a PDF document can contain rotated pages and even pages of different sizes. (You can't create multi-page PDF files in Photoshop, but you can combine individual pages created in Photoshop using Adobe Acrobat.)

EXPORT A PDF FILE FOR PRINT

1. **With house_final.psd open, choose File>Save As.**

2. **Navigate to your WIP>Realty folder as the destination and choose Photoshop PDF in the Format/Save As Type menu.**

3. **Deactivate the Layers check box.**

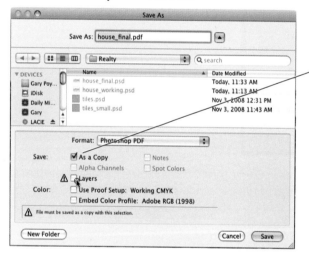

The As a Copy option is checked when you turn off the Layers option; since you are saving as a different format with a different file name, nothing else changes.

4. **Click Save, and then click OK in the warning message.**

   Before the PDF is saved, you have to define the settings that will be used to generate the PDF file. Some options (such as color profile information) can be changed in the Save Adobe PDF dialog box; those choices will override the selections in the Save As dialog box.

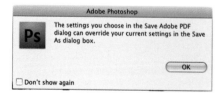

5. Choose High Quality Print in the Adobe PDF Preset menu.

The Adobe PDF Preset menu includes six PDF presets (in brackets) that meet common industry output requirements. Other options might also be available if another user created custom presets in Photoshop or another Creative Suite application.

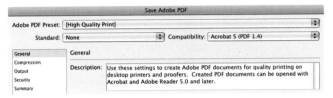

Because there are so many ways to create a PDF — and not all of them are optimized for commercial printing — the potential benefits of the file format are often undermined. The PDF/X specification was created to help solve some of the problems associated with bad PDF files entering the prepress workflow. PDF/X is a subset of PDF, specifically designed to ensure that files have the information necessary for and available to the digital prepress output process. Ask your output provider whether you should apply a PDF/X standard to your files, and if so, which version to use.

The Compatibility menu determines which version of the PDF format you will create. This is particularly important if your layout uses transparency. PDF 1.3 does not support transparency, so the file will require flattening. If you save the file to be compatible with PDF 1.4 or later, the transparency information will be maintained in the PDF file; it will have to be flattened later in the output process (after it leaves your desk).

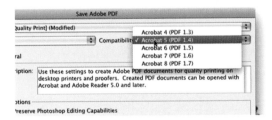

6. Review the options in the General pane.

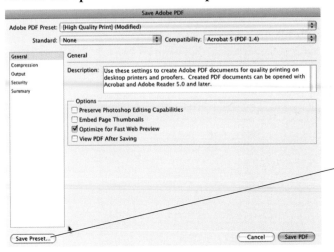

Click this button to save your choices as a preset so you can use it again later.

7. Review the Compression options.

The Compression options determine what — and how much — data will be included in the PDF file. This set of options is one of the most important when creating PDFs, since too-low resolution results in bad-quality printing, and too-high resolution results in extremely long download times.

Before you choose compression settings, you need to consider your final goal. If you're creating a file for commercial printing, resolution is more important than file size. If your goal is a PDF for posting on the Web for general consumption, file size is equally important as (if not more than) image quality.

You can define a specific compression scheme for color, grayscale, and monochrome images. Different options are available, depending on the image type:

- ZIP compression is lossless, which means all file data is maintained in the compressed file.

- JPEG compression options are lossy, which means data is discarded to create a smaller file. When you use one of the JPEG options, you can also define an Image Quality option (from Low to Maximum).

If you don't compress the file, your PDF file might be extremely large. For a commercial printing workflow, large file size is preferable to poor image quality. If you don't have to submit the PDF file via modem transmission, large file size is not an issue. If you must compress the file, ask your service provider what settings they prefer you to use.

Note:

Since you chose the High Quality Print preset, these options default to settings that will produce the best results for most commercial printing applications.

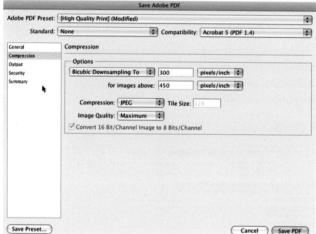

Note:

The Output options relate to color management and PDF/X settings. Ask your output provider if you need to change anything for those options.

8. Click Save PDF. When the process is finished, close the Photoshop file.

Project Review

fill in the blank

1. The _____ dialog box can be used to change the resolution of an image without affecting its physical size.

2. The _____ command can be used to share color swatches between Photoshop and Illustrator.

3. The _____ tool is used to fill areas with a solid color or pattern by clicking the area you want to fill.

4. _____ is the percentage of a brush's diameter that is completely opaque.

5. The _____ brush mode option is useful for filling gaps left by other painting methods.

6. The _____ removes pixels from an image while attempting to maintain edges of an object in the foreground.

7. The _____ can be used to restore specific areas of an image back to a previous state.

8. The _____ tool is similar to the Brush tool, but can only create hard edges.

9. The _____ tool is used to paint with patterns, either painting a stroke of the pattern or revealing more of the solid pattern with each brush stroke.

10. _____ store specific settings for a specific tool; they can be accessed in the menu on the left end of the Control panel.

short answer

1. Briefly explain the difference between a bitmap (line art) image and a regular raster image.

2. Briefly explain how layers made it easier to complete this complex project.

3. Briefly explain three advantages of the PDF file format.

Use what you learned in this project to complete the following freeform exercise.
Carefully read the art director and client comments, then create your own design to meet the needs of the project.
Use the space below to sketch ideas; when finished, write a brief explanation of your reasoning behind your final design.

art director comments

The client is very happy with the house painting, and would like to hire you again to create color renderings of the other two models that will be available in the complex.

To complete this project, you should:

❏ Use the sketches in the RF_Builders>Realty folder as the basis of your paintings.

❏ Convert the bitmap sketches to RGB mode at 300 pixels/inch.

❏ Create a custom pattern to fill in the roof areas of the houses.

❏ Experiment with custom brushes to create realistic looking grass and trees around the houses.

client comments

Buyers for the new community will actually have three models to choose from. We'd like to have paintings for the other two models as well so buyers can compare apples to apples when they're choosing which model they prefer. We would be happy with one more color rendering, but we'd be thrilled if you could do both of the other two house sketches.

When you paint the other houses, use colors from the same color palette, but none of the houses should look exactly the same. Buyers are shown the same paint swatches as those in the palette you used to paint the first house; they can pick any combinations of those colors for the main stucco and up to two shades for the trim.

Remember, these houses are all going to be in the same development, so try to be consistent with the plant life. We can't have one house look like it's in a rainforest and another surrounded by desert scrub.

project justification

_____
_____
_____
_____
_____
_____
_____
_____
_____
_____
_____
_____
_____
_____

Project Summary

Drawing and painting from scratch requires some degree of creativity and natural artistic talent; however, learning the technical aspects of drawing and painting will help you as you complete many different types of projects — and might even help you to develop and refine natural artistic skills.

Creating original artwork in Photoshop — including artwork that starts as a black-and-white pen sketch — can be a time-consuming and sometimes repetitive process. If you learn how to use the painting and drawing tools, you will have a unique advantage when you need something unique. Mastering these skills also gives you an advantage because few people take the time to learn the intricacies of creating original digital artwork.

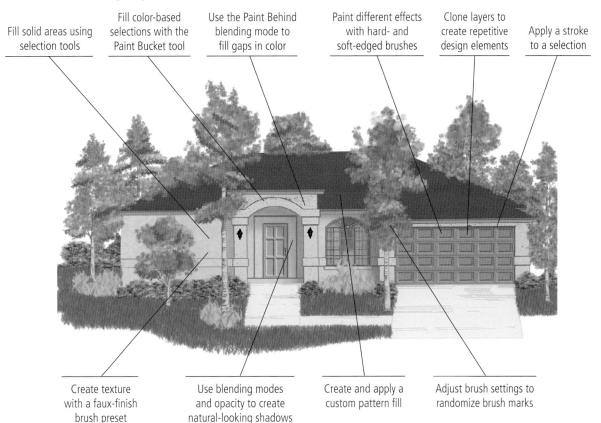

Fill solid areas using selection tools

Fill color-based selections with the Paint Bucket tool

Use the Paint Behind blending mode to fill gaps in color

Paint different effects with hard- and soft-edged brushes

Clone layers to create repetitive design elements

Apply a stroke to a selection

Create texture with a faux-finish brush preset

Use blending modes and opacity to create natural-looking shadows

Create and apply a custom pattern fill

Adjust brush settings to randomize brush marks

Photo Gallery Web Page

Your client is a company that specializes in "extreme tourism" — mountain climbing, ice hiking, white-water rafting, and other outdoor adrenaline boosters. Your agency was hired to build the company's Web site. As part of the team assigned to the project, your role is to build the photo gallery page and animate the company's logo to add visual interest to the site.

This project incorporates the following skills:

❏ Using actions and batches to automate repetitive processes and improve productivity

❏ Creating and optimizing frame-based animation in a Photoshop file

❏ Slicing a page into pieces and defining settings for individual slices

❏ Saving images and pages in appropriate format for display on the Web

Project Meeting

client comments

We're happy with the basic layout you created, but we'd like to see one of the pages completed. I know the timing is our fault since we haven't yet finalized the copy; but we have the images we want to use in the photo gallery, so we'd like to see at least that page completed. Of course, the images are all rather large. We'd like the gallery page to include thumbnails of each image, so when users click a thumbnail, the full-size image opens in its own window.

One other thing: I know that most of the site is purely informational, but the whole concept of our company targets active, high-energy people — so we want action on the site. We'd like to see some kind of animation incorporated, although we really don't know what that could or should be. We'll leave that up to you.

art director comments

The basic look of the site has already been defined, and the other members of your team are still waiting for the actual content of each page before they can finish their work. Since we have the images for the gallery, you can complete your part, even though everyone else is on hold.

Since this part of the site will be completed first, you're also responsible for building animation into the page so we can show the client what the animation will look like on a completed page. I want you to animate the client's logo to appear in three phases; when the logo is entirely visible, I want the page header to fade in.

I've forwarded the basic file that was used to create the first samples. Unfortunately, we lost the final version when the server crashed last week, so the version you're getting doesn't include the slice and link information. You'll have to recreate that part of the file.

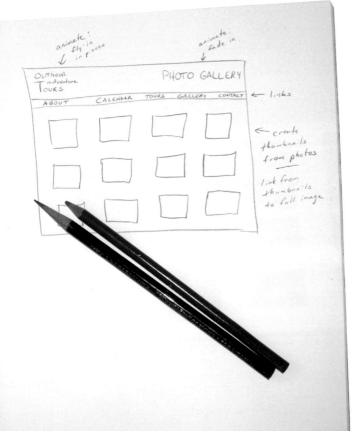

project objectives

To complete this project, you will:

- ❏ Create and save an action
- ❏ Batch-process multiple files
- ❏ Create individual animation frames
- ❏ Create an animated tween
- ❏ Control animation timing
- ❏ Optimize an animation
- ❏ Create slices from guides
- ❏ Create and divide manual slices
- ❏ Create slices from layers
- ❏ Test your page in a Web browser
- ❏ Define slice and page export options

Stage 1 **Automating Repetitive Tasks**

Actions are one of the most powerful (yet underused) productivity tools in Photoshop. In the simplest terms, **actions** are miniature programs that run a sequence of commands on a particular image or selected area. An action can initiate most of the commands available in Photoshop — alone or in sequence — to automate repetitive and potentially time-consuming tasks.

Running an action is a fairly simple process: highlight the appropriate action in the Actions panel and click the Play button at the bottom of the panel.

Some actions work on an entire image, while others require some initial selection before the action can create an effect. If you use the actions that shipped with the Photoshop application, the action name tells you (in parentheses) what type of element the action was designed to affect.

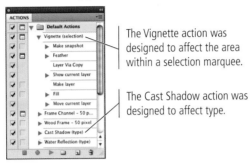

The Vignette action was designed to affect the area within a selection marquee.

The Cast Shadow action was designed to affect type.

Note:

It's important to remember when creating actions that, "just because you can, doesn't mean you should." There are many powerful tools in Photoshop that require human judgment and intervention if they are to be effective. Color correction, for example, is different for every image, and should never be left entirely to a computer to implement.

In most cases, you can run an action on other elements without a problem. However, running an action that requires a selection results in an error if you haven't yet made a selection.

EXPLORE THE SAMPLE SITE

1. **On your desktop, copy the Adventures folder from the WIP folder on your Resource CD to the WIP folder where you are saving your work.**

   This folder includes a number of files that are required for some steps later in the process to work properly.

2. **On your desktop, double-click the file index.html (in the WIP>Adventures folder) to open it in your default browser window.**

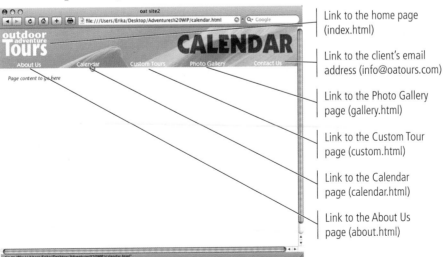

Link to the home page (index.html)

Link to the client's email address (info@oatours.com)

Link to the Photo Gallery page (gallery.html)

Link to the Custom Tour page (custom.html)

Link to the Calendar page (calendar.html)

Link to the About Us page (about.html)

3. **Click through the links in the horizontal navigation bar to open those pages in your browser.**

4. **Click the Contact Us link to open your default email application with the client's email address in the "To:" line.**

5. **Close your email application without sending.**

6. **Close the browser window and continue to the next exercise.**

The Actions Panel in Depth

The default Actions panel (Window>Actions) shows the Default Actions set, which contains several pre-built actions. A folder icon indicates an **action set**, which is used to create logical groupings of actions. You can expand an action set to show the individual actions contained within that set, and you can expand a specific action to show the steps that are saved in that action; any step in an action marked with an arrow can be further expanded to see the details of that step.

The left column of the Actions panel shows a checkmark next to each action set, individual action, and step within an expanded action. All elements of pre-recorded actions are active by default, which means that playing an action initiates each step within the action. You can deactivate specific steps of an action by clicking the related checkmark. (If the checkmark next to an action is black, all elements of that action are active. If the checkmark is red, one or more steps of that action are inactive.)

Labels around the panel image:
- Action set
- Individual action
- Steps involved in the expanded action
- Toggle item on/off
- Toggle dialog on/off
- Stop Playing/Recording
- Begin Recording
- Play Selection
- Create new set
- Create new action
- Delete
- Button Mode / Choose Button Mode to view actions in the panel as buttons.
- New Action... / New Set... / Duplicate / Delete / Play
- Start Recording / Record Again... / Insert Menu Item... / Insert Stop... / Insert Path
- Set Options... / Playback Options...
- Clear All Actions / Reset Actions / Load Actions... / Replace Actions... / Save Actions...
- Commands / Frames / Image Effects / Production / Text Effects / Textures / Video Actions — Built-in actions for a variety of purposes
- Close / Close Tab Group

Modal Controls

The second column in the Actions panel allows you to control the degree of user interaction required when running an action. If an icon appears in this column, the Photoshop dialog box relevant to that step opens when the action runs. These are called **modal controls**; the action pauses until you take some required action. You can deactivate modal controls for:

- An entire action set by clicking the dialog box icon next to a set name
- An individual action by clicking the icon next to the action name
- A single step by clicking the icon next to the step

If the modal controls are turned off, Photoshop applies the values that were used when the action was recorded. This increases the automatic functionality of the action, but also offers less control over the action's behavior.

Some actions require a certain degree of user interaction, in which case the modal controls can't be entirely deactivated. In this case, the dialog box icon appears grayed out in the panel, even when the remaining modal control icons are turned off. (If an action shows a black dialog box icon, all modal controls within the action are active. If an action shows a red dialog box icon, one or more modal controls within the action have been turned off.)

Button Mode

Choosing Button Mode from the panel Options menu makes running an action one step easier. Each action in the panel is represented as a colored button, which you can simply click to run the action. Any modal control that is active when you choose Button Mode is active when you click a button.

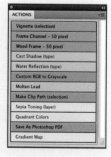

SAVE AN ACTION SET

Whenever you need to perform the same task more than two times, it's a good idea to automate as much of the process as possible. This project requires you to create thumbnails from twelve images. Creating one thumbnail requires at least four steps:

1. Open the file (any number of clicks, depending on the default location in the Open dialog box).

2. Resize the image to 125 pixels wide (at least two clicks, possibly three if the Resample check box is active), as well as typing the new dimensions.

3. Save the file in a new folder with a revised file name (any number of clicks, depending on the default location in the Save dialog box), as well as typing the new file name.

4. Close the file.

This process can be streamlined by using an action, which you have to record only once.

1. **Choose Clear All Actions from the Actions panel Options menu.**

Rather than editing an existing action set, you are going to create your own action set to store the action you define. If you did not clear the existing actions, the set you define would include all of the default actions as well as the one you create.

Note:

You don't need to have a file open in Photoshop to change the Actions that are available in the Actions panel.

Note:

You can add actions to the Actions panel by choosing a defined set or by choosing Load Actions in the panel Options menu.

2. **Click OK in the warning message dialog box.**

Clear All Actions removes everything from the Actions panel. You can also remove a specific action or set from the panel by highlighting the item in the panel and clicking the Delete button, or by choosing Delete from the Actions panel Options menu.

These commands remove the actions or sets from the panel, but they do not permanently delete saved actions or sets. If you delete an action from one of the built-in sets, you can reload the set to restore all items that originally existed in the set.

3. **Click the Create New Set button at the bottom of the Actions panel.**

Note:

Reset Actions *restores the default set to the Actions panel. You have the option to replace the existing actions or append the default set to the current sets.*

Replace Actions *replaces the current action sets with whatever set you load in the resulting dialog box.*

4. **In the New Set dialog box, name the new set Portfolio Actions, and then click OK.**

You can name the set whatever you prefer, but the action set name should indicate what the set contains, whether it's a set of actions for a specific type of project, for a specific client, or any other logical group.

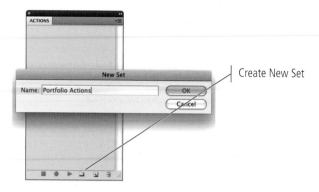

Create New Set

5. **With the Portfolio Actions set highlighted in the Actions panel, choose Save Actions from the panel Options menu.**

Note:

Action sets are stored by default in the Presets>Actions folder in the Photoshop Application folder on your computer. You can also load an action from another location, such as when someone sends you an action that was created on another computer.

6. **In the Save dialog box, make sure the Save As field shows Portfolio Actions.atn and click Save.**

Action sets are saved by default in the Photoshop>Presets>Actions folder with the extension ".atn" (the extension is automatically added for you).

If you make changes to a set — whether you delete an existing action from the set or add your own custom actions — but you don't save the altered set, you'll have to redo your work the next time you launch Photoshop.

7. **Continue to the next exercise.**

CREATE A NEW ACTION

Recording an action is a fairly simple process: Open a file, click the Record button in the Actions panel, and perform the steps you want to save in the action. Click the Stop button to stop recording, either permanently when you're done or temporarily if you need to do something else in the middle of creating the action. (If you stop recording, you can also select the last step in the existing action and start recording again by clicking the Record button.)

1. **In Photoshop, click the Launch Bridge button in the Control panel.**

2. **In Bridge, navigate to the WIP>Adventures>photos folder to review the client's images for the gallery.**

   The images are not consistent in size, which means the thumbnail images will not be consistent either. To make the gallery page as clean as possible, you are going to resize all the images to be 125 pixels wide so they will form a clean grid on the page.

3. **Close the Bridge window and return to Photoshop.**

4. **Open the file biker.jpg from your WIP>Adventures>photos folder.**

5. **Click the Create New Action button at the bottom of the Actions panel.**

Stop Playing/Recording

Begin Recording

Play Selection

Create New Action

6. **In the New Action dialog box, type** `Create Web Thumbnail` **in the Name field.**

By default, new actions are added to the currently selected set. You can add the action to any open set by choosing from the Set menu. The Function Key menu allows you to assign a keyboard shortcut to the action, so an "F" key (with or without modifiers) can initiate that action. The Color menu defines the color of the button when the Actions panel is viewed in Button mode.

Note:

As with any user-defined element, you should use descriptive names for your actions.

7. **Click the Begin Recording button.**

Anything you do from this point forward is recorded as a step in the action until you intentionally stop the recording by clicking the Stop Recording button.

Note:

You can change the name, keyboard shortcut, and/or button color of any action by selecting it in the Actions panel and choosing Action Options from the panel Options menu.

8. **With biker.jpg open, choose Image>Image Size.**

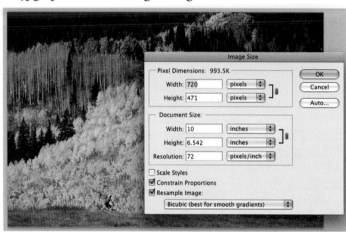

9. **Make sure the Constrain Proportions and Resample Image options are checked.**

You want the thumbnails to be proportionally sized, and you want them to remain at 72 ppi.

10. **Change the Pixel Dimensions width to 125 pixels.**

Because the Resample Image option is checked, changing one field in this dialog box affects others; reducing the number of pixels results in a proportionally smaller document size.

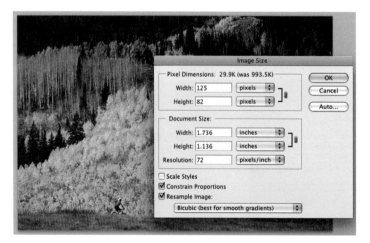

11. **Click OK to close the Image Size dialog box and apply the change.**

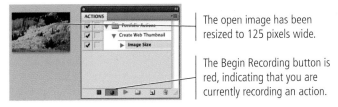

The open image has been resized to 125 pixels wide.

The Begin Recording button is red, indicating that you are currently recording an action.

12. **In the Actions panel, click the Stop Recording button.**

13. **Expand the Image Size item in the Create Web Thumbnail action.**

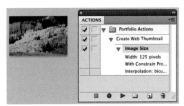

14. **Close the biker.jpg file without saving.**

You don't need to save the changes since this file will be processed when you run the action on the entire photos folder.

15. **Select the Portfolio Actions set in the Actions panel and choose Save Actions from the panel Options menu.**

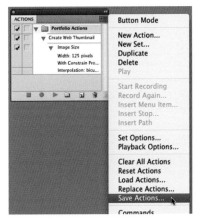

16. **Accept the default options in the Save dialog box and click Save.**

17. **When you see a message asking if you want to replace the existing set of the same name, click Replace.**

    If you don't resave the set after adding the action, the Create Web Thumbnail action will be lost when you quit Photoshop.

18. **Continue to the next exercise.**

Inserting Action Stops and Menu Options

When you record actions, you can insert a stop (an intentional pause) by choosing **Insert Stop** from the Actions panel Options menu. When you insert a stop, the Record Stop dialog box allows you to type a message that displays when the action runs. This message can include specific instructions or reminders to the user, such as a prompt to make a selection before the remainder of the action runs.

When the action reaches a stop, the message you entered into the Record Stop dialog box displays. The user must click Stop, perform the required step, and then click the Play button in the Actions panel to complete the rest of the action. The Allow Continue option in the Record Stop dialog box adds a Continue button to the Stop message; if the user clicks Continue, the action resumes (if possible).

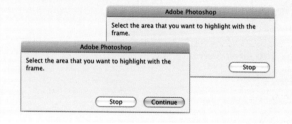

You can also cause an action to open a specific dialog box or execute a menu command by choosing **Insert Menu Item** from the Actions panel Options menu. When the Insert Menu Item dialog box appears, you can make a selection from the application menu, and then click OK. When the action runs, the specified dialog box opens or the menu command executes.

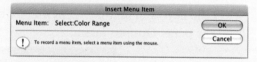

When you insert a menu item that opens a dialog box (such as Select>Color Range), you are adding a modal command that can't be turned off. When the action runs, even with modal commands turned off, the dialog box opens and requires user interaction. Although an action can automate many steps in a repetitive process, there are still some things that can't be entirely automatic.

BATCH-PROCESS FILES

The ability to batch-process files further enhances and automates productivity. If you have a large group of files that all require the same adjustments, you can build an action, set up a batch, and go to lunch (or, depending on your computer processor and number of files, go home for the night).

For example, when we write the Portfolio books, we take screen shots in RGB mode at 100%. Before the books are laid out for print production, the screen shots are converted to the U.S. Web Coated (SWOP) v2 CMYK profile and resized (not resampled) to 40%. As you have probably noticed, there are a lot of screen shots in these books. Rather than sitting for several days and modifying each file (or even sitting for one full day and running an action on each file), we set up a batch that converts all screen shots for an entire book in about 25 minutes.

1. **In Photoshop, choose File>Automate>Batch.**

   At the top of the Batch dialog box, the Set and Action menus default to the active selection in the Actions panel. In this case, there is only one available choice, so the Create Web Thumbnail action is already selected. You can choose to run a batch for any action in any open set.

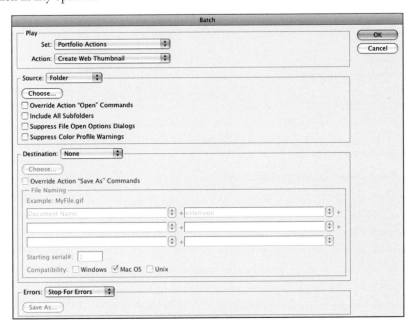

2. **Choose Folder in the Source menu.**

   The Source menu allows you to choose which files are batched:

   • Folder processes a group of images on your computer.

   • Import acquires and processes a group of images from a scanner or digital camera.

   • Open Files processes all files currently open in the application.

   • File Browser processes files selected in the File Browser.

   When Folder is selected, you can also choose to override "Open" commands that are recorded in the selected action, include subfolders within the selected folder, and suppress color profile warnings for the files being processed.

3. **Click the Choose button and navigate to the WIP>Adventures>photos folder and click Choose/OK.**

4. **Make sure the Suppress Color Profile Warnings option is checked to prevent the batch from stopping if color management policies are violated.**

   This is a matter of some debate, but when processing images for the Web, color management is not considered as critical as it is for print.

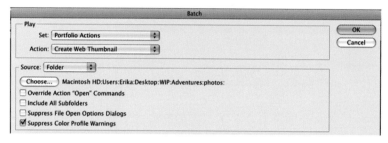

5. **Choose Folder in the Destination menu.**

   The Destination menu in the Batch dialog box presents three options:

   - **None** simply means that the action will be run. If the action saves and closes the files, those commands will be completed. If the action does not save and close the files, you might end up with a large number of open files and eventually crash your computer.

   - **Save and Close** saves the modified file in the same location with the same name, overwriting the original file.

   - **Folder** allows you to specify a target folder for the files after they have been processed. This option is particularly useful because it saves the processed files as copies of the originals in the defined folder; the original files remain intact.

6. **Click the Choose button and navigate to the WIP>Adventures>thumbs folder and click Choose/OK.**

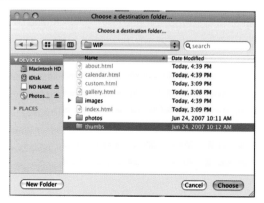

Note:

*You can create a **droplet** from an action, which allows you to run the action using a basic drag-and-drop technique (as long as Photoshop is running). The Create Droplet dialog box (File>Automate>Create Droplet) presents most of the same options as the Batch dialog box, with a few exceptions. Clicking Choose at the top of the dialog box allows you to define the name of the droplet and the location to save it. The dialog box does not include Source options because the source is defined when you drag files onto the droplet.*

7. **In the File Naming area, open the menu for the first empty field and choose document name (lowercase) from the menu.**

   The File Naming fields allow you to redefine file names for the modified files. You can choose a variable from the pop-up menu, type specific text in a field, or use a combination of both. The example in the File Naming area shows the result of your choices in these menus.

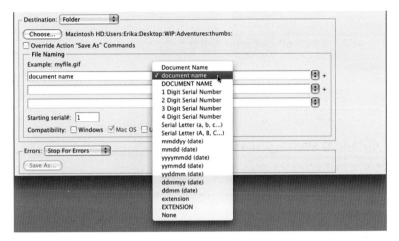

Note:

These options are only available when Folder is selected in the Destination menu.

8. **In the second field, type _sm.**

   This identifies the images as thumbnails, differentiating them from the full-size images with the same names.

9. **Choose extension (lowercase) from the menu for the third field.**

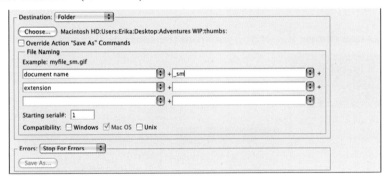

10. **Click OK to run the batch.**

    When the process is complete, you will have 12 thumbnail images in your WIP>Adventures>thumbs folder.

11. **Continue to the next exercise.**

Note:

*The last section of the Batch dialog box determines what happens if an error occurs during a batch. **Stop for Errors** (the default setting) interrupts the batch and displays a warning dialog box. **Log Errors to File** batch-processes every file and saves a record of all problems.*

PLACE AND ALIGN THUMBNAILS ON THE PAGE

Now that the thumbnail images have been created, you can arrange them in the gallery file so it can be animated, sliced, and saved for the Web.

1. **Open the file OATsite.psd from the RF_Photoshop>Adventures folder.**

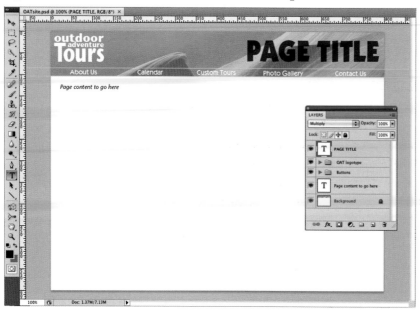

2. **Select the PAGE TITLE layer to make it active. Using the Type tool, select the text on the active layer and type PHOTO GALLERY.**

3. **Control/right-click the layer and choose Rasterize Type from the contextual menu.**

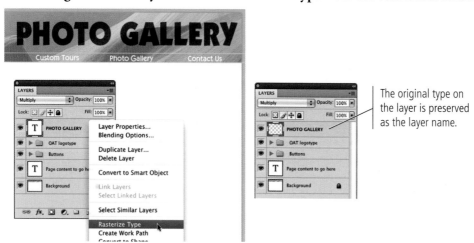

The original type on the layer is preserved as the layer name.

4. **Delete the "Page content to go here" layer.**

The text layer that was here for positioning isn't necessary.

5. **Select the top layer in the stack (PHOTO GALLERY) to make it active.**

6. **Place all 12 thumbnail images (from your WIP>Adventures>thumbs folder) into the OATsite file as Smart Objects, leaving them at their default locations (stacked on top of one another).**

   Unfortunately, you have to place (File>Place) the files one at a time, and press Enter to apply the placement. You align the thumbnails in the next exercise.

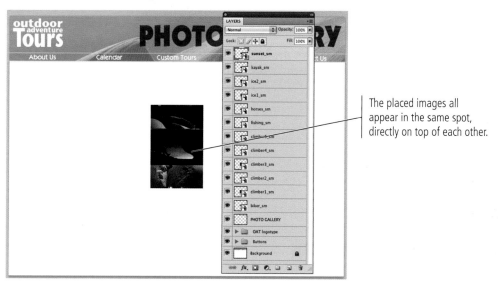

The placed images all appear in the same spot, directly on top of each other.

7. **Rasterize each Smart Object layer into a regular layer.**

   Because you selected the previous top layer before placing the thumbnails, the thumbnail image layers appear above the layers that were stored in the file when you opened it. The names of the thumbnail layers are based on the names of the thumbnail files you placed.

Note:

You can press Shift to select the multiple layers and rasterize them all at once.

8. **Save the file as** gallery_working.psd **in your WIP>Adventures folder and continue to the next exercise.**

ARRANGE THE THUMBNAIL IMAGES

The Align and Distribute options in the Control panel offer the easiest solution when you need to arrange the content of multiple layers in relation to one another. You can simply select the specific layers you want to arrange, and then click the appropriate buttons to align edges or centers; or you can distribute layers across a specific amount of space.

1. **With** `gallery_working.psd` **open, select all 12 thumbnail layers and create a layer group named** Thumbnails.

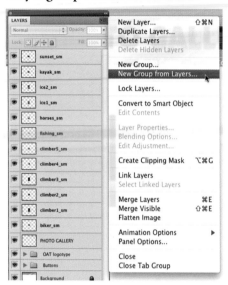

Note:

Shift-click to select contiguous layers; Command/Control-click to select non-contiguous layers.

2. **Expand the Thumbnails layer group. Select only the ice2_sm layer, and drag that layer to the top of the stack within the Thumbnails folder.**

3. **Drag climber3_sm, ice1_sm, and climber1_sm (in that order) below the ice2_sm layer.**

These layers are the four portrait-orientation images (they are higher than they are wide); they will make up the first row of the thumbnail grid.

Although layers don't have to be contiguous to use the align and distribute options, it's easier to manage the layers when the ones on the top row are on the top of the layer stack, the ones in the middle row are in the middle of the stack, and so on. In fact, some users might even create nested layer groups for each row of thumbnails.

4. **Hide the eight thumbnail layers you didn't drag to the top of the stack.**

   It's easier to manage the first row of images when the other eight are out of the way.

5. **Select the Move tool, and then select the ice2_sm layer.**

6. **Drag the layer contents to the top-left corner of the gallery space (below the Outdoor Adventure Tours logo).**

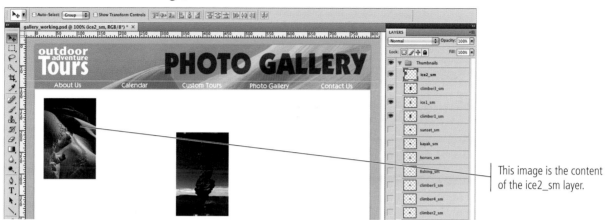

This image is the content of the ice2_sm layer.

7. **Select the climber1_sm layer and use the same method to position it in the top-right corner of the thumbnail area.**

8. **Shift-click to select all four of the visible thumbnail layers.**

9. **In the Control panel, click the Align Top Edges button.**

10. **With the same four layers still selected, click the Distribute Horizontal Centers button.**

    This option places an equal amount of space between the horizontal center point of each selected layer. Because these four thumbnails have the same width (caused by your earlier action), the four images are exactly spaced in relation to one another.

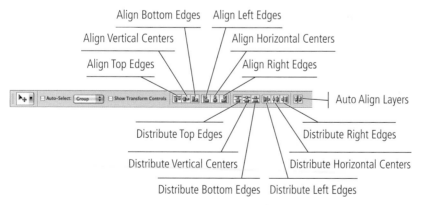

Align Bottom Edges   Align Left Edges
Align Vertical Centers   Align Horizontal Centers
Align Top Edges   Align Right Edges

Auto Align Layers

Distribute Top Edges   Distribute Right Edges
Distribute Vertical Centers   Distribute Horizontal Centers
Distribute Bottom Edges   Distribute Left Edges

Selecting multiple layers allows you to access the Align functions in the Control panel.

climber1_sm
climber3_sm
ice1_sm

11. With the same four layers still selected, click the Align Vertical Centers button.

Because these four images aren't exactly the same height, aligning their centers looks better than aligning their top edges.

12. In the Layers panel, rearrange the rest of the thumbnail image layers in the following order (below climber1_sm):

climber4_sm

climber5_sm

climber2_sm

kayak_sm

biker_sm

sunset_sm

horses_sm

fishing_sm

13. Make the climber4_sm and biker_sm layers visible.

14. Using the Move tool, drag the biker_sm layer contents to the bottom-left corner of the gallery space.

15. With the biker_sm layer selected, Command/Control-click to select the ice2_sm and climber4_sm layers.

These three layers make up the left column of thumbnails.

16. In the Control panel, click the Align Left Edges button, and then click the Distribute Bottom Edges button.

By placing equal space between (i.e., distributing) the bottom edges of the selected layers, you are not affecting the position of the top image in the column. The middle image is moved so there is equal space between the bottom edges of all three images, based on the current bottom-edge positions of the top and bottom images.

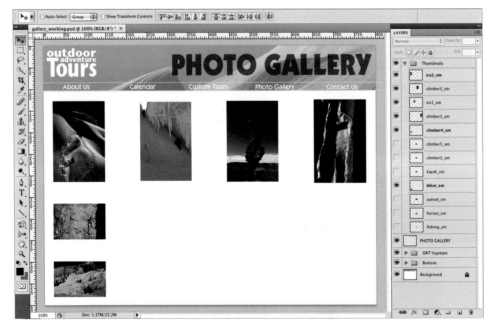

17. Continue arranging and aligning the rest of the thumbnails. Use the Align and Distribute buttons in the Control panel to create a visually pleasing arrangement (our solution is shown below).

18. Click any of the thumbnail images and apply a drop shadow style with the default settings.

19. Control/right-click the styled layer and choose Copy Layer Style from the contextual menu.

20. Select all the other placed thumbnail layers, Control/right-click any of the selected layers, and choose Paste Layer Style from the contextual menu.

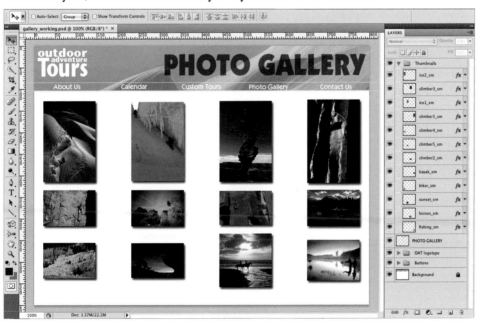

21. Save the file and continue to the next stage of the project.

Stage 2 Building Frame Animations

Animating objects on Web pages can be an effective way to hold visitors' interest. In Photoshop, animation is created as a series of frames displayed in rapid succession, creating the illusion of movement. For each frame in the animation, you can change the position of objects, the opacity and visibility of a layer, the color of objects, the applied styles, and other options.

Photoshop animations are created and controlled using the Animation panel (Window> Animation). In Frame mode, you can create or delete frames; control looping options, frame delay, and tweening; and preview the animation within Photoshop.

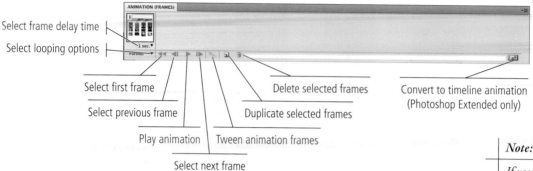

Select frame delay time
Select looping options

Select first frame
Select previous frame
Play animation
Select next frame
Tween animation frames
Duplicate selected frames
Delete selected frames
Convert to timeline animation
(Photoshop Extended only)

Note:

If you have Photoshop Extended, you can work with the Animation panel in Timeline mode, which gives you more sophisticated control over animations — closer to what you can accomplish using the Timeline in Adobe Flash or Dreamweaver.

- The **looping** option determines how many times the animation plays. You can choose Once, Forever, or Other (a specific number of times).

- The **frame delay** for each frame determines the amount of time before the next frame appears. Short or no delays help create smoother transitions; longer delays create a more choppy flow (which might not be what you want).

- **Tweening** creates intermediary frames between two selected frames to smooth transitions from one frame to the next.

PREPARE LAYERS FOR ANIMATION

Photoshop combines layers with frames to create the illusion of movement. For each frame in an animation, you can change the position, opacity, visibility, and effects applied to a layer, as well as add new layers, paint on existing layers, and more. In short, what is visible in the Layers panel for a selected frame is what you see when the animation reaches that frame during playback.

1. **With gallery_working.psd open (from your WIP>Adventures folder), open the Animation panel.**

   In the gallery file, you're going to build a five-stage animation:

   - Reveal the first word in the company logotype
   - Reveal the second word in the company logotype
   - Move the third word into place from the left side of the page
   - Add a Bevel style to the entire logotype
   - Fade the page header into view

   You need to determine what needs to be done in the first (default) frame of the animation to accomplish these steps, and then apply those settings to the various layers.

2. **If you have Photoshop Extended, make sure the Animation panel is displayed in Frame mode.**

3. **In the Layers panel, collapse the Thumbnails group and expand the OAT logotype folder.**

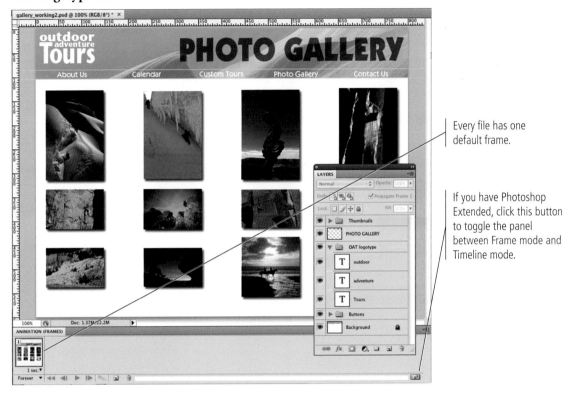

Every file has one default frame.

If you have Photoshop Extended, click this button to toggle the panel between Frame mode and Timeline mode.

4. **Hide the outdoor and adventure layers, and then zoom in to the top-left area of the document (where the logo was positioned).**

These two layers will be revealed in sequential frames, so you can simply toggle the layers' visibility to achieve your goal.

5. **Select the Tours layer. Using the Move tool, press Shift and drag left until the word is entirely past the page edge.**

To reveal this layer, you move it from this location and back into place, and animate the change in position.

Shift-drag to move the Tours layer content horizontally off the page.

6. **Select the PHOTO GALLERY layer in the Layers panel and change the opacity to 0%.**

   To reveal this layer, you will set the opacity back to 100% and animate the change in opacity.

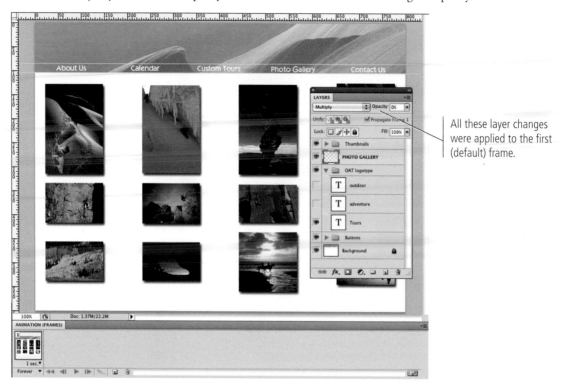

All these layer changes were applied to the first (default) frame.

7. **Save the file and continue to the next exercise.**

CREATE NEW FRAMES

When you build a frame-based animation, you need to add a new frame every time you want something to change. As we stated at the beginning of the previous exercise, the animation you're building has five basic stages or changes, so you need at least five frames in addition to the default frame that appears when you open the HTML file.

1. **With gallery_working.psd open, click the Duplicate Selected Frames button at the bottom of the Animation panel.**

   The second frame is an exact duplicate of the first.

Duplicate selected frames

2. **With the second frame selected in the Animation panel, use the Layers panel to make the outdoor layer (in the OAT logotype folder) visible.**

When this animation is played, the word "outdoor" will become visible as soon as the animation reaches the second frame.

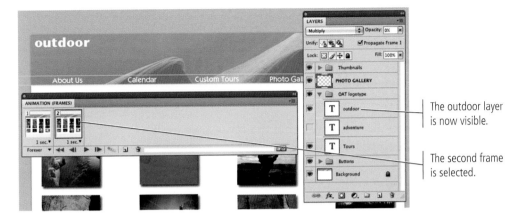

The outdoor layer is now visible.

The second frame is selected.

3. **Duplicate Frame 2 in the Animation panel.**

4. **With Frame 3 selected in the Animation panel, use the Layers panel to make the adventure layer (in the OAT logotype folder) visible.**

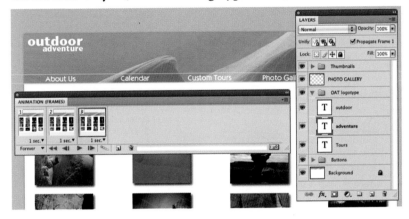

5. **Duplicate Frame 3 in the Animation panel.**

6. **With Frame 4 selected in the Animation panel, select the Tours layer in the Layers panel. Using the Move tool, press Shift and drag the layer right, returning the layer to its original position.**

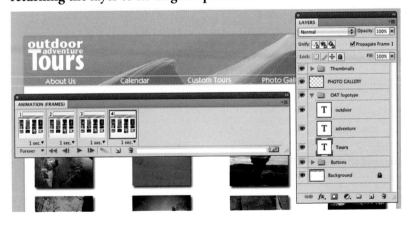

7. **Duplicate Frame 4.**

8. **With Frame 5 selected in the Animation panel, apply a Bevel and Emboss layer style to the Tours layer, using the following settings (if a setting isn't listed, use the default settings):**

Style:	Inner Bevel
Technique:	Chisel Soft
Size:	2 px
Shadow color:	Sample a brown from the background image at the top of the page

9. **With Frame 5 still selected, copy the layer style from the Tours layer to the other two layers in the OAT logotype layer folder.**

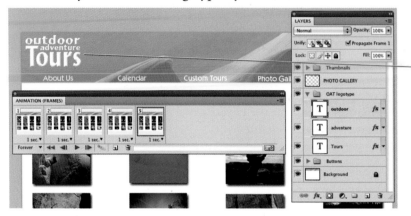

In Frame 5, the layer style appears on all three pieces of the logotype.

10. **Duplicate Frame 5. With Frame 6 selected, change the opacity of the PHOTO GALLERY layer to 100%.**

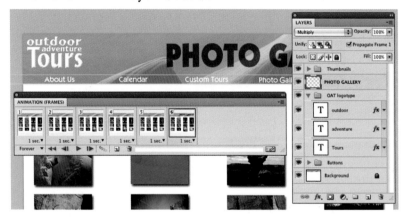

11. **In the Animation panel, make sure Once is selected in the Select Looping Option menu.**

You don't want the logo to repeatedly appear. Setting this option to Once makes the animation play a single time when the page loads.

12. Click Frame 1 to select it, and then click the Play Animation button to preview your animation.

When the animation plays, each frame is revealed sequentially. The second and third frames correctly reveal the first two words of the logotype. However, the switch from Frame 3 to Frame 4 makes the word Tours appear suddenly instead of sliding into place (the same problem occurs between Frames 5 and 6, when the page header simply appears instead of fading in). You fix these problems in the next exercise.

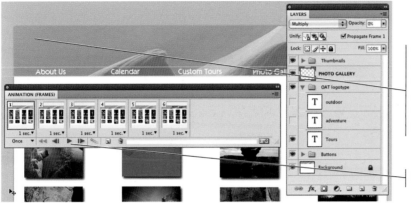

When you select Frame 1, the document window displays the layer visibility, position, and other attributes that are active in Frame 1 (everything is hidden, moved off the page, or entirely transparent).

Play the animation

13. Save the file and continue to the next exercise.

CREATE A TWEEN

To create the appearance of movement, such as a word sliding onto the page or an image fading in, you have to use a sequence of frames between the starting position and the ending position. Each intermediary frame changes the object slightly so, when the frames play in quick succession, the objects appear to make a smooth transition from their original state to their ending state.

For very precise control, you could create each intermediary frame manually, but that method would be very time consuming for even a simple animation. Fortunately, Photoshop includes an option to **tween** frames, which means the application creates intermediary frames for you based on specific parameters.

1. With `gallery_working.psd` open, select Frames 3 and 4 in the Animation panel.

2. Click the Tween Animation Frames button at the bottom of the Animation panel.

In the Tween dialog box, Selection is automatically chosen in the Tween With menu. Using this option, the new frames will be placed between (hence the name) the two selected frames.

Note:

Shift-click to select contiguous frames.

Note:

If only one frame were selected in the Animation panel, you could choose Tween With Next Frame or Previous Frame to determine where the tween would be created.

3. **Change the Frames to Add field to 7, make sure All Layers is selected in the Layers area, and make sure the Position option is checked in the Parameters area.**

A tween can create transitions for layer position, opacity, and effects — and any combination of those three attributes.

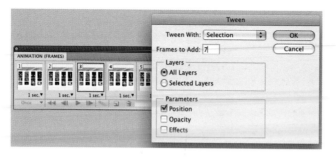

Note:

If the Selected Layers option is active, the tween frames will include only the layers currently selected in the Layers panel; the rest of the page (the background, buttons, and so on) will not be visible during the tween frames' playback.

4. **Click OK to create the tween frames.**

When Photoshop creates the tween, the specified number of frames is added to the animation. Each frame varies the selected parameters (in this case, position) slightly to create the transition. In this animation, each frame moves the word Tours one-eighth of the distance from its position in Frame 3 to its position in the original Frame 4.

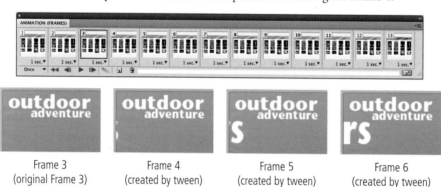

Frame 3
(original Frame 3)

Frame 4
(created by tween)

Frame 5
(created by tween)

Frame 6
(created by tween)

Frame 7
(created by tween)

Frame 8
(created by tween)

Frame 9
(created by tween)

Frame 10
(created by tween)

Frame 11
(original Frame 4)

5. **Create another tween between Frames 12 and 13 that adds 8 frames that change the opacity parameter.**

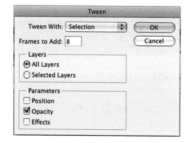

The PHOTO GALLERY layer currently has 0% opacity in Frame 12 and 100% opacity in Frame 13. You need to tween this transition to allow the header to fade in instead of suddenly popping into view.

Each new frame alters the layer opacity by approximately 11%, or one-ninth of the difference between 0 and 100.

6. **Select Frame 1 in the Animation panel and play the animation.**

7. **Save your work and continue to the next exercise.**

 ## CONTROL ANIMATION TIMING

As it stands now, the animation is very choppy because each frame in the animation has a one-second delay. In other words, each frame appears for one full second before the next frame appears. Some frames might actually require longer delay times; but in other cases, a long delay can ruin the effect (as in the case of the two tweens you created in the previous exercise).

The one-second delay for tween frames prevents the word Tours from moving smoothly into place.

1. **With gallery_working.psd open, Shift-click to select Frames 4 through 11.**

   Frame 4 is the first tween frame that brings the word Tours into the image. Frame 11 is the final frame in the animation, when the word Tours is in position.

Note:

By selecting all eight frames, you can change the delay for all eight frames at once.

2. **Click the arrow next to the current delay interval for any of the selected frames, and choose No Delay from the resulting menu.**

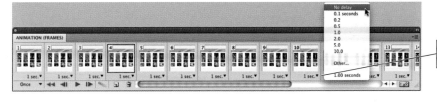

Click here to open the Delay menu.

3. **Repeat this process for Frames 13–21 (the first and last frames that fade in the page header image).**

4. Select Frame 1 in the Animation panel and play the animation.

The two transitions move much more smoothly now. If you see a slight delay between frames, don't worry; it will be less apparent when the final animation file is exported. Photoshop is a good tool for building this type of animation, but its previewing capabilities are limited.

5. Save the file and continue to the next stage of the project.

Optimizing Animations

If bandwidth is a concern (and it should be) you might want to optimize animations to reduce the size of the file that will be exported. Frame disposal and overall optimization options are built into the Photoshop Animation panel. Control/right-clicking a frame in the Animation panel displays three options for frame disposal; these choices determine what happens to the current frame during a transition.

- **Automatic** discards the current frame if the next frame contains layer transparency. This is the default setting, and it is desirable for many animations. This method must be used when optimizing images using the Redundant Pixel Removal optimization option.

- **Do Not Dispose** preserves the current frame as the next frame is added, allowing the current frame to show through transparent areas of the next frame. To preview an animation accurately, you should use a browser with this option.

- **Restore to Background** deletes the current frame before the next frame loads. The current frame does not appear through transparent areas of the following frame.

You can also reduce the final file size by cropping frames until you are left with only the important parts of the animation.

Photoshop can move through the frames of an animation, looking for identical information in two sequential frames; when it finds such a situation, it crops the frames so they include only the information that changes from frame to frame. Static areas are eliminated, saving system resources.

If you choose Optimize Animation from the Animation panel Options menu, you have two choices. The Bounding Box option crops each frame to include only the areas that have changed. The Redundant Pixel Removal option replaces every static pixel with transparency.

Stage 3 Slicing the Page

Now that you've finished designing your page and building the animation, the next step is to cut the image into pieces (called **slices**) that can work properly on a Web page. At the very least, each element that needs to link to a different location should become a slice, as should any element that requires unique output options (such as file format).

When you export the page, Photoshop can create an HTML file with the necessary information for assembling the slices into a functional Web page — which is useful for previewing your work. However, Photoshop is not a Web design application. A more common workflow for developing live Web sites is to create the pieces in Photoshop, and then hand them off to a Web developer who uses specialized products (such as Adobe Dreamweaver) to reassemble the pieces using proper HTML structure and code.

CREATE SLICES FROM GUIDES

Photoshop includes three options for creating slices: based on guides, based on layers, and based on a manually defined area. Each of these methods has its own advantages, which you will see as you use all three to slice the photo gallery page.

1. **With gallery_working.psd open from your WIP>Adventures folder, make sure guides are visible (View>Show>Guides).**

2. **Choose the Slice tool (nested under the Crop tool) in the Tools panel.**

3. **In the Control panel, click the Slices From Guides button.**

   Eah slice is identified by a small number and icon in the top-left corner. Slicing this page based on the guides resulted in three slices, each of which can have unique settings.

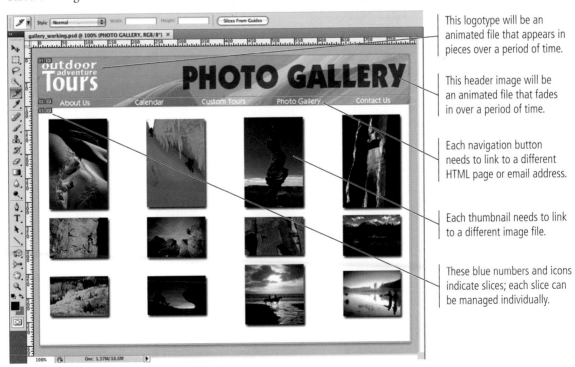

This logotype will be an animated file that appears in pieces over a period of time.

This header image will be an animated file that fades in over a period of time.

Each navigation button needs to link to a different HTML page or email address.

Each thumbnail needs to link to a different image file.

These blue numbers and icons indicate slices; each slice can be managed individually.

4. **Choose the Slice Select tool in the Tools panel (nested under the Slice tool).**

5. **Double-click Slice 01 in the top-left corner.**

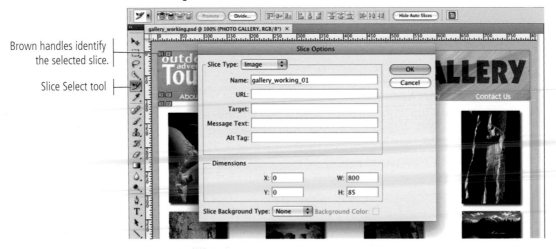

Brown handles identify the selected slice.

Slice Select tool

For every slice, you can define a number of settings:

- **Name** is the file name that will be used when you save the slice for the Web.

- **URL** is the file that opens if a user clicks the slice. (Slices don't have to be links; if you don't want a slice to link to something, simply leave the URL field blank.)

- **Target** is the location where the URL opens when you click the slice. Although there are other options available in full-scale HTML development applications such as Dreamweaver, you will primarily use "_self" to open the link in the same window or "_blank" to open the link in a new window.

- **Message Text** appears in the browser's status bar. If you don't type a specific message, the URL link will display.

- **Alt Tag** appears in place of an image when image display is disabled in the browser, or when a Web page is being read by screen-reader software.

Note:

The Dimensions fields are automatically filled with the current size of the slice. You can also change the slice background type and color if the slice contains areas of transparency.

6. **Click Cancel to close the Slice Options dialog box.**

7. **Save the file and continue to the next exercise.**

DIVIDE SLICES AUTOMATICALLY

In some cases, you need to define slices manually to select a certain area. In this page, you need to create an individual slice for each text button so each word will link to the appropriate page.

1. **With gallery_working.psd open, use the Slice Select tool to double-click the 02 slice.**

2. **In the resulting Slice Options dialog box, define the following settings, then click OK to close the dialog box:**

Name:	btn
URL:	[None]
Target:	_self
Alt Tag:	Outdoor Adventure Tours

None of this information is complete. However, you are going to divide this slice into further slices, and this information will be the same for each slice. By defining the information for the primary slice, it will be copied into any slices you create from this one.

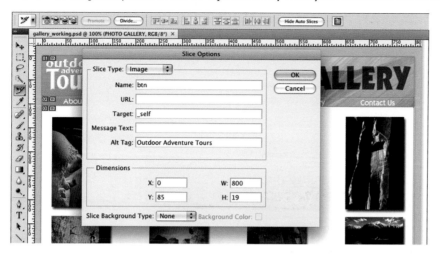

3. **In the Control panel, click the Divide Slice button.**

4. **In the Divide Slice dialog box, make sure the Preview option is selected, and then divide the slice vertically into five pieces (one slice for each button).**

Note:

You need to use the Slice Select tool to access the slice options in the Control panel.

Dividing the main slice into five vertical pieces creates the slices required to generate all five buttons.

5. **Click OK to divide the slice.**

6. **Using the Slice Select tool, double-click Slice 02.**

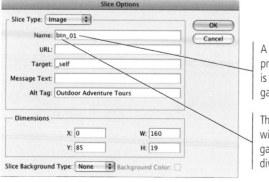

A sequential number, preceded by an underscore, is added to the name you gave the master slice.

The name of the slice starts with "btn" — the name you gave to the slice before you divided it.

7. **Make the following changes to the slice options, and then click OK:**

   In the Name field, change the "01" to about.

   Type about.html in the URL field.

   Add About (including a space after the word) to the beginning of the Alt Tag field.

By defining the information for the main slice, you saved a bit of unnecessary typing. Remember — whatever you can do to minimize repetitive tasks will improve your overall workflow.

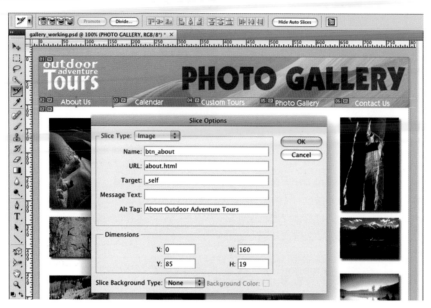

8. **Change the remaining button slices using the following information:**

   Slice 3   Name: button_calendar

              URL: calendar.html

              Target: _self

              Alt Tag: Outdoor Adventure Tours Calendar

   Slice 4   Name: button_custom

              URL: custom.html

              Target: _self

              Alt Tag: Outdoor Adventure Tours Custom Packages

   Slice 5   Name: button_gallery

              URL: gallery.html

              Target: _self

              Alt Tag: Outdoor Adventure Tours Photo Gallery

   Slice 6   Name: button_contact

              URL: mailto:info@oatours.com

              Target: [None]

              Alt Tag: Email Outdoor Adventure Tours

Note:

To create an email link, you have to type "mailto:" followed by the email address. Do not add a space between the colon and the email address.

9. **Save the file and continue to the next exercise.**

CREATE MANUAL SLICES

For the resulting HTML to work properly after the page is exported, every area of the page must be a slice. When you manually create a slice (whether from guides, from layers, or by drawing with the Slice tool), Photoshop automatically creates extra slices as necessary to support the ones you create.

Slices you create (called **user slices**) have bright blue tags; the ones Photoshop generates to support your manual slices (called **auto slices**) have gray tags. You can convert an auto slice to a user slice by double-clicking it with the Slice Select tool and defining slice options, or by selecting an auto slice and clicking the Promote button in the Control panel.

1. **With gallery_working.psd open, click the top slice (01) with the Slice Selection tool to select it.**

2. **Zoom in to the top-left corner of the document, and then show the Info panel.**

3. **Click the left-center handle of slice 01 and drag right until the X field shows 140 px.**

   In this step, you are dragging what will become the left edge of the title slice, so the X position will be 140 px.

   When you release the mouse button, a new slice 01 automatically appears in the top-left corner. The slice you just resized is now slice 02.

Note:

Because the document rulers display pixels as the unit of measurement, the Info panel shows measurements and positions using pixels. You can change the panel units in the Panel Options dialog box, which you can open from the panel Options menu.

4. **Click the 01 auto slice, and then click the Promote button to convert it to a regular slice.**

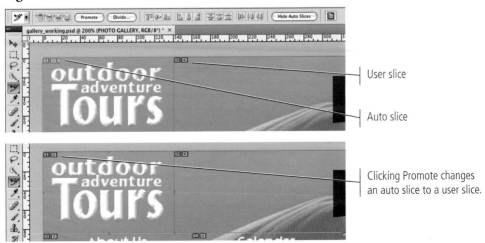

User slice

Auto slice

Clicking Promote changes an auto slice to a user slice.

5. **Double-click the new slice 01 and define the following settings:**

Name:	oat_logo
URL:	index.html
Target:	_self
Alt Tag:	Outdoor Adventure Tours Home Page

6. **Define the following settings for slice 02:**

Name:	gallery_title
URL:	[None]
Alt Tag:	Outdoor Adventure Tours Photo Gallery

7. **Save the file and continue to the next exercise.**

Creating No Image Slices

PHOTOSHOP FOUNDATIONS

In the Slice Options dialog box, you can change the slice type to No Image, which is useful if you want to create a slice to contain editable HTML text instead of a graphic representation of text. When No Image is selected in the Slice Type menu, you can define the HTML text that will appear in the slice after the page is exported. This text won't appear anywhere in Photoshop, except within the Slice Options dialog box.

Double-clicking a slice in the Save For Web preview opens the Slice Options dialog box with most of the same options as in the main interface. Several additional options allow you to define the horizontal and vertical alignment of text within the exported slice (the word "cell" is used in this case because the exported text area is actually a table cell rather than an image slice).

We converted slice 05 to a No Image slice with text content.

This text will not appear anywhere within the Photoshop document.

The defined text appears in the cell when the page is viewed in a browser.

If you open this dialog box from the Save For Web dialog box, you can define the position of text within the HTML cell.

CREATE SLICES FROM LAYERS

You can also create slices based on selected layers, which can be far easier than manually drawing slices around individual images (such as the thumbnail images that make up the gallery).

1. **With gallery_working.psd open, expand the Thumbnails layer group and select all layers in the group.**

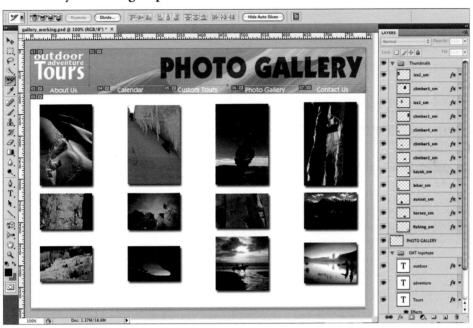

2. **Choose Layer>New Layer Based Slices.**

   The thumbnails area is automatically cut into a number of slices. The important slices are the ones that surround each thumbnail (and the applied drop shadow). The other thin slices are necessary to align the thumbnail slices in the exported HTML file.

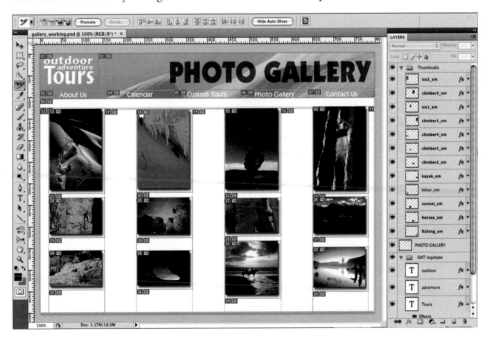

3. **Using the Slice Select tool, click in the page head area to deselect the new layer-based slices.**

4. **With the Slice Select tool active, double-click the top-left thumbnail slice (Slice 13 in our example) to open the Slice Options dialog box.**

   Unfortunately, there is no way to define the common settings for this group of files, so you have to define the options for every thumbnail individually.

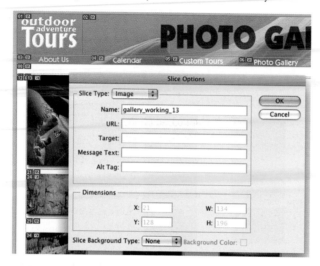

5. **Use the following information to define options for each thumbnail slice:**

Name:	Use the layer name
URL:	Type photos/, use the layer name without the _sm, and then add the extension .jpg
Target:	_blank (each larger image will open in a separate browser window)

   This is why you placed the thumbnail files, and then rasterized the Smart Objects. Remember, the thumbnail names are based on the original photo names with _sm added; this method allows you to know the target file name without having to hunt through folders on your desktop.

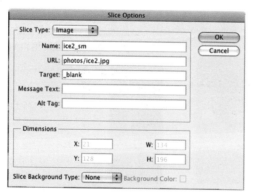

Note:

The "photos/" part of the URL tells the HTML code to look in the folder "photos" within the folder where you export the HTML page. All the full-size images, as you may remember from the batch-processing exercise, are saved as JPEG files in the photos folder.

6. **Using the same process as in Steps 3 and 4, link the slice for each thumbnail to the larger version of the image so the larger versions open in separate browser windows.**

7. **Save the file and continue to the next exercise.**

PHOTOSHOP FOUNDATIONS

When optimizing files for the Web, the format you use will affect the display of the colors in the exported file, as well as compression and transparency capabilities. The Save For Web dialog box allows you to save images or slices in one of five formats (JPEG, GIF, PNG-8, PNG-24, or WBMP), and then define options specific to the format you choose.

JPEG

JPEG is the format of choice for continuous-tone images (such as photos) since it can store up to 24-bit color. The JPEG format compresses information using lossy compression, which means information is lost in the resulting file. It is not well suited for text or graphics, since its compression method introduces a blurring effect to the graphics.

You can choose a predefined compression level (Low, Medium, High, Very High, or Maximum) or define a specific quality percentage. These choices refer to the quality of the resulting image, not the amount of compression applied; the higher quality you want, the less compression you should apply.

- The **Optimized** check box creates an enhanced JPEG with a slightly smaller file size. Some older browsers don't support this feature.

- The **Progressive** option allows the image to appear in stages as more data downloads; this option is only available if the Optimized check box is selected.

- The **Blur** option applies a Gaussian blur to the exported image, which allows higher compression without destroying the image.

- The **ICC Profile** preserves the profile of the image in the exported file.

- The **Matte** option defines a color for any pixels that were transparent in the original image. The JPEG format does not support transparency.

PNG-8 and PNG-24

PNG is another format used for Web graphics and images. Two versions of the format — PNG-8 and PNG-24 — support 8-bit and 24-bit color respectively. For the PNG-8 format, the options are the same as for the GIF format, except that PNG-8 files cannot be compressed. PNG-24 can support continuous-tone color as well as transparency.

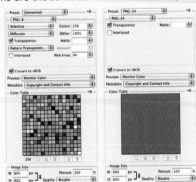

GIF

GIF is an 8-bit format typically used for graphics and artwork that don't have a large range of color. It is ideally suited for files with large areas of solid color, but it is ill suited for continuous-tone images that have subtle color variations.

When you save a file in the GIF format, all the colors are mapped to a color table (called **indexed color**). Indexed color is an 8-bit color model in which the specific 256 values are based on the colors in the image. You can remap the indexed colors using a number of options:

- **Perceptual** gives priority to colors to which the human eye is more sensitive.

- **Selective** is similar to Perceptual, but favors broad areas of color. This usually produces the best results.

- **Adaptive** samples colors appearing most commonly in the image.

- **Restrictive (Web)** uses a standard 216-color Web-safe color table. This option can result in drastic color shift.

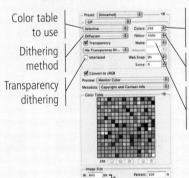

The **Lossy** option reduces file size by selectively discarding data; higher settings result in more data being discarded.

The **Dithering Method** option applies **dithering**, which blends two available colors to simulate additional colors. A higher dithering percentage creates the appearance of more colors and more detail, but can also increase the file size.

The **Transparency** and **Matte** options determine how transparent pixels are treated. If Transparency is checked, semi-transparent pixels blend into the defined Matte color.

The **Transparency Dithering** option allows you to dither transparency in a similar manner as dithering colors.

The **Interlace** option allows the image to display in stages as more data downloads (similar to progressive JPEG files).

The **Web Snap** option specifies a tolerance level for shifting colors to the closest Web palette equivalents.

OPTIMIZE IMAGE SETTINGS AND EXPORT HTML

Once all the slices have been defined, you can safely export the page and all the necessary image files for the Web. Before exporting, however, you should define the file formats, compression, and color settings that will work best for each slice. This process is made easier using the File>Save For Web command.

1. **With the file gallery_working.psd open, choose File>Save For Web & Devices.**

   The Save For Web & Devices dialog box defaults to show the optimized version of the image. You can use the tabs at the top of the preview to show the original image or split the window into two or four panes; each pane can have different settings for experimentation/comparison.

Note:

The tools in the Save For Web dialog box serve the same purpose as the related tools in the main interface.

2. **Using the Slice Select tool, click the top-left slice (01) where the logotype appears.**

   Animated files must be saved using the GIF format. If you review the optimization settings, you can see that the optimized file will download in 5 seconds over a 56.6 K modem.

   Don't assume that all users have high-speed Internet access. Many people, especially in the general consumer and international markets, still use dial-up modems. If your target audience is one of these, you should optimize your files for slower download speeds.

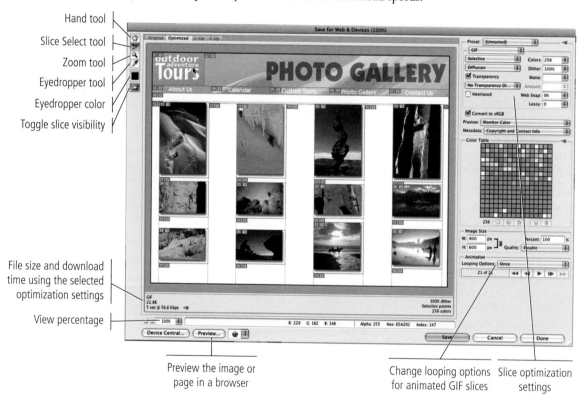

Hand tool
Slice Select tool
Zoom tool
Eyedropper tool
Eyedropper color
Toggle slice visibility

File size and download time using the selected optimization settings
View percentage

Preview the image or page in a browser

Change looping options for animated GIF slices

Slice optimization settings

3. **Select the first thumbnail image slice (Slice 13 in our example) in the preview area.**

   Because this is a photograph, the JPEG format is a better choice than the default GIF.

4. **Click the Format menu, choose JPEG, and then review the Optimization settings.**

Using the High compression option, the image will download in 4 seconds on a 56.6 K modem. This is an acceptable download time, and the image preview shows that the quality will be fine for a small thumbnail image.

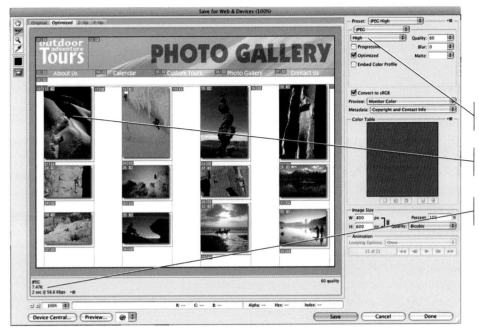

Default (High) optimization settings for a JPEG file

Optimized preview of the selected slice

File size and download time using a 56.6 K modem

5. **Change the remaining thumbnail images to the JPEG format using the default settings.**

The remaining slices will work well using the default format options. You can now export the page and slice images.

6. **Click the Save button and navigate to your WIP>Adventures folder as the location for saving.**

This folder already contains the files from the first samples. When you export the gallery page into this folder, the links to other pages will work properly (assuming you typed the URL links properly for each button).

Note:

You can Shift-click each thumbnail slice to select multiple slices, and then change the export options for all selected slices.

Note:

Clicking Done closes the dialog box and saves your slice optimization settings. Clicking Cancel simply closes the dialog box; your choices are not saved.

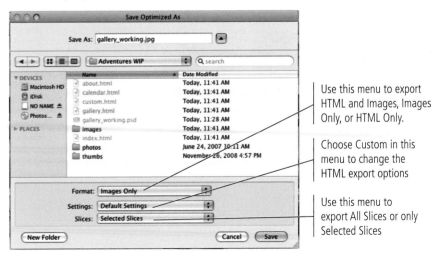

Use this menu to export HTML and Images, Images Only, or HTML Only.

Choose Custom in this menu to change the HTML export options

Use this menu to export All Slices or only Selected Slices

7. **Remove "_working" from the file name.**

8. **Make sure HTML and Images is selected in the Format menu, and All Slices is selected in the Slices menu.**

9. **Click Save to generate the HTML and image files for the photo gallery page.**

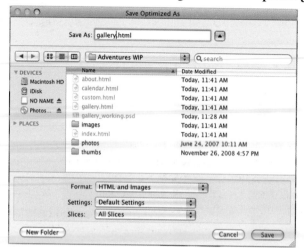

Note:

HTML settings include options for tag formatting in the resulting code; creating an HTML table or cascading style sheet (CSS) to reassemble the slices; default slice-naming conventions; background settings; and default image file and path options. You can almost always use the default settings since most HTML from Photoshop is ultimately imported into Dreamweaver or another Web design application for finetuning.

10. **Review the information in the Replace Files dialog box, then click Replace.**

   These files already exist from the first sample export (without the animation or photo gallery content). When you replace these files, the new (animated) logo_animation file will be correctly read by all HTML pages in the folder.

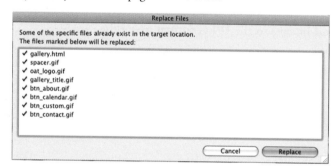

11. **On your desktop, double-click the gallery.html file in your WIP>Adventures folder to open the file in a browser.**

12. **Click any thumbnail image to view the larger image.**

The large image opens in a new window because you used the _blank target.

13. **Close the browser windows and return to Photoshop.**

14. **Save the Photoshop file, and then close it.**

   Using the Save For Web dialog box does not save your work in the native Photoshop file. You have to save the Photoshop file separately after the HTML and images have been exported.

HTML Output Options

When you use the Save For Web dialog box to output HTML, you can change the options for the resulting HTML by choosing Other in the Settings menu of the Save Optimized As dialog box. (Background Image, Default Settings, and XHTML are saved sets that you can call without opening the Output Settings dialog box.)

The Output Settings dialog box has four panes, which are accessed in the menu below the Settings menu. Most of these options require a good understanding of HTML, CSS, and Web design structure; if you don't understand these concepts, you can safely use the default settings for most basic Web pages that you design in Photoshop.

Background Options

The **View Document As** option defines a specific image or color to use as the Web page background. If Image is selected, the page displays an image or color as the background behind the image or page you are exporting. If Background is selected, the page will display the optimized image as a tiled background.

In the **Background Image** field, you can define an image to use as the page background. The background image will be tiled behind the optimized image on the Web page.

The **Color** field and menu allow you to define a color that will be used as the background of the exported page.

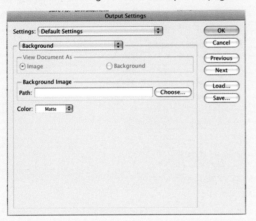

Saving Files Options

The **File Naming** options change the default file naming conventions for files created when you export an image or page for the Web. These options are similar to those that you used to assign names to batch-processed files.

The **Filename Compatibility** options make the filename compatible with Windows, Mac OS, or UNIX servers.

The **Put Images In Folder** option defaults to "images", which is a standard convention for Web site folder structure. If a folder named "images" does not exist where you save the optimized file, the images folder will be created for you.

The **Copy Background Image When Saving** option preserves a defined background image as a single image.

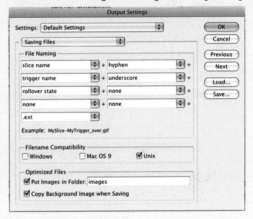

PHOTOSHOP FOUNDATIONS

HTML Options

The **Output XHTML** option creates Web pages that meet the XHTML standard. This option disables options that might conflict with this standard; when this is selected, the Tags Case and Attribute Case options are automatically set.

The **Formatting** options determine how the resulting HTML code will be formatted:

- **Tags Case** defines the capitalization for tags.
- **Attribute Case** defines the capitalization for attributes.
- **Indent** defines a method for indenting lines of code.
- **Line Endings** defines the platform for line ending compatibility.
- **Encoding** defines the default character encoding for the page.

The **Coding** options determine what will be included in the resulting code:

- **Include Comments** adds explanatory comments to the HTML code.
- **Always Add Alt Attribute** adds the ALT attribute to images to comply with Web accessibility standards.
- **Always Quote Attributes** places quotation marks around tag attributes, which is required for compatibility with some older browsers.
- **Close All Tags** adds closing tags for all HTML elements in the file for XHTML compliance.
- **Include Zero Margins On Body Tag** removes default internal margins in a browser window, and adds margin tags with zero values to the body tag.

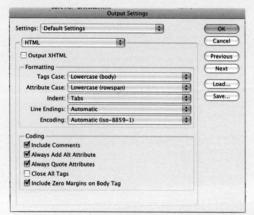

Slices Options

The **Generate Table** option creates an HTML table to reassemble the slices in the exported Web page.

- **Empty Cells** defines how empty slices are converted to table cells.
- **TD W&H** defines when to include width and height attributes for table data.
- **Spacer Cells** defines when to add empty spacer cells around the generated table.

The **Generate CSS** option creates a cascading style sheet to reassemble the slices in the exported page. The **Referenced** menu defines how slice positions are referenced in the HTML file (By ID, Inline, or By Class).

The **Default Slice Naming** options are, again, like the options that you used to name batch-processed files.

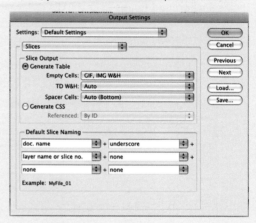

1. The _____ command can be used to run an action on all files in a specific folder without user intervention.

2. Align options are available in the _____ when multiple layers are selected in the Layers panel.

3. _____ is the process of automatically creating frames to animate a change between the beginning and ending states of a layer.

4. The _____ for each frame determines the amount of time before the next frame appears.

5. Use _____ at the beginning of a link target to create a link that opens a pre-addressed email message.

6. When defining slice settings, the _____ option defines the file that should open when a user clicks that slice.

7. The _____ tool is used to manually cut apart a page into smaller pieces for Web delivery.

8. When setting image optimization settings in the Save For Web & Devices dialog box, the _____ format allows lossy compression and does not support transparency; it is best used for photos.

9. The _____ format supports transparency but not a large number of colors; it is best used for artwork or graphics with large areas of solid color.

10. The _____ format supports both continuous-tone color and transparency, but is not universally supported by Web browsers.

1. Briefly explain how actions can be used to improve workflow.

2. Briefly explain two advantages of designing a Web site interface in Photoshop.

3. Briefly explain two disadvantages of designing a Web site interface in Photoshop.

Use what you learned in this project to complete the following freeform exercise.
Carefully read the art director and client comments, then create your own design to meet the needs of the project.
Use the space below to sketch ideas; when finished, write a brief explanation of your reasoning behind your final design.

Every professional designer needs a portfolio of their work. If you've completed the projects in this book, you should now have a number of different examples to show off your skills using Photoshop CS4.

The projects in this book were specifically designed to include a broad range of *types* of projects; your portfolio should use the same principle.

Using the following suggestions, gather your best work and create printed and digital versions of your portfolio.

❏ Include as many different types of work as possible — book covers, image retouching, art projects, etc.

❏ Print clean copies of each finished piece that you want to include.

❏ For correction or compositing jobs, include the "before" image as part of the sample.

❏ For each example in your portfolio, write a brief (one or two paragraphs) synopsis of the project. Explain the purpose of the piece, as well as your role in the creative and production process.

❏ Design an interactive Web page with thumbnails of your work; link the thumbnails to larger versions of the files so potential employers can review your work digitally.

❏ Create a CD version of your digital portfolio so you can present your work even when an Internet connection is not available — you never know when you might meet a potential employer.

_____
_____
_____
_____
_____
_____
_____
_____
_____
_____
_____
_____
_____

The graphic design workflow typically revolves around extremely short turnaround times, which means that any possible automation will only be a benefit. Photoshop actions can be useful whenever you need to apply the same sets of options to more than one or two images. Every click you save will allow you to do other work, meet tight deadlines, and satisfy your clients. In the case of running a batch on multiple images, you are completely freed to work on other projects, be in other places, or even (technically) "work" while you're gone for the evening.

Although many developers use dedicated Web design software like Adobe Dreamweaver to build sophisticated Web sites, the images for those sites have to come from somewhere. It is very common for a designer to build the "look and feel of a site in Photoshop, then slice and export the pieces so the developer can reassemble them in the Web design application. And as you saw by completing this project, Photoshop can be used to create complete (although basic) pages including frame animation and hyperlinks.

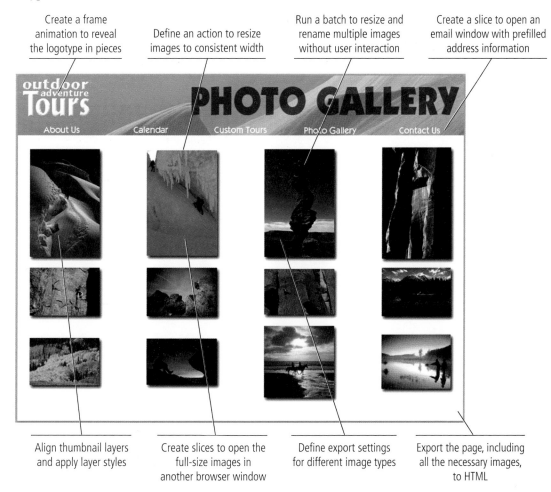

Create a frame animation to reveal the logotype in pieces

Define an action to resize images to consistent width

Run a batch to resize and rename multiple images without user interaction

Create a slice to open an email window with prefilled address information

Align thumbnail layers and apply layer styles

Create slices to open the full-size images in another browser window

Define export settings for different image types

Export the page, including all the necessary images, to HTML

PROJECT PORTFOLIO
Design Awards

The **Against The Clock Project Portfolio Design Awards** are your chance to gain recognition for your creative and technical design skills. Prizes range from your work being displayed in the Against The Clock Web Gallery, to cash prizes, to having your design published in an upcoming ATC book.

The **Project Portfolio Design Awards** are designed to test both your creative talents and technical skills. Submit your Portfolio Builder project from any of the Professional Portfolio Series books for your chance to win. Entries will be judged on design quality, originality, understanding of client needs, and technical skills.

Go to **www.againsttheclock.com/contest.html** for complete contest details and rules, and to download the official contest entry form.

Use our portfolio to build yours.

The Against The Clock Professional Portfolio Series walks you step-by-step through the tools and techniques of graphic design professionals.

Order online at www.againsttheclock.com
Use code **PFS409** for a 10% discount

Go to **www.againsttheclock.com** to enter our monthly drawing for a free book of your choice.

AGAINST THE CLOCK
mastering graphic technology